THE SECRET MULRONEY TAPES

Flame of Power: Intimate Profiles of Canada's Greatest Businessmen

Renegade in Power: The Diefenbaker Years

The Distemper of Our Times: Canadian Politics in Transition

Home Country: People, Places and Power Politics

Bronfman Dynasty: The Rothschilds of the New World

The Canadian Establishment, Volume 1: The Old Order

The Canadian Establishment, Volume 2: The Acquisitors

The Establishment Man: Conrad Black, a Portrait of Power

*True North, Not Strong, and Free:
Defending the Peaceable Kingdom in the Nuclear Age*

*Company of Adventurers: Volume I of the Unauthorized History
of the Hudson's Bay Company*

*Caesars of the Wilderness: Volume II of the Unauthorized History
of the Hudson's Bay Company*

Sometimes a Great Nation: Will Canada Belong to the 21st Century?

Canada: The Great Lone Land

*Empire of the Bay: An Illustrated History of the Hudson's Bay
Company*

*Merchant Princes: Volume III of the Unauthorized History of the
Hudson's Bay Company*

Canada 1892: Portrait of a Promised Land

The Canadian Revolution: From Deference to Defiance

Defining Moments: Dispatches from an Unfinished Revolution

The Canadian Establishment, Volume 3: Titans

Here Be Dragons: Telling Tales of People, Passion and Power

THE SECRET MULRONEY TAPES

—

Unguarded Confessions of a Prime Minister

—

PETER C. NEWMAN

RANDOM HOUSE CANADA

www.randomhouse.ca

ISBN-13: 978-0-679-31351-9
ISBN-10: 0-679-31351-6

Jacket and text design: CS Richardson

Printed and bound in the United States of America

10 9 8 7 6 5 4

ACKNOWLEDGEMENTS

I wish to thank Taivo Evard and Mario Canseco for their valuable
assistance in organizing and double-checking the quotations from
Chairman Mulroney, and Brian Bethune for his meticulous fact-checking.
I am particularly grateful for having been allowed to log into the talent
and energy of Anne Collins, chief editor and publisher of Random House
Canada. She has been bountifully creative in her editing and charged me
up with the enthusiasm and resolve that made this
difficult book possible.

Charles Parnell Cassidy, God rest his soul, was the perfect specimen of an Irish politician. They're a migratory tribe, so you can find them everywhere—Boston, New York, Chile, Vatican City, Liverpool, Peru and Sydney, Australia. They're hardy, resistant to infection by disease or new ideas, little modified by regional influences. The accent drifts a bit, maybe. The dialect adapts itself to the local patois: but that's a chameleon's trick: protective colouring, no more. The rest of it, the sinuous mind, the easy passion, the leery eye, the ready smile, the fine, swaggering, billycock-and-shillelagh-walk, the flexible moralities, the bel canto oratory, the black bilious angers, these never change.

—Morris West, *Cassidy*

Contents

The Mulroney Years

———

March 20, 1939	Martin Brian Mulroney born to Ben and Irene Mulroney in Baie-Comeau, Quebec.
1961	Graduates from St. Francis Xavier University with a bachelor of arts in political science.
1962	Attends Dalhousie Law School, and fails to pass his year.
1963	Graduates from Laval University with a bachelor of law degree. While there, helps organize the Congress of Canadian Affairs.
1972	Becomes partner in Montreal law firm Howard, Cate, Ogilvy.
1973	Marries Mila Pivnicki.
1974	Appointed to the Cliche Commission investigating union violence during the building of the James Bay hydroelectric project.
1976	Loses Progressive Conservative leadership race to Joe Clark.
1977	Appointed president of the Iron Ore Company, a subsidiary of Hanna Mining in Cleveland.

1980	Works in the "No" campaign during the first Quebec referendum.
June 11, 1983	Defeats Joe Clark to become leader of the Progressive Conservative Party.
August 29, 1983	Wins a by-election in Nova Scotia's Central Nova riding to claim a seat in Parliament as leader of the Opposition.
July 9, 1984	Prime Minister John Turner calls an election for September 4.
August 25, 1984	In a televised debate, Mulroney derides the patronage record of the Liberals and criticizes Turner for accepting appointments designated by Pierre Trudeau. Turner replies, "I had no option."
September 4, 1984	The Progressive Conservatives win a record 211 seats in the House of Commons, in a campaign marked by Mulroney's promise of "Jobs! Jobs! Jobs!" Mulroney easily carries Quebec's Manicouagan constituency.
September 17, 1984	Is sworn in as Canada's eighteenth prime minister, and appoints a forty-member cabinet.
November 5, 1984	The Mulroney government delivers its first Throne Speech.
February 12, 1985	Defence Minister Bob Coates resigns after visiting a topless bar in West Germany while carrying classified NATO documents.
March 17, 1985	Mulroney hosts U.S. president Ronald Reagan at the Shamrock Summit in Quebec City. The two leaders begin preparations for a free trade agreement.
March 23, 1985	Holds national economic conference, chaired by Stanley Hartt.

May 23, 1985	Finance Minister Michael Wilson's first budget de-indexes old age pensions.
June 6, 1985	Government defangs the Foreign Investment Review Agency (FIRA).
June 27, 1985	Mulroney promises to restore pension indexing after widespread protests from seniors.
July 15, 1985	Transport Minister Don Mazankowski unveils a plan to deregulate rail, roads and airlines.
July 25, 1985	The U.S. icebreaker *Polar Sea* begins a voyage through the Northwest Passage, setting off controversy about Canadian sovereignty of the Arctic.
September 1, 1985	Canada suffers its first bank failure in sixty-two years, as the Canadian Commercial Bank, based in Edmonton, collapses.
September 23, 1985	Fisheries Minister John Fraser resigns after CBC Television reveals he allowed a New Brunswick firm to place tainted tuna on the market.
September 30, 1985	Northland Bank of Calgary collapses despite federal intervention.
November 8, 1985	Simon Reisman appointed to negotiate a trade deal with the U.S.
December 18, 1985	U.S. ambassador Clayton Yeutter calls for no-holds-barred trade talks.
December 31, 1985	Junior Transport Minister Suzanne Blais-Grenier leaves cabinet after repeated unjustified trips to Europe and other foul-ups.
January 30, 1986	The government orders a partial de-indexation of family allowances.
February 26, 1986	Finance Minister Wilson delivers his second budget with new taxation measures.

March 19, 1986	Mulroney and Reagan agree to launch a $5 billion research program into acid rain. Sondra Gotlieb, wife of the ambassador to the United States, slaps her social secretary.
April 23, 1986	The U.S. Senate authorizes "fast-track" free trade negotiations.
April 29, 1986	*The Globe and Mail* reveals that Noreen Stevens— wife of Regional Industrial Expansion Minister Sinclair Stevens—arranged a loan for the family business from a firm that depended on federal aid.
May 6, 1986	Canada joins the exclusive club of industrial powers, as a member of the G-7.
May 12, 1986	Sinclair Stevens resigns from cabinet, protesting his innocence; nineteen years later he is exonerated.
May 12, 1986	Tory MP Michel Gravel is charged with fifty counts of influence peddling; he is eventually sentenced to a year in prison.
May 23, 1986	The U.S. imposes a tariff on cedar shakes and shingles. Mulroney derides the decision as bizarre and unacceptable.
June 2, 1986	Canada imposes an $80 million package of duties aimed at various American imports. Provincial premiers authorize Ottawa to launch free trade talks.
July 4, 1986	Following a cabinet meeting in Saskatoon, Mulroney announces his intention to open the Constitution to include Quebec.
August 16, 1986	More than 150 Tamils are found drifting in lifeboats off the east coast. Mulroney agrees to grant them refugee status.
October 31, 1986	The government awards the lucrative CF-18 fighter maintenance contract to Montreal-

based Bombardier over a lower bid from Bristol Aerospace of Winnipeg.

January 17, 1987   Mulroney fires Junior Transport Minister André Bissonnette after learning of a complicated land-flip scheme in Bissonnette's riding, involving Oerlikon Aerospace.

February 6, 1987   Mulroney vows to restore public faith in his ministers.

February 19, 1987   Minister of State Roch LaSalle resigns amid revelations that he had arranged a $5,000-per-person party at which business leaders were promised government contracts.

March 27, 1987   A first ministers' meeting called to entrench Native self-government into the Constitution fails.

April 30, 1987   The premiers and the prime minister meet at a government lodge on Meech Lake in the Gatineau hills and hammer out a constitutional accord.

June 3, 1987   The Meech Lake Accord, which sought to bring Quebec into the Constitution, is finalized after an extraordinary nineteen-hour negotiating session.

June 5, 1987   A Defence white paper calls for the acquisition of ten nuclear submarines.

June 18, 1987   Wilson introduces a new reform package, giving the biggest break to Canada's wealthiest taxpayers.

June 30, 1987   The House of Commons rejects the death penalty by twenty-one votes after an eight-day debate.

September 14, 1987   Following an emergency summer sitting, the House of Commons approves a bill cracking down on illegal immigrants.

October 3, 1987   Canada and the United States reach a free trade agreement.

December 3, 1987   Health Minister Jake Epp introduces a national daycare strategy designed to double the number of spaces by 1995.

January 2, 1988   Mulroney and Reagan sign a formal trade pact, promising to push for ratification in their respective legislatures.

February 3, 1988   Mulroney fires Supply and Services Minister Michel Côté after a conflict-of-interest scandal.

March 31, 1988   Mulroney shuffles cabinet, bringing in his long-time friend Lucien Bouchard as secretary of state.

June 22, 1988   The House of Commons approves the Meech Lake Accord.

July 20, 1988   Liberal leader John Turner urges the Senate to block the free trade bill, ensuring it cannot be passed without an election.

September 22, 1988   Mulroney apologizes to Japanese Canadians for their internment during the Second World War, and offers $300 million in compensation.

September 26, 1988   The House of Commons approves the daycare bill and sends it to the Senate.

October 1, 1988   Mulroney calls an election for November 21. Sixteen bills—including the daycare program— die on the Order Paper.

November 21, 1988   The Conservative Party remains in government with 169 seats in the House of Commons. Mulroney earns a second term as prime minister, only the second Tory PM to do so since Sir John A. Macdonald.

December 12, 1988   Parliament opens; approving the free trade bill leads the agenda.

December 15, 1988   The Supreme Court strikes down Quebec's French-only sign law in a landmark decision.

December 18, 1988   Quebec premier Robert Bourassa uses his constitutional veto (the notwithstanding clause) to override the Supreme Court ruling on the sign law.

December 24, 1988   The House of Commons approves the free trade bill after a two-week fight.

December 30, 1988   The free trade bill receives Senate approval and royal assent.

April 3, 1989   Parliament opens with Mulroney's agenda for his second term, which includes a new federal sales tax (GST), more focus on the environment and an overhaul of unemployment insurance.

April 26, 1989   Media leaks force Wilson to table his lean financial plan at a hastily called news conference. The budget includes tax increases and spending cuts.

May 30, 1989   Quebec Tory backbencher Richard Grisé resigns after pleading guilty to breach of trust.

July 15, 1989   Consumer Affairs Minister Bernard Valcourt is seriously injured in a motorcycle accident at Edmonston, NB. Blood samples show illegal alcohol levels.

August 2, 1989   Valcourt resigns from cabinet after pleading guilty to impaired driving.

August 8, 1989   Wilson unveils the proposed goods and services tax as a 9 per cent federal sales levy.

September 7, 1989   The Conference Board of Canada reports that business confidence is plummeting, foreshadowing a probable recession.

October 4, 1989   The government announces plans to cut passenger rail service in half.

October 30, 1989   Newfoundland premier Clyde Wells declares he will rescind his province's approval of the Meech Lake Accord.

November 10, 1989   Three provinces—Newfoundland, New
Brunswick and Manitoba—oppose the Meech
Lake Accord at a first ministers' conference.

November 27, 1989   A parliamentary committee urges Wilson to lower
the proposed GST from 9 to 7 per cent.

December 2, 1989   Audrey McLaughlin wins the New Democratic
Party leadership race, and replaces Ed Broadbent.

December 19, 1989   Finance Minister Wilson reduces the GST to
7 per cent.

December 21, 1989   The Organisation for Economic Co-operation
and Development (OECD) predicts a mild
recession in Canada.

January 24, 1990   Sports Minister Jean Charest resigns from
cabinet following revelations that he phoned a
judge about a case involving a track coach.

February 20, 1990   Wilson warns of tough economic times ahead
in a budget that targets provinces for the
biggest spending cuts.

March 22, 1990   In a televised address, Mulroney announces the
creation of a parliamentary committee to try to
break the deadlock over the Meech Lake Accord.

May 17, 1990   The committee proposes that a follow-up
resolution be passed after the Meech Lake
Accord, explaining the limits of Quebec's
status as a "distinct society."

May 21, 1990   Environment Minister Lucien Bouchard leaves
the Conservative Party after accusing his
colleagues of trying to weaken the Meech Lake
Accord.

June 3–8, 1990   Mulroney and premiers meet for six days to
devise a plan to save the accord, which requires
the approval of Newfoundland and Manitoba.

June 11, 1990	*The Globe and Mail* publishes an interview in which Mulroney claims that the deal with the premiers worked because he knew when to "roll all the dice."
June 12, 1990	Mexico announces it is seeking a free trade deal with the United States. Trade Minister John Crosbie promises that Canada will monitor the talks.
June 22, 1990	The Meech Lake Accord collapses when Newfoundland and Manitoba fail to vote on its provisions.
June 23, 1990	An exhausted and dispirited Mulroney assures Canadians that the failure of the Meech Lake Accord was "not the failure of Canada."
June 23, 1990	Jean Chrétien is elected leader of the Liberal Party.
July 11, 1990	In a shootout between Quebec provincial police and Mohawks in Oka, one officer is killed.
July 26, 1990	The separatist Bloc Québécois—with Lucien Bouchard as its leader—presents its nationalistic platform.
August 20, 1990	Mulroney sends troops to end the Oka standoff.
August 24, 1990	Following Iraq's invasion of Kuwait, Canada dispatches three ships to the Persian Gulf to participate in a naval blockade.
September 26, 1990	The Oka standoff ends as Mohawks surrender.
September 27, 1990	Mulroney relies on a seldom-used constitutional provision to enlarge the Senate, appointing eight Tories in a move to approve the GST.
October 5, 1990	Senate members stage an eleven-week filibuster to block the GST.

October 31, 1990	Statistics Canada confirms that the country has been in a recession since the beginning of April.
November 1, 1990	Mulroney announces the creation of the Citizens' Forum on Canada's Future, headed by former *Ottawa Citizen* publisher Keith Spicer.
November 29, 1990	Canada helps sponsor a landmark UN resolution authorizing the use of force to drive Iraq out of Kuwait.
December 13, 1990	The Senate passes the GST legislation.
January 1, 1991	The GST comes into effect.
January 16, 1991	Mulroney declares that Canada, along with most of the Western world, is at war with Iraq.
February 5, 1991	Trade Minister John Crosbie announces that Canada has joined trilateral trade negotiations with the United States and Mexico.
February 8, 1991	Mulroney calls on the UN to convene a summit limiting weapons of mass destruction.
February 26, 1991	Finance Minister Wilson tables a tough budget and forecasts that Canada will be out of recession by summer.
March 13, 1991	An acid rain agreement is signed with U.S. president George H. Bush, who refuses to endorse Mulroney's proposal for a disarmament summit.
March 15, 1991	Housing Minister Alan Redway resigns from cabinet after joking to an airport security guard about carrying a gun. He is the twelfth minister to leave under a cloud.
March 27, 1991	The commission on Quebec's future—headed by Michel Bélanger and Jean Campeau—issues a report urging Bourassa to hold a referendum on sovereignty by October 1992.

April 21, 1991   Joe Clark leaves the External Affairs portfolio to become the Mulroney government's constitutional affairs minister.

June 20, 1991   The Quebec legislature passes a bill authorizing a referendum on sovereignty association.

June 27, 1991   Spicer presents the report of the Citizens' Forum on Canada's Future, claiming that there is "a fury in the land against the Prime Minister."

September 24, 1991   Mulroney unveils a sweeping new constitutional reform plan.

October 3, 1991   The government orders public servants back to work after a seventeen-day strike.

October 21, 1991   The U.S. proposes Mulroney as a candidate for secretary-general of the United Nations.

October 28, 1991   Mulroney takes himself out of the secretary-general race, saying he cannot leave during a constitutional crisis.

November 7, 1991   The parliamentary committee on the Constitution nearly collapses due to poor organization and partisan bickering.

November 13, 1991   Clark announces that the government will hold five regional conferences on the Constitution.

January 14, 1992   The Conference Board of Canada claims there is little hope for strong economic growth over the next two years.

January 19, 1992   Delegates to the first constitutional conference, in Halifax, say Quebec should be allowed greater powers than other provinces.

January 26, 1992   Delegates to the second constitutional conference, in Calgary, call for an elected, but not equal, Senate.

February 2, 1992	Delegates to the third constitutional conference, in Montreal, throw out Ottawa's proposals for economic union.
February 9, 1992	Delegates to the fourth constitutional conference, in Toronto, agree that Quebec should be recognized as a distinct society.
April 1, 1992	Mulroney tells MPs he will hold a national referendum if the first ministers fail to agree on a national unity pact.
April 22, 1992	The International Monetary Fund forecasts that Canada will have the strongest economic growth in the industrial world during 1993.
June 4, 1992	The House of Commons passes a bill authorizing a national referendum.
June 15, 1992	The House of Commons passes a new "no means no" rape bill.
July 7, 1992	Clark and the provinces (excluding Quebec) reach a constitutional deal that includes a Triple-E (effective, equal and elected) Senate.
July 10, 1992	Mulroney, unhappy with Clark's deal, says more time is needed for "fine-tuning."
August 4, 1992	Bourassa ends his two-year boycott of constitutional talks and returns to the bargaining table with the other first ministers.
August 12, 1992	Canada, the U.S. and Mexico agree in principle to the North American Free Trade Agreement (NAFTA).
August 22, 1992	The first ministers reach a constitutional deal in Ottawa after five days of intense closed-door negotiations.
August 28, 1992	The new constitutional agreement is finalized in Charlottetown.

September 3, 1992	Mulroney calls for a national referendum on the Charlottetown Accord, with polls showing two-thirds of Canadians would vote "Yes."
September 15, 1992	A Quebec radio station obtains and airs tape of two top Quebec bureaucrats agreeing that Bourassa caved in at the constitutional bargaining table.
September 20, 1992	Former prime minister Pierre Trudeau warns that Quebec nationalists are insatiable and will continue to blackmail Ottawa until federal leaders say no.
September 25, 1992	The Royal Bank of Canada releases a study warning that the breakup of Canada would mean a $10,000 drop in family income and unemployment rates of 15 per cent.
September 28, 1992	Mulroney is criticized for tearing a sheet of paper, meant to represent Quebec's gains from Confederation, during a speech at Sherbrooke, Quebec, warning that a "No" vote on the Charlottetown Accord would start the dismantling of Canada.
October 1, 1992	Trudeau joins the "No" forces with an influential speech at a Montreal restaurant.
October 6, 1992	British Columbia constitutional affairs minister Moe Sihota claims Bourassa was outgunned by the other premiers at the bargaining table.
October 26, 1992	The Charlottetown Accord is defeated in six provinces. Mulroney vows to turn his attention to the economy.
October 29, 1992	Mulroney tells his caucus that he will lead the party into the next election.
November 12, 1992	Admits he misjudged the severity of the recession.
November 22, 1992	Tells Canadians to expect an election in the fall of 1993.

November 23, 1992 Informs senior Tory organizers he will lead the party into a third general election.

December 17, 1992 Mulroney signs the North American Free Trade Agreement.

January 4, 1993 In a minor cabinet shuffle, Kim Campbell is shifted from justice to defence.

January 16–17, 1993 Mulroney is invited to Camp David to spend the final weekend with outgoing American president George H. Bush.

February 1, 1993 Liberal leader Jean Chrétien dares Mulroney to call an election. The PM boasts he has already beaten the Liberals twice; "the triple crown is just around the corner."

February 5, 1993 Mulroney meets U.S. president Bill Clinton, securing his support for NAFTA.

February 19, 1993 Mulroney tells the House of Commons, "I feel young and frisky, compared to some people I know," and that he will be happy to call an election as soon as Chrétien figures out where he stands on free trade and the GST.

February 24, 1993 Mulroney announces his resignation.

June 12, 1993 Kim Campbell becomes the new leader of the Progressive Conservatives.

June 24, 1993 Mulroney officially steps down; Campbell becomes prime minister.

September 8, 1993 Campbell calls an election for October 25, claiming Canadians "are well beyond the glib glad-handing of the past."

October 14, 1993 A television advertisement featuring still pictures of Chrétien's face along with derogatory comments is severely criticized. Campbell claims she did not see the spot before it aired.

October 25, 1993   The Liberals secure 177 ridings in the election. The only Progressive Conservatives to win seats are New Brunswick's Elsie Wayne and Quebec's Jean Charest. Campbell loses in her Vancouver Centre riding. Lucien Bouchard's Bloc Québécois becomes the official opposition.

Mulroney Unplugged

———

What a bizarre phenomenon he was,
this backwoods combination of
Machiavelli, leprechaun and Dr. Phil.

THE PHONE RANG AT AN AWKWARD MOMENT,
which turned embarrassing when my wife walked into
our living room and declared, "It's the prime minister. He
wants to speak to you."

Her announcement was met with jeers from our neighbours, gathered for a pre-Christmas tipple in 1986 at our
seaside house, cantilevered over a cliff, facing Haro Strait
on Canada's extreme western edge. Across the water I
could spot the shores of San Juan Island and the
American flag being whipped by the winter wind.

"Why would 'Lyin' Brian' be phoning you?" asked
Ross, our immediate neighbour. "Maybe he wants advice
on when to quit. I can tell him: Yesterday!" Frank, the
retired English gentleman who helped with our garden,
and several others chimed in, making it very clear that
none of these hardy and practical west coasters believed for

a minute that anyone in Cordova Bay, the tiny village nestled into a notch on the coast of Vancouver Island where we lived, would be likely to receive a call from a prime minister— even Brian Mulroney, whose reputation ranked just below that of the harbour seals that fouled local fish nets.

I picked up the phone in the kitchen to hear that resonant, rain-barrel voice of his ask, "Where are you, Peter?" This was his standard opening ploy. While the PMO switchboard could always locate me, he never knew if I was in a suitable place for one of his rants about "those myopic, incestuous bastards" in the Ottawa press gallery, or the latest perfidy by "that asshole" Pierre Trudeau.

"I'm at home," I replied, "entertaining the neighbours . . ."

"Lookit, I just wanted to tell you something." He sounded unusually subdued. "We recently celebrated my mother's seventieth birthday and she cooked asparagus flavoured with bread crumbs melted in butter. When I asked where she got the recipe, she said, 'from Peter Newman's mother.' We really enjoyed it. I thought you'd want to know."

He bid me a gentle Merry Christmas and hung up. It was nearly Silent Night, Holy Night, and the Big Guy was feeling mellow.

The call was a typical grace note from a man I had known and admired for twenty-five years, a man who had never failed to honour the appropriate occasion. My mother, the last and closest member of my family, had recently suffered a prolonged and tormenting death from cancer. She had enjoyed meeting the Mulroneys many years earlier when she and Brian's mother were both visiting Ottawa, where I then lived. Now he was subtly acknowledging the agony of my mother's passing, and how much I must be missing her.

Such compassionate gestures were one source of his power. His entourage, which consisted of his chums from St. Francis Xavier University and the Laval law school, had learned to appreciate this side of the man. It wasn't just for show. Those of us who were beneficiaries of his generous sentiments and frequent phone calls could never figure out how he made time to govern the second biggest nation on Earth without forgetting our birthdays, wedding anniversaries and deaths in the families.

Now I had a problem. How could I explain to my expectant guests that the prime minister of the second largest nation on Earth was calling me ostensibly because he had enjoyed my mother's asparagus recipe?

As I walked back into the living room, looking as if I had just kissed the Pope's ring, my guests began shouting: "So, what did he want? Is he lonely? Hope you didn't tell him about that marijuana stash up on Dover Street!"

I silenced them with a wink. "If you must know," I confided, "I advised him to invade Zimbabwe."

It had been a typical Mulroney moment.

HE BUGS US STILL. During the Mulroney years, most Canadians stopped being languid spectators of the Ottawa minstrel show. Instead, the country's benign burghers, mobilized by their loathing for the blarneyed smoothie who occupied the nation's highest elected office, turned federal politics into a killing field. What was it, exactly, that prompted such visceral contempt for this down-to-earth politician with charm to burn and the guts to tackle some of the country's toughest problems? Even now, almost a generation later, it remains a puzzle, in the same league as trying to figure out why Japanese kamikaze pilots wore safety helmets or how wild deer manage to read those DEER CROSSING signs on country roads.

Perhaps the suicide pilots wanted to keep the hair out of their eyes, and probably the deer just follow their cousins' spoor, but the Mulroney mystery demands a better explanation. This book attempts to provide it through his unfiltered thoughts and uncensored words. By reviving the echoes of his presence in this unplugged, informal, one-on-one format, I hope to resolve the riddle—to trace his mutation from the genial poster boy of U-turn politics into a reform-minded statesman who became a high-stakes player, rolled the dice and lost.

Mulroney's time in office was a harsh, unsettling decade. No journalistic formula can convey the sheer velocity of events, the patterns of response and denial that shaped the stewardship of the rowdy Irishman who headed Canada's federal government for most of ten crucial years. It was a time of few heroes, yet there was no shortage of heroic confrontations, providing some of the most hair-raising clashes in Canada's generally tepid political history. But instead of emerging from these pivotal encounters with victor's laurels, Mulroney seemed diminished by them.

THE SECRET OF GOVERNING CANADA is knowing what not to touch. The first (and only) irrevocable law of politics in these northern latitudes is to make the necessary possible. The most successful prime ministers have been ideological acrobats. They could square any circle and allow pragmatism (a fancy word for where the votes are) to decide where they stood.

Brian Mulroney was by temperament and inclination the most traditional of politicians. Yet he championed fundamental changes, cracked open social, political and economic verities, and attempted to alter the country's political landscape while at the same time placing its future in play. He became embroiled in an accumulation of tumbling paradoxes in the midst of which anything might happen, and did.

He was the most radical prime minister in Canadian history—radical in the dictionary meaning of "going to the root of things and advocating fundamental changes in social and economic structures." Initially condemned for being an unprincipled opportunist (stuck in his shillelagh pan-Canadianism), he ended up trying to rewrite the country's social contract.

He came to power at a time when Canadians were searching for emotional anchorage in an increasingly alien, fast-paced, technological world gone global. The Canada he was governing was far removed from Northrop Frye's peaceable kingdom, a nation grown hard and cynical. Instead of being able to tackle an orderly succession of issues, Mulroney's political agenda was set by the winds—or, more precisely, by the hurricanes—of change. He might have been expected to escape those social and economic upheavals by hunkering down and doing as little as possible. Instead, he behaved like an obsessive beekeeper, patrolling the buzzing apiary that Canada had become, punching holes into every hive he could find. More often than not, the liberated bees stung the man who had set them free.

In those accusatory times, the contradictions in the country's character grew so acute that no simple show of authority or patriotic appeal could have quelled the public's twitchiness. Any police officer knows that it's safer to confront professional killers than to intervene in family quarrels. That was why our internal squabble grew so combustible. During Mulroney's time, Canadians mirrored their neuroses, performing the psychic act that Norman Mailer described as "taking our national anxiety, so long buried, and releasing it to the surface, where it belongs."

From being self-satisfied facsimile Brits living in a quiescent, faintly backward society, we became ardent if neurotic pseudo-Americans reaching out for a future modelled on imported values. The Protestant ethic that worships moderation (not merely as the safest course between extremes, but as the essential ingredient of social change) remained our state religion, but in its purest form it had become as rare as the Sunday suits that had symbolized it. Canada was transformed into an inflammable collection of 27 million characters in search of an author.

Once that defiant new mood took hold, Mulroney became the poster boy for Canadians' individual anger and collective rage. The dispirited country he announced he was leaving behind in the gloomy winter of 1993 bore little resemblance to the Canada whose governance he had eagerly embraced in the hopeful autumn of 1984. During the interval, he roused more hostility and controversy than any Canadian prime minister before him. It was as if he were responsible for every sparrow that fell from the sky. The more vulnerable he appeared, the more blame was directed his way. He became the nation's designated lightning rod, living out Bertrand Russell's hard-hearted admonition that "democracy is the process by which people choose the man who'll get the blame."

A fatal weakness was his tendency to assume personal blame for most of his ministers' many pratfalls. At crisis points in past administrations, his predecessors had backed away from politically wounded colleagues, cut them out of the loop, demanded their resignations, then carried on as if they had never existed. Mulroney too often supported his offending ministers and MPs when they were not just walking wounded, but walking dead. His time in office turned out to be a long siege marked by few calm interludes. When he resigned, he'd been in power longer than all but four Canadian heads of government (King, Macdonald, Trudeau and Laurier), outlasted an astonishing nineteen provincial premiers and survived nearly every leader of the Western world. But it cost him.

A good argument could be made that Brian Mulroney was a daring agent of change; a better case can be made that he was its victim.

I FIRST MET BRIAN MULRONEY in 1961 at a one-day symposium held in Quebec City by a group of Laval law students calling themselves the Congress of Canadian Affairs. The meeting, organized mainly by Mulroney and Peter White, who later became Conrad Black's business partner, provided the first platform for an intelligent discussion of Quebec separatism. I was inordinately impressed by this youngster from Baie-Comeau, and we decided to keep in touch.

The son of an electrician who held two jobs to make ends meet, the youthful Brian had attended St. Francis Xavier University in Antigonish, Nova Scotia. There he came under the influence of the co-operative teachings of Father Moses Coady, who implanted the notion in his students that an active social conscience was life's highest goal. Mulroney joined the college's Progressive Conservatives because he calculated that his chances for personal advancement were more promising than with the moribund campus Liberals. "The Grits were no fun—they took themselves too seriously," was his ready explanation.[1]

When Mulroney applied for a Rhodes scholarship, the Nova Scotia selection committee invited candidates to a formal luncheon as a test of their social graces. "I was living in Halifax," recalled Patrick MacAdam, Mulroney's friend from St. Francis Xavier who later became one of his key operatives, "when Brian called looking for a bed for the night. He was having his Rhodes interview the next day and wanted me to show him which knife, fork and spoon to use. I had been a raggedy-assed kid from Cape Breton Island but had joined the Reserve Officers Training Corps while at university, and knew about cutlery." Brian used the right fork but didn't get the scholarship.

---

1. Remarkably, Mulroney contested no elections, even for internal posts at university, until his 1976 run for leadership of the federal Conservative Party. He was determined not to have a single defeat on his CV.

By the time he and I met, he was already deep into Tory politics, having attended the 1956 party leadership convention as vice-chairman of the Youth for Diefenbaker movement. Later in 1961, when *Maclean's* published an all-party panel discussion about young politicians (hosted by Peter Gzowski and me), I picked Mulroney (and Ted Rogers) to represent the Conservatives. At one point I asked the assembled group, "Will the politician of the future be different? What will be his attitude towards patronage?"

"His attitude will be drastically changed from the attitude of those who are in government today," Mulroney jumped in. "The young people of today are going to strengthen the nation at the cost of partisan politics. They are going to have a much more idealistic view of things twenty years from now than we do today." I should have got him to reproduce that in needlepoint.

From then on, every time I visited Quebec City during the 1960s, we would meet. In his early twenties, Brian lived in a modest boarding house at 71 rue Saint-Louis, dividing his time between chasing nurses and drinking at the Aux Délices tavern, as well as devoting spare moments to his law studies at Laval. Always nattily dressed, he was the best-informed source in town and was busy trying to boost the federal Tories' waning chances in the province. *Renegade in Power*, my 1963 history of the Diefenbaker years, mentions that the Conservative prime minister "had only one enlightened advisor in the province of Quebec, by the name of Brian Mulroney. He was politically mature beyond his years and had a perfect appreciation of Quebec's political aspirations. Unlike most of the other men who had access to the Prime Minister, he was unafraid to be openly critical. It was largely because Mulroney's advice went unheeded that the Tories lost the confidence of Quebec, and thus the 1963 election." (The Chief believed that his edict of issuing bilingual cheques for French-speaking federal civil servants was enough to keep Quebeckers content.)

Mulroney's mentor was Daniel Johnson, leader of the Union Nationale, who later became Quebec's premier. They spent many an afternoon talking politics at La Place de la Fontaine, the ground-level bar at the Château Frontenac hotel, where I occasionally joined them. Poking fun at me for taking seriously *la grande politique* of the reigning Liberals, Johnson would expound his own political philosophy, or rather his lack of any. One evening after a round of kir, he told me, "You know, in politics it's very dangerous to have a philosophy. In a democracy you should have politicians who settle the problems that exist, not set out to prove philosophical ideals." No matter what the weather or circumstance, Johnson always appeared impeccably dressed, not a hair out of place, looking more like a mannequin than a down-home ward politician. During our chatter, Johnson confided that the secret of maintaining effective leadership of any political party was to concentrate on keeping its caucus happy. Just about everything Mulroney did later in life carried Johnson's imprint, from his thrice-daily shirt changes to his emphasis on the value of a contented caucus, his struggle to grant Quebec distinct-society status and his admiration of all things American, especially tug-size black limousines as symbols of authority.

He was moving up within the Quebec wing of the Conservative Party, but his ideological dedication was always skin deep. When I asked Alberta premier Ralph Klein—the Grandma Moses of Canadian politics, in the sense that one was never sure whether his wisdom was intentional—what kind of a Conservative he considered Mulroney to be, he deadpanned, "I never knew him as a Conservative. I only knew him as Brian."

Our off-hand meetings took on new urgency in 1976, when Mulroney decided to run for the party leadership being vacated by Robert Stanfield. Along with Ian MacDonald of the Montreal *Gazette* and Peter Desbarats of *Global News*, I attended one of his final pre-convention strategy sessions at a cottage in Quebec's Eastern Townships, near Magog. For someone who had never tried to get elected to anything, his bid for the leadership seemed more than a little presumptuous, particularly since Pierre Trudeau was solidly entrenched in power at the time.

It was during that weekend in Magog that this book was born. We were sitting on the steps of the cottage, looking toward the river's outlet to Lac Memphrémagog, when Brian said, out of the blue, that if he won office, he would appoint me Canada's ambassador to Austria. I laughed and shook my head, explaining that while Vienna might be my birthplace and while I still spoke the language, being an ambassador and having to lie for my country was not my preferred career option. But since he had brought up the subject of some sort of collaboration, I told him that if he was ever elected PM, I wanted to write a book about his time in power, providing it was not a commissioned effort. My tentative title would be *The Burden of Power*, I said, because I intended to document from the inside how difficult Canada was to govern, even on good days. Mulroney's only control over the project would be its timing. He and I agreed that since I intended to present an unadorned portrait of him and his administration, such a book would be published after he left office. "I don't want a puff job," I can distinctly hear him telling my tape recorder. "I find myself so goddamn frustrated, as a modest student of history, wanting to know, what was the guy really like? Did he get laid? Did he look after his family? Did he swear? Did he get drunk? It's safe to say that the only bloody Canadian prime minister who really comes across as a human being is Macdonald. I've always said that if I were ever lucky enough to be in that position as prime minister myself, I would not object at all to people reading about my warts and my failings. They're part of me. So as I say, I don't want a puff job."

We shook on it.

My favourite moment of his unsuccessful 1976 leadership run was the midnight phone call I received, presumably while he was cornered in some Edmonton hotel room by a well-briefed journalist. "What do I think about Rhodesia?" he whispered into the mouthpiece, his voice a muffled foghorn. At the time, white minority rule, unilaterally declared by Prime Minister Ian Smith, was still in effect. I advised him to support the British policy of trade sanctions, imposed to restore democratic rule.

The race was lost because his campaign was too ostentatious and because he had yet to plant his roots deep enough in the party outside Quebec. Joe Clark emerged as everybody's second choice, which left Mulroney bitter and vindictive enough that his drinking and dark moods threatened his marriage. The situation improved when he moved into the corporate arena by becoming CEO of Iron Ore of Canada, a valuable subsidiary of Hanna Mining of Cleveland. He thus joined the Canadian Establishment, became a member of the Mount Royal Club and settled into a life of luxury and leisure—with one exception. During that time he became a member of the royal commission headed by Judge Robert Cliche, a thoughtful professor-politician charged with cleaning up the rot in the province's construction industry. The testimony of 279 witnesses revealed the corruption and violence triggered by the clash of unbridled unionism and irresponsible capitalism. A worker had been stabbed in the back and one union official had driven his bulldozer into a Hydro-Québec generator, causing damage worth $32 million. The commission's 132 recommendations brought peace to the construction scene, but for Mulroney it was a valuable lesson in controlling mayhem—the ideal preparation for becoming leader of the Progressive Conservative Party of Canada.

When my book on Conrad Black was published in 1982 to a controversial review in the *Globe and Mail*, Mulroney invited me to Montreal for a weekend and took me to a

Canadiens' hockey game just to cheer me up. I had attended his wedding to the beautiful Mila in 1973, and he was one of my best men when I married Camilla Turner in 1979, and offered to fly us to an exotic honeymoon spot aboard his corporate jet. We went sailing up the Murray Canal, off Lake Ontario, instead.

In 1983 I accompanied Mulroney to the key Tory policy convention in Winnipeg, where his platoon of search-and-destroy commandos successfully undermined Joe Clark's leadership to create the vacancy Mulroney intended to fill. This was a brutal Irish power play that would have made the IRA proud. Watching the Tory party in conclave was a sobering experience, even if the delegates themselves drank enough booze to pickle a pharaoh. They were all there: the bushy-tailed Mulroney disciples, with smiles on their faces and murder in their hearts; the defrocked zealots from the Age of Diefenbaker, worn out by years of political outrage; the prime-time guys who had jetted in from Bay Street and who scrutinized Clark through pawnbroker eyes, trying to calculate the downside risk of sticking with him. Then there were the hang-loose mystics from British Columbia, tuning their chakras and quizzing their inner children about whom to support, along with the mouth breathers from Saskatchewan, sipping Styrofoam coffee out of Styrofoam cups, cursing a world they never made. What these and other delegates had in common—the sentiment which then (and now) unites Conservatives—was that no statute of limitations applied to the their internal feuds. They not only eat their young, they swallow their old.

I still have the perceptive internal memo written by John Thompson, the Toronto industrialist who was then Mulroney's campaign manager. "People are scared of your candidacy because they don't trust you," he confided to his candidate. "They don't trust you because of the slickness, the smoothness, the pat answers, the feeling that you are not your own man, but somebody else's candidate in your perfect Christian Dior shirts and Ken doll image." Thompson's contribution was key, but his heresy kept him from sharing the spoils of eventual victory.

The actual leadership selection, held in Ottawa, could have gone another way if Joe Clark had agreed to support John Crosbie, whose combination of being unilingual and boasting about it made him too tempting a stand-alone target. But Joe remained the ever-dutiful pedestrian who would never set the world on fire except by accident, and made no move. Smiling through the sweaty proceedings was David Crombie, a good man in the wrong place at the wrong time, his followers (including the redoubtable Barbara McDougall) huddling around the few campfires of decency that illuminated the Tory landscape on that historic day. Of all the contenders, Crombie sold the smallest piece of himself that afternoon, and suffered the consequences.

Michael Wilson had about him the brooding diffidence of a man waiting for something that had already happened. His campaign literature featured his photograph, racquet at the ready, with a caption claiming, "Wilson is an accomplished athlete and one of the few on Parliament Hill who beats Finance Minister Lalonde at squash." All through Wilson's therapeutic nomination speech, the delegates assumed their sermon-enduring positions as their mood alternated between mild boredom and mild despair. Then there were the fringe candidates, led by John Gamble, all chest and no neck, blowing through his moustache, a touch of hermit madness in his eyes.

Mulroney was selected leader on the fourth ballot by only 259 votes over Clark. He stepped onto the platform, a winner at last, with all the chutzpah of P.G. Wodehouse's fictional butler, Jeeves, who entered any room "like a procession of one."

The 1984 election that followed was a love-in. Although most voters recognized Mulroney as an amiable lightweight, something significant happened during that campaign that only became clear to me when I attended a late-afternoon rally at a Montreal shopping centre. When I arrived, the crowd was milling about with the kind of excitement that greets the annual bull run in Pamplona, Spain. Then it started to rain. Mulroney came out bareheaded and began dispensing his brand of blarney, even though he was getting soaked. Mulroney shouted. The audience not only lapped up his performance, but spontaneously began to collapse their umbrellas, presumably wanting to be blessed by the same raindrops that were wilting Mulroney's cowlick. The man next to me sported the blank, pomaded look of a jowly, haunch-grabbing primate, with a composite-drawn face that gained character mainly from the angle of his cigar—not your typical Mulroney acolyte. But even he succumbed to the Irish charm, ignoring the rain and croaking in his raspy voice, "Way to go, Brian!" He gave me a dirty look because I was taking notes instead of cheering. That was the moment I knew this was going to be a sweep.

And it was. After starting ten points behind the Liberals, Mulroney won 211 of the Commons' 282 seats, a margin of victory unrivalled in Canadian history. When Trudeaumania was its height in 1968, Pierre won 56 fewer ridings.

Immediately after the election, Canadians felt good about themselves and their country. But during the campaign, Mulroney put his reputation on the line with his hyperbolic rhetoric, promising that the day after he was elected, "there will be tens upon tens of thousands of new jobs!" He pledged to end patronage and guaranteed he would run an open government. At one point, Dalton Camp, who served briefly as a Mulroney advisor, took him aside and said, "Damn it, Brian, you cold-turkeyed on smoking. You cold-turkeyed on drinking. Why can't you cold-turkey on hyperbole?" But he never did. By promising too much and not being able to deliver, he was caught having to choose between manoeuvrability and credibility, a deadly political dilemma.

Tom Kierans, then head of the C.D. Howe Institute, was convinced that Mulroney was ill prepared for the top slot. "Brian's background left him totally unsuited to deal with the country's problems, especially from Ottawa, which is like passing into a spaceship it has so little to do with how Canadian society actually works," he claimed. "You can't leave the corporate boardroom to become prime minister and know what the hell you're doing. Mulroney may have been qualified to negotiate free trade, but he had no more idea of how to reform social policy than how to fly to the moon. He sat there, isolated in that crazy vacuum called Ottawa, listening to the special interest groups as if they represented the country, or any part of it. Canada was changing—race, creed, colour, male-female—and most of the people he talked to were totally irrelevant. He didn't have any touchstones. I mourned his lack of political sensibility."

SHORTLY AFTER MULRONEY TOOK OFFICE, I wrote the new prime minister my only letter of advice: "There is only one thing that can defeat you: if you begin to believe that the version of Canada reflected in Ottawa has any reality. You won the leadership and you won the election by going into the country, where real people live and real things happen. A desk in Ottawa is the very worst place from which to govern this country. So even if you get too busy to breathe, don't ever forget that your power base is outside the confines of Ottawa's castles in the air that house so many misguided mentalities . . . Even the man who occupies the nation's highest office must realize that he has been chosen, not to seek historical vindication, but to preside over the available options. *Bonne chance.*"

Soon afterwards, we concluded the formal arrangements for my book through an exchange of letters in which I promised not to publish while he was still in office. He understood that this would in no way be an official or sanctioned biography but pledged to supply me with documents, including secret party memoranda and strategy papers, as well as the journal in which he chronicled his personal impressions of what had been going on. Our agreement's key paragraph, as drafted by me and signed by him, read, "Life is unpredictable and just to make it official, please initial this letter, which will make official the fact that you are keeping certain personal and highly confidential but not classified reminiscences of important events during your stewardship in your personal possession—and that these are destined to be shown to me and only me when I come to write my book about the Mulroney years." That understanding launched my arduous cycle of chronicling Brian's stewardship.

DURING THE MORE THAN THIRTY YEARS I knew Brian Mulroney and the two decades when I actively interviewed him, he granted me access never before allowed any journalist by a Canadian PM. I took full advantage of that unique gift of time and confidence. Between these covers are gathered a selection of brutally frank comments from the prime minister and his entourage who governed our collective destinies from 1984 into 1993.

The tapes of our conversations were transcribed by Frances McNeely, who has been my empathetic right hand since I hired her at *Maclean's* in 1978, and still is. My 330 interviews with the two dozen men and women closest to the PM, including the 98 interviews I had with Mulroney, amounted to 7,400 pages of transcripts—about 1.8 million words. I was a freelance writer by the time Mulroney assumed office, and for the next decade I took quarterly interview trips to Ottawa on my own nickel. I would fly in for a couple of days and interview members of his entourage, who had been instructed to confide in me. (Their names, titles and interview dates, as well as the chronology of my sessions with the PM, are listed in Appendix A.) Early evenings or on weekends I would see Mulroney himself, either at 24 Sussex Drive or at his country place on Harrington Lake. Various staff members would drive me up to the Gatineau cottage, the most mysterious of them being Roger Mazerolle, a federal civil servant who, I discovered, was the prime minister's official food taster, though Mazerolle told me nothing but his name, rank and serial number, and that his boss preferred meat and potatoes. (I later found out he had a backup named Jacques Ouellet, who seemed to specialize in pretasting lobster.) This was a defensive move adopted not in the face of the PM's plummeting popularity, but as a cautionary measure dictated by the RCMP.

Watching Mulroney during my visits, I realized the unusual significance he placed on prime ministerial toys. He revelled in those official Cadillacs with the Canadian flag on their portside front fenders, their red NORAD telephones, back-seat TVs, and self-important police outriders gunning their Harleys. I could sense that he savoured walking by the supplicants waiting outside his office, watching them hastily put down the magazines they were nervously browsing, as if such pastimes were a frivolity forbidden in the presence of *le grand fromage*. Wherever Mulroney went, people monitored his every move, followed his gaze, prayed to be noticed. To the ultimate outsider from Baie-Comeau, being PM meant that he not only had made it, but had it made. Mulroney didn't need to be reminded that the sixteenth-century navigator Jacques Cartier had described Mulroney's birthplace, the St. Lawrence's wild North Shore, as "the land God gave to Cain."

In his lengthy and uneven political journey, Mulroney was handicapped by being out of phase with the mood of the country. He belonged to the Old Canada, where a sense of the land and the protection of the family hearth were palpable notions that defined people's lives. Mulroney's childhood in Baie-Comeau was the governing influence of his life. He never saw himself apart from the child he had been. It was a simple existence pegged on physical survival in a harsh universe light years removed from the cities of glass inhabited by the people whose political leader he would become. The mill town offered little comfort and no prospects. As elsewhere in rural Canada, its main cultural facility was the community hockey rink, but here, pollution from the stacks of the local paper mill had also defoliated every tree in town. There were two seasons: winter and August. The little community's plain, hard-working people frequented the Taverne aux Amis to drink so they could remember the good old days, then drink some more to forget them. The Mulroney house at 132 Champlain Avenue was cozy and filled with a loving atmosphere, but the town itself was a prison. Young Brian's genes as a mediator came to him naturally, since the Irish historically mediated between the French and the English, sharing language with the one and religion with the other.

He was our one and only working-class prime minister, and was all too aware of his origins. He felt he had to take on a new guise to persuade us into believing he deserved office. Precisely because he had to keep proving that he could fill his own shoes, he got trapped into delivering more substantive policies than a more secure leader like Jean Chrétien, who accomplished virtually nothing in ten years. In the process of trying to live up to the role he was playing, Mulroney created a political revolution that altered the Canadian landscape.

Most of his biographers, detractors and hagiographers maintained that the defining experiences of his youth were the occasional songs he performed for Colonel Robert McCormick, the proprietor of the *Chicago Tribune*, who visited his paper mill in the private company town once a year aboard his converted B-17 bomber. Nearly everyone there depended on their foreign landlord for their livelihood. The image of the eight-year-old Brian, dressed up in his white shirt and black tie, standing on the piano at the Manoir guesthouse, warbling "Dearie" and other McCormick favourites, then pocketing a fifty-dollar bill for his performance (which went straight into his mother's grocery account), created an irresistible metaphor. That innocent vignette was routinely offered as proof that Little Brian would mature into Big Brian who, half a century later, would give Canada away to the Yanks for a song. To my mind, the real significance of these musical interludes was not the youngster's fawning performance (every kid enjoys the approbation of adults) but the colonel's patronizing presence. Growing up in that pinched milieu, Mulroney learned that deference to higher authority might pay the occasional dividend—but that possessing authority was far better than catering to it. That small epiphany was the emotional trigger that led him into politics, and eventually to the top.

It was in his hometown that the young Mulroney was also baptized by the mineral waters of progressivism. He wore the conservative label but never became a neo-con and seldom practiced any faith except to reach for personal power. The fact that he was Canada's first working-class prime minister ought to have been an advantage, but he didn't celebrate it. "The problem with Brian," his friend Sam Wakim told me, "was that his story is not really a Canadian story. No Canadian had ever done this before, a poor working stiff from Baie-Comeau who joined the party when he was a teenager and reached the top job. In the States, a guy coming from any occupation can become president, and his background is honoured."

By the time he was fourteen, when he left to attend a boarding school in New Brunswick, Mulroney knew that his future lay elsewhere—that he would have others sing to *him*. That was his ticket to ride. He never spent another winter in Baie-Comeau. During his triumphant 1984 election campaign, he repeatedly proclaimed that Canada was "a land of small towns and big dreams," which applied to no one more poignantly than himself. It gave resonance to his quest, as it would to so many lives in a country where the only way to pursue your dreams was to leave home.

Now the whole damn country was his to command. Now he could choreograph the capital's power groupies and make them jump to his tune. Ottawa politicians need constant affirmation of their omnipotence, even if its only outward sign is the casual wave from the commissionaire on duty at Parliament's front doors. They *saluted* when Muldoon waltzed in.

FROM THE START, OUR INTERVIEWS had quickly turned into soliloquies. I became an offstage voice, prompting and goading him as he initially portrayed himself as the ambitious plotter, followed by the newly elected PM who could do no wrong, then the scandal-ridden victim of gossipmongers, and finally the increasingly disappointed loner in his cave, surrounded by villains and evildoers. That was the arc of his story. Throughout, he displayed an ironic awareness that he was speaking with an eye to history. He wished me to portray him as he wanted to be seen. In this sense, our exchanges were less Socratic than narcissistic. Mulroney knew exactly what he was doing but thought that I didn't. I knew what he was up to but didn't want him to know that I did. Despite this little game, *Secret Tapes* paints an unvarnished profile of my subject.[2]

The transcripts are exact. But I allowed myself one liberty: if the PM or any of my other interviewees talked on separate occasions about the uprising at Oka, for

---

2. The tapes, transcripts and floppy disks of our interviews are lodged in the Fisher Rare Books Collection at the University of Toronto and will eventually be accessible to academics and the public.

example, I felt it was within my rights to stitch those comments together into a coherent whole. It's the narrative line that counts. Narrative, after all, is character revealed by action over time. Stories unfold—always have, always will. This one does, through the words of the men and women who lived them.

Though he had an audience of only one, Mulroney put on a show compelling enough to sway the most cynical and the most innocent—two qualities in which I abound. What he never understood was that charm doesn't constitute a belief system. Brian Mulroney was a very private person, an Irish charmer who needed the electorate to love him yet who hesitated to reveal to the voters who he really was. Between wanting to be loved and wishing to be respected, he came down on the wrong side. Making enemies is sometimes essential, but they must be chosen with great care. It can even define you, as Pierre Trudeau discovered to his delight.[3]

Mulroney's political ambition was relentless but not blind. Despite his magnificent victory, he could sense that the contradictions in the country's character had grown so acute that no single symbol of authority, even that of the prime minister, could reconcile them. The vulnerable public mood required a leader whose thoughts and aspirations—like the country's—remained in flux, so that his subjects could hang their varied aspirations on his destiny. That tactic required a magus with the ambiguity of a Trudeau to carry it off. Mulroney was about as ambiguous as a speed bump. His style of governing—long, brooding silences interrupted by avalanches of new policy announcements—spawned confusion and alarm. No one knew what to expect, least of all Mulroney. "Our government," admitted Charley

---

3. When the French sage Voltaire was on his deathbed, an attending priest asked if he was ready to renounce the devil. The dying man shook his head. "This," he said, "is no time to make new enemies."

McMillan, his chief policy advisor, "is 5 per cent planning and 95 per cent scrambling."

As the interviews that follow illustrate, the defining mark of Mulroney's character was his need for approval. Lacking internal validation, he spent a lifetime in scarch of himself. We are all insecure, but it is how we handle those 3 a.m. feelings of inadequacy that decides what kind of men and women we are. The profile that emerges from *The Secret Mulroney Tapes* may be one-dimensional, but it's the dimension that counts, because it is the way he saw himself. He reveals little sustaining philosophy beyond "you dance with the one who brung you."

What a bizarre phenomenon he was, this backwoods combination of Machiavelli, leprechaun and Dr. Phil. Yet Mulroney's impact was enormous. He deconstructed the country's economy through free trade with the Americans, seriously rejigged our tax system with the introduction of the GST, deregulated the transportation and energy sectors, privatized dozens of Crown corporations and revolutionized social policy with precedent-shattering budgets. At the same time, he seemed to believe that public consent could be bargained for, forgetting that people don't like to feel bought and that they resent the purchaser as much as the transaction. That attitude, along with his presidential style, triggered the rise of the Bloc Québécois and Reform parties, fatally weakening his original power bases in French and Western Canada.[4]

His contradictions knew few bounds. He professed never to have read the three crucial anti-Mulroney texts: books by Stevie Cameron, Claire Hoy and, to a

---

4. The emergence of the Bloc Québécois stole great material from comedians attempting to satirize the political scene. Here was a party driven entirely by its members' death wish for Canada, sitting in a Parliament where they could hold the balance of power, calmly sabotaging our future—always careful, of course, not to pull the plug until its members qualified for their parliamentary pensions.

much lesser degree, John Sawatsky. Yet he could quote them from memory. I was part of a group of sympathizers who in 1990 advised him to resist reading the papers so that he could stop obsessing about what the media thought of him. As my interviews so abundantly reflect, he could always be counted on to interrupt whatever was occupying his mind by launching into an achy-breaky lament about how the press was ruining his life. (It played well, if you went heavy on the pedal steel guitar.) And yet he snorted news and commentary as if it were the kind of stuff they seize at the border. His self-imposed media ban had lasted less than a week when he phoned me to triumphantly announce that an editorial in the *Lethbridge Herald* had praised his Meech constitutional caper. At the same time he complained to me that "It's been twelve weeks since I was on the cover of *Maclean's*." (By then I had left the editorship of that magazine and had nothing to do with choosing its covers.)

I even tried to console him by offering to rewrite the Lord's Prayer, urging reporters to recite, "Give us this day our daily bread and forgive us our press passes . . ." Nothing worked.

It really hurt him. Sam Wakim, Mulroney's soul-buddy, used to taxi over late every evening to the loading docks behind the *Globe and Mail* building in Toronto to grab a paper fresh off the press so he could report what was being written about the PM. When Wakim phoned Brian and Mila to read them Stevie Cameron's story about his alleged Gucci shoe collection, Mila came close to breaking down. Their son Mark hugged her, and said, "Why can't we just go home?" To which his father, close to tears, replied, "Out of the mouths of babes . . ."

Politically, the prime minister operated in a chilly climate, made worse by his flurries of patronage appointments. I wasn't excluded. He invited me to become the chairman of the CBC, which was a compliment of sorts because I had been offered the same position by Pierre Trudeau. Neither offer tempted me. I wanted to retain my independence, and recognized that trying to ride herd over the cats who run the CBC was an impossible assignment.

While the Mulroney government was worse than it should have been, it was better than it appeared to be. But try as he might, Mulroney was never able to fashion a strong enough following for his constitutional agenda, which he saw as his chief legacy. Following his triumphs in the 1984 and 1988 elections, his approval ratings went into free fall. They eventually sank to 11 per cent, the lowest ever recorded for any PM.[5]

As the polls kept slipping, Mulroney called me for a heart-to-heart. "Lookit, Peter," said he, "tell me the truth. What's going on? Why am I so unpopular?"

"Okay, Brian," I said flat out. "It's simple: nobody believes a word you say." After that he didn't call for six weeks.

No one told him the truth. Most members of his entourage were not so much his acolytes as his idolators, too deferential to speak out. Nor did he want them to. "The staff was trained to believe that criticism of the prime minister was disloyal no matter how constructive," recalled Stanley Hartt, who served as both deputy minister of finance and Mulroney's chief of staff. "He was actually convinced that if you tolerated a system where it was okay to criticize the prime minister, even among a very limited circle of people who wanted nothing but good for him, that before long the distinction between creative and constructive criticism and negative and destructive criticism would blur. He would not be seen as a god, and if he were not a god, he couldn't lead. His 'prime ministeriality' didn't permit him to allow criticism even by his top aides."

---

5. By coincidence, that equalled the proportion of Americans who believed that Elvis Presley was alive and well in a suburb of Memphis.

INEVITABLY, THIS VOLUME digs into the echoing canyons of Brian Mulroney's psyche. What he said into my tape recorder during nearly a hundred interviews both illuminates and condemns his brand of politics. This is not a history of the Mulroney years but rather an impressionistic journey through a prime minister's mind and temper. It is less Mulroney Unplugged than Mulroney Undressed. From interview to interview he paints his self-portrait with broad yet subtle strokes. More often than not he is on the defensive, convinced that his unacknowledged triumphs and perpetual betrayals were legion. Few imagined insults were small enough to claim his forgiveness.

I vividly remember coming to interview him at 24 Sussex Drive, his official residence, a couple of months after he took power. Like most visitors, I was given a personally conducted tour: "That was where John Diefenbaker had his desk; that was the chair where George Hees sat and cried when he resigned from cabinet; those are the stairs Maggie Trudeau used to sneak her boyfriends upstairs . . ."

After one of our interviews, he called me into his study, where he proudly presented me with a sheaf of blank stationery bearing the golden prime ministerial imprint, as if to prove conclusively that he really was the first among equals. The same afternoon, he confessed when that realization first hit him: "I remember thinking that I must be prime minister, because I was signing a thank-you letter to Fidel Castro. This was not something I had done every day."

Those who saw only the stiff public Mulroney will be surprised by his emergence on my tapes as one of the great stand-up comics of Canadian politics. His humour is wry and clever, not at all pedantic. To my comment that he was selling out Canada, he looked surprised, cocked his head to one side and asked in pretend bewilderment, "Who would buy it?" When I asked him about his

Guccis, he replied with mock seriousness, "We had a family crisis the other night. Nicolas was lost for three hours in my shoe closet. The kid obviously doesn't have much sophistication. We found him in the Wallabee section." Joking about his extravagant use of political patronage, he quipped, "We practise neither nepotism nor extravagance at 24 Sussex. It's true, we did put in a dumbwaiter. It was the least we could do for Uncle Larry."

His most trusted confidante, Senator Marjory LeBreton, revelled in Mulroney's sense of humour: "I was actually laughing my head off most of the time at the way he described people and recounted events. It was almost like a sitcom. My husband, Doug, couldn't get over it because I would be on the phone with the PM and when I hung up, he'd say, 'Who were you talking to and laughing so hard?'"

WHEN OUR INTERVIEWS started in earnest, my main concern was how candid Brian would be. That turned out not to be a worry, except that what he told me, not surprisingly, was *his* truth. He would recite his take on some pivotal event, and could easily have passed a battery of lie detectors testing his veracity. But the details he provided sometimes had only a tangential relationship to what had actually happened. Truth is a difficult enough concept, and the prime minister had so ardently convinced himself of his own version of events that he had genuine difficulty separating objective reconstructions from his rose-tinted memory. If I was going to do a full-scale biography I would need to rely on independent sources as well as on his personal recollections. (What I'm trying to say here, in my stumbling Canadian way, is that he Reconstructed, Confabulated and Revised. If he lied, he seldom realized it.) "Brian Mulroney is the principal of the school of revisionism, particularly fond of reconstituting events," wrote Andrew Cohen, the talented political commentator, who noticed the same tendency. "His rewriting of history inflamed passions, created misunderstandings and sowed division."

The stories Mulroney told were based on his understandable wish to create his own version of history. But, being a politician, he was also looking for audience reaction, even if it was only two hands clapping. (I did try applauding once and he gave me a decidedly quizzical look.) Mulroney never stopped editing his flights of fancy and rearranging the past. Interpreting his most opportunistic gestures as responses to the summons of history, he was, without a doubt, Canada's most consummate political animal. Ever. His almost physical inability to take a single step without tailoring it to his personal political agenda was bred in the bone. It was as much a part of his being as the belief among nineteenth-century Catholic women that to marry a divorced man was to burn in hell.

Some politicians and theologians whine when they preach, using the superficial nasal twang of old-time cowboy singers. Not Mulroney. His basso profundo tones have the consistency of treacle. More elegantly put, his manner of speech is operatic in its *recitativo* echoes. Anchorman-modern, it is a compromise between intimacy and authority. When I asked about the way he used his voice, he said, "I was born with it, and I believe it's an asset by any objective criteria, unless you think that a politician should have a high, squeaky voice. They say I'm unctuous, mellifluous, glib. Hell, you can't even be yourself. Am I supposed to sound like Clark or Chrétien, or have a whiny, tiny voice like Trudeau's?"

I found Mulroney a compelling conversationalist, his lingo bolstered by wild exaggerations and wilder curses. Because I felt that cleaning up Mulroney's language would interfere with the mood and authenticity of the interviews, I shortened but did not clean up the transcripts. Mulroney never actually said, "That fucker Bouchard fucked me over on Meech and now that fucker Turner is fucking me over on free trade," but he might as well have. Much of what he told me was crude and vicious. Yet during our interviews another Mulroney emerged: warm, witty, street-smart, yet kind and considerate.

POLITICIANS MUST BE JUDGED not by what they do from day to day, but by their greatest moments, when they determine how they intend to be remembered. The first of these occasions for Brian Muloney came on December 10, 1984, shortly after his first election victory, on the occasion of his address to the Economic Club of New York, where such giants as Woodrow Wilson, Winston Churchill, Dwight Eisenhower, Nikita Krushchev, Jawaharlal Nehru, François Mitterrand, Henry Kissinger and John F. Kennedy had previously sung for their suppers.

Mulroney could not number himself in such august company, but his appeal to this crowd was no mystery. He already knew most of them. He had, after all, spent the six previous years as president of the Iron Ore Company. The firm may have been the Canadian storefront for Cleveland's Hanna Mining Co., but Hanna was at the centre of mighty spokes, uniting five great family fortunes: the Mellons of Pittsburgh, the Hannas and Humphreys of Cleveland, the Bechtels of San Francisco and the Graces of New York. Mulroney may have been the titular head of a branch plant, but he had ready access to the platinum heart of the U.S. business establishment, and he used it. His pro-American orientation was most boldly expressed in an aside to Charley McMillan, at the end of a lengthy late-night strategy session: "When this foolishness is over," he sighed, "we can all retire to Palm Beach." Not the dream of most Canadian patriots. Political columnist Roy MacGregor believed that Mulroney was simply out of touch with the aspirations of Canadians: "The one crucial matter about this country that Mulroney had not the background to grasp was that we are willing to pay to be Canadians. Our souls have no bottom line. He failed to comprehend this simple truth, which to most of us is self-evident. If only Brian Mulroney were a novel, a wild-eyed account of a CIA plant or fifth column sent in to destroy a civilization and hand the icons over to America, then at least we would have the option of not buying it."

On this particular evening in New York City, rising to address Wall Street's chief animators, he was happy to declare that his country's highest objective was to grab a slice of the American apple pie. His audience lapped it up. The euphoria of the glittering event was best caught by Mulroney's buddy, Nabisco chairman Ross Johnson, the cowboy capitalist of *Barbarians at the Gate*, who introduced Canada's newly elected prime minister to the glittering Fortune 500 audience: "Having another CEO of a multinational become the head of a government gives us all an unexplainable tingling feeling." Johnson brought the house down when he reminisced about "the fact-finding missions" he had shared with Mulroney, touring "such trouble spots as Paris, Palm Beach and Venice." Johnson purchased a full-page ad in next morning's *New York Times*, proclaiming the Canadian prime minister to be "the right man in the right place at the right time."

By the simple stratagem of dressing up in my father's black-tie outfit, made for him by an Austrian tailor in 1935, I was able to drift around the private receptions before the meeting, the only journalist to do so. (In those primitive days, security judged you by how you dressed. If you looked to be part of the in crowd, no one stopped you from joining them.) I found it hard to name any Canadian power brokers who had stayed home. They had turned out to pay homage to their leader's American debut. More remarkable was the heft of the representatives from the U.S. investment community, including David Rockefeller, Jack Welch and Pete Peterson, decision makers who distributed American billions across the world's time zones. So many Yankee bigwigs wanted to sit close to the Big Bopper from

Baie-Comeau that an extra dais had to be set up to accommodate the forty-two head-table guests.

The Grand Ballroom of the New York Hilton was incandescent with those "masters of the universe" who would happily finance another assault on the Alps by Hannibal, providing he could keep his books straight. Many of their wives were also there, attracted by the reputation of Mila and Brian as the continent's newest dazzling power couple. These were the kind of women who raised Lhasa Apsos, wore aviator glasses for walks in the country and discreetly discarded the bread part of their lobster canapés. "Listen, Malaura"—I overheard one of these creatures breathlessly brief another—"this is really a big deal. That guy with the chin is the president of Canada!"

What Mulroney understood about the CEOs in his audience was that even more than craving fat bottom lines (and thin female ones), the Yankee tycoons wanted to be appreciated. It was a time when any Third World or European politician could get elected by depicting President Ronald Reagan as a senile Dr. Strangelove and Americans as hamburger-chomping imperialists. (Just like now.) Flanked by twin red-coated Mounties, Mulroney delivered a simple message in his most beguiling Kirk Douglas whisper: send us your megabucks and we'll be your cuddle-buddies. These merchant adventurers (okay, pirates) were not frightened off by investment risks and had never been particularly bothered by Pierre Trudeau's anti-Americanism.[6] What Mulroney's listeners could not tolerate was politicians who changed the rules of the game in midstream. That was why the loudest ovation of the evening greeted Mulroney's declaration that "There shall be one game—building Canada—and one set of rules. These shall not be changed after the game has started to

---

6. U.S. undersecretary of state for political affairs Lawrence Eagleburger privately referred to Lucky Pierre's end-of-term peace initiative as "akin to pot-induced behaviour by an erratic lefty."

the detriment of any of the players. Our message is clear. Canada is open for business."

Then Mulroney interrupted himself to ruminate on the undefended border between the United States and Canada: "There hasn't been a shot fired in anger between our two countries since 1812," he ad libbed. "That wasn't much of a war. We captured Detroit, took one look around and gave it back."

As the evening ended and the crowd dispersed, the faces of New York's Economic Club members were relaxed in a postcoital glow. The guy with the chin in charge of America's attic was user-friendly, they decided. Canada was A-okay.

MULRONEY'S BIGGEST PROBLEMS were the overprotectiveness of his staff and his own, curious approach to his position. He was certain that prime ministers must reassure their subjects by appearing perfect and thus invulnerable. He was almost always trotted out in public, aloof and untouchable, impeccably groomed and waving to crowds in slow motion, his pants pleated sharply enough to cut Wonder Bread. He genuinely believed that he could not govern if voters saw him sweat. "If they think I'm just another guy, they won't follow me," he once told me. Strangely, that attitude was in place almost from the day he declared his serious candidacy in 1983. "There is something not quite straight about him," wrote Michael Valpy in the *Globe and Mail*. "He's too unrumpled. The face is too conventionally handsome, the suits a little too expensive and too well tailored, the voice too smooth, what he says too lacking in 'ums,' 'ers,' and grammatical stumbles."

When he hosted a televised National Economic Conference in early 1985, Mila, watching it on TV, called in to report there was an open air vent over her husband's head. "It's blowing his hair all over the place," she complained. "Turn it off!" Stanley Hartt, the loyal Mulroney follower who was chairing the conference, was bold enough to challenge her. "Look," he said, "it's not that terrible for people to see his hair out of place. He's human. He's not made of plastic—his hair flutters in the wind."

Not *that* wind—the vent was promptly shut.

Dress codes even applied to rural cabinet retreats staged to demonstrate how the Mulroney government was "keeping in touch with the grass roots." The PM would dress informally for these down-home chinwags, relaxing in sweaters and slacks. Unfortunately, the sweaters appeared to have been flown over for the occasion direct from Rome's fashionable Via Condotti; he looked more like a model than a Canadian PM on a rural retreat.[7]

All this hokey posturing perpetuated the image of a prime minister who chose not to acknowledge human frailties. Not a single picture exists, if ever one was taken, of the PM looking rumpled, much less showing any signs of zits, hickeys, blackheads, goobers or volcano boils.

In private, Mulroney was loose-limbed and endearing, but as soon as he gave a press conference or appeared on television, his arms seemed to be welded to his shoulders. Faced with the routine chore of laying a wreath on a cenotaph, he would rehearse every vowel and consonant of his body language: when to turn left, whose hand to shake, how vigorously to pump it. Anthony Wilson-Smith, who was *Maclean's* Russia correspondent, and later the magazine's editor-in-chief, recalled a typical example of his rigid formality. "My favourite, enduring memory of Mulroney's visit to Moscow in 1989 was when, rather than walk two hundred metres, he waited more than ten minutes to be driven by a limousine for about twenty seconds to the next ceremony—which, as it happened, celebrated the importance of exercise and physical fitness."

---

7. Lest readers doubt my sartorial expertise, I should point out that my name appeared two years running in the Vancouver *Province*'s list of "Ten Worst-Dressed Canadians."

His motives may have been worthy, but he looked and sounded like a robot encased in cement. It was as if he decided he would rather *play* himself than be himself. What most Canadians want in their prime minister is an ordinary individual attempting extraordinary things, so that they can connect with him or her on a human level.

Mulroney seemed to believe that he could somehow bridge that gap through photography. Partisan feelings aside, there was no doubt that he and his family came closer than any previous PM to portraying a handsome and beautiful ideal, four wonderful children included. In a reversal of the feeling among primitive tribes who refused to allow visiting anthropologists to photograph them because they believed that pictures imprisoned their spirits, Mulroney regarded political life as one big photo op: if he had his and the family's photographs taken often enough, he assumed that Canadians would forgive whatever else might be upsetting them. It was not to be.

"I did a lot of thinking about this, and I concluded that the major problem we had was that we never knew which Brian Mulroney it was we were trying to sell," said Tom Long, a PMO advisor. "Ronald Reagan remained pretty much the same guy within the normal bounds of behavioural changes. But with Mulroney, it was hard to tell who we were selling. There was this sombre, almost sonorous guy who appeared at state occasions; there was the fellow who was upbeat and joked a lot; and then there was this guy on amphetamines who showed up in Commons' Question Periods. That sent a lot of contradictory signals. Since there were a variety of different guys for a variety of different occasions, most Canadians concluded that he wasn't a genuine sort of person."

"The kid from Baie-Comeau that used to be in the man had been largely suppressed," Dalton Camp once lamented. "It was hard for many who knew him to believe this prime ministerial model was real; only the truest of sycophants didn't worry about the disappearance of the real Mulroney. A number of people came to the conclusion they had gained a prime minister and lost someone they had known."

If there is a remnant still in existence of the bouncy boy who thundered out of the North Shore wilderness to conquer the world, he lives in these pages.

AS I PREPARED TO BEGIN WRITING my planned biography of the Mulroney years, I waited impatiently to be handed the documents and personal journals Mulroney had pledged were to be mine. He had remained enthusiastic about my project throughout our interviews, never once asked to see my manuscript before publication or set any conditions on its contents. "You're doing what I hope will be the definitive book or books on the administration," he told me. "It will be very helpful, Peter, to the whole process when you see these guys that you'll be talking to, to put the questions right to them: What do you think of the prime minister? How has he been to work with—and so on."

He saw the biography not only as his vindication but as my gold mine. "Your book is going to be such a bestseller because it's a colourful, astonishing story," he told me. "It's absolutely unbelievable. The publishers don't have to worry about whether this thing is going to sell. The only question they're going to have to wonder about is whether they've got enough paper in the forest to print the fucking books. That's all they have to worry about. I'll tell you this, if there ain't a good book in this, there's not a good book in Canadian history. So there you go. I don't know about your other books, but boy this one's going to sell. I mean the others, you've done okay, but I'll tell you, you're going to be able to retire for sure. If this thing holds, it's going to be quite remarkable. I'd be very surprised, Peter, if by the time it's all over if there weren't two books in this thing for you. Let's let the books go out first, and then do the television."

"I'm going to tell you the truth, no self-serving bull-shit whatsoever," he had promised at the start of our interviews. "I'll tell you the reason: I know goddamn well that if you're off by one inch, they're going to kill you."

He was right. To my mind, a full-scale biography would have worked only if I had obtained the documents he had promised. Had I written the book he visualized with no supporting documentary evidence, I would have been slaughtered by readers and critics alike. And rightly so. Mulroney withdrew that privilege from me in the spring of 1995, explaining that his notes contained material that might hurt innocent bystanders. Still, he urged me to carry on and do the project based mainly on our interviews. At the time I felt that while the interviews had given me invaluable material, they couldn't carry the factual load of a volume mandated to be a full-scale, unbiased examination of ten critical years in Canada's history. That required documentary rather than rhetorical evidence. (In retrospect, I recognize that his reason for changing his mind may have been the realization that he wanted to write his own autobiography.)

Yet I didn't want to simply discard ten years' work collecting those invaluable interviews, knowing that they could never be duplicated and that they provided the only first-hand accounts of how the prime minister viewed his tempestuous mandate.

So I decided to publish this book, not breaking any confidences since my conversations were on the record and are being made public more than a long decade after the Mulroney government's demise. Not to mention the disappearance of the Progressive Conservative Party itself, the faith that brought these men and women into public life. This then, is their monument, or more likely their epitaph.

BRIAN MULRONEY had been very specific. He told me that he didn't want a puff job. He's not getting one.

The Secret Tapes

I

"Canadian people like me, you know?"

—

Mulroney on His Rise to Power

SINGING FOR COLONEL McCORMICK

Even before he became a politician, Brian Mulroney consisted of equal measures of ambition and insecurity.

Mulroney's law partner and friend Arthur Campeau:
If I had to do a psychological profile of Brian Mulroney, I would stress his sense of inferiority despite all his achievement. I don't know whether this came from Baie-Comeau or being an English Catholic, which is a sort of minority within a minority, but he never saw himself as part of the establishment, never saw himself being accepted even as prime minister. He always had to play this role, this perfection. At least once every two or three weeks, when Brian and I were practising law together, we would have lunch and the whole discussion had to do with how far he had come

from Baie-Comeau. He wanted me to recognize what he had managed to accomplish despite his humble origins.

I once thought that if I were going to write a book on Mulroney, my title would be *Singing for Colonel McCormick*. When he was a kid, the whole town would know that Mulroney was singing for Colonel McCormick, the *Chicago Tribune* publisher who owned the local paper mill, and basically owned Baie-Comeau. Brian's relationship with Ronald Reagan was very similar to the one he had with the colonel. There was this incredibly powerful American who held the fate of his people, and Brian was their little man who could appease this great type who with a sweep of the pen could destroy the entire town.

Patrick MacAdam, who later became Mulroney's caucus liaison, on the first time he met the future prime minister at St. Francis Xavier University:
He arrived at St. FX full of pith and vinegar, and broke every rule there was. Hazing went on for a week, and it was just brutal, some of the most cruel and inhumane punishment and physical abuse. You were humiliated. Not him. It seemed from the very first day he arrived there, Brian was running for something. We didn't know what.

Stanley Hartt, Mulroney's Montreal friend and fellow lawyer, who went on to become his chief of staff and a deputy minister of finance:
He's overwhelmed by the fact that the boy from Baie-Comeau is prime minister. He knows that he's a friendly, outgoing, back-slapping human type, yet he has cautioned himself against showing those sides, especially on formal occasions.

Clerk of the Privy Council Paul Tellier:
He was coming from a modest background, so he wanted to make sure about his table manners, the way he dressed and so on. He couldn't afford a slip. Nelson Rockefeller

could, maybe, but Mulroney, because of where he came from and so on, cannot afford to.

Senator Lowell Murray, another St. FX alumni:
The so-called French side of Brian's development and upbringing was absolutely minimal until he arrived at Laval University. He could speak a bit of French when he was at St. FX, but it was only street French. The other students and professors at Laval used to poke fun at him. He never had any formal education in French, never learned any grammar or syntax.

Mulroney's long-time finance minister Michael Wilson:
Mulroney is a progressive; he does concern himself with the underdog, people who live in the regions of the country. His upbringing in Baie-Comeau always influenced his thinking. He had concerns for people who did not have the things he has now. He saw his father die when he was young, so the pressures on his family were just that much greater. But he also had the conservative part. He was director of a bank; he knew a lot of people in the corporate community and could talk easily and understand their points of view. He understood the difficult economic financial decisions that had to be taken.

OPPORTUNITY LOST

Robert Stanfield resigned as leader of the Progressive Conservatives in 1976 and Mulroney decided to seek the party's leadership. Months before the actual vote of party faithful, an overconfident Mulroney was already assembling his cabinet and offering posts to friends. In the end, he didn't make it to the final ballot. Claude Wagner, a Quebec Liberal judge whom Mulroney had recruited for the Tories in 1972, took the support of Quebec delegates with him as he faced off against Joe Clark.

**Mulroney originally saw Wagner as an ideal replace-
ment for sleep-walking Tory leader Robert Stanfield:**
MULRONEY: We decided to run a survey on Stanfield and
hired Robert Teeter of Market Opinion Research in
Detroit, Richard Nixon's personal pollster. The results
were very realistic. With Stanfield, we were going to get
7 per cent of the vote. In our view, Wagner had to be
there instead of Stanfield to win in BC and Ontario.
Whatever we got in Quebec would be a fringe benefit.

NEWMAN: But Wagner didn't know about the survey
until after he announced he was a candidate.

MULRONEY: We never showed it to him. We gave Wagner
the code name "Houlihan" because we didn't know what
the hell was going on with our telephones. All I can tell
you is that getting Wagner in was a long goddamned
negotiation. Wagner is a very bright guy, a great family
guy. He loves his wife and his family. He likes to stay at
home, never runs around. He doesn't smoke—maybe a
cigar sometimes. Anything that sort of diverts from the
pattern is uncomfortable. Wagner doesn't believe in political parties; he sees them as vehicles. He's a religious guy,
a guy who doesn't swear. I have never seen a greater
Conservative with the great traditional values.

**After deciding to launch his own bid for the leadership
in 1976, Mulroney was already visualizing a head-to-
head contest against Pierre Trudeau. The Boyo from
Baie-Comeau would emerge as Quebec's natural leader,
eradicating Trudeau and separatist leader René
Lévesque in one blow:**
If it comes down to Quebec, I'm going to be in there, and
Trudeau won't get in there. Then I'll get the mandate.
There will be no constitutional niceties that will keep me
out. This thing about, "Oh, the leader of a federal party
can't get involved in a provincial election." Like hell. I

plan to go into that bloody race and—this will sound pretentious as hell—but I plan to dominate it. I'm always trying to leave the delegates I meet thinking, "This guy can beat Pierre Trudeau." I think I'll be running against Trudeau—that's just my own feeling. If he calls an election now, I'm going to beat him.

Mulroney felt certain that Canadians would warm up to everything—good and bad—that he represented:
You know the Irish: smoke too much, drink too much and swear too much. They've got all the failings, but they have good hearts. They're generous and warm and funny, and I've got both the qualities and the failings in a substantial measure. I'm perceived by some people as being reasonably tranquil and unflappable. I don't yell very much.

Mulroney was already ruminating in a prime ministerial vein before the Conservatives even got a chance to vote:
It's the growing realization that you're responsible for thousands of people. I was very careful in my decision to run. I got in very reluctantly and very prudently, travelling the country. No one was paying any attention to me, so I was free to roam like a vagabond, looking for votes and building an organization. When I made the decision to go, I knew I was going to do well. In other words, I wouldn't disgrace me or my family.

Mulroney on his rivals in the race:
Without being unkind to anybody, let's say this party elects Flora MacDonald as its leader. The great debate, the great fight, is going to take place in Quebec. And what is Flora going to say? She can't even set foot in the province of Quebec and say a word. I've always thought, and I've felt this now for months, that the last ballot will come down to two names: Brian Mulroney and Sinclair Stevens.

In the end, Mulroney's 369 votes in the third ballot were not enough to keep him in the race. Mulroney blamed Wagner:

It turned out we didn't know him as well as we thought. I don't say that to besmirch the guy—he just didn't have the capacity for growth, or openness, or generosity that a leader must have. You've got to have a leader who can end the enormous rupture between the Conservative Party and one-third of society, namely the French Canadians.

Conrad Black's partner Peter White, a prominent Tory, heard Mulroney blame more than Wagner for his defeat:
Brian was particularly bitter at two or three people. Number one on the list was Lowell Murray, and number two was [New Brunswick premier] Richard Hatfield. I suppose Flora, too, although he had given up on Flora by then. Also, Joe Clark represents the antithesis of almost everything that Brian is. Brian could never stomach the fact that he had been defeated by Joe Clark. It would have been different if he had been defeated by Claude Wagner. When Joe was prime minister in 1979 and 1980, Brian hardly ever heard from him unless there was some crisis in Quebec and Joe needed help, such as fundraising dinners and this sort of thing. As Brian put it, he saved Joe's ass at least twice with fundraising dinners in Quebec.

Lawyer Richard Holden, a personal friend, on Mulroney after the 1976 loss:
Before the convention, he kept calling me "Senator" and "Judge." I said, "Brian, you'd better wait." During that period after the 1976 convention, he would get more bitter when he drank. We'd be into the cognac and after the cognac, it was always "that fucking Flora" and "that fucking Hatfield" and "that fucking Lowell." It was a litany, and it was unhappiness, really. His drinking certainly didn't make him jolly.

Senior policy advisor Charley McMillan believed Mulroney thought he wouldn't get a second chance:
A lot of people said he was bitter because he lost. He was incredibly bitter, but it was not just that he had lost. In the first three months of the Clark period, Brian had basically made up his mind that Clark would be there for twenty years. The last thing on his mind was running for the leadership again.

Mulroney's friend Sam Wakim says Mulroney offered to run as a Tory candidate for Clark:
Roch LaSalle had gone from federal politics to lead the Union Nationale, and fought the disastrous provincial campaign that saw the Union Nationale wiped out. So there LaSalle was, wanting his federal seat back. Brian left that option to Joe. "If you want me to run, fine, I'm prepared to look at it." But Joe was quite happy to have LaSalle run again instead. I could never understand why Joe never made a public declaration urging Brian to run. Brian made a speech in which he outlined the various steps that should be taken to strengthen the party in Quebec. Joe should have picked up the telephone and said, "You're right, we look to you to do it."

Frank Moores, former Newfoundland premier and Ottawa lobbyist, had a different take on Mulroney's 1976 defeat:
Look, the best thing that ever happened to Canada and Brian Mulroney is that he didn't win that damn thing in 1976. He was not even close to being ready for it. The biggest thing that happened to him is he got out and met a lot of ordinary people on their terms. He is awfully loyal to the people who have been loyal to him. He's unbearably Irish in that regard. He's emotionally loyal to a degree that is wonderful to see, but it's almost naïveté in the world he's in. Mulroney is the sort of friend who it's amazing the things you'll do upon request. I mean, if he asks you

quietly for something, you can't wait to do it for him. The son of a gun pulls you in to a degree that's totally disproportionate to his intellect. If you can imagine a charming Machiavelli, that's what you've got. Even a decent Machiavelli—which doesn't seem to go together—but the bugger is awfully good at both. He was one of these kids who, I'm sure, said when he was eleven years old, "I'm going to be prime minister" and meant it. After the 1976 defeat—he didn't take defeat lightly, by Jesus—I don't think the expression "burning ambition" ever applied to anyone to any greater degree than it did to Brian.

Mulroney's last word on 1976:
I had a pretty sexy, razzmatazz campaign. What the hell's wrong with that? So it didn't fly with some of the delegates. I wasn't a member of the caucus. I didn't have any pros working for me. So what the hell, we made mistakes. Now they all sit around saying, "He did this wrong, he did that wrong." Well, I must have done something right. Christ, I came in third and it took the biggest gangbang in history to stop me.

Patrick MacAdam said Mulroney hit bottom on a trip to Romania in 1980 to sell his company's iron ore:
Romanian president Ceaușescu said to Brian, "Mr. Mulroney, twelve years ago, Richard Nixon sat in the very same seat you're sitting in. Mr. Nixon didn't give up—don't you give up either." After that, he drank up a storm. One night we were in the Intercontinental Hotel, and at closing time, he turned vicious, telling me, "What the fuck's wrong with you? Why don't you smile? You're sitting there like a goddamned sphinx!" And he's saying that with eight Remy Martins lined up in front of him. Before coming back to Canada, he told Bob Coates and myself, "Boys, I've just made a decision: I'm going on the wagon. I'm going to play tennis this summer and get my shit together and my head in shape." That was June 1980 in Bucharest.

WINNING THE LEADERSHIP

Joe Clark's 1979 campaign produced a Tory minority government. Two decisions altered Clark's political life forever. The first was to allow a no-confidence motion to proceed in the House of Commons on December 13, which the government lost by six votes—leading to Pierre Trudeau's comeback in the 1980 election. The second was Clark's resolution to call a leadership convention for 1983, after deciding that the support of 66.9 per cent of the PC delegates did not represent the endorsement he needed to carry on as leader. Seven years after his first crack at federal politics, Mulroney returned to the race and defeated Clark by 259 votes on the fourth ballot.

Sam Wakim remembered the reaction of the Mulroney faithful to the vote at Clark's leadership review:
We were in Brian's hotel room at the Winnipeg Westin when the vote was announced. We all said, if Clark gets one vote less than he got in the previous year, he is out. If he had one more vote, he was in. After the numbers came out, we almost said, fine, let's get going and have a drink. When Joe said he was calling a leadership convention, we all had to pick ourselves off the floor. We couldn't believe it. He's a dumb bastard. Mila was there, Pat MacAdam was there. MacAdam looked at me and said, "I don't know, Sam, is there something cooking? You can smell the dead meat all the way here."

So Clark won the vote and still called a leadership convention. That just had to be enormously bad judgment. In politics, it's a numbers game. Guys win by fifteen votes and go on to have tremendous political careers. Clark was a useless, very poor leader and poor manager and poor administrator and poor many other things he didn't have the nerve to tell the folks back home. Calling the convention was a terrible mistake.

Mulroney credits his close friend Michel Cogger for urging him to try again:
Cogger said, "Now, do you seriously think that Joe Clark or someone else can form a government?" And with no malice towards Clark I said, "No, obviously he can't do it, and history will establish that."

Other people were of a different view, including Newfoundland MP Jim McGrath:
MULRONEY: McGrath called me, and to my absolute consternation and disbelief, asked me if I really thought I should run for the leadership. And I said, "What do you mean?" And he said, "Finlay MacDonald and Flora MacDonald say things look a little tied up in Quebec." And I said, "McGrath, four months from today, when you call me up, you're going to be talking to the leader of the Opposition. Good day." McGrath was so unpopular in Newfoundland that if I hadn't intervened, they were going to throw him right into Conception Bay.

In the earliest stages of his second leadership bid, Mulroney decided to take a different tack with the media:
I had made up my mind that the Ottawa press gallery really didn't have the foggiest idea of what was going on in the country. But even more important, it would probably be an advantage to have them against me, because they are held in such disrepute.

Arthur Campeau recalled how Mulroney was worried about details of his life leaking out, even before he ran for the Conservative leadership a second time:
It must have been 1980 or 1981 when he was to appear on some French-language television program here in Montreal, so the researcher called and asked me for a few sort of vignettes about Brian that most people would not know. So I told her this story of how he failed his bar

exams twice—he just could not get procedure, civil procedure, into his head—and how we all wanted him as our
partner. Anyway, he calls me later in the day and says,
"Did you speak to her?" And I said, "Yes." "What did you
tell her?" I said, "Well, I talked to her about the goddamn
bar exams and all that." And he said, "Oh, geez, you didn't
tell her that, did you? Arthur, Jesus Christ, you call her
back right now and you tell her that you don't want that
to be brought up during the course of the interview."

**Tory supporter and Mulroney aide Keith Morgan, on
the Clark camp's tactics in 1983:**
It was the first time that my daughter was exposed to politics. Clark's people tried to disqualify her as a delegate,
and she broke down and cried. It was an awful mess;
there was a lot of fuss. We had problems with certain individuals. There were a lot of underhanded tactics, but it
was understandable. The leader of the party had the
machine and the national personnel.

**Mulroney's executive assistant Bill Pristanski said his
boss had the linguistic edge:**
Clark stood up and tried to defend himself in French. He
got booed. When Brian spoke French, there was no booing. That's when I first saw the guy could really win it. He
was on the right side of expectations.

　　After he won, it took Flora months to accept it. Joe
came to accept reality a lot faster than a lot of the people
around him. Now Maureen McTeer, I can remember she
came up to me and said, "It's just awful, Bill, you don't
know who you're fighting." I guess it was kind of a hell-
ish thing to go through, but she was very bitter.

Mulroney on how he differed as a leader from Clark:
I make a point of including people. Clark always excluded
all people like Dan McKenzie [a right-wing MP from
Manitoba]—he let the press paint them all as crazy right-

wingers. You disagree with Clark, you get excluded. Now they're all in there; McKenzie is deputy critic for public works. My line to caucus has been simple. I told them, "The time has come for the Conservative caucus to make a fundamental decision. Do you want to form a government or spend the rest of your time writing letters to the editor?"

Mila Mulroney's biographer, Sally Armstrong, on the Mulroney mystique:
I remember people were mad about him—he was this new hotshot, sexy guy from Montreal. I was there the night he won the by-election [in Nova Scotia's Central Nova riding], and I was standing up on a table to see over all the rest of the reporters, and I looked at him and thought, you'd have to be God almighty to deliver what everyone thinks you're going to deliver to them. That's what we do in this country: we raise them up so high, and then we start to take the shots.

Mulroney—who stopped drinking three years before becoming leader—said he encountered a small problem in the Tory ranks:
In the party, there is staff fighting staff. It's come about because of the booze. Somebody with a bad attitude doesn't know how to handle people, and be it through frustration or what have you, too much gin or too much wine, there'll be an explosion at the table. Unfortunately, there's someone sitting at another table. In Ottawa, chances are that it's either a journalist or somebody who knows a journalist.

Policy advisor Jon B. Johnson on how Mulroney passed his first big test as leader of the Opposition:
The first thing we have is that whole French-language issue emerging out of Manitoba, and the need to reaffirm the principles of the Official Languages Act. The way he brought the Tory caucus around to support official bilin-

gualism was quite remarkable. He made two speeches in the House, and his speech in Winnipeg in March 1984 where he had RCMP with guns around us. There were death threats, dozens of death threats. In the end, those speeches were probably the best speeches he ever gave because he really cared about the subject and also cared enough to get really involved in the process, instead of the way he frequently behaved later, where you'd provide him with a text and he'd look at it more as an editor than as a policy person, and wouldn't get into its guts.

Mulroney thought there was no way Prime Minister John Turner would call an election with official visits from the Queen and the Pope looming:
FRANK MOORES: Brian was going to take a month off during the summer, because he had been busy for a couple of years. He planned to give Turner free hash for the summer—there's nothing you can do about it, you can't go in and picket the Queen, or the Pope, who were coming to Canada.

And then Turner called the election. We were three days late getting the campaign going because we were grinning so much.

2.

"You had an option, sir!"

———

The 1984 Coronation

IN THE SUMMER OF 1984, when Brian Mulroney first hove into public view as an alternative to the philosopher king who had ruled Canada for sixteen interminable years, he was welcomed like the coming of green buds at the end of winter. During that luminous season, Canadians found themselves playing host to temporal, spiritual and extraterrestrial visitors, come to scatter their tributes across the land. People waved happy hellos to Queen Elizabeth II, Pope John Paul II and Marc Garneau, Canada's first astronaut. Polls confirmed that most of us felt satisfied or very satisfied with our economic lot, and an even larger percentage of us were optimistic about the future. In that rosy outlook, Brian Mulroney appeared as an added bonus, in tune with the general euphoria.

The election waged that summer turned into a Mulroney love-in. Except for the Joe Clark hiccup of

1979, the Conservatives had not been in serious contention for two long decades, and they had been out of power for forty-two of the previous fifty years. Now something was blowin' in the wind that indicated not so much a change in the political weather as a shift in the nation's very climate. It had happened to the Tories twice before: in 1930, when R.B. Bennett defeated the Liberals in the bear pit of the Great Depression; and in 1958, when John Diefenbaker turned the Liberals' arrogance during the pipeline debate against them and swept into office with the largest parliamentary majority up to that time.[1] By 1984, Pierre Trudeau had become vulnerable. His grandeur had grown in exact proportion to his aloofness; he had not changed, but the country had. His streak in power had lasted nearly sixteen years—most of a generation—and the demand for new political blood could no longer be denied. Lucky Pierre had outstayed his welcome.

Looking at his situation, Mulroney was well aware that he could win only if he captured a good portion of Quebec's seventy-five seats. He also realized, from bitter experience, how difficult that would be. Since 1885, when Sir John A. Macdonald had refused to commute the hanging of Louis Riel, it had meant next to nothing to be

---

1. Diefenbaker's dramatic victory included forty-two French-speaking Quebec MPs, elected through an alliance with the provincial premier, Maurice Duplessis, who saw supporting the federal Tories as a way of protecting provincial rights. To put it kindly, these new MPs were a mixed crew. They included a Montreal parliamentarian on the lam from a rival gang of municipal thugs, who arrived on Parliament Hill in a bullet-proof limousine and spent his entire time in Ottawa with a pistol concealed in his shoulder holster. Just as another MP was about to be named Diefenbaker's chief Quebec lieutenant, he went on a drinking spree that reached its climax when he relieved himself in a potted palm at Dorval airport. Instead of merely unzipping, he insisted on pulling down his pants—an unwise move since he was accompanied by the editor and a photographer of one of Quebec's largest dailies.

a Conservative in French Canada. Mulroney had grown up in a province tightly in the grip of the federal Liberal machine, which maintained power with an iron fist and patronage galore. Though they were very different men and vastly different politicians, Mulroney saw himself as the natural heir to the Trudeau mantle—minus the intellectual Jesuitry. Certain that the only way to build his majority was to negotiate a partnership with the province's nationalists, Mulroney offered them a decentralized federalism that would grant the province special dispensations. He had convinced himself that despite Quebeckers' separatist impulses, most of them were looking for reasons to stay in Canada, if they could do so with honour—or with the appropriate electoral goodies. Instead of treating the province with tough love, as Trudeau did, Mulroney cast himself as the great conciliator, always careful to stay on the right side of the touchstone language and constitutional issues. That was why he became a champion of French rights in Manitoba when such a stand took extraordinary courage in a caucus that still harboured a residual platoon of unreconstructed rednecks. By so doing, Mulroney touched the microchip embedded in most Canadians' souls that is pledged to the country's continuity.

But the essence of Mulroney's electoral strength was best summed up by a Tory organizer who phoned me a week into the campaign. "At last," he said, with a sensuous sigh of contentment, "we've got product." Allan Gregg, the pollster, voiced a more earthy description: "The biggest differences between selling Brian Mulroney and selling soap are that soap doesn't talk and its competitors don't say it's a crock of shit."

Out on the hustings, Mulroney was an equal-opportunity dispenser of promises, pledging everything to everybody, whether they were naughty or nice, Grit or Tory. He spread the wealth wherever his campaign jet touched down, campaigning from the political left at the same time as he granted recognition to the right. His opponents immediately accused him of being a pretend share-the-wealth Liberal. That was just plain wrong. Anyone who added up the cost of his promised giveaways would easily conclude that he was a real one. "There are any number of reasons why a guy gets elected prime minister," he told me during a break in his electioneering, "and I couldn't give a damn what they are, as long as I have one of them."

Throughout the campaign of 1984, Mulroney was careful not to antagonize Ed Broadbent, the NDP leader, in case he won with a minority and required the socialists' support to gain office. On July 18, Peter White, his former classmate at the Laval law school, had sent Mulroney a for-your-eyes-only memo on the touchy subject, with some advice for the Tory leader: "Say nothing during the campaign that might personally offend Broadbent or the NDP establishment, and constantly keep in mind the possible necessity of his support," because "if neither party wins a clear majority on September 4, Ed Broadbent immediately becomes the most important politician in Canada . . . Under these circumstances, our best course is to predispose Broadbent to prefer us over the Liberals in the event of a minority government. Turner is highly unlikely to make a deal with Broadbent before September 4, so the field is open." White went on to outline steps in the wooing of Broadbent, including designating "a few qualified people to follow the NDP campaign on a daily basis . . . and recommend how some of their policy proposals might be accommodated by a PC government."

My favourite moment of the campaign was Mulroney's opening gambit when he spoke to a group of Estonians in Nathan Phillips Square in front of Toronto's city hall. "Today," he purred in his most endearing basso profundo, "we are all Estonians." I was standing between two sons of Tallinn, who instantly burst into tears, perhaps not aware that the son of Baie-Comeau had taken his cue from John F. Kennedy on his historic visit to Berlin. Most of those Baltic faces around me were nodding their heads in approval; only a few exchanged whispers about this startling revelation of Mulroney's ancestry.

Throughout the campaign, Mulroney proved to be equally at home soothing the yearnings of small-town Canadians who belonged to organizations like the orders of Elks and Moose (and other quadrupeds) or stroking the fiscal imperatives of the big-buck boys in Westmount, Rosedale and Shaughnessy Heights. His campaign was based not on ideas or policies, but on the promise and premise of power. It was fuelled by the most efficient electoral organization in Canada's history, better known as Ontario's Big Blue Machine, run by Norman Atkins, a former army quartermaster (and later a senator) who had run four successful campaigns for Ontario premier Bill Davis. Atkins was Mulroney's true political godfather. It was his application of modern polling and marketing techniques that provided Mulroney's political crusade with its impregnable infrastructure.

Mulroney was also fortunate in his Liberal opponent. On paper, John Turner looked to be the best of Canadian prime ministers (until Paul Martin came stumbling along with an equally impressive curriculum vitae). But as Trudeau's successor and Mulroney's alternative, Turner turned out to be a bit player who propelled himself to well-deserved obscurity. His dated locker-room expletives and 1950s lingo, his unfashionably cut suits, foot-long cigars and habit of publicly patting female party officials on the bum left him struggling to remain relevant (and alive). Although the Liberals started the election with a decisive lead, Turner marched his party steadfastly backwards. His clash with the freshly minted Tory leader climaxed in their television debate, three weeks into the campaign. By then, Turner and Mulroney had learned to expect the worst of one another, and they were seldom disappointed. But the televised debate was their defining joust.

In a confidential memo before the debate, Michael Wilson, the Toronto investment advisor who would be the new government's finance minister, warned his future boss not to be too tough on Turner: "I believe very strongly that you should take the high road and leave the negative stuff to other heavy hitters in Caucus. I have received a number of comments that you are being too personal in your attacks on Turner, and that you diminish your own stature by this action." Mulroney ignored Wilson's advice, and not for the last time.

Turner committed his biggest electoral gaffe before the campaign even began, by agreeing to make nineteen patronage appointments on behalf of the departing Trudeau. This unprecedented dollop of retroactive patronage added up to an $84 million gift from the Treasury to ill-deserving Grits.[2] It seemed like an obvious issue for him to avoid during his TV faceoff, but Turner couldn't help himself; he had to raise it.

"We have this patronage issue," he tentatively began. "Mr. Mulroney has told his party that every job would be made available to every living, breathing Conservative."

"I beg your pardon, sir," Mulroney interrupted, hardly believing his luck.

"I would say, Mr. Mulroney," Turner went on, unaware he was about to commit hara-kiri on public TV, "that on the basis of what you've talked about getting your nose in the public trough, that you wouldn't offer Canadians any newness in the style of government."

Mulroney reacted with the confidence of a gladiator, pointing his sword at the throat of his prey: "Mr. Turner, the only person who has ever appointed around here, for the last twenty-odd years, has been your party, and 99 per cent of them have been Liberals. The least you should

---

2. Turner was well aware that he had been dumb to obey Trudeau's dicta. After leaving his meeting with the retiring PM, he confided to an enquiring aide, "Turn away when I tell you this, because you're going to vomit."

do is apologize for those horrible appointments. You, sir, owe the Canadian people a profound apology for having indulged in that kind of practice with those kinds of appointments."

"I told you and told the Canadian people," Turner replied, his knife now poised above his own vitals, "that I had no option."

"You had an option, sir. You could have said, 'I'm not going to do it. This is wrong for Canada and I'm not going to ask Canadians to pay the price.' You had an option, sir, to say no, and you chose to say yes, to the old attitudes and the old stories of the Liberal Party."

"I had no option," Turner muttered, to himself as much as to the television cameras, the blood running into his shoes.

The 1984 election was over.

From that moment on, Mulroney began every speech by imitating Turner's pathetic plea that he had "no option," adding in mock grief, "The devil made him do it!" His voice would drop an octave: "He could have said no to the baser instincts of the Liberal Party. He could have said yes to Canada."[3] Turner bravely continued his campaign, as Jeffrey Simpson noted in the *Globe*, "the way a dead man's fingernails continue to grow."

On election day, the Conservatives won 211 of the Commons' 282 seats, earning a majority in every province and territory, something no party had ever done before. It was the biggest absolute majority ever and represented the largest electoral shift of votes since the beginning of Canadian polling. The Liberals suffered their most humiliating defeat, obtaining only 28 per cent of the votes. Mulroney walked away with his home riding of Manicougan, overcoming a previous 16,000-ballot

---

3. In a subsequent TV debate on women's issues, Mulroney was not nearly as audacious. "How did you like my courageous silence on abortion?" he asked an aide as he walked off stage.

Liberal majority. He won fifty-eight of Quebec's seventy-five seats, harvesting 50.3 per cent of the popular vote, compared with 47.4 per cent in True Blue Ontario. The Mulroney coalition between Quebec nationalists and western populists held; his triumph was complete. As he awaited the results at Le Manoir Comeau, the mill manager's house (originally wired by his father), he looked back on a triumphant campaign and looked forward to a well-deserved stint running the country. Only the odd whisper could be heard warning that the shift to his banner had been too swift to signal a permanent realignment of political loyalties, and that continued support would be contingent on his government's performance.

Before he was sworn in, Mulroney paid a brief, informal call to 24 Sussex Drive, the official residence of Canadian prime ministers. "Come on," he told Pat MacAdam, "you're going to be part of history. I'm paying my first visit to Sussex as prime minister." The two men climbed out of an armoured government Cadillac and walked in, unannounced, through the front door, noticing that hasty renovations were being completed for the new occupants. "We are three or four steps from the entrance," MacAdam later recalled, "when all of a sudden, this discombobulated voice booms from afar: 'Get the hell off the floor, it was just stained this afternoon!' We both recoiled, went down to the basement, and walked through the tunnel to see Trudeau's swimming pool. Brian noted the area where he would put his Exercycle and his weights, but we never did see the rest of the house. We got kicked out by some workman who doesn't know to this day that he was yelling at the prime minister of Canada."

Two weeks after the election, while Brian Mulroney was being driven to Government House to be sworn in as Canada's eighteenth prime minister, he took inordinate delight in the fact that his new Tory Cabinet numbered forty, not by coincidence the total number of Liberals represented in the new Parliament. In the bravado of the moment, he boasted to a friend that no Grit administration above the municipal level held power *anywhere in the country*. At his first cabinet meeting, he startled the gathered ministers by announcing, "The next election campaign begins today!"

The proud new Conservative PM was determined that the transfer of power would not "merely be the exchange of one nuisance for another," as the philosopher-scientist Havelock Ellis once complained about a British election. He would establish the Progressive Conservatives as Canada's new Government Party. "Give us twenty years," he exclaimed during his first appearance in the Commons, "and you will not recognize this country!" (A truer prediction was never made.)

Seldom if ever had the nation's vested and popular interests been so closely aligned as they were in the election of 1984. It was one of those rare moments when everyone could sense the continuity of an age being cut. What came now would be very different from what had come before.

———

As his first electoral battle approached, Mulroney was already counting his chickens:
MULRONEY: Canada is essentially a nation of regions whose interests often conflict. Probably the greatest failing of Trudeau was his disinclination to recognize this as a fact of Canadian life. The most recent example is medicare. We had a good system going. But what Trudeau did was delegate the responsibility to Monique Bégin—whose competence is less than overwhelming— and instructed her clearly to go out and pick a series of street fights, first with the medical profession, then with the nurses, and finally with the provinces. The result was

bitterness and uncertainty. That's Trudeau's style of government, which of course is at complete variance with my own. The only way you can conduct the affairs of the country is to act on the basis of competence, recognizing that there are regional considerations. You can't exclude an entire region or part of a region from the decision-making procress. That's what the Liberals have done to Western Canada—that's why the alienation is so profound.

Mulroney had to be nimble ideologically, which was easy for such a political pragmatist:
I had moved to the right during the Tory leadership campaign because that's where the party should have been. I was pro-American, pro-NATO, pro-Israel—I was all-pro, all the things I've always been for. But I knew goddamned well I wasn't going to get elected if I let people accuse us of privatizing medicare and all of this stuff. So we had to make some strategic decisions, and we made them.

Pollster Allan Gregg on what Mulroney had to offer the Canadian electorate:
I believe this Boy from Baie-Comeau stuff is real, the boot-strap kind of stuff. The guy is ruthlessly pragmatic and ruthlessly clever. I use the words together advisedly; a part of it scares me sometimes when I see it. He will never do anything too wrong because he is so ruthless—he knows that he can't get away with it, and so his eye is always on the ball. He does have a fairly strong sense of what's good and what's bad on a moral plane.

For Lowell Murray, Mulroney was a miracle worker:
When Turner threw his hat into the ring, the Tories being the Tories, they saw it slipping again. They started running around like chickens with their heads cut off. Mulroney handled that very well. He said in caucus, "I'm not the slightest bit impressed with John Turner. If he

calls an election in August, he'll be back at that law firm by September."

Mulroney loved poking a stick in the eye of Liberal entitlement:

MULRONEY: The Liberal position was "Mulroney can't win the convention." Then it was "This party's going to be split asunder." Then the issue was "He can't win in Central Nova." Then "He can't win in the west because he's an easterner." Then "We are going to eat him up in the House." Then the issue was medicare. And now this bright, unsullied Liberal minister of finance was supposedly going to present a pre-election budget that was going to inspire the confidence of the business community. I know the business community, having been a senior member of it. Nothing will turn them off collectively more than Marc Lalonde's numbers. There is nothing Lalonde could have done by way of a budget that could terrify the business community more than what he did. Nothing. He could pass retroactive legislation, confiscate their salaries, but all they'd say is that he's a son of a bitch. So, if you look at the sequence of Liberal predictions . . .

NEWMAN: The next one is Mulroney can't win the election.

MULRONEY: The polls have an obvious like/dislike factor, and Canadian people like me, you know? If they say, "I hate the son of a bitch," the next question is "Why?" Well, he looks competent, he knows what he's talking about, he doesn't yell and scream, and he's got a good sense of humour. The *Globe and Mail* CROP poll showed us with fourteen more points than the Liberals from the feminine side. And the Liberals were going around saying there was a gender gap. There is no goddamn gender gap—we're fourteen points ahead. This is crap from

[Liberal senator] Keith Davey. I love Davey. I love him, you know why? He's a lot less smart than he thinks he is.

His senior policy advisor, Charley McMillan, was just as confident:
My prediction is that this election will be like Ronald Reagan versus Jimmy Carter in 1980. You put Brian against those two guys, John Turner and Jean Chrétien, and, especially if there's a debate, the vote will just collapse and it'll be a sweep.

Bill Pristanski recalled that campaign co-chair Norman Atkins suggested the candidate needed to elevate his discourse:
Atkins was always after Mulroney at the beginning of the campaign to back away from the humour stuff, because the thirty-second clips on the radio would be the one-liners that would begin the speeches. Pat MacAdam used to write ten one-liners for a speech, and Mulroney used five or six of them. They told him, "The strategists think you've got to be more serious, you should be more prime ministerial." It was tough, though, because he wanted to go up there and ham it up.

Mulroney felt underestimated by Turner—and by some members of the press:
Turner dropped the writ and then called me. This never happens. He was feeling sorry for me—he was fourteen points ahead and the great Liberal machine was going to win, as best evidenced by one of their skilful propagandists, Richard Gwyn. On CTV's *Question Period*, Gwyn said, "Well, what are you going to do after the election? It looks very much like a commanding Liberal majority." And I said, "Richard, you really never have gotten it, have you? You don't understand what's going on in the country. We're going to win the election." He said Turner had some great candidates. I said, "I beg your pardon? The

last time I saw Bob Blair, he was in Calgary at a Conservative fundraising dinner, and Iona Campagnolo is a defeated candidate from the last election who is president of the Liberal Party."

But he admitted that some of his own team acted like losers:
Liberals arrange—not that they're responsible for it, but they take the credit—they give you a nice big office, then they give you Stornoway [the official residence] with a staff, a car and a chauffeur and lots of prestige. The objective of all of this is to convince us that we won something, when we haven't won a goddamned thing. I said to caucus, "Now, you see that building over there, that's the Langevin Building. They want us to forget that that building exists because they think—and they've got us pretty well persuaded—that the Conservative leader goes to Stornoway and he's happy to stay there. They want us to think that's our place, and that other place, 24 Sussex, that's for them.

"I don't want any quibbling. I don't want recriminations. I don't want any backbiting and I will fire anybody who does. What I want is everybody onside. I don't have any enemies in the Conservative Party—all I got are friends, and all my friends are on the campaign team, everybody is in this together and we're going over there as an army and take these people out. I won't stop at Stornoway . . . I'm going right to 24 Sussex."

Pat MacAdam on how Mulroney tended his caucus members:
If a member called, the call came to me. If he had a problem, he had an immediate solution. If he wanted to see the leader, he saw him the same day. If he wanted an autographed picture for his wall, he got it the same day. Brian loved it. Autographed books, pictures, we sent them out by the ton.

Bill Fox, Mulroney's communications strategist, recalled the campaign trail:

I felt a revolution was coming. I remember a day in London, Mulroney was there with the local candidates, and a city bus came by full of students. There was a squeal that came out of the bus when they saw him, hands thrusting through the windows. He was the personification of the Canadian dream, that you can make it if you work hard. People get really excited by that. He was very confident; he knew all along that he would be better than John Turner. I remember talking to him, saying, "Boss, you will kick the crap out of this guy."

But Mulroney had to have something beyond his charm to do it with, and the campaign team was not a well-oiled machine.

JON JOHNSON: There was little new party policy on the shelf or in process when our policy advisory group came together in September 1983. The policy development exercise carried out by our Opposition critics from October 1983 to May 1984, with our assistance and direction, was not very successful and so, in the end, it was mainly our group that finalized party policy with the approval of Mulroney and the critic. The Office of the Leader of the Opposition was full of old Mulroney friends, most of whom spent their time jockeying for position with him to earn favour in the government to come— and taking credit for the work of others. Several staffers were particular offenders, speaking and leaking frequently to the media when, in fact, their substantive roles were minuscule.

Navigating through these people was an exhausting daily ritual. Since none of our group had strong personal ties to Mulroney, we survived by the fact that we did the work that none of the others could do, or were prepared to do. On a daily basis, I literally pushed my way into Mulroney's office, or worked through his secretary or driver, to get past various assistants and to get speeches and other material to him for approval. This sometimes caused resentment, particularly among some colleagues whose titles suggested they had policy-related roles but who, in fact, did little. The sad part is that, because his friends often took credit for work that others did and monopolized access to him, to this day Mulroney does not fully realize who really got him elected in 1984. His own contribution as a campaigner cannot be denied. But the rest of the job was not done by his old pals; it was carried out by a cadre of long-time, skilled Tory professionals—the campaign team—and young turks, our policy advisory group.

Mulroney himself never hesitated to roll up the shirt sleeves:
JOHNSON: No speech I ever wrote for him ended up looking the way I wrote it. He was his own editor and he wanted to change a lot of the stuff—I always felt for the worse, but he disagreed.

Mulroney gauged his campaign's impact on his home province:
In early August 1984, when the goddamned polls came out saying I was going to win two hundred seats, René Lévesque—who had crapped all over me before—came onside. But I was going to win anyway, at this point in time. The night I won the Conservative leadership in 1983, Lévesque was on TV saying, "This is terrible. What we wanted was Joe Clark."

Liberal strategist Jack Austin, reading Mulroney's mind:
In a perverse way, Mulroney will portray himself as the real political heir in Quebec of Pierre Trudeau. He was careful throughout the whole time never to knock Trudeau in public, only Turner. In constructing a cabinet,

he will neutralize Clark by putting him in External Affairs. Or the High Commission in London. London is even more neutral than External Affairs.

Mulroney, on his knockout punch to John Turner, delivered during the televised leaders' debate on August 25, 1984:
Turner referred to a clipping about Union Nationale patronage or something like that, to say I was not a paragon of virtue. And that's when I said, "I beg your pardon? You're talking about patronage? You? The leader of the Liberal Party, who has just appointed these twenty-nine people to Liberal heaven? I wasn't going to raise it, but now that you've raised it, this disgraceful performance, unparalleled in the history of Canada, you did that, you and Trudeau did that?" And he said, "I had no option."

At this point, I know there's been a dramatic, historic exchange, but I wasn't sure whether I had helped or hurt my case. I really wasn't. As the debate ended, I could see from Ed Broadbent's attitude that I had scored heavily. I was tired, I was very tired, and I'm sure they were too. When we met in Toronto for the women's debate, Turner reacted. You know, Turner is a profane guy. He said, "Holy Christ, it's brutal out there, it's goddamn brutal out there, I'm getting killed."

Pat MacAdam, on the impact of the nine-second exchange:
Brian was a different man the next day. When John Turner held up his hands in abject surrender, Brian rode it like a stake into his heart.

How they won:
MULRONEY: Trudeau said to Turner, "Look, I was going to make these appointments, and if you don't make them, I'm going to make them." So Turner undertook to make them. I don't think he realized the magnitude of it, or the

nature of the list, which was scandalous. How did we win the 1984 election? Right there.

A number of people, including Norman Atkins, strongly advised me against using the patronage story during the campaign, and I disagreed completely. Norman thought we had good policies, he didn't see much value in the patronage appointments—it was a 72-hour story to him. I said, "This is not a 72-hour story, this is dynamite—nothing like this has ever happened before. And besides, this thing has enormous comedic possibilities. I'm going to entertain the troops with this across the country in a manner you've never seen."

Pundit Hugh Segal and journalist Tom Gould had prepped Mulroney:
SEGAL: My responsibility was facts, figures, tactics and strategy. Tom Gould was stance, how you look, how you address the other candidates, whether you lean, whether you stand, what you should wear, how to manage a TV studio, what the cameras are going to be doing to you. This is vital information to have. If nothing else, it gave Brian a sense of comfort with what was going to happen to him. I don't think anybody did that for Turner—that was one of the reasons he looked so unpleasant. It was like telling a guy he's going to perform surgery without telling him what he'll find in the operating room. It was very unfair to John.

We'd rehearse the questions. Sometimes I would play Turner, or I would play Broadbent. I think we played Turner better than Turner did. Sure enough, at the actual debate, Turner went right into the patronage thing, the dumb son of a bitch. Brian just knocked the ball out of the park, and the guy kept throwing it over the plate. I must say, for the kind of pressure that those debates represented, Brian was very cool, considering he had also given up smoking and drinking. He had no props, except a glass of Turkish coffee every fifteen minutes and a Nicorette.

Senior policy advisor Ian Anderson recognized the impact of the performance:
It was Brian Mulroney at his ultimate best. He was thinking on his feet. There is probably no other politician in the Conservative Party who would be able to move that quickly for the jugular. For the first time since John Diefenbaker, the Conservative Party had seen a leader just pummel—not just dash, but pummel—a Liberal leader into speechlessness.

After the debate, the tenor of the campaign changed:
BILL PRISTANSKI: In the first stage of the campaign, the crowds were literally there to see Mila. After the debates, the crowds were there to see both of them, because he had performed so well and they were excited—they wanted to see this guy who had put Turner away. At the end, there was another difference in the crowds: they were coming out to see their new prime minister. You could see it in how people acted with their babies; they were presenting their children to Brian, like they were holding them up for the blessing.

After his victory, Mulroney concentrated on a new message:
I ran two campaigns in little more than one hundred days, without a day off. What I'm trying to convey first of all— with regard to this town here [Ottawa] that leaks like a sieve—is that I'm in charge of the government and the cabinet. Anybody who's out of line is gone. Then we convey the impression of coolness and competence, a good sense of humour. "Mind your own business, do your own business." I'll be there with the Pope, there with the Queen, there with President Reagan, still doing my job. They get the impression of competence and Canadians can feel good about their country.

Some of his own people had their doubts:
JON JOHNSON: We won the campaign in 1984 not because of the TV debates—we won it because, as Allan

Gregg indicated, there was an inexorable desire for change. People wanted a change in the style of government and Mulroney really embraced this—he thought Trudeau was too confrontational, while he would be consensus-oriented. That was his natural predilection, and he took it to heart.

We kept telling him, "Brian, when you get to government, we've got a plan, you know what has to be done, you can hire all the talent to implement it, let's get it done." What does he do? He goes back to his natural tendency for caution, pragmatism, consensus, everybody loving him psychologically, right?

When Mulroney won the prime ministership, he didn't jettison the people who may have been great in opposition but wouldn't be good policy wonks and thinkers in government. They kept moving forward with him, much to the consternation of those of us who worked with them and knew they could not make the jump. We just couldn't believe that he was taking some of those people with him. And that was the time I left and the reason I left. I just didn't think I could work in government with some of these people, who I knew would not be able to implement the agenda. The fact of the matter is that every one of those people was terminated by Brian himself within two years. That's when he brought in Stanley Hartt, first, and then Derek Burney, his best chiefs of staff by far.

But Mulroney was enjoying his honeymoon:
I stroll into all these places, I arrive at restaurants and there's a riot. I went out before Christmas to buy some presents. I arrived at the biggest shopping centre in Ottawa with the kids, and it was almost a riot. It's just a tremendous good feeling. People say, "You're doing a good job, keep it up, we're with you." We have polls that show us at 58 per cent, the NDP at 20 per cent and the Liberals at 16.5 per cent. There's a tremendous feeling out there— there's a lot of goodwill in the country.

3

"What did I do wrong?"

———

Patronage and the Art of Politics

Mulroney was amazed at the flak his appointments drew in the months after the election. At first he pointed the finger at rookie mistakes:
We were new at this, there were so many things going on, we didn't know how everything was controlled or what have you. It was a watershed and it caused us enormous trouble and set us on a road where we got blamed, irrespective of our nomination record, which was very good on women, minorities and the judiciary. Nevertheless, we got branded, tarred and feathered with this thing, with a compliant and mediocre press gallery. They just refused to look at any facts.

Nova Scotia MP Bob Coates, the defence minister, was the first to screw up:
MULRONEY: There was a corporation in Nova Scotia and

I don't remember what it's called—some think tank down there, the International Oceans Development or something . . . They had good people on the board, it was an inoffensive agency, and unbeknownst to me or to anybody—I didn't even know that the agency existed—one day in the *Globe and Mail* there was a huge front-page story on Bob Coates firing all of the directors of this Nova Scotia agency to replace them with Conservatives. This was the first problem, and caused outrage because, first of all, it was needless, and second, I had made such a point of the patronage thing in the campaign and we were genuinely trying to reform it by referring the appointments to committees in the House of Commons. This allowed Turner to be able to say, "The prime minister is a hypocrite."

Michael Wilson thought the prime minister was his own worst enemy:
Two comments kind of have left people with the impression that if Brian Mulroney can appoint a crony Conservative, that's his first choice. "No whore like an old whore" and "Everybody in this room is going to be a senator" have coloured so many people's judgment that they don't see beyond them. I've seen the other side of Brian Mulroney, who agonizes over these appointments to make sure he's got the best people. I've seen him send a whole slate of appointments for a new board because the balance doesn't reflect multiculturalism or sex. He feels very strongly about these things.

Frank Moores said no one needed to act ashamed:
I think it's only fair to appoint Tories to key boards, since they represent 56 per cent of the Canadian population. Still, it would be better to do it all at once and give the press less to criticize. Mulroney seemed to have a two-week lag time between each appointment, and each damn appointment that came up was a new news story. After

six months, that gets to be patronage. And anyone who is a friend of Brian is looked upon as a crony. He has no friends, only cronies. It's a very, very sick climate.

National Progressive Conservative director Janis Johnson thought the government was naïve:
Patronage is a normal part of politics, like the 35,000 Liberal appointments of years past. Not one of them wasn't a Liberal, but the Liberals get away with it because they know how to do it. Mulroney wants people he likes and trusts, he wants to do things for them and he can't help himself. I mean, if he could have given everybody in Canada an appointment, he would have—something to make them happy. He put people in ridiculous jobs sometimes.

Peter White was initially placed in charge of appointments during Mulroney's tenure:
Mulroney does agree that we have to target specific voter blocs and try to make more inroads, for instance in what he calls the Mediterranean Catholics who did not vote for us in the last election. A major way of doing that is through the appointments process, and so he has charged us with really larding the appointments heavily with representatives of the various ethnic and cultural communities.

Brian intends to take a very active hand in all appointments, whether or not they have traditionally been prime ministerial appointments. If it's a vacancy that catches his eye and he has a name in mind, he's just going to tell the minister that's who it's going to be. That might cause a little tension at the outset, but everybody has to agree that if the prime minister wants to make an appointment, it is his right to do so. He's an excellent judge of people and he sees fit where other people don't. Brian wants to restore the balance somewhat, but that does not mean that all the appointments will be Tories. It means that very few of them will be Liberals.

White thought the media were naïve:
You've got to recognize that the government was given the right by Parliament to make these appointments. These are considered as executive appointments, and it's only natural for the party in power to appoint people of like mind, people it knows. When the country voted for change as massively as it did, one has to assume that they wanted change at all levels, not just at the cabinet. And so, the government is right to do what it does, but what we have to avoid is the egregious appointments of un-qualified people.

In the press everything's become "patronage." Every time you appoint somebody who met the prime minister before he became prime minister, it's a patronage thing. Now, how can you get to know a person if you've never met him? How can he judge how good a man is if he's never met the guy?

Though White had to admit the prime minister had built his own fire under charges of hypocrisy:
In his campaign book, *Where I Stand,* he said that a certain number of economically important deputy ministers should be subject to review by Parliament. In the television debate with Turner, he said that other senior appointments—and again he referred to heads of Crown corporations—some of the quasi-judicial agencies should be subject to parliamentary review. He obviously hadn't thought the whole thing through, and both of these statements were made when he was in opposition. This will cause him all kinds of problems: it's going to give the Opposition a field day, it's going to deter good candidates and it's going to keep the whole patronage issue constantly on the front pages.

Bill Pristanski recalled that Mulroney was still able to joke about it:
One of the most hilarious days we had here was January 22,

1985. It was the day Lord Carrington [then secretary-general of NATO] was here, and the day that Finlay MacDonald and the new senators Mulroney had appointed just before Christmas were here to be sworn in. All things were happening at the same time. The prime minister met with Lord Carrington in his office, and we were walking down to the Senate dining room for a luncheon. There, standing at the elevator, was Finlay MacDonald. So they stopped and the prime minister said, "Oh, Lord Carrington, let me introduce you to our newest senator." And of course, the TV cameras were following us. The lord met him and said, "Does this mean that his son will become a senator, too?" The prime minister turned and looked at Finlay, and said, "Well, we're working on that." That night, we went up to the reception they'd thrown for Finlay up in room 601, and his son was there. The boss repeated the story, and of course all of Finlay's cronies and friends thought it was hilarious.

Marjory LeBreton took over the unofficial patronage portfolio after Peter White's departure:
Leading up to the leadership, people used to say, in the party, "You know, Brian Mulroney would be a great leader, but boy, I am worried about his friends." You would hear that, and I used to say, "Don't be so silly, everybody has liabilities—Joe Clark has got a fair sprinkling of them, I don't mind telling you."

LeBreton dealt with dozens of demands and requests, particularly when Senate seats became available. Seven prominent Tories explicitly asked for appointments:
I had John Reynolds on the phone lobbying for a Senate seat for himself, and giving me this pitch that it should be someone that could go on the talk shows. I said, "Gee, John, I haven't noticed you being out there."

Gerry St. Germain wrote a letter to the prime minister talking about the sacrifices he's made. I actually felt sorry when I read it. It said something to the effect that he would want to serve in the Senate and then he ended the letter by saying, "If you decide to choose someone else, please know that you will have my absolute loyalty." Jim Doak, who was seventy-four, was actually going to sign a letter saying that he would only stay there for a year, just to be called a senator. Doak was originally the president of the party in Manitoba under Diefenbaker. Duncan Jessiman was another of the old party bagmen stalwarts, but he had supported the prime minister financially when he ran for leadership. He was seventy years old, and he sent the Prime Minister a kind of "you owe me" letter, and you know the prime minister—people have helped him out. He [didn't make him a senator but] put Dunc in the best appointment he could give at the time, which was on the board of Air Canada, and of course we privatized Air Canada and they didn't keep him on the board, but they gave him a lifetime pass. We had Kate Schellenberg [later Kate Manvell] in BC. She was married to Ted Schellenberg, who was the MP from Nanaimo. She wrote a long letter to the prime minister just before Christmas. As the prime minister was reading it, he said, "There must be some reason she's writing." The last paragraph was, "I'd like to be named to that vacant Senate seat from BC." We made her a citizenship court judge. Pat Carney asked for the Senate seat too, but claims she didn't.

We've had some outrageous ones, like a former MLA in New Brunswick named Jim Gordon, who lobbied for the Senate seat and then said, "If it's a woman you're looking for, my wife Tilly would be pleased to . . ."

LeBreton was grumpy about the ingrates:
I'm going to have to start putting pressure on people like Janis Johnson to start to consider how they got where they are. Mila and the prime minister were really angry with her over her abortion stand in the Senate when she voted against the government position. Jim McGrath—all

the things he said and did for him. Not only did the prime minister make him lieutenant-governor, he also made him a commissioner of the National Transportation Agency. The prime minister saw him at Pat MacAdam's house between Christmas and New Year's and said, "Hello, Commissioner." McGrath did not even have the decency to say "Thanks, Prime Minister." David Angus [whom Mulroney appointed to the Senate] is quite mischievous and quite troublesome at times. Honest to God, I could kill him for the things he says.

She thought the boss was a saint to put up with it:
One day he said to me, "Don't tell me any more, it makes me so goddamned mad that they beg like that." I sometimes said to him about people he appointed, "You just amaze me—if that were me, I'd be throwing them off the Peace Tower on their head, and hoping they don't tilt over onto their feet." And he'll say things like, "Well, they did their best."

Mulroney's friend Arthur Campeau:
Brian walked a very thin line. On the one hand, promising a higher degree of integrity and transparency, yet meeting the expectations of a party that had been out of power for so long that it was their turn for appointments. Ultimately his attempt to do that gave him the aura, created the impression, that he was duplicitous, that he was a liar. So he carried this stigma that just got worse and worse and worse. And of course, it sells newspapers. It's wonderful; we love those kinds of scandals.

Mulroney received the most flak after appointing Mila's hairdresser to the board of the Federal Business Development Bank:
You see, it's the vulgar and corrupt nature of the Ottawa press gallery. Rinaldo Canonico is a small businessman, an Italian immigrant who is a success story, who has forty-two people working for him, who is a leader of the Italian

community. And we got him from Pierre Trudeau. He was Pierre Trudeau's personal hairdresser!

Some Mulroney appointments created problems, including the reward to his loyal caucus liaison, Pat MacAdam:
MacAdam is getting a terrible pounding. Of course, partly it's his fault, if you want to know the truth. He wrote me a confidential letter, which I have here, at Harrington Lake, asking for the job [displacing a career diplomat in a posting for External Affairs]. I thought about it, and gave him a call, and said, "I think we can do it, on a very, very confidential basis. I don't want a word said to anybody." And the next thing I knew, it was in the newspapers. And the reason was because MacAdam called External Affairs to get a description of the perks, the salary and all of this stuff. And of course, the leaks began. It was even worse than that. The person that he spoke to at External Affairs was close to former Liberal cabinet minister Mark MacGuigan. I'm not very goddamn happy about that. Obviously, she tells the guy who's supposed to be going over there instead of MacAdam, and they start leaking to Jeffrey Simpson.

Unperturbed, Mulroney fiercely defended his record:
I appointed more Liberals, NDP and non-Conservatives to key positions than any prime minister in the history of Canada. I appointed more Liberals to the Senate and NDPers to high jobs in the decision-making process than anybody else. I appointed more women to the judiciary. When I became prime minister, there were 33 women who were on the federal courts. When I left, there were 107. I appointed two women to the Supreme Court of Canada. There were two women ambassadors when I became prime minister, there were twenty-one when I left. There had been three or four women [deputy ministers]; there were twenty-three or twenty-four when I left. Everything from David Lam as lieutenant-governor of British

Columbia to Lincoln Alexander in the same position for Ontario, you name it. All of these appointments were never mentioned. You cannot deal effectively with this media in the trivialization of a nation's business—it cannot be done—so you just go ahead and do your business. I'm sure you think I'm a little bit nuts or paranoid talking about the media. I'm not at all. Wilbert Keon, [the eminent and non-partisan cardiologist appointed to the Senate by Mulroney] for instance, was totally abused by the media, and he's a guy who's constantly transplanting hearts and saving people's lives.

Two years after leaving public life, Mulroney thought that his successor at 24 Sussex was the real patronage artist:
Find a Conservative, one Conservative that Jean Chrétien has appointed in a year and a half. The answer is none. John Fraser got appointed, but you have to appoint former Speakers.

Mulroney remained bitter:
Christ, it does get irritating. As if I did something wrong. What did I do wrong? Consider it for a second. Patronage? What? Are you kidding me? Roméo LeBlanc sitting in government house with his son working for Chrétien; Chrétien's niece working in the Privy Council Office; Chrétien's nephew as our ambassador to Washington; Sharon Carstairs in the Senate . . . What? I did something wrong? *I* did something wrong?

—

DANCING THE PATRONAGE POLKA

Nothing damaged Brian Mulroney's record more profoundly or more permanently than the tidal wave of patronage he freely dispensed to his friends and supporters. Within the first year of taking office, Mulroney made 1,337 political appointments, and after that the parade of partisan popinjays never stopped. He elevated John Buchanan, a former Nova Scotia premier, to the Senate while he was still under active police investigation. He appointed Louise Dion to the board of the Canada Council, the country's top cultural funding agency, although her only administrative experience was founding a branch of Weight Watchers in his riding. By the end of his time in office he had named fifty-four senators and thirty-six diplomats. That was nearly twice as many senators and diplomats as had been named by his predecessor, though Trudeau had been in office almost twice as long.[1]

Mulroney came dangerously close to fulfilling the pledge he uttered during the 1983 Tory leadership campaign, when he confided to several closed-door party gatherings, "I look around this room and see a roomful of senators, maybe one or two judges. A Conservative government will give jobs to people in other parties only after I've been prime minister for fifteen years and can't find a single living, breathing Tory to appoint." That cynical attitude became public when he joked aboard his campaign plane about Trudeau's intended appointment of Bryce Mackasey as ambassador to Portugal, "There is no whore like an old whore." Everyone assumed he was referring to the former Liberal labour minister, but the

---

1. Pierre did win the gold in the patronage Olympics by ramming through 225 appointments in one week during the winter of 1984, just before resigning.

seldom-quoted remark that followed made it clear that Mulroney was really referring to himself. "If I'd been in Bryce's position," he said, "I'd have been in there with my nose in the public trough like the rest of them."

What made Mulroney's patronage orgies so much more lethal to his reputation than the equivalent partisan appointment binges of his Liberal predecessors was that he had gained office on a platform specifically pledged to end the practice. "The Liberals have dishonoured the system," he repeatedly declared during the 1984 campaign, "and it shall never, never happen again under a Conservative government. I'm sending out a dramatic signal of renewal in this area of Canadian life." He had scored impressively when he lectured Turner on the evils of patronage and when he turned out to be as two-faced on the issue as every other PM, the effect was devastating. Mulroney had swept the country promising that voters' concerns would be integrated into his government's priorities. Yet nothing is more exclusionary by its very nature than patronage—looking after your own, regardless of their ability or talent.

With a few exceptions, Mulroney's appointees were burned-out cases from his personal entourage or the loyal regional fixers who had grown grey in the service of the Tory diaspora. Sometimes even the recipients of his favours didn't know why they had been chosen. When Gayle Christie, a Tory municipal politician from Toronto, was named to the board of Air Canada, she confessed she was puzzled because her only experience with transportation was driving her car. When Rinaldo Canonico was named a director of the Federal Business Development Bank, some bystanders joked that it was because he added perpetual shine to Mila's hair with his cellophane highlighting technique.

Mulroney reserved the most outrageous patronage for his own riding of Manicouagan in the remote northeast corner of Quebec. By his personal edict, the riding was allocated more than $288 million in federal funding for a national park, a new harbour, a rebuilt airport runway, St. Lawrence River cleanup, aid to the fishing industry, local road construction grants, regional development subsidies and other projects. On top of that, Mulroney personally intervened in the construction of a new federal prison at Drummondville, between Montreal and Quebec City. More than $1 million had already been spent on the planning phase and the land had been acquired when the PM decided the $68 million facility would be located 582 kilometres to the east, at Port-Cartier—in his riding. According to the auditor-general, this wilful relocation cost taxpayers an extra $41 million, as well as causing serious hardship to prisoners' families, who now faced a fourteen-hour bus trip from Montreal on visiting days.

Even as he was attacking Turner on television for rubber-stamping his predecessor's paroxysm of political appointments, Mulroney's own patronage apparatus was already being mobilized. Skippered by his party's deputy leader, Erik Nielsen, it was designed to produce true-blue Tories for every empty slot that existed or could be created within the federal system. The operational code of the killer-force patronage machine was outlined in a meticulously detailed secret memo Neilsen wrote to Mulroney on May 25, 1984. (It is reproduced in Appendix B.) Two months before Mulroney beat Turner to a pulp in the debate, Nielsen was already recruiting provincial advisory committees (PACs) to put forward the names of eligible Tory appointees. Seven weeks later—still twelve days *before* the televised debate—Nielsen, with Mulroney's full blessing, activated the PACs, ordering them to round up actual patronage candidates. When I asked Mulroney, shortly after the fact, whether Nielsen had indeed covertly recruited patronage candidates before the election was even won, he replied without a moment's hesitation: "The fellow who is co-ordinating all this is Neilsen. He is playing an absolutely indispensable role. As deputy leader, he is very much in control of the entire party apparatus. I put the structure together and I put the people in place, but Erik runs it."

There was nothing haphazard about this computer-driven operation. It could justifiably be called the Mulroney government's smoothest-run (and busiest) department. Appointments were evenly distributed. The Yukon, for example, had 0.8 per cent of Canada's population and received precisely 0.8 per cent of the job handouts. In British Columbia the ratio was almost even at 11.2 per cent population to 11.4 per cent patronage positions, in Ontario just a fraction apart at 36.6 per cent to 35.5 per cent, and so on throughout the country. The mix was designed to cover all the bases, including gender balance and cultural diversity. The appointment of the first three Tory directors to the board of Canadian National, for example, was a work of art: a black entrepreneur from Toronto, a Ukrainian farmer from Draper, Alberta, and a francophone housewife from northern Ontario. (But not an Estonian in sight.) Nine of the ten PAC chairmen received immediate senior patronage appointments; the tenth had to wait a few weeks. In a 1990 marathon, when he needed partisan support in the upper chamber to pass the GST legislation, Mulroney appointed a record twenty-four senators in one month.

No one's record was too shameful for a dip in the trough. Few MPs gave Mulroney more trouble than backbencher Dan McKenzie, who was unalterably opposed to bilingualism and had been fired by the PM as a parliamentary secretary. But when it came time for McKenzie to retire, Mulroney appointed him as a one-man task force to study the prospects of economic association with the impoverished Caribbean islands of Turks and Caicos, which happened to be the Winnipegger's favourite winter hangout. It turned out to be an onerous responsibility that required much intensive research (and a bounteous expense account) before McKenzie, a former telephone company supervisor, concluded that the laidback inhabitants of the island paradise should not enter Confederation.

Mulroney did make some excellent appointments, such as naming his friend Yves Fortier to the post of Canadian ambassador to the United Nations, and Stanley Hartt as deputy minister of finance. But these were outweighed by the sheer volume of his questionable choices. Amazingly, the Tories' patronage net even (tentatively) extended to Jean Chrétien. On June 25, 1984, just after the Liberals had picked John Turner as their next leader and Chrétien seemed to be at loose ends, Fred Doucet, then Mulroney's chief of staff, suggested to Brian that he ought to "check with Jean since our news is that he's having a tough time settling for the terms Turner is offering him." Doucet recorded in his journal, "My suggestion is, based on the fact that there's nothing to lose, we should call Jean and suggest to him that he would be well looked after later, in terms of an appointment. If Chrétien stays with the Liberals and accepts Turner's offer, there would still be some gains in that Chrétien would see a measure of kindness extended his way in these, his tough times— and this would help us either way. We don't think he will accept any of the offers but we think there are some points to be made by chatting with him and we're going to do that tonight." Later the same day, Doucet's journal entry recorded the outcome: "Mulroney has now spoken with Jean and he confirms our suspicions that indeed, he is not very happy, he's a pretty disgruntled man, but however bad that might be, he still remains a Liberal. We still think there was something positive in chatting with him." After John Turner retired from politics and returned to Bay Street, Mulroney sounded him out on becoming Canadian ambassador to Italy and to the Vatican, but it was not to be.

Those Mulroney supporters left out of the patronage loop shared the wealth by becoming Ottawa lobbyists. The city ran on a simple principle: proximity to power *was* power. Operating below the radar range of public notice, such fixers minted fortunes from the sale of access to the PM and his ministers. Harry Near, a former aide to Energy Minister Pat Carney, made so much money lobbying for the oil patch, he built himself a pretentious mansion in Rockcliffe Park, a ritzy Ottawa suburb. His mansion warming, attended by most of cabinet, produced one of the great quotes of the Mulroney era. Harvie Andre, a bright and lively Albertan who as minister of corporate and consumer affairs was one of the lobbyists' chief targets, stepped into the marbled foyer of Near's Alhambra and mused aloud, "I've never understood why it's so much more profitable to *know* Harvie Andre than to *be* Harvie Andre."

One of the chief benefactors of the Mulroney patronage machine was none other than its creator, Erik Nielsen. "The problem with Erik's chairmanship of the patronage committees," Mulroney admitted in one of my later interviews with him, "was that he was so partisan, I had to remove him. And as for this guy opposing patronage, he asked to become ambassador to Washington, and I had to turn him down for obvious reasons." Although Nielsen portrayed himself in his autobiography, *The House Is Not a Home*, as the slayer of "patronage, political favoritism and influence-peddling, wherever I found them," when he decided to leave federal politics in 1986, he nominated himself for several jobs, including not only the ambassadorship but also chief justice of the Yukon. Mulroney asked Ray Hnatyshyn, then minister of justice, to see what he could do. The answer came back: the idea would never pass the local bar association. Instead, Mulroney appointed Neilsen to the highest-paying job in the public service, as head of the Transport Board, at $143,000 a year (later raised to $155,000) plus $44,000 in fringe benefits including a chauffeur and limousine and a special retirement package. Neilsen refused to operate out of the agency's palatial offices in Hull, Quebec, rented at a cost of $333,490 per year, and instead leased a luxurious suite at Minto Place in downtown Ottawa for $55,200 annually— at government expense, of course. Mulroney even put through a special order to stipulate that Nielsen couldn't be removed by any future government.

The only cabinet minister brave enough to criticize Mulroney's patronage binge was Joe Clark, who sent him a confidential letter on July 2, 1985, which read in part, "We were elected to be both national and new. So far, we have been remarkably successful as a national government but the patronage issue has tarnished our newness; among other things, it has distracted us from defining ourselves in terms of the real changes we have accomplished—on the deficit, energy, federal-provincial relations. We must consciously develop, and convey, a distinctive reform reputation for the government." No one paid any attention. Instead, the Mulroney insiders revelled in their good fortune.

In mid-January of 1985, Mulroney and some of his closest buddies—Charley McMillan, Patrick MacAdam, Guy Charbonneau, Sam Wakim, Michel Cogger and a few others—were having dinner in the Senate Speaker's Gallery, where the wood panelling is carved with Latin inscriptions. Late in the evening they were speculating about what the carvings meant when they were brought up short by Wakim, who quipped, "Well, I don't know about you guys, because I was never that good in Latin, but the way I see it, this stuff on the walls means, 'Thank God for patronage!'"

Mulroney himself liked to tell the story about a legendary New York lawyer and lobbyist who accompanied John F. Kennedy on his successful 1960 presidential campaign. Everywhere the candidate's plane landed, the lawyer would jump out and walk Pushinka, Kennedy's dog. After watching him perform this pedestrian task on several occasions, R.W. Apple of the *New York Times* went up to him and said, "I gotta tell you, I've lost a lot of respect for you. Here you are, at the top of your profession, a millionaire lawyer from New York who is supposed to know everything that's going on, and you're walking this silly mutt."

"That might look like a dog to you," the lawyer replied, as he was pulled along the tarmac by his charge, "but it looks more like an embassy to me."

During my interviews with Mulroney I found his devil-may-care comments about his promiscuous use of patronage astonishing. He obviously regarded the ability to reward his loyalists as his due—and theirs. His tenure tested the capacity of Canadians to be shocked. Every swath of partisan appointments was interpreted as another of the prime minister's moral lapses. Of his liabilities, this was the most obvious and the least forgivable. His election as a reformer, specifically pledged to end shoddy patronage, proved to be a tragic masquerade.

4·

"Goodbye Charlie Brown!"

Scandals, Retreats and Flip-Flops

Once the euphoria of his 1984 victory had faded, Brian Mulroney discovered that instead of cutting him some slack and treating the series of embarrassing government scandals that erupted with irritating regularity as the minor annoyances they were, Canadians were unforgiving and peevish. During the Trudeau years, they had pardoned Pierre for many transgressions; his shrug had a disarming effect. Even if he was a smartass, he was *our* smartass, and the world envied us for having elected him.

Mulroney had no such protective aura at his disposal. Within eighteen months, most of the goodwill he had earned during the 1984 election evaporated as his government stumbled from one crisis to the next, none of them life-threatening but all of them embarrassing.

It wasn't so much what Mulroney did that drove

Canadians batty; it was that they expected him to be as different as he claimed to be, and he turned out to be worse. Ordinarily placid citizens grew so cynical that even when offending Mulroney ministers admitted they had lied, nobody believed them.

The ephemeral nature of the Tory mandate became clear as polls showed the party consistently running behind the Grits. By the end of Mulroney's second year in office, an astonishing 60 per cent of voters wanted him to resign. Exhausted by a decade and half of Trudeau's petulance, Canadians had voted in a new government believing that it would not only be more accommodating and more competent than the Liberals, but be the answer to all their prayers. By delivering a huge majority to Mulroney, Canadians deposited their hopes, dreams and expectations on his unshrugging shoulders—and hung him with expectations no government could fulfill. The succession of ministerial resignations and the government's inability to follow through on its promises robbed its supporters of their illusions.

Driven to distraction by Mulroney's presidential style and the government's questionable ethics, Canadians of the late 1980s became increasingly convinced that they were being governed by dysfunctional nabobs with few core values to call their own. Mulroney needed to overcome this defeatist gospel, first in the exhausted psyches of his entourage, then among the distracted, disaffected population. By trying too hard to win friends and influence people, he did neither. He also overestimated his buddies in the private sector who had assured him that the entrepreneurial spirit would burn bright once "that commie Trudeau" was relegated to purgatory. Mulroney had naïvely subscribed to the wisdom of those Chamber of Commerce valedictorians, Business Council on National Issues factotums and Mount Royal Club habitués, who kept assuring him that the floodgates of capital investment would open after he was elected. Jobs would follow dollars. That was why Mulroney felt able to promise "Jobs! Jobs! JOBS!" during his 1984 campaign. In government, he followed the business community's counsel—dropped corporate taxes, privatized nearly everything except the Canadian Mint and tried to confiscate pensions. But the rich and powerful went on bloating their corporate bottom lines with little regard to job creation, and the poor gave up, leaving little middle ground between smugness and despair.

And yet Canadians still expected the electrician's son from Baie-Comeau to be their king, sugar daddy, fixer, babysitter and prime minister. Mulroney's triumphant campaign shattered the Liberal hegemony; he had fielded a truly national caucus and united the PC Party for the first time in almost a century. That should have been the hard part. But it soon became apparent that neither he nor most members of his inner circle had planned much beyond the election night victory party. He was prepared to govern, yes, but based on what policies and according to which priorities? No one knew what to expect from the Age of Mulroney, least of all its creator. Mulroney could articulate no inspiring vision behind which to mobilize political commitment.

Deprived of the enlightened leadership they had expected, Canadians declared a limited state of class warfare. They had traditionally considered themselves to be members of a classless society—as George Orwell so cleverly put it, part of "the lower-upper-middle class." But now, for the first time since the Great Depression, hints of class consciousness began to emerge in Canada. Allan Gregg reported in *Maclean's* that "the most significant trend is a growing and potentially dangerous class disparity. This is the beginning of class-based thinking." Core middle-class values, essential to the Canadian experience, were being eroded by rising taxes, false promises and just plain anger. For most citizens that was disquieting; for Brian Mulroney it meant a political lynching. Here was a prime minister elected mainly because his thousand-watt smile suggested that he could reconcile the country's social and economic interests. Instead, he stood accused of ripping asunder Canada's social fabric.

His most immediate concern was to make some visible dint in the gargantuan deficit bequeathed by the spend-thrift Trudeau regime. Everyone agreed that federal spending had to be slashed, so long as not a penny was removed from their own pockets. Demand for deficit reduction remained as strong as the resistance to the means of achieving it. By 1986, Mulroney decided to forego hopes of balancing budgets and went on a seven-year spending spree, trying to buy back his fading popu-larity. As finance minister from 1984 to 1991, Michael Wilson accumulated more public debt than all of his peacetime predecessors combined.

A good case could be made that what happened wasn't Mulroney's fault but rather the inevitable legacy of the size and the nature of his mandate. "His parliamentary majority, the largest in Canadian history, gives him no mandate at all for decisive leadership," commented Reg Whitaker, a professor of political science at York University, a year after the original Mulroney victory. "The irony is that the wider the electoral victory, the weaker the mandate. If a country is deeply fragmented by language, region, class and economic interests, the more representative the government, the more representative it becomes of all the divisions and the more politically par-alyzed it appears. After a year of post-Trudeau politics we find a majority government wallowing immobile, in the political centre, up to its armpits in rancid tuna, patron-age and resigning cabinet ministers. Worst of all they are increasingly perceived as incompetent economic man-agers, bailing out failed businessmen with wads of tax-payers' money."

In his efforts to prop up failing communities, Mulroney had learned from history. He knew that

Shelburne, Nova Scotia, for example, once had 15,000 inhabitants and now was almost a ghost town. As head of Iron Ore, he had lived through the agony of closing down the model company town of Schefferville, Quebec. He realized how thin was the membrane between prosperity and extinction, and that communities and even regions can atrophy and die.

In *Candide*, Voltaire wrote about the English military habit of executing someone "to encourage the others." For Mulroney, it didn't work out that way, though during his terms in office there was no shortage of political executions and self-immolations, eventually involving a dozen cabinet ministers. Another nine MPs were charged with varieties of fraud, breach of trust and influence peddling. All resigned, but only a couple went to jail. The worst was Michel Gravel, charged with ten counts of bribery, thirty-two of defrauding the government and eight of breach of trust in connection with construction of the Museum of Man in Hull. Gravel pleaded guilty (which precluded any detailed discussion of his crimes) and was incarcerated for a year. Unlike the Chrétien sponsorship scandal, which involved the systematic plundering of the federal treasury by a network of corrupt politicians and lobbyists, the wrongdoing during Mulroney's time was largely limited to dishonest individuals taking advantage of their positions to illegally pocket graft and bribes. All of the culprits resigned, voluntarily or otherwise.

Still, I vividly recall Norman Inkster, the commissioner of the RCMP, confiding that his horsemen were conducting twenty-two investigations into wrongdoing by members of the Mulroney administration. That prompted me to speculate in print that in order to maintain a quorum, cabinet meetings might have to be held when ministers were out on day passes. The political atmosphere became so charged that nobody would admit to anything. Although Brian and Mila vowed not to charge taxpayers for their nanny, her name (Elizabeth MacDonald from

Guysborough County, Nova Scotia) soon appeared on federal expense accounts. With a straight face, Fred Doucet staunchly denied that MacDonald was actually a nanny, describing her function as being "to interface with the children in a habitual way." At least that mini-scandal produced some badly needed comic relief.

The most incendiary incident was a flash confrontation between Mulroney and Solange Denis, an angry pensioner who picketed Parliament Hill in June 1985, after the first Conservative budget de-indexed old age pensions. "You lied to us!" she shouted at the PM. "You made us vote for you, then goodbye Charlie Brown!" That exchange crystallized the nation's discontent: this was a government content to let the rich get richer while everyone else grew poorer. The same budget that cut old age pensions allowed millionaires to claim (by about an equal amount) tax-free capital exemptions for their old masters and young mistresses. At the same time as the budget, the federal government bailed out the depositors of two bankrupt Alberta banks and allowed the Reichmann brothers to claim a tax break worth $600 million to purchase the Canadian operations of Gulf Oil. These moves, which only reinforced the incipient class split, collapsed the government's approval ratings. The barriers to social and economic advancement were being institutionalized. Just to rub it in, Ottawa chose this particular moment to launch a brutal tax audit of Newfoundland fishermen.

Universality had been a wondrously compassionate hallmark of Canada's social welfare net: if everyone was entitled to payouts, those who really needed them could accept financial help with no stigma attached.[1] Stung by mounting criticism, Mulroney reversed himself and ordered

---

1. Peter Curry, for example, was a high-ranking executive of Power Corp. and a millionaire many times over. He married his son's youthful babysitter and sired a daughter by her, then boasted that he was collecting both family allowance and old age pension cheques, though he needed neither.

Wilson to retreat on the de-indexing budget provisions. But that only meant he lost the support of both rich and poor. One result of the policy flip was a sharply worded confidential memo to Mulroney from Joe Clark, who had been appointed to External Affairs. "The Jeffrey Simpson thesis—that Brian Mulroney undercuts his colleagues—could become conventional wisdom," he wrote. "Many people believe that Mike Wilson and Jake Epp have been seriously diminished by the old-age pension de-indexing episode; and the implication is that you did not do enough to support them. I can think of nothing but time to turn that around. In the meantime, you must be extraordinarily careful that nothing you say or do lends credence to that thesis."

To resurrect the voters' confidence in him, Mulroney toured the country endlessly, held private mutual admiration sessions with friendly journalists (both of them) and set Mila, his most effective propagandist, loose among the heathen. But changes of mood cannot be legislated or artificially created. Only inspired leadership can achieve such a shift in public opinion. Brian Mulroney operated according to the maxim of most politicians who are in trouble: appear confident but run scared. By mid-1985, he looked and acted as if he really might be running scared—and then he *was*, and only a miracle could save him.

—

"HE WENT TO A BAR": THE FIRST DISGRACE

Bob Coates became the first Mulroney minister to resign, in February 1985, after it was revealed that he had visited a shady West German nightclub while on official business. The jaunt was considered a security risk since he was carrying a briefcase of classified NATO documents at the time.

As usual, Mulroney blamed the media:
Bob Coates went to a bar and had a drink with somebody who was less than the daughter of Isabella. The media took these isolated things and conveyed the impression that this was a corrupt, indecent group, without offering any perspective.

Lowell Murray was left scratching his head:
As Mulroney went through the chronology in caucus, I kept asking myself, "Why the hell did he resign? Why did Mulroney accept his resignation? What the hell did he do that was so serious?" He blundered into the damn place. If somebody said to me, "Let's go for a drink," and I felt like it, I might go, but it's hard to find a place where everybody has all of their clothes on.

"DID YOU LIE TO THAT LADY, DADDY?":
PENSION FLIP-FLOP

In 1985, Mulroney was forced to roll back his decision to de-index pensions after being publicly scolded by pensioner Solange Denis for breaking a "sacred trust."

A foot in his mouth:
NEWMAN: When you talked about maintaining "a sacred trust," what did you have in mind?

MULRONEY: Medicare. I decided to deal with this medicare thing right off the bat. I said, "This is a sacred trust—it will not be violated. Period." The media, of course, then generalized. That was a typical press gallery distortion. It's all nonsense.

Stanley Hartt heard it the way the press gallery did:
What happened was, this little old francophone lady from Quebec, Solange Denis, basically said, "You lied to us—

you told us these were sacred trusts." And Mulroney went home and found his wife and kids watching TV and the kids said to him, "Did you lie to that lady, Daddy?" And he was hurt by that—he was really physically hurt by that. I mean, he *had* lied. Yes, he had said they were sacred trusts, in typical Mulroney hyperbole. He had promised he wouldn't hurt them.

Being hit by his political enemies was bad, but shots were also coming from his own finance minister:
MULRONEY: Broadbent called me a liar in the House, and he'll pay for that. He doesn't know when or how, but I guarantee it. What he said about me was false. And Wilson . . . Well, you know, Wilson's statement about sacred trusts was the stupidest statement I've seen. I told him how bad it was. He's not a stupid man, but he doesn't have any political intent, and he has bad staff.

Mulroney kept making excuses:
I thought that given the artificial insults crusade started by the CBC and everybody else, I would remove one element that was tending to obscure Michael Wilson's budget completely, namely the indexation of the pensions. I found out then that what would be construed as reasonableness and a thoughtful approach to management in the private sector was construed as a sign of weakness. The unfairness of the Ottawa press gallery at the time was such that they portrayed me as weak and vacillating. They crapped all over me. So I just said screw you. If reasonableness is construed to be a sign of weakness, you'll never catch me at it again.

Minister of National Revenue Perrin Beatty:
The first political mistake was to de-index. The second was to change positions on it. I remember well when he announced the decision to us, and that was it. The decision was taken.

Policy advisor Geoff Norquay:
The Liberals clearly decided that they would set some huge traps for Brian and his leadership. The Liberals and the NDP played that sacred trust thing very well. The biggest error in judgment was to assume that there was a widespread understanding of the need to cut the deficit and, second, a consensus on the need to target better social programs.

It was a half-baked proposal, the de-indexation. It was half-baked in the sense that it hit an element of society that is perceived to be almost universally at risk, and it attempted to apply that reduction to them all. There was no distinction between well-to-do elderly, getting-by elderly and really, really poor elderly.

"NO ONE WAS EVEN SICK": TAINTED TUNA

Fisheries Minister John Fraser was forced to resign on September 23, 1985, after he overruled his ministry officials to release tainted tuna to the Canadian public, and offered a different version of the events than the prime minister's.

Once again Mulroney was on the defensive:
You would think that ten thousand people died because of rancid tuna. No one was even sick. At the same time, in September of 1985, there were I think ten or eleven people who died in an elderly home in southwestern Ontario. There was a big problem, but it hardly even made the media. I just regret that it was our administrative incompetence that allowed this to happen. The media gave more publicity to tuna than to the Gulf War. I'll never forget the editorial in the *Wall Street Journal* talking about this, where they said, "Only in Canada would these things be referred to as scandals." Black September, because John Fraser, poor John, got involved in something with tuna.

Ian Anderson had the inside track:
Fraser's problem was that he had basically a war within his department. What he said to his fisheries inspector was, "You're not going to tell me what to do." Then the *fifth estate* story came out, and the prime minister told Fraser that the cans had to come off the shelves. Fraser, I guess, was going through a lot of stress and got into conflict coming to the House of Commons on Friday. He let loose that the Prime Minister's Office had been briefed in detail, while he had first learned about it on the *fifth estate*. It was a horrible, horrible experience.

Charley McMillan:
What happened was, on the Wednesday we told Fraser, "You're in big trouble. The fish has got to be withdrawn." You know, cut your losses and withdraw it. Ironically, if you look at the transcript of that day, Fraser got up [in Question Period] and said that he had requested the minister of health to withdraw the tuna. It could have been the end of it. He should have disappeared for three weeks and gone to Hong Kong or Florida, but then he got into this crazy scrum and blamed the PM. We couldn't believe it, just couldn't believe it. I called the PM and said, "This thing's a lot more serious than Fraser thinks, and he may lose his head on this thing tomorrow."

Fraser didn't lose his job because of the tuna:
MULRONEY: It was agreed that John would not say anything anymore, and we had it pretty well under control, but he left the House of Commons and went to a microphone and made his statement there at variance with what I had said, thereby opening himself—and me—to criticism. That was when John's career as fisheries minister came to an end.

Once again, Bill Pristanski said, the PM had great fodder for wisecracks:

We had the publisher of *Time* for lunch, and about thirty senior American business people. The PM started the speech by saying, "President Mitterrand has somebody running around his government blowing up ships. Chancellor Kohl has spies in every office in his administration. I've got tuna."

"SLIT HER THROAT": SUZANNE BLAIS-GRENIER

Mulroney's first environment minister was shuffled to Transport in August 1985, and left the cabinet on the year's last day ostensibly over the closure of an oil refinery in Montreal but actually because the powers-that-be thought she was in over her head. Her many unjustified junkets had made her stay impossible.

Mulroney blamed himself:
That was my mistake in terms of believing that she could handle that kind of portfolio. I didn't know her as well as I should have, and it turned out to be too much to ask of a newcomer, who is a woman in politics, new to the party, new to the language, new to Ottawa, new to the ministry, new to the House of Commons.

Pat MacAdam saw the early warning signs:
Mme Blais-Grenier and her husband, who was her chief of staff and consort, were going to Auckland. It was the inaugural flight of Air New Zealand from Vancouver. She said, "It's a freebie." We cancelled it and told Brian, who was in Nassau. "Slit her throat," he said.

We had also received a snarky letter from her chief of staff complaining that she was changing flights in Paris and she had a four- or five-hour stopover and no one from the diplomatic mission came out to meet her. We didn't know she was in Paris, and on her way to Algeria. I mean, thank God stupidity is not contagious.

Peter White said Mulroney contemplated firing Blais-Grenier after her first problems:
So Brian says to himself, well, shit, who am I going to put in my cabinet from Quebec if I drop Blais-Grenier? He doesn't know. The fact is that there are probably five people out there who are twice as good as Blais-Grenier, but he doesn't know who they are. As a result, he decided not to drop Blais-Grenier. That's another sort of indecisive half measure. It's going to look terrible.

Lowell Murray joined the chorus:
He could have dropped her out, clunk. Instead of that, he made her minister of transport. He even said, "Every time her name is mentioned, we lose 25,000 votes."

"PHONE YOUR MOTHER, PHONE YOUR RELATIVES!": SINCLAIR STEVENS

On April 29, 1986, the Globe and Mail *revealed that Noreen Stevens, the wife of the regional expansion minister, negotiated a $2.6 million loan to his holding company, York Centre, from a firm that depended on federal aid. Stevens was actually exonerated of any conflict of interest in 2005, nineteen years after he was forced to step down.*

Mulroney was travelling when the scandal broke.
BILL PRISTANSKI: The Prime Minister was very frustrated, and he called Bill Davis and some other people, and said, "What's your perception of the perception, because I'm not in Canada. I'm not seeing any of these reports. How bad is it? Where are we now?"

Finally, do you know what he did? He said, "Okay, go back to your rooms, phone your mother, phone your relatives and ask them about Sinclair Stevens. Ask them how they feel and come back and see me." So they did, they all did. They phoned their mothers and relatives, and it became pretty clear that Stevens had to resign.

Charley McMillan:
I was listening to Sinc that morning when we went into cabinet, and he said, "There's nothing to it." I asked him if he was going to do anything about it, and he said no. When we finally got him talking about it, we were in Tokyo. Frankly, if there's one lesson from Richard Nixon's stonewalling strategy, it's that it never works. Sinc was holding back in terms of the potential allegations and all that kind of stuff. I mean, if you want to write an article that said I was with a bunch of hookers in Montreal last night, I would categorically deny it. But Jesus, if somebody asked me if I was in Montreal last night, and I said, "Well, yeah, but I can't tell you about it. . ." I think Sinc wasn't as forthcoming on a lot of things, you know. Sinc didn't face up to it.

Geoff Norquay, on Stevens's defence strategy:
One of the problems early on was that Erik Nielsen and Bernard Roy met with Sinc and did not come away from their meeting confident that they knew the whole story. That was the fatal flaw. How could Sinc speak and how could he defend himself when the whole basis of his defence was that he didn't know anything?

Mulroney's take on the Stevens scandal:
What was that? It was a conflict of interest, which by the way was also new—the whole concept of conflict of interest began in 1984. It existed in embryonic form, but now it was institutionalized and it was new.

"THE ONLY ONE": MICHEL GRAVEL

*The Tory MP from Gamelin, Quebec, was charged with
fifty counts of influence peddling the same week that
Sinclair Stevens left cabinet. He pleaded guilty and spent
a year in jail.*

Mulroney:
Michel Gravel was a member of Parliament who was obviously corrupt and who went to jail for a small period of
time, and that unfortunately happens in all political parties. But I think that's the only one.

"NOT EVEN A THANK YOU": CF-18

*In a decision that fuelled western alienation and encour-
aged the formation of the Reform Party, the Mulroney government awarded an aircraft maintenance contract to
Montreal's Bombardier instead of Winnipeg-based Bristol
Aerospace, whose bid had offered better value at a lower
price.*

Mulroney was angered by the reaction of Montrealers:
We made a very major decision at the cabinet level, ordering the CF-18 contract into Montreal to ensure that
Montreal and French Canadians have a technological foot
in the twenty-first century. What was the response from
Montrealers? "Give us the fucking Space Centre." Not
even a moment to say thank you. Why would I be
spending any time in Montreal? And why would any of
my people? What they really need in Montreal is an NDP
government. Then you've got everything on the agenda
from the dismantling of our defence, the chasing away of
foreign capital, the drying up of our markets, the end
of our relations with the United States, and interest rates
at 25 per cent. Then you're going to see the fucking trucks

in there, moving everything out of Montreal again back into southern Ontario.

The party line, as expressed by Bill Pristanski:
Ontario has everything that's snazzy, spiffy, that you can have pride in. The only thing Montreal has—and it's a small thing, but at least there's some pride left for the francophones in Montreal—is the aerospace industry. If you rape the aerospace industry in Montreal and allow it to die, they have nothing, and will lose their pride.

"IT LOOKS PRETTY BAD": OERLIKON

In April 1986, Canada's Low Level Air Defence contract was awarded to Swiss firm Oerlikon-Buhrle, which began construction of a facility in Saint-Jean-sur-Richelieu. On January 18, 1987, the area's MP—André Bissonnette— was dismissed from his junior cabinet position as transport minister over a complicated land-flip scheme, a scandal that rocked the Mulroney government.

Pat MacAdam:
The boss had Bissonnette in and asked for his resignation. Bissonnette's last words as he left the office were, "I'll be back." There was this rumour that Brian had kicked the wall. He told me, "Kicked the wall? I just about kicked his fucking head out the window."

There were no easy excuses when it came to this one, no blaming the media:
GEOFF NORQUAY: The prime minister's been through a real trying time in the last—well, ever since the Bissonnette thing. You can dress the Bissonnette thing any way you want, but in the minds of the public, it looks like that individual is very probably a crook. You really can't bullshit your way out of that, and Mulroney knows it. He

will put on a brave face about it, but on several occasions he's said to me, "You know, you really can't sweep that under the carpet, there's no question about whether it's inappropriate or not appropriate. It looks pretty bad." He's had to do a lot of thinking about the people around him.

The way forward:
MULRONEY: I can't blame a guy in Baie-Comeau. Give him a choice to discuss the fact that interest rates are down by four points or Bissonnette's wife putting a million dollars in her pocket—what do you think he's going to talk about? What we've got to do now is govern in a dull manner, without any Oerlikons jumping out at me.

"HE'S GOT TO HAVE A MERCEDES": MICHEL COGGER

One of Mulroney's closest friends, Senator Michel Cogger, was the subject of a lengthy RCMP probe after reports surfaced about alleged influence-peddling from a private company:

Mulroney:
I'm very upset by what happened, but not half as upset as my wife is. The reason I put Cogger in the Senate was to keep him out of this kind of stuff. I thought that with a position in the Senate and a modest association with the law firm, he could earn a nice living and be happy for the rest of his life. But he just can't seem to resist. He's got to have a Mercedes and not a Chevy. If he has a business opportunity, it seems to me that he has an obligation to look at it very carefully and say, "Is there any possibility that this could do damage to the prime minister? Because if it will, I won't touch it."

Still, Mulroney thought the press made too big a deal out of it:

Reporters just became enveloped in the malice. Everything had to be wrong. Look at what they tried to do to Cogger. For Christ's sakes, there was a special detachment of the RCMP set up to try and suborn the guy. You and I would have succumbed to the goddamned temptation. I'm flabbergasted. Then if you read those books—what they tried to do to catch him, to entice him, to lure him, he never did. That thing [my tape recorder] is not running, is it?

NEWMAN: Yes it is.

5.

"The sweetest deal ever known
to man"

———

The Meech Lake Accord

IN "SILVER BLAZE," Sherlock Holmes solves a mysterious murder when he realizes why a guard dog didn't bark. The failed Meech Lake Accord—the designated centrepiece of Brian Mulroney's second term—was the "dog that didn't bark" of his controversial time in office. From the initial meeting at a government lodge in the Gatineau Hills on April 30, 1987, where the constitutional agreement between the PM and provincial premiers was breech-birthed, to the day the accord died in the Newfoundland and Manitoba legislatures— June 23, 1990—the issue dominated the national agenda. It proved that what doesn't happen can be as significant as what does.

Someone once defined Canada as being the only nation in the world where books on federal-provincial relations are sold at airports. Meech Lake roused hope and anger in equal proportions, but at least it proved that thesis to be true. Canadians went to the wall over complicated constitutional subtleties that no one, including those books' authors, fully understood. At one point in the debate, Jean Chrétien, the Liberal leader and a Meech opponent, told a *Maclean's* reporter, "Lac Meech, Lac Meech. Eventually people dream about Lac Meech. Nobody knows what it is."

Mulroney's legitimate reason for Meech was not to make history, but to rectify it. In his 1981 rush to patriate the Constitution, Trudeau failed to create the conditions that might have allowed Quebec premier René Lévesque to buy into the deal (which was hardly surprising since making the country work better was not exactly part of Lévesque's separatist agenda). In return for signing on to the constitution, the Mulroney accord granted Quebec distinct society status. But the offer was extended in typically Canadian fashion: nearly everyone outside Quebec was against it, except its sponsors, who claimed that deep down distinct status was virtually meaningless. What could be better?

Having no familiar framework in which to fit the inexorable nationalistic impulses of a large number of Quebeckers, the rest of the country interpreted Meech as the hot breath of revolution. Yet all that moderate Quebec nationalists really wanted was reassurance in writing that they were different. That was demonstrably true: French and English Canadians live in different languages by separate legal codes, enjoy diverse cultures and have a common past but little common history.

Meech was a unique phenomenon. The analysis of its 7,425-word text became a growth industry with its own momentum. At its most intense, the Meech Lake debate threatened reputations in academic halls and triggered fisticuffs in beer parlours. The process by which Meech was created bypassed established bureaucratic forms and customs. There were no formal minutes of the tense negotiating session at Meech Lake. Subtle agreement among the participants was transmitted mainly by body language. As Andrew Cohen, who wrote the best book on Meech (*A Deal Undone*), described it, "Glance rather than stare, stare rather than wink, wink rather than nod, nod rather than whisper, whisper rather than speak, speak rather than write. No doubt many wanted to frame the constitution that way. Ambiguity meant flexibility. It allowed the drafters to avoid fixed positions. Making hard decisions meant a flaring of tempers, a clash of wills and, ideally, a meeting of minds."

Robert Bourassa, the Quebec premier who ended up on the firing line, declared, "You can break modern Quebec history into two stages: pre- and post-Meech. Without Quebec's signature on the Constitution, there is a hole in the heart of most Quebeckers. I thought that with Meech, we could heal that."

The agreement was far from perfect. It made no provision for the constitutional future of the First Nations and the special concerns of women's groups. But neutral observers concluded that the legitimate reason for giving Meech priority was that it made so little sense not to. Meech became a totem, crossing party lines, corralling such disparate supporters as Ed Broadbent, Bob Rae and Stephen Lewis of the NDP; Liberals John Turner, Paul Martin and Sheila Copps; as well as most community leaders, unionists and pundits, myself included.

The Opposition was field-marshalled by a ghost come to life. During the original Meech Lake meeting, Joe Ghiz, the premier of PEI, noted an invisible presence haunting the conference: "There was another man in the room that day. We talked about him quite a bit. He was there. He was there in spirit. He was Pierre Trudeau." That phantom of the Meech Lake opera morphed into the dominant presence in the debating that followed. Instead of supporting Bourassa's willingness to opt into his constitution, Trudeau came out, mouth blazing, and cursed "the snivelling eunuchs of premiers" and "the wimp of a prime minister" who wanted to render "Canada totally impotent." He then toured the country, musing in TV studios and newspaper offices that Canada had no claim to immortality and that he, for one, would not "hang himself in a loft" if Quebec were to separate.

In response, Mulroney became a heat-seeking missile, speaking (it seemed) to each Rotary Club and in every church basement from sea to sea. Even visitors to Canada were not exempt from his proselytizing. At a private breakfast he hosted at 24 Sussex for Robert and Elizabeth Dole, then America's most distinguished power couple— he was the senior senator from Kansas and later the Republican presidential candidate, she the secretary of labour in the first Bush cabinet—he spent most of the meal explaining Meech.

"Forget Canada," he told them. "Let's assume that the United States decided they had to have a new constitution, and all the states met with the federal administration for an extended period of time. Finally, they came up with a new document. But it was not endorsed by New York, California and Texas. That's approximately the breakout equivalent of Quebec's population in this country."

The Doles looked baffled as to how any such thing could happen.

"It gets better," Mulroney sarcastically assured them. "In those negotiations, the governors of the fifty states wound up with the power to override every provision of the American Bill of Rights and all decisions of the U.S. Supreme Court."

Elizabeth Dole, who had been a candidate for the Supreme Court, couldn't resist. "Are you telling me that the governor of Mississippi would have been given the right to overrule Supreme Court decisions on issues of civil rights?"

"That's exactly what I'm telling you," Mulroney shot back.

"Who did this?" she demanded.

"Guess who? Pierre Trudeau, the same fellow who today is demanding perfection in the Meech Lake Accord!"

HAD THE DOLES STUCK AROUND for the final chapter in the Meech saga, they would have been even more incredulous.

Enter Clyde Wells. Although he had made a fetish out of refusing to move on Meech Lake without consulting "the people," the Newfoundland premier announced unilaterally on the day after his party was elected—April 20, 1989—that he now had a mandate to renegotiate Meech Lake, an intention absent from his platform. Without holding any public hearings during the fourteen months of his premiership, Wells rescinded his predecessor's signature on the accord. Like Trudeau, who was Wells's friend and mentor, Wells was adamantly opposed to Quebec's being recognized as distinct in any respect. Such a position was particularly galling for a Newfoundland premier to take because that province's own terms of union with Canada in 1949 contained "several provisions conferring powers and imposing obligations quite distinct from those of any other province."

At the final week-long bargaining session in Ottawa that ended on June 9, 1990, Wells himself drafted the communiqué that pledged him to use "every possible effort" on behalf of the accord by putting it to either a referendum or a free vote in his legislative assembly. To demonstrate that intent, Wells invited Mulroney, as well as the premiers of Ontario, Saskatchewan and New Brunswick, to make their case to the Newfoundland legislature, with the clear pledge that a vote would follow. On the Thursday evening before the Meech deadline, at a private dinner at his home with Mulroney, Wells was still reassuring the PM that he would call the vote. An informal poll taken that evening showed that Meech would have passed in the Newfoundland legislature by a margin of two votes.

Wells's view of the nation's future, bound up in the dreams and past glories of Pierre Trudeau, added up to obstruction for its own sake. The premier attacked the accord like an old-fashioned prosecuting lawyer delivering his final summation in a series of righteous thunderbolts, his arguments marshalled not to prove that he was right, but to prove that no other version of events dared exist. When he was in private legal practice, Wells eschewed partners. He preferred wet-eared juniors who would do his bidding. In cabinet meetings, he treated most of his ministers like superannuated flunkies. An apocryphal story then making the rounds in St. John's had Wells inviting his nondescript cabinet to the Hotel Newfoundland. "And what would you like for lunch, Mr. Wells?" asked the waitress.

"Roast beef."

"And the vegetables?"

"Oh," replied the premier, gesturing around the table, "they'll have roast beef, too."

Flexibility was not Wells's strong suit. The east coast broadcaster and columnist Michael Harris told me a story that perfectly defined the man's mentality. One of the tasks of Wells's private secretary was to balance the firm's books. One day, the books were one cent short. Knowing how fussy her boss was, she made a one-cent deposit, which he discovered when the bank statements arrived. Instead of being pleased, he called her into his office and sternly lectured her that two wrongs do not make a right. That was Clyde Wells.

MEANWHILE, A TENSE DRAMA of a different kind had been evolving in Ottawa. On the Sunday morning after obtaining the late-night signatures on his accord, Mulroney started calling around to various "friends of

Meech" to share his triumph. On the list was William Thorsell, then the editor of the *Globe and Mail* and the PM's most compliant media confidant. They agreed Mulroney would give the paper an exclusive interview for Monday, recounting his impressive negotiations. Assigned to the story were Ottawa bureau chief Graham Fraser, political columnist Jeffrey Simpson and Parliament Hill reporter Susan Delacourt. The *Globe* journalists treated their assignment as a chance to record Mulroney's sense of triumph against impossible odds. No prime minister in modern times had managed to obtain unanimous approval for a constitutional amendment that included Quebec.

"I can say that, yes, the interview was amiable, and from our perspective deliberately so," Simpson wrote to me later. "We discussed how to approach the interview at some length beforehand. We knew that with Trudeau, for example, it was often best to be aggressive since that might elicit the most information. With Mulroney, it was obvious that he loved to talk about himself, his triumphs. Since he had just recorded one, or so he thought, and had phoned Thorsell to brag about it and relive it, we deliberately decided to offer him soft questions so that he would be relaxed, self-congratulatory, revelatory—which of course he was. The rest, as they say, is history, including his attempt subsequently to recast what he had said."

The journalists arrived at 24 Sussex at eleven o'clock on the Monday morning. Though Mulroney looked sleep deprived, he was exhilarated, anxious to expound on his negotiating triumph. Asked why he had opted to call a first ministers' conference for the first week of June— ominously close to the accord's final implementation deadline—he replied, "I decided, after consultations with my colleagues, mostly Lowell Murray, Paul Tellier, Norman Spector, and people like this, that . . . I remember when I told them, I called them right here, I asked them to come and see me, and I told them when this thing was going to take place. I told them a month ago when we were going to start meeting. It's like an election campaign: you've got to work backwards. You've got to pick your dates and you work backwards from it. And that . . . and I said that's the day I'm going to roll all the dice. It's the only way to handle it."

"And this was a month ago?" asked Fraser.

"About a month ago," said the prime minister.

"Roll of the dice . . . This was a conscious, obvious decision," Simpson reiterated, to make sure he had heard right.

"You had to roll all the . . . the only way that this could be done was to roll all the dice," the prime minister emphasized.

The next day's *Globe* led with the story, under the heading, "Marathon Talks Were All Part of Plan, PM Says." Its third paragraph included that fateful "roll of the dice" metaphor, which was widely interpreted as Mulroney's willingness to gamble with Canada's future. "In the minds of just about everyone," wrote Allan Levine in *Scrum Wars,* his book on the politics of the press, "but especially Clyde Wells, poker talk of this sort confirmed yet again what many people had thought of Brian Mulroney for more than a decade: that he was a partisan, manipulative deal-maker who was willing to play 'Russian roulette with Canada,' as Christopher Young put it in his *Ottawa Citizen* column. Serious damage to the fragile constitutional agreement had been done."

Stanley Hartt, Mulroney's chief of staff, was being driven to work by his wife when he heard the "dice" quote. "It was instant," he later recalled. "I mean, it didn't take me half a millisecond. I asked her to pull the car over, stopped and said, 'He's finished. It's over. I think he blew it. I really do.'" Hartt had been carrying out secret negotiations with Chrétien, who had at last seemed willing to voice his reluctant support for the accord, and who as a result backed off.[1]

Mulroney insisted that the *Globe* had got it wrong. Claiming he had been quoted out of context, he complained vociferously to Thorsell, who agreed to publish the transcript made by the PMO of the taped session, which showed only one inconsequential deviation from the reported interview. Instead of, "That's the day I'm going to roll all the dice," Fraser had hurriedly scribbled that the PM had said, "That's the day *we're* going to roll the dice." The transcript conveyed Mulroney as an unbuttoned PM—the same private Mulroney profiled in this book, a wild contrast to his public persona of sulking statesman encased in a lawyerly cloak of self-protection. Mulroney had never allowed the press to get so close.

The final irony of this newspaper war was that what Mulroney said about picking a date and rolling the dice was simply not true, and he knew it. During the two months preceding the final conference, Norman Spector and Lowell Murray had been commuting to the provincial capitals and returning to Ottawa to warn the PM to postpone the meeting as long as he could because several premiers had cooled on the "distinct society" idea. Several foreign visits (including a drop-in by Gorbachev) also disrupted the schedule. But eventually Mulroney decided he had to go to war and "shoot the wad" (a less delicate but more appropriate description) because time was running out. In other words, the timing of the conference was not a gamble but a necessity, dressed up as a "roll of the dice" by the PM's Irish bravado.

Using the story as a pretext to claim he had been manipulated, Clyde Wells went back on his word and his signature on June 22, 1990, and disallowed a vote on Meech in his legislative assembly. The Manitoba legisla-

---

1. Although he used the "roll the dice" remark as his excuse, it was more the objections of his wife, Aline, that influenced him.

ture similarly failed to vote on Meech, held up by the absence of the unanimous approval required for ratification. The agent of protest was the vote (cast with an upheld eagle feather) of MLA Elijah Harper, who was a member of the Red Sucker Lake First Nations band. Ottawa tried to find a way of extending the Manitoba deadline to lay the blame on Wells alone. The following day, at the Liberal leadership convention in Calgary, the TV image imprinted on the public mind was that of a smiling pair of Wells's co-conspirators, Trudeau and Chrétien, patting the Newfoundland premier on the back and congratulating him for a job well done.

Mulroney's reaction was blind rage against Wells. "You know all politicians take liberties—that's the nature of the beast, getting kicked around and trying to get things done in an imperfect system," he told me a few days after the last gasp of his love child. "But nothing has ever compared to the lack of principle of this son of a bitch. Lookit, on the night before the vote I was standing in the rain on the doorstep of his house and I asked him what the odds were. He told me that after my speech, they were good—at least fifty-fifty. This was *after* he had already made up his mind to cancel the vote." Mulroney's evidence for this claim came from many sources. The previous evening, Wells's chief of staff had confided to Dan Gagnier, Ontario premier David Peterson's chief of staff, that Wells had made up his mind that there would be no vote. Charley McMillan had similar intelligence from a New England conference of premiers and governors. Broadcaster Bill Cameron confronted Wells on CBC's *The Journal* with the direct question, "You mean to tell me that you had the prime minister of Canada in your house for three hours and you never told him that you had decided to cancel the vote the next day?" Wells's only reply was, "I don't remember."

The legacy of the Meech Lake debate outlasted its thirty-eight-month run. Its failure was the trigger that drove Lucien Bouchard out of the Progressive Conservative Party to establish the Bloc Québécois and later to become his province's most successful separatist. It was also the catalyst that created the feud between Jean Chrétien, who opposed Meech, and Paul Martin, who was an enthusiastic supporter. At a Liberal rally in Montreal during the leadership contest between the two men, unilingual Paul Martin supporters bussed in from Toronto, feeling bored, started a meaningless sing-song using the French word for the melted cheese dish they had enjoyed at a restaurant the previous evening, "*Fondue!*" The Chrétien contingent swore they heard the taunting chant "*Vendu!*" ("Traitor!"), and went ape. As improbable as it sounds, this misunderstanding was the spark that lit the flame of the Chrétien camp's intense resentment of Martin and his followers.

Meech Lake turned into a drowning game. Nearly all of its architects were stripped of power within three years of its denouement, including David Peterson, one of its most enthusiastic backers. He had his political head chopped off in an election only eleven weeks after the accord's collapse. Meech's demise also prompted its backers to try out new variations on the theme, behaving like troubled sooth-sayers counting angels on Margaret Atwood's head.

The failure hit Mulroney the hardest. His superb negotiating skills had won the day only to have a province with 2 per cent of Canada's population, which existed mainly on federal grants, sabotage his efforts. Together with free trade, Meech had been his claim to greatness, and it had turned to dust. His despair found expression in his personal journal. On January 13, 1991, six months after the event, Mulroney gave voice to his anguish. At the end of one of our interviews, after a melancholy reprise of Clyde Wells's treachery, he read his journal entry for that day into my tape recorder: "Last night I told Mila of an enormous sadness in my heart that I have carried since the Wells decision to sabotage Meech. It is like a dark cloud that smothers the joy one would normally associate with the privilege of being prime minister of such a great country. For thirty years I have felt that the successful resolution of the question 'what does Quebec want,' would solidify the federation once and for all. The danger with 1981–1982 was that, unlike 1867, Quebec was no longer a willing partner in the agreement on Confederation. Indeed, by proceeding without Quebec, Trudeau gave rise to a new arrangement that Quebec could perhaps one day make—that since they never signed the 1982 convention they were neither morally nor legally bound by it. Accordingly, they would claim, we are not in violation of national or international law if we secede because we never formally accepted the Constitution in the first place. Twice in 1987 and then again in 1990 we achieved unanimity, although the 1990 document was qualified by Newfoundland and Manitoba. Meech was not perfect and it no doubt would have given rise to some controversy in the future. But by signing Meech, Bourassa truly became a Canadian and would have been forced by circumstances to defend his signature, hence Canada, against the onslaught of the anti-federalists. His enthusiasm for fence-sitting would have been dramatically lessened. By signing the document he took himself off the fence forever. Wells destroyed the Bourassa legacy as a Canadian nation builder. He may well have forced Bourassa into a process where the notion that the nation that emerges is not Canada, but two Canadas, both diminished and forever banal, is living proof of the failure of honourable compromise. When reason is replaced by ideology, the essential dynamic of a federation as a living, changing political entity has been fundamentally stunted. The greatest irony of Canadian history may turn out to be the one underlined by Jack Pickersgill [a former Liberal cabinet minister who sat for a Newfoundland riding]. Namely, Pick says, it was a Québécois, Louis St. Laurent, who engineered the compromises that in 1949 enabled Newfoundland to enter Confederation. It was a Newfoundlander, Clyde Wells, who repudiated the compromises in 1990 which encouraged Quebec to leave Confederation. All of this does not lessen my own personal sense of grief for Canada. The experience since June has been like a death in the family, and I have not been able to shake fully the feeling of loss. To have come so close twice and to have it snatched away so needlessly to satisfy the vanity and arrogance of a few who themselves failed to bring unity when they were in office is like a throbbing pain that refuses to go away."

———

Mulroney just couldn't understand how Trudeau could have done it:
If you said to me, "We'd like a constitutional arrangement with the government of Canada and the nine English-speaking provinces," my question to you would be, "Would you like it for breakfast tomorrow morning or for dinner tomorrow night?" This is not a big challenge; anybody can do that any time. The challenge is the nine Anglo provinces and Quebec, because that's Canada.

If a constitution is supposed to unify people, how could you ever have a constitutional amendment of this dimension while leaving out one of the founding peoples? With Trudeau, not only was the end result a screw-up, the process was lost forever. Trudeau said we've got a thousand years before we've got to worry. Let's say he's wrong, and in fifteen years you're staring a referendum in the face—don't worry about it, because the country that you will have ruined is not yours, it's your children's. The country that you will have thrown away with a bunch of assholes like Trudeau and Chrétien is not yours anymore.

He wasn't the one to blame for the Americanization of Canada, Mulroney maintained:

The Americanization of Canada didn't come from me. It came from the Charter. When the government brought in the Charter, it Americanized Canada. This was the beginning. It wasn't the free trade agreement; it was the Charter of Rights, which undertook to fund every interest group that the country has ever seen. The national interest began to be submerged in special interests. That's what I inherited in 1984, everybody from women's groups to Native groups to regional groups to gender groups—you name it. They were all in Ottawa in nice offices funded by the federal government.

The Meech Lake Accord was part of an overarching vision of national reconciliation and economic renewal. It's all part of what I said I was going to try and do. And my critics say, "Well, Trudeau had a vision of a strong central government." Isn't that interesting? The Anglo literati and glitterati would celebrate him for leading a strong central government, where he actually crippled the government with debt and undermined its credibility by giving away a notwithstanding clause. And he renders the country immobile constitutionally by proceeding without Quebec. This is the work of a strong man? This is a vision?

Chief of Staff Hugh Segal said Mulroney had a different view of the subject before entering politics:
Brian's position on the Constitution, as a private lawyer speaking out on the issue, was for a Charter of Rights, was for patriation, was for as much power as necessary in Ottawa.

But Mulroney was now prepared to move in another direction:
We had very limited time in which all of this had to be done. I met all of the premiers separately, hours on end. Four hours and forty minutes with Clyde Wells alone. It was just the most exhausting and intensive thing that's happened in Canadian history. Meech was an extraordinary thing.

What was never captured by anyone was how hard we worked, and how much we cared. I can't tell you the effort and the anguish and the devotion to Canada which was there, that was trivialized and discarded.

Stanley Hartt, on Mulroney the negotiator:
Mulroney is, without a doubt, the most skilled cold negotiator that I've ever met, and the reason is, he fixes in his mind the objective, and he simply will not countenance that he won't get it. And he will just doggedly come back after it until your resistance has been pulled away. But secondly, he starts from a position of "I'm smart enough as a professional negotiator to know what you want, because if I just say what I want, give it to me, you'll just say no. But if I say, I know what you want and indeed I have great sympathy with what you want and it's important, your wanting it, and I'm going to help you get it—all of a sudden I have an ally."

I used to see that all the time in his labour negotiations. When he settled the *La Presse* strike, he was about two weeks out of law school and it had been going on for three years. He settled it in about six weeks because he's so good. He said, "Look, let's talk about what we have to get done. You need this, but I need that. There's no reason you can't give me what I need, and, guess what, I can give you what you need." That's how he did it.

But he could also blow it, too. In the case of the Meech negotiations, "roll the dice" came back to haunt him:
NEWMAN: If you had said "Give it our best shot" instead of "Roll the dice," the consequences would've been very different.

MULRONEY: When I said that we were going to roll the dice, all it meant is we had that time frame imposed upon us, and we were going to give it our very best shot. That's all it meant.

Remember when Pierre Trudeau said, "I'm planning a coup d'état. That's why I'm firing [Clerk of the Privy Council and constitutional advisor] Gordon Robertson." How do you like that for a statement? I was planning a coup d'état, but Gordon Robertson was too refined a gentleman, too respectful of the law, and I needed somebody who would organize and co-operate with me in a coup d'état, something that would damage irreversibly Canadian society if we had to. How do you like that for a stink? How do you like that compared to "roll the dice"?

Ontario premier David Peterson rolled his eyes:
A very good friend of his—not mine—who worked for him told me that he knew Brian was going to do that stupid "roll the dice" thing. He said, "I knew his braggadocio, I knew he could not stand other people getting any credit, I knew he would crack within three weeks." Mulroney killed it. All he had to say was, Clyde Wells is a great Canadian, Gary Filmon put the national interest first, it was very difficult and I'm very sorry we took all this time, but we had to try to work to narrow the differences, and that's the genius of this great country. At the end of the day, we all pulled together. He could have had them sucked in . . . Oh, God, I wept when that happened.

Robert Bourassa's support of Meech effectively ended Mulroney's friendship with Lucien Bouchard:
MULRONEY: Bourassa made that memorable speech, where he said, "Signing this document tonight, I feel like a real Canadian." And guess what? Bouchard's at home watching the television, and he just falls right through the floor. Because I did exactly what I said I would do. And therefore at that point in time, Bouchard's a dead man. He's a dead man. Separatists are done like dinner, at this point in time. But then Clyde Wells went back and revoked a constitutional amendment for the first time in British parliamentary history. Then he dishonoured his

signature on a constitutional document, and in his dis-
honour he relieved Bouchard of his. Bouchard—who is at
this point in time paralyzed with fear because of what is
going to happen—is [now] able to say, "I was for Meech
Lake all along, but Clyde Wells and those Anglos wouldn't
pass it."

Mila Mulroney was out doing her bit:
I said to friends, "There are minimal conditions to Meech
Lake." And after I told them, I would ask, "Do any of these
minimal conditions bother you?" And they would all say
no. The fact is, very few people understood them. What
they did understand is that the premiers met behind
closed doors and they had lavish dinners, and that the
media wasn't in, and the Natives were not represented.

Mila was harsh on the media:
You can't deliver a message in a country of this size with
forty people in your cabinet if those meetings aren't being
properly represented in the media and the newspapers.
On the news, Meech was treated as a holdup in a gas sta-
tion at six o'clock in the morning. My beef with Meech
Lake was, why was Brian the only one selling it? And I
was told, "Believe me, all of them are selling it, it's just not
being reported." When people said to me, "Why isn't
Brian selling it?" I said, "He is, but they're not reporting
it." I'd ask that same question to Brian, and he'd say,
"Mila, John Crosbie is out there in Newfoundland trying
to do the best he can, but they're not reporting it."

**One thing the Canadian media widely reported was
Mulroney's flash visit to St. John's to seek support for
the Meech Lake deal, when Wells was still giving the
accord a fifty-fifty chance:**
MULRONEY: What he actually said was, "I wouldn't have
given this thing a plug nickel." Then he said, "After your
speech down here and your efforts, it looks good." And I

said, "On a scale of one to ten what does it look like?" And he said, "I'd give it a five." Which coming from him was extraordinary.

As he was telling me that on the doorstep of his home in the rain, he had made up his mind to cancel the vote. He's amazing. God, I tell you. In a country where the WASPs have always said a man's word is his bond, it's amazing that a guy would put his signature on a constitutional document wherein he undertakes to do something, and then betrays everything—including the country—and he gets applauded in English Canada for doing it. Nobody would believe that anybody could be that dishonest. No vote. Clyde Wells dishonoured his signature and didn't put it to a vote. There's nothing wrong with losing a vote in a democracy—you like to win, but there's nothing wrong with putting something to a vote and it being defeated. If Meech Lake had been put to a vote in the Newfoundland legislature and had passed, then I think we know the consequences. Today you'd have a united country—not perfectly united, because the separatists would still be around, but you'd have a signed constitutional document, which really would have changed profoundly the way we do business in Canada.

Wells was philosophically opposed to the entire effort: I've long been a proponent of a constituent assembly. Really, when you get down to it, what does it matter what the premiers or the government leaders of the territories and the leaders of the Aboriginal people, what does it matter what they agree on in a room with horse-trading back and forth? It's really academic what the premiers say. What we've got to do is try and build a consensus that has a reasonable prospect of acceptance by the Canadian people. In the end, that's where we are.

The other big stumbling block, Mulroney believed, was Trudeau's ego:

Point of fact, there was nothing wrong with Meech Lake except one thing: Trudeau's vanity. He didn't want anybody to succeed where he had failed. Trudeau's contribution was not to build Canada but to destroy it, and I had to come in and save it. Three times I've achieved unanimity. In sixteen years, he couldn't do it once, the "great statesman." No wonder they're all laughing behind his back around the world. He couldn't even do it at home; you can imagine what they thought of him around the world.

His constitution was done at night in the kitchen. The constitution is supposed to be an instrument of unity. He brought in a constitution that was repudiated by one-third of the population, and one of the two founding peoples. You give away the power of the Supreme Court to become the instrument of law because you give the provincial premiers an override clause, which makes the whole thing meaningless. This concession does not exist anywhere in the civilized world.

Former Liberal cabinet minister Mitchell Sharp offered a counterpunch:
I don't like Meech Lake. I don't think the Canadian interest was well defended during the negotiations. My view of what happened was the prime minister said to all the provinces, "Tell me what you want and I'll get it for you." The purpose of Meech Lake was to make Quebec more distinct than it is now, to differentiate it from the other provinces, to make that a policy. Meech Lake would not prevent the withdrawal of some privileges from the English-speaking in Quebec, and in the rest of the country would not result in very much of an improvement for the French-speaking minority.

Mulroney himself downplayed the significance of the concept of a "distinct society":
A distinct society doesn't mean a goddamned thing. It does not confer on Quebec any powers whatsoever that

are not given to any other province. It's an interpretive section of the Constitution, the same way that multiculturalism is there, the same way that Aboriginals are there. That's all it is. It's whatever the Supreme Court thinks it is. The distinct society clause, as I said to Wells, "All it means is dick to me. Means dick."

Mulroney was certain there was a conspiracy to kill Meech Lake:
NEWMAN: Was the lawyer Deborah Coyne Trudeau's agent in this?

MULRONEY: Yes, and Trudeau himself. There were conversations between [former Liberal cabinet minister] Don Johnston, directly between Don Johnston and Clyde Wells, Pierre Trudeau and Clyde Wells, and Deborah Coyne.

NEWMAN: Deborah Coyne was then going out with Trudeau?

MULRONEY: That's when she was impregnated.

NEWMAN: Do you draw any connection?

MULRONEY: Yes, that's exactly what happened. They were together, persuading Wells, and Trudeau wound up persuading her and that's where she became pregnant, exactly at that time. That's when the kid was born.

NEWMAN: Well, conceived . . .

MULRONEY: Lysiane Gagnon [the *La Presse* columnist] wrote, "What a disgraceful performance. Only a farcical English Canada could remain unaware of the fact that a conspiracy so bloody blatant that it produced a child is going on to get Meech killed off by Clyde Wells and with no responsibility." And the fact that a former prime minister at seventy-three years of age can go out and father a child out of wedlock and have people comment on it approvingly tells you everything you want to know. Like it's kind of an accomplishment for you and I to go out and pick up with somebody overnight, knock her up. This has been going on since the apes.

Clyde Wells, on Trudeau's influence:
I'm not in any manner a disciple of Trudeau. There's not one iota of truth in that. As it turns out, my view of the constitutional structure is quite similar to Mr. Trudeau's . . . but I mean, there's a marked similarity in the views of millions of other Canadians.

NEWMAN: About Meech, Frank Moores told me that if the vote in the legislature had been held, you would have lost . . .

WELLS: No, he's totally wrong, no question whatsoever. The federal government knew it, and John Crosbie knew it. I was committed to having a free vote with no role in trying to persuade people to vote one way or the other, and I didn't tell anybody how I was going to vote. Although anybody who listened to the opinions that I was expressing generally on the issues shouldn't have had any doubt about my personal view. I couldn't hide it. You can't be that dishonest.

Crosbie was there all that day orchestrating the performance of the Opposition and, as things developed in the course of the afternoon, when it became clear what was happening in Manitoba [Elijah Harper's filibuster], I spoke with Crosbie and Lowell Murray, and told them what the situation was. Later that day, we went back into the House to conclude the debate and we adjourned at the request of the Opposition. The leader of the Opposition, Tom Rideout, the government house leader and myself met with Crosbie, told him the way the vote would be, and the Opposition agreed that it would be defeated. In the meantime, Murray was saying, "We have time now, we are going to take a reference to the Supreme Court to see if we can roll back the deadline." And here was Newfoundland, having forgone its referendum that it wanted to hold because of time pressures. Now, all of a sudden, they have time to accommodate Manitoba, yet they didn't have time to accommodate Newfoundland.

But that wasn't the telling factor. What I said to Crosbie was if the vote is taken, you know and understand it will be defeated. Now, what will be achieved with Manitoba having already failed to support it? It can't pass because it has to have unanimous approval. So it's dead in the water as of now. If we can get the Supreme Court to agree, by that time maybe you might be able to change more minds and you might be able to get it approved, but if a vote is taken now, it will be defeated. Now, what's going to be achieved by Newfoundland causing an affront to Quebec by rejecting it? If you're right about the Supreme Court, then I suggest we adjourn this debate so that a vote can always be taken—if you solve the problem in Manitoba. And we can bring it back. But if you go now, be assured that it will be defeated. Why don't you get the prime minister to agree that the sensible thing to do would be to defer the vote in Newfoundland until you resolve this problem with Manitoba and if you do, then we can bring it back?

So he went to the prime minister, and he would agree with Newfoundland adjourning the debate to allow time for the matter to be resolved in Manitoba, but only on one condition: that I personally express my support for Meech Lake. How do you live with that? I couldn't live with it. I can't operate that way. It would be fundamentally dishonest. I didn't support what was in it, and I couldn't sell my soul that way. The prime minister thought it was appropriate to pressure me to do that.

So we adjourned the debate anyway and that's what

we did—it wasn't voted against: the motion was still on the Order Paper, and could have been brought back had they resolved the problem in Manitoba. Even if I had made that declaration, it wouldn't have done any good, but it would have made me look like eighty-four kinds of a fool and I couldn't do that. I'd sooner resign than have done that.

Trudeau advisor Michael Pitfield thought Mulroney should look to his own government:
I don't believe Trudeau prompted Wells to do anything—I think Mr. Wells did his own thing. He had his views and he used Deborah Coyne, who was a common link with Trudeau, a better link than some of us thought. He and Trudeau found common cause together.

If the government had handled Meech with more skill, they would have succeeded. If they had proceeded quickly and with dispatch, instead of leaving this thing on the table. If the government had sought to include in and reached out, instead of taking all the glory itself. If they had tried to dispel in their documentation some of the contradictions in the document itself. If they had not locked the premiers away from their advisors all the time, including at the end, they would have had premiers who understood what they were signing. We had two or three premiers saying right afterwards they didn't understand what they had signed. Manitoba's Howard Pawley had no idea.

Stanley Hartt agreed with him:
Meech Lake was the crowning achievement of Brian's negotiating technique. The one mistake he made was that he didn't say, "Now, the Constitution says there are three years to ratify. We're not going to take three years to ratify—too much time for opposition to build up. Some of you guys might get defeated and change your minds. Let's agree on an order, and I don't care if we bunch the order,

like a group of three, then a group of two, but I want this done in six months."

Hanging Louis Riel all over again:
MULRONEY: I'm discouraged by the fact that we had the sweetest deal ever known to man and it was thrown away. I'm discouraged for Canada because I know what's going to happen with these vain, stupid people in a short period of time. There's a televised picture of Chrétien at the Calgary leadership convention, where he hugged Clyde Wells for killing the Meech Lake Accord. That was the modern equivalent of hugging Macdonald for hanging Louis Riel. This is like the hanging of Louis Riel on videotape. "Thank you, Clyde, for all your work." This is like sitting back and watching the boys hang Louis Riel.

Mulroney found Wells's attitude mind-boggling:
Could I have known what Wells was going to do? It's like somebody saying, well, I suspect that this Oklahoma City bomber Timothy McVeigh down in the United States is a killer. You might've suspected that, but until you've seen him blow up the building, you had no reason to think that the guy was really going to do that.

He believed all the blame should be laid at Wells's doorstep:
Aboriginals are not to blame for Meech's failure, despite Elijah Harper's stupidity. I said to my caucus, "I don't want anybody blaming the Aboriginals. How can you blame people whose lands were taken away from them, whose lives are infected with prostitution and drunkenness, malnutrition, lack of opportunity, all of this inflicted on them by the industrialized society? How can you go out and blame them?" I was very emotional because they were ready to rush out and lynch them, all because of Elijah Harper's stupidity. He turned down a sweetheart deal.

Ontario premier David Peterson was even more vituperative than Mulroney:
I know Clyde well. I'm going to tell you, he is the most arrogant son of a bitch I've ever met in my life, as in "I'm right and you're wrong." We spent a week with the bastard, and the whole discussion was convincing Clyde. He would never admit it, but he's wrong in law and he's wrong in politics. The tragedy is that we were that close.

John Crosbie:
I didn't think the Meech Lake Accord ever had a chance of passing once Wells got elected. I knew he had this fetish about Meech Lake, although it wasn't a big issue in the provincial election. I've known Clyde for a long time and he's like a dog with a bone. Once he has an opinion, it never changes, never varies. People were mad because Mulroney said something about Newfoundland being a small province, come into Confederation late or something like this, and surely it shouldn't hold up the unanimity approving this Meech Lake Accord. But the person who destroyed Meech Lake was Clyde Wells.

Mulroney, ruminating obsessively on Wells:
I'm staying away from the argument on Meech Lake, which is "I told you so." It's very interesting—the Maritime premiers now have cut Wells out of their action. I personally just can't stand to be in the room with him. He's the most unprincipled guy. You know, all politicians take liberties. That's the nature of the beast, getting kicked around and trying to get things done in an imperfect system. And I've run into a fair amount of it and have probably contributed a small amount myself, but nothing has ever compared to the lack of principle of this son of a bitch.

But, according to Stanley Hartt, Mulroney held no long-term grudge:

The accusation is made constantly: "He's punishing Aboriginal peoples for Elijah Harper having blocked Meech Lake." That isn't true and it really hurts him. The credibility issue is not an ego thing—this is not him wanting to be thought well of. He isn't the kind of person who would say, in the case of Newfoundland because of what Clyde Wells did, "Not a red cent for those bastards."

Senator Lowell Murray on the impact of the Meech rejection:
It was the last chance we had to keep the old Canada and try to build on it. Mulroney's metaphor of the bridge was very apt. Like him, I never saw Meech Lake as a solution to a problem, I saw it as a bridge. If we could put it in place, then you've got the status quo for a certain time and you've got some breathing space over that time to evolve and to work out perhaps somewhat different arrangements, but in a completely different context.

Had Meech Lake passed, then Quebec would have become one of ten at the table and whatever new constitutional demands she might have would have to be worked out with us and with the other provinces. Now Quebec is isolated again, and her minimal conditions have been turned down.

At the time, Mulroney foresaw serious consequences:
You're going to be confronting a referendum in between ten and fifteen years, and the night before the referendum takes place, when the whole country is holding its breath, the elements of the Meech Lake Accord are going to look very reasonable indeed.

Five years later, on the eve of the Quebec referendum in 1995, Mulroney predicted revenge against Chrétien:
In the 1980 Quebec referendum, we had a message: "Vote No and we are going to deliver a new constitution." Now, in 1995, Jean Chrétien is the prime minister, with very

little credibility in Quebec and he's sinking fast. We have no message, because the message last time was believe us, stick with us and we'll give you a constitution of which you can be proud. They wound up with a constitution that they wouldn't sign. Chrétien, who played an active role in sabotaging Meech, would have been enormously better off as the prime minister of Canada to have Meech, to have it done and to be able to say, "This is what Canada stands for."

6.

"Canadians think I'm an arrogant bastard—that's not a bad position to be in"

———

The Second Mandate

EVERY NATIONAL ELECTION is a contest between heritage and impulse, as the verities of the past compete with the risks of the future. But in the eleven hours it took thirteen million Canadians to cast their ballots on November 21, 1988, something very different happened. A nation that less than a decade earlier had defeated a Conservative government for daring to impose a minor excise tax on gasoline audaciously opted for a revamped economic order at home and a hazardous new partnership with its largest trading partner abroad. By voting for Mulroney's free trade agreement with the United States, Canadians bestowed a revolutionary mandate on a prime minister who only months before had held what seemed like a permanent lease on the basement of popularity polls. Although his government had passed 232 pieces of legislation during its first mandate, only weeks before the 1988 campaign started, Mulroney's popularity was scraping 20 per cent. At the same time, the Tory campaign war chest was brimming over with $25 million, collected largely from Bay Street, which was jubilant about President Reagan's recent approval of free trade.

His wrist still sore from having signed 352 patronage appointments in the days before he called the election, Mulroney pulled the plug on Parliament and hoped for the best. I covered that campaign and recall that it felt more like a blitzkrieg than an election. We had a hurried lunch together in a Victoria hotel room when the polls were still against him. But Mulroney was pacing the floor like a trophy-hungry prize fighter, hardly able to contain his exploding impatience to get back on his tour bus. I had never seen him so energized. "His performance was one of the most remarkable I have ever witnessed," recalled John Tory, one of Mulroney's senior advisors at the time, who later became leader of the Ontario Progressive Conservatives. "He demonstrated absolutely unflagging energy, getting the job done in very difficult circumstances, and never wavered."

Caught up in the contradictory emotions of this pivotal debate, candidates stumped the land calling one another traitors, liars, power-hungry rats and, on one occasion, power-hungry scumbags. With her customary penchant for understatement, Sheila Copps compared the free trade debate to the War of 1812, declaring, "We pushed back the Americans then and we'll do it again!" Not to be outdone, Simon Reisman, Canada's chief free trade negotiator, suggested that if the talks didn't succeed, he would make the ultimate sacrifice. "I'm putting my reputation, which is considerable, on the line," he told a Global Television interviewer. Then, looking directly into the camera, he stoically added, "I'm putting my life on the line."[1] That offer was

---

1. To me, the most vicious comment in the debate was the accusation by Peter Cook, in his *Globe* financial column, that in order to get re-elected the Tories were "throwing money around like drunken sailors." Sir, sailors get drunk on their own money.

mercifully never redeemed, but Copps escalated the debate by charging that the real victims of free trade would be the unborn. Once the agreement was signed, she blustered, American lawyers would pour across the border searching for surrogate mothers whose wombs would be cheap to rent because of medicare and the low value of the Canadian dollar.

Weird outfits such as BAD (Billiards Against the Deal), DAD (Dancing Against the Deal) and RAD (Rock Against the Deal) sprang up across the country. Near Vegreville, Alberta, a farmer stomped an anti–free trade slogan into his wheat field in 250-foot-wide letters. Possibly the most bizarre manifestation of the debate was an interview by the *Ottawa Citizen*'s resident humourist, Charles Gordon, with his dog.

"How will you feel when we have free trade with the United States, Fido?" Gordon asked.

"Rough!" responded the pooch.

It was that kind of debate.

This and all the other nonsense that went on helped mask the 1988 election's radical impact. Mulroney made the free trade issue and his re-election inseparable, and it was never entirely clear just how much support he harvested for the issue or for himself. But there was no doubt that Mulroney's victory was the most miraculous resurrection since Lazarus.

Once dismissed as a lucky and untried opportunist, Mulroney emerged from the campaign as a shrewd and mature opportunist. The win endowed him with a surge of self-confidence and encouraged him in the purring, effortless possession of power that he had heretofore denied himself. Most of the campaign's winning strategy had been his own. His first two decisions turned out to be crucial. Despite intense pressure from many of his advisors to drop the writ in early September, Mulroney held off the election call so that he could spend that month crisscrossing the country, sprinkling favourable news clips that gradually improved public perception of his government. When the campaign started on October 1, he resisted his entourage's advice and insisted that the leaders' television debate be held within the first four weeks and that there be no separate discussion on free trade. He figured going early would give him a chance to recover if he couldn't repeat his virtuoso outing of 1984.

And he didn't. It was Turner who put on the most persuasive performance of his political life, not Mulroney. The Liberal leader, who had been making Tarzan-like noises ("Me tear up treaty"), acquired unexpected legitimacy when Mulroney downplayed free trade, which he had previously been trumpeting as being essential to Canada's economic salvation. During the debate, for reasons that he never explained or justified, Mulroney described the agreement as being "cancellable on six months' notice." This was astonishing from the man who in the same debate had endowed the treaty with magical qualities, and it reminded voters just why they had grown to distrust him during the previous four years. Turner emerged from the television confrontation as a lively candidate, having successfully turned free trade from an economic policy into a social and cultural issue that would decide Canada's future. Most of the seven million or so Canadians who watched switched their allegiances overnight, placing the Liberals on top in what the pollsters reported was the most dramatic mid-election crossover ever recorded. But as Mulroney had predicted, he still had time to make up for lost ground.

Allan Gregg, watching his boy get slaughtered in the polls, turned to a friend and proclaimed what he considered to be one of the great political truisms of his time: "The bridge between the fear of free trade and John Turner is Turner's credibility. We've got to bomb the bridge." It was a good thing that most Mulroney operatives didn't have the faintest idea what he was talking about. And it didn't matter in the end, because Turner jumped off the bridge all by his lonesome. That gave Mulroney the chance to live out one of Napoleon's favourite dicta: "Never interfere with the enemy when he is in the process of destroying himself."

Whether it was bad luck or ill fate, the Liberal campaign began to fall apart immediately after their leader's successful TV performance. It imploded like the slow-motion film of a collapsing bridge, to pick a random metaphor. Turner had the wittiest slogan ("Guts or Guccis") and the most impassioned cause (Canada's independence), but his crusade was constantly being sabotaged by his own troops, who first circled the wagons, then turned inside the perimeter and started shooting at one another. Throughout the campaign, weekly plots were uncovered planning the leader's overthrow, which destroyed the Liberals' claim to be an alternative government.

Turner came across as Don Quixote, gathering wayward passions but exercising little political clout. Like jazz musicians who stop playing live concerts and retreat to studio work, he had lost rapport with his audiences and the ability to improvise—that spark of spontaneity that propels and inspires great performers, in both jazz and politics. Turner had spent nearly a decade in a Bay Street law factory, the equivalent of a musician's studio, and that was his undoing. During those ten lost years he had become a fervent disciple of North American capitalism, so that his fierce attacks on free trade as a conspiracy of Big Business left his listeners with unresolved doubts about his conviction and intentions.

As election day approached, Mulroney's popularity soared, with surveys claiming that 35 per cent of Canadians believed he would make the best prime minister. Turner trailed with a token 17 per cent. In the final hectic week, when he knew he was winning, Mulroney hit his stride, laughing all the way to the voting booths. After former Tory leader Robert Stanfield endorsed him "warts and all" at a rally in Yarmouth, Nova Scotia, Mulroney joked that it was no wonder John Turner wanted to cancel the purchase of nuclear-powered submarines for Canada's navy: "If you've been torpedoed as many times as he has, you wouldn't like submarines either." Turner had vowed that if he was elected he would rip up the Free Trade Agreement, and Mulroney drafted a pretend endorsement for Turner from President Reagan: "Let's win this one for the Ripper!" The audiences lapped it up.

On November 21, the Conservatives were returned with a solid majority of 169 seats. The Liberals had won in 83 ridings, their second worst showing since Confederation, while the NDP elected an impressive 43 MPs. Mulroney became the first Conservative leader to win a second straight majority since John A. Macdonald in 1891. His was the first back-to-back majority for any party since 1953, and the first time any democracy had re-elected a political party since beginning to televise its legislative sittings. The thrill of electoral battle, the passion of the Tory leader's message and the self-destructive proclivities of his Liberal opponent combined to mask Mulroney's negative image over the preceding four years. But while his new government was blessed with a majority, it would now be held accountable for the human costs of free trade. The price of remaining Canadian was about to rise.

That election night, I joined Mulroney and his inner circle at the Manoir guesthouse in Baie-Comeau. This was where, as a boy, he had sung his organ-grinder's-monkey serenades to Colonel McCormick and dreamed of wilder shores. I found myself in the company of a newly incarnated politician. The 1988 election changed the way Mulroney walked, his ability to look into a TV camera lens without turning into cement—and mainly, the way he felt about himself. As Graham Fraser noted in his masterful book on the campaign, Mulroney emerged "as a shrewd, hard-edged, colloquial and street-smart politician who understood the subtleties of the country he [was] governing." It was time for Mulroney to abandon his chief political asset to that point: being perennially underestimated by his opponents. His record might or might not withstand the chill of history, but his decisive win would allow him to undertake the kind of radical reforms a party leader panting for re-election could never attempt.

After concession speeches from Turner and Broadbent that night, calls of congratulation came in from Ronnie, Maggie, Robert Bourassa and Jeanne Sauvé, the Liberal-appointed governor general, who gushed, "Hey, you've still got us as your neighbours!"

The gathered retinue had watched the TV coverage that night in a glow of self-congratulation. They burst into wild applause only twice: when Barbara McDougall won the bellwether riding of St. Paul's in Toronto, and when Maureen McTeer lost her bid to sit as a Tory for the Ottawa Valley riding of Carleton-Gloucester.

Three days after the election, Mulroney was relaxing at 24 Sussex when he decided to call Fred Doucet, the closest of his advisors. "I'm all alone—Mila went shopping and I'm lying here reading a book," he mused. "You know what you said to me yesterday, that I should savour this moment because I dreamed so long of being re-elected with a majority—that's true, especially if I try to conjure up what a defeat would have felt like. So, I'm lying here in bed, nibbling at the ears of my funny half-glasses, and really enjoying myself. Then I look down at my feet, and there's Clover, my shaggy dog, in a state of deep oblivion. I roar at him and he doesn't blink an eye. So I say to myself, 'Wouldn't you know it, he's already ahead of me. He doesn't want me to move out of Sussex—and now we don't have to!'"

—

Many were confidently predicting his downfall, but Mulroney believed he had several aces up his sleeve:
What I'm doing is just learning history. I'm in the process of co-opting all these worthwhile groups into the party, large groups of society. Let's take Quebec and the west. With those two, we can't be defeated. By the time I get through with goddamned Broadbent and Turner in the election campaign, all these so-called experts are going to be sitting on the fucking snowbank saying, "Holy Jesus, how did he do that?"

I take nothing for granted, but the mood is good. I just came back from the [PC party] headquarters and I told them two things. First, I learned a long time ago that national unity is the most important issue. Second, we need the skills required to manage a complex economy. Those to me are the issues of this campaign: it's competence and it's leadership.

An early poll confirmed his optimism:
The CROP poll has us at 42.5 per cent, with the Liberals at 30 per cent and the NDP at 26 per cent. We've moved to a 10-point lead in the Island of Montreal. Paul Martin Jr. is going to lose his deposit. He's going to lose. If you went back to Quebec now and surveyed again, you would see the Liberal Party with nothing.

Other surveys showed that Canadians had reservations about him as a leader:
MULRONEY: The accusation was that the government was sleazy and Mulroney was wishy-washy, he can't make up his goddamned mind. The press gallery continues to make the same mistakes. Allan Gregg says the downside is Canadians think I'm an arrogant bastard who won't listen to anybody and is going to go ahead with whatever he wants, irrespective of their views. Personally, I think that's not a bad position to be in.

Running his first campaign as an incumbent, Mulroney claimed that the press was censoring him:
We've got this goofy bunch travelling with us. I gave four scrums, a no-holds-barred interview to the editorial board of the *London Free Press,* plus two major speeches. Nothing was reported, because we have a bunch of idiots. Corrupt, venal people like Linda McQuaig of the *Toronto Star* and airheads like [CBC reporter] Wendy Mesley. Those are the facts.

If you watch television, the double standard is pretty visible. The Toronto media, they just call up the same people all the time. It wouldn't occur to them that maybe somebody from Saskatchewan would have a valid point of view. The *Toronto Star* has been telling us, and the *Globe and Mail* and the *Toronto Sun*, that Mulroney's finished, but the son of a bitch is going to win in Quebec.

Turner received more media attention in the role of challenger:
MULRONEY: I saw somebody last night saying, "Well, Mulroney is running a good campaign, but he's tightly scripted, and that's not good." The same reporter then says, "John Turner has made himself available to the press." So they promptly cut his throat and ruined him forever. Well, they're right. It's good for them, but it's not good for John Turner. And still, Canadians don't know why Turner's opposed to free trade, they think he's snotty and snarky, he's in trouble in his own province. He lost his hometown in a by-election—that's got to tell you something.

Mulroney seemed captivated by the sudden success of the New Democratic Party:
The fascinating development is that the Opposition may turn out to be the NDP. That is awful for the country, but it will keep us there for an awfully long time. And Broadbent is a phony; he can't draw flies, for God's sake. There's nothing to his media-oriented, all-union haul. It's

a disgrace, but I don't say anything about it because I figure any vote that's going to Broadbent is a vote that's not going to the Grits.

The gloves came off after Broadbent called Mulroney a liar:
BILL PRISTANSKI: Mulroney said, "Forget it. I'm going to write Broadbent and the boys off. No more Mr. Nice Guy. If Broadbent comes and asks any of you for a favour, I don't want you talking to his staff—cut him off." And he did, after he had courted Broadbent for three years, because he figured someday, minority government, might need Broadbent. He said, "Forget him, he's not a man I want to work with."

Mulroney didn't want to debate Turner and Broadbent:
I think we're going to put the whole country to sleep. After the Canadians get a look at us three birds for six hours, they're going to say, give us a break for God's sake, give us a bloody break. It's not written in the Constitution that we have to put up with this.

Mulroney never wavered in his conviction that he was going to win:
Canadians have a tendency to view leaders in the fulcrum of adversity. They'll say, we gave this son of a bitch our best shot, and he's still standing, looking good, he's got a big smile and we're going to give him another one. I'm the only one in this party who can understand where Quebec fits into all of this, where Bourassa fits, all of these things.

And he was right. His party was re-elected with a historic second majority, winning 169 seats to the Liberals' 83 and the NDP's 43. Most pundits described the 1988 election as a referendum on free trade, but Mulroney disagreed:
It was a referendum on who you want as prime minister. What happened was this: after the leaders' debate, 55 per

cent of the people believed Turner when he said opposing free trade was the cause of his life, but by the time the election was over, 79 per cent of the Canadian people thought he was a liar. The Liberals are beautiful. They're unbelievable. They defined their citizenship as fundamentally anti-American. Vicious, bitter, mean-spirited and anti-American.

Given the choices they had, Mulroney claimed, Canadians were only being sensible:
Are you going to vote for Mulroney? Not a goddamn bit, he's a real pain in the ass. Well, who are you going to vote for? The alternative is Turner. Well, guess not. Well, you can vote for Mr. Perfection, Broadbent. That asshole Broadbent? Well, maybe Mulroney is not so bad. He has brought prosperity and relative peace to the country. Maybe I'll give him another shot. That's what life is about.

I knew goddamned well in 1988 the expectations of Turner were subterranean, and I told our people, all this guy has got to do is show up for the TV debate, just show up, and the media is going to declare him the winner. So you can imagine if he takes a couple of jabs at me—I mean, the Don McGillivrays and the Pamela Wallins are going to go berserk. [*Toronto Star* reporter] Carol Goar is going to have a goddamned orgasm over this kind of stuff, which will probably be fairly unique.

Looking ahead, Mulroney didn't think the Liberals had what it took to beat him:
It's hard for me to believe that for the 1990s, the Liberals are actually going to reach back to [Chrétien] and get somebody who was elected in the 1960s. I've got my eye right on Chrétien, Wells, McKenna, Carstairs, and I give you a personal guarantee that there will never be a Liberal government elected in my lifetime with these people holding these positions.

Mulroney, on the winners and losers among the opposition in the House:
I don't see much talent in terms of leadership. The fact is that Turner is the most talented one over there. If you want to know what's being said on the floor of the House of Commons, and not the fluff that's being written in the press gallery, I can tell you the two strikeouts of the early session. The biggest one is [former BC premier and NDP MP] David Barrett, he's just a total flop. They're sending messages to Broadbent, telling him, "Your job is safe." The second strikeout is young Paul Martin.

Given his record in his second term, Mulroney couldn't figure out why he was still labelled as wishy-washy:
Since the 1988 election, we brought in the toughest budget since the end of World War II. We brought in the goods and services tax, we cancelled the committees and subcommittees on the Via Rail thing. We totally changed the UIC thing. We put an abortion law out. This is from a prime minister who—according to the media—likes to be liked, and seeks to avoid difficulties? What a crock of shit.

As the term progressed, Mulroney began to defend his accomplishments even more forcefully:
If I had gone the Liberal route, the spending route, we would be finished. We may still be finished politically—by that I mean we may be defeated in the next election—but we will be defeated on a record of profound historic accomplishment, whereas had we gone the spending route like the Liberals, we would have been defeated and disgraced.

Not that Canada's new five-party political landscape made things easy:
We now have five parties, and two of them are cutting away directly at our bases—Reform and Bloc

Québécois. The idea of why we're so low in the polls doesn't mean that we have done anything particularly wrong, or that I am particularly odious. Our support has fallen because voters have found a more attractive alternative. People who would sympathize with us have found a regional attraction, a one-trick pony. Anything that I can do for the west, Preston Manning can do better. Anything that I can do for Quebec, Lucien Bouchard says he can do more.

Toward the end of his second term, with Chrétien now Liberal leader and Audrey McLaughlin the head of the NDP, Mulroney was less cocky about the future:
I'm not going to sit here and tell you that Jean Chrétien will not be elected prime minister, or that Audrey McLaughlin will not be elected prime minister, because anything can happen. But I'll tell you this. Right now, Canadians are in a funk, in a sulk; they're bitchy, they're crabby, a lot of it for understandable reasons—we have very serious economic problems.

Still, he thought his chances for a third term were good:
It's pretty hard to tell somebody who won 211 seats the first time out, having started way behind, and then 169 the next time out, that he can't do it a third time against Jean Chrétien, Preston Manning and Audrey McLaughlin. Give me a break.

Yet it was hard to ignore the steep decline in his popularity in the public opinion polls. Governor General Ray Hnatyshyn offered some advice to the prime minister at Harrington Lake on New Year's Eve:
I said, "Prime Minister, have I ever told you the story about my dog?" Brian said, "No, but I think I'm going to hear it now."
I said, "In 1979, I was in the Clark cabinet as minister of energy, world oil prices were out of sight, all hell was

breaking loose and I was working eighteen-hour days. I got a phone call from my kids in Saskatoon saying the dog had died. It was Friday night, so I went home. The kids told me they needed $285 for the funeral. My wife, Gerda, said they had made arrangements with a perpetual cemetery for the dog. So I gave them the $285. Three weeks later, the local outlet of the CBC did an exposé on scams, and one of them was on pet cemeteries, where these fly-by-night operators took the money and didn't live up to their promises. They zoomed in on a headstone, and it said, 'Here lies Tippy, Faithful Family Friend and Pet of the Hnatyshyn Family,' and Hnatyshyn was misspelled. My whole political life flashed before my eyes. Who is going to vote for someone who parted with $285 like a village idiot? Well, would you believe that two weeks later I had one hundred letters of support from people commending me for being such a wonderful animal lover? Later I got an offer of an honorary title in the Saskatoon Kennel Club."

I turned to Brian and said, "You're only at ten points in the polls. I could arrange to have your dog killed."

Mulroney took a good hard look at his poodle, and in feigned sympathy told his favourite pooch, "That's it, Clover. I love you, but you're a goner."

Frank Moores tired of the Mulroney blame game:
It's as if Brian was trying to adapt to a presidential system, where everybody can be wrong except himself, à la Reagan, if you like. I mean, Reagan did that very, very successfully. No matter how much trouble Reagan got into, it was always someone else's fault. Brian is doing that very well.

"WHAT PEOPLE HAVE AGAINST HIM": GUCCI-GATE

Mulroney came under intense fire after newspapers reported that his closets were filled with dozens of Gucci shoes.

Stanley Hartt said the PM could never figure out why his shoes became a lightning rod:
He would deny that what people have against him is his style. He thinks that they're mad at him for his policy, that they turn to style as the excuse to get him. It's like being angry at Stockwell Day for coming to a press conference in a wetsuit, instead of because he stands for cockamamie ideas.

Mulroney insisted it was all a misunderstanding:
Well, I suppose that in terms of pairs of shoes at any given time, I have three or four pairs of Gucci shoes, a couple of pairs of running shoes, a couple of pairs of beach shoes and a couple of pairs of loafers. That would be what I would have had in the closet.

But I mean the story was so preposterous. How did this happen? Where did this come from?

Well, I figured out how it was done. On the second floor, my dressing room, on the second floor—there were no closets and no place to put closets. So when we moved in, rather than have them build closets into the wall, Mila bought closets that were movable. And this famous architect Giovanni whatever-his-name-was [Mowinckel], who gave his documents to Stevie Cameron and who is now a felon on the lam from Canadian justice and who was the source for all of this information for Stevie Cameron—he can't come back to Canada or he's going to be arrested for fraud. But this guy apparently in the process of doing this thing said to Mila, well, we'll get this kind of a closet, in here he'll be able to put suits, here he will be able to put shirts, and over here he'll be able to put shoes.

Apparently this particular closet was designated in his files as a shoe closet, which was never used as such, and because it was known in the press that I had a few pairs of Gucci shoes and I used to wear Gucci shoes—not exclusively at all, but I would wear them—somebody figured out how many pairs of Gucci shoes you could put in that closet, in the space. And somebody said, well, geez, you can put fifty-eight pairs of shoes in there. Look, Peter, you can probably put eleven children in this house, but I don't have eleven children, I only have four. All I had were three or four pairs of shoes plus the normal knockabouts.

Pat MacAdam:
I don't know how many pairs of shoes he has, and neither does the *Globe and Mail*. He said his closet could accommodate fifty-eight pairs; that's not to say he's got fifty-eight pairs. I thought every truck driver in Baie-Comeau had a dream of growing up and owning Gucci shoes.

Press secretary Bill Fox, trying to get the countervailing message out:
Here's a man who doesn't smoke, doesn't drink and he's not running the ropes. This is a guy that you give a hamburger and a club soda, and he'll work for eighteen hours a day.

Mila, with the real scoop:
There was very little cupboard space so what we did was we built a cupboard that had three drawers for shoes, and I think that what it works out to is ten shoes per drawer. There's three drawers so that's thirty shoes. And then there's the shirt section and there's a section for tuxedos and his morning coat, but it's not a big cupboard. I could even show it to you.

Now anybody that knows Brian—the reason Brian wore Gucci shoes is—that's my fault. As prime minister he has never really gone . . . he doesn't go into a store . . .

so I know the make, I know the size and once a year or twice a year I buy him two brown and two black. I can get those in Florida or I can get them in New York if I'm there. It's all done very quickly, I don't spend time in stores and so that's where the nonsense with the Guccis came from.

But I think it was also Giovanni getting back at us; he made it up. He was a very sick man and so he took us on in a vulnerable area, which was expenses. I mean what he doesn't tell you, for example, is that final bill he sent us, we went through the accounts and he had over-billed me by $38,000. I mean this was a man desperate and when you look back at things, he had spent too much money and he had over-extended himself and he had a condo here and a condo there.

The thing is that Brian cares about shoes as much as he cares about anything—I mean for him it's totally irrelevant. He puts his shoes on, if they work with the suit . . . do you know what I mean? You've known him a long time. Have you ever heard him discuss clothes or shoes?

"DRUGGED UP, HYPER INDIANS": THE OKA CRISIS

In 1990, a proposal to build a nine-hole golf course in Oka led to a confrontation between Mohawks and law enforcement officials, first from the Sûreté du Québec and later from the Canadian Army. The seventy-seven-day crisis cost Canadian taxpayers $112 million and cast a shadow on Mulroney's claim of sympathy toward the First Nations.

According to the PM, it was the Mohawks who upped the ante:
They didn't give us much choice. We've intercepted a lot of their telephone conversations. The Indians not only had a very good cause, they had a lot of public sympathy, but you can't move ahead with a gun at your forehead. They just made the biggest mistake of their lives. They

got carried away on this thing and they'll find out that there's not much a country can do when it's fighting for its survival. We've got to try and find some way out for them because there are twenty-five or thirty of them drugged up pretty well and pretty hyper. The army has been excellent, I can tell you that.

Marjory LeBreton:
The prime minister was dismayed by the whole thing. He still is. He was very sympathetic with the Aboriginals but came to realize that they were held hostage in many ways to the warrior society.

For reporter Christopher Walmsley, the media did a terrible job in covering Oka:
The stakeout at Oka, which was just a travesty, with the reporters on the inside literally directing the public relations—that's not what I want to be involved with.

Archbishop Michael Peers, head of the Anglican Church in Canada:
The prime minister chose a certain path of dealing with Oka, which at first was just ignoring it and letting the Mohawks take the lumps with the police, and then of course they ended up making Oka a household word around the world. When I went to Canberra in Australia six months after Oka, that was what everybody asked me about. Still at meetings in England in 1994, people would ask about Oka.

"THEY'RE MAKING FORTUNES HERE": OTTAWA'S LOBBYISTS

Mulroney had mixed feelings about the influential figures who roamed the capital during his tenure, using his name as an entree.

Mulroney insisted that he wasn't the one who created the plague:
As bad as the cronyism thing is—Michel Cogger and Sam Wakim—there's the people who don't get blamed, the lobbyists—Bill Neville and Norm Atkins and Harry Near—all that bunch. They're all making fortunes here, in much the same way as the Liberals made fortunes. Some of these people were needlessly aggressive in promoting themselves. I'd go a little further and say some of them, if they didn't abuse their position and abuse the trust of people, they came awfully close.

The second thing has to do with the growth of the lobby industry. Under the Liberals, Senator Harry Hays used to answer his senator phone by saying "Gulf Canada." He was on the payroll. All the Liberal senators were on the payrolls of the banks. They were the lobbyists. There were four or five Conservative senators around, they chaired the banking committee. And then Bill Lee and Bill Neville started it, they got lobbying going. It was a big business when I came to office. What happened then was that you saw the proliferation of lobbying in the United States in the 1980s, so there was a commensurate growth here.

Mulroney tried to sanitize the lobbying industry:
I brought in legislation—the first legislation—to curb lobbying, to render it more transparent. But the assault was on by the media. The conspiracies were everywhere. Then there were people here who got into the lobbying business who were friends and supporters of mine, close to the party, who were extremely visible and who, as it turned out, were extremely unethical. As it turns out, they didn't do anything illegal. They did enough to add some justification to the

malodorous smell surrounding lobbying generally, here or in the United States. It was just enough for a Frank Moores, or a whatever, to do enough, and to do it so visibly, that there was an assumption that everything was corrupt and venal and so on. Whereas, in point of fact, I suppose, they were just as good or bad—with some exceptions—as any other time.

After he left office, he admitted he should have been tougher on the lobbyists, but also pointed the finger at Chrétien:

That was my responsibility. That was a mistake I made. I must tell you. Should I have known about Frank Moores and these guys selling our friendship? I think the answer is yes. I think [Deputy Prime Minister] Don Mazankowski and I should've known. I can't tell you now why we didn't. Was it because of the rush of events? The hostility of the atmosphere? The fact that we were constantly being bombarded every day by the media and the Rat Pack and the headlines? "Pair of shoes, pair of shoes."

I'll tell you something else, history repeats itself. The same thing is happening. It's on a larger scale now. And he's getting much more indulgence than I got. But it was my fault. And even though it was exacerbated by the media and the Opposition and the unfairness, that happened on my watch. I in particular, but Maz and I should have known about it. And we should have dealt with it even more harshly. Lots of things happened without my knowing. Most of it.

But look at what's going on today. How does the prime minister justify putting his niece—who was a researcher for the Liberal Party of Canada—in the Privy Council Office, the most sensitive job? How can he justify putting the governor general's son in charge of Maritime patronage? How can he justify putting his nephew in Washington?

My friends got blamed for being my friends. I didn't have any friends. I had "cronies."

7

"Grab 'em by their privates, and their hearts and their minds will follow"

The Mulroney Gang

BRIAN MULRONEY DISPLAYED terrier determination for making and keeping friends. Fuelling the long march to the 1984 electoral sweep was a band of brothers (and the occasional sister) who were hard-ass operatives, dedicated to his cause and none other: Jean Bazin, Michel Cogger, Paul Creaghan, Fred and Gerry Doucet, Keith Hamilton, Bert Lavoie, Cam McArthur, Michael Meighen, Charley McMillan, Lowell Murray, Bernard Roy, Jean Sirois, Sam Wakim, Peter White and Patrick MacAdam. They were later joined by Ian Anderson, David Angus, Arthur Campeau, Guy Charbonneau, Jonathan Dietcher, Bill Fox, Janis Johnson, Marjory LeBreton, Pierrette Lucas, Michael McSweeney, Hubert Pichet, Frank Moores, Roger Nantel, Rodrigue Pageau, Bill Pristanski and Ginette Pilotte. Precisely how each of them fitted into the putsch to make "Bones" (as he was known before he became "the boss") prime minister—and how each was later amply rewarded—was less important than what held them together.

The most important addition to the gang was Stanley Hartt, one of Mulroney's mentors, who came to Ottawa in 1985 to be deputy minister of finance and later became Mulroney's chief of staff. He was the only real mensch among the rowdy crew, set apart from the other insiders because he had an original mind and was in Ottawa strictly to perform a public service—at less than half the money he had been making at a Montreal law firm. ("Stanley's most important job," Mulroney confided, "is reminding my old friends of the difference between lobbying and influence peddling. It's about two years.")

They were a talented bunch, bound to one another less by creed than loyalty, inside jokes, jibes at the pretentious pols who held real power (known among them, sarcastically, as "Great Canadians") and, as often as not, the black cross on the gold ring that marked them as alumni of St. Francis Xavier University. These loyalists from Mulroney's university days (which included the 1963 Faculty of Law graduating class at Laval) alternated between acting like Green Berets on a search-and-destroy mission and the gossipy knitting circle gathered around the French Revolution's guillotines. They were adept at crisis management of the political wars that they had either started or that raged around them and became experienced at putting out the many fires that might have charred Mulroney's candidacy. They were very different from the *Weltschmerz* groupies bent on saving the country from itself who had assumed the burden of governing under the tutelage of Pierre Trudeau. These fancy-pants philosopher-princes (serving their philosopher-king) believed that in order to conduct the affairs of state one first had to serve the required apprenticeship at

Oxford, Harvard or the Sorbonne, preferably all three.[1]

The Mulroney brigade's organizational command post was the Maritime Bar at the Ritz-Carlton Hotel in Montreal (or the Mount Royal Club across the street), the location less a convenience than a statement that they had arrived. They dealt in various levels of sincerity with Robert Stanfield, Joe Clark, Claude Wagner and the serial nobodies who followed Daniel Johnson as leaders of the Union Nationale. There was a changing of the guard in the fall of 1987, when Derek Burney, a professional foreign service officer, became Mulroney's chief of staff. Most of the originals became lobbyists, publicists and other "ists," hawking their connections to the Big Guy.

The Mulroney entourage was usually dismissed as a nest of cronies. But they were better than that—they were street-smart realists who went into politics for fun and profit, in that order. Their operational code, aimed at persuading Mulroney doubters, was simple and direct. As one of them put it, "Grab 'em by their privates, and their hearts and their minds will follow."

---

1. The only Rhodes scholar within the Mulroney circle was Montreal lawyer Yves Fortier, but he was a Liberal and more a personal Mulroney friend (and law partner) than a member of the entourage. The two PhDs in the crowd were McMillan (the world's leading non-Asian authority on Japanese productivity) and Fred Doucet, who held a doctorate in administration.

8.

First of the great betrayers

———

Lucien Bouchard

NO BETRAYAL—PERSONAL OR POLITICAL touched Brian Mulroney more profoundly than the unexpected defection of Lucien Bouchard in the spring of 1990. The man who had been his schoolmate and soulmate jettisoned his Tory affiliation and crossed over to lead the separatist political movements dedicated to his former friend and mentor's political destruction. This was the most poignant of the betrayals that would plague Mulroney's years in power.

Bouchard and Mulroney had been self-described "buddy-buddies" at the Laval law school during the 1960s. They complemented one another: Mulroney was the man of action and Bouchard the man of intellect. They had enjoyed the kind of closeness that allowed them to finish not only one another's sentences, but one another's thoughts.

As prime minister, Mulroney was well aware that politics and gratitude are strangers, but his best friend's defection was like a death in the family. For once, his upset was measured not in anger but in sorrow. "Even in the political world, where imperfection often dominates and loyalties can be fleeting, Bouchard's conduct was of a new and impressive dimension," he lamented to me one evening. "I have never known a more vulgar expression of betrayal and deceit."

Five years earlier, Mulroney had named Bouchard ambassador to France, and three years after that he and his family campaigned hard to get Bouchard elected in the rural Quebec riding of Lac-Saint-Jean. He then immediately appointed Bouchard secretary of state and later promoted him into the high-profile environment ministry and named him his chief Quebec lieutenant. The friendship seemed immune to the vagaries of Ottawa's political precedents. It was Mulroney who held the wedding reception at Sussex Drive for Bouchard when he was married for the second time, to Audrey Best, his American sweetheart (they have since divorced). When their elder son, Alexandre, was born, Lucien's first call was to Brian.

Bouchard's breach of faith was best described by Stanley Hartt: "Lucien turned himself into a human car bomb, designed to go off at a time and place when it would do the most damage. He acted when he did because he recognized there was a way for the Meech provisions to work and thus disarm Quebec separatism. The tactic of not coming to see his friend to talk things over was deliberate. He saw a chance to make himself both a hero and a martyr at the same time, and the opportunity to catapult himself into being Jacques Parizeau's successor as Quebec premier. And that was exactly what he did. I don't know anybody else like that. And I'm glad."

A soulmate no more, Bouchard became first the leader of the breakaway Bloc Québécois in the House of

Commons and later Quebec's almost successful separatist premier. The two men have never spoken since.

What bothered Mila most about the defection was the fact she and the whole family had sacrificed Caroline's fourteenth birthday in the cause of Bouchard's initial election to Parliament. Mila regards birthdays as sacrosanct occasions to be celebrated with joy and enthusiasm—only the most pressing of reasons would justify messing up such a day. Yet Caroline and her parents spent her birthday in Bouchard's riding helping him. His defection to follow his destructive ambition was one of the few events that truly enraged Mila during her whole time in Ottawa.

Mulroney's wounded feelings about Bouchard— which also involved Caroline—spilled over into his private journal. "When the infamy of Lucien Bouchard was made public," he wrote, "the gesture we now know designed to undermine Meech itself before its possible ratification in June, my daughter Caroline walked into my den at 24 Sussex and quietly placed on my desk a letter she had received less than two years earlier from Lucien Bouchard. She just walked in, just like that, put it on my desk. A long, handwritten letter. On her birthday, I always take them out and I told her on her birthday, the 11th of June, 'I can't take you out. I am going to have to take you campaigning because Lucien Bouchard is in very serious trouble.' And we went in on the Saturday. I came back to Ottawa that evening and left again on Sunday with Mila. We were there on Sunday night, all day Monday and Tuesday morning, to pull out the by-election for him. In the long handwritten letter, he thanked her effusively for spending her fourteenth birthday getting him elected in the Lac St. Jean by-election. He then went on to extol—I have the letter by the way—went on to extol the extraordinary efforts Mila and I had deployed on his behalf and expressed to Caroline his deep, personal gratitude for all that we as a family had done for him over so many years. I was not aware of the existence of the letter until that very moment, but as Caroline left my den, you could sense the feeling of overwhelming betrayal in her eyes. She was not quite sixteen, but you could tell she shared my pain and astonishment that flowed from the wilful actions of one who only days earlier had spoken of the enormous debt of gratitude he owed the Prime Minister for his unfailing generosity, support and friendship over thirty years. Caroline had spotted, with the innocence of a child, the grotesque hypocrisy of which Bouchard was capable."

—

In 1985, Mulroney candidly explained his rationale for offering a key diplomatic post to the unknown Bouchard:
As long as he was just a Chicoutimi lawyer, that's all he was. Now—if we decide to run him or whatever—he's the former ambassador to France, and that makes a big difference. We're three years away from an election, so he has lots of time to be purified. I think it's a great appointment; a lot of the WASP journalists don't like it. They haven't the foggiest idea who he is.

Bouchard was elected in 1988. Only two years later, he left cabinet, protesting the Charest Commission report, which, he charged, diluted Quebec's constitutional position. Mulroney believed that was merely window dressing for a personal betrayal:
We've got it all documented. Bouchard was knee-deep, very deeply involved in destabilizing our caucus while he was a minister of the Crown. This was not spontaneous at all. It was well organized. How can he say that he resigned over the Charest report when I have in writing from a guy he had dinner with in Bergen, Norway, three days before the Charest Commission report came out, that he was going to resign?

I put [Jean] Charest on the committee at Bouchard's request. Here was young Charest trying to get hold of his friend Bouchard, who wouldn't take his calls. Things are not usually clear in politics, but this one is as clear as hell. Bouchard thought he would take twenty-five or thirty people to the Bloc Québécois. I never thought that. Bastard. He was holding meetings with [Parti Québécois member] Bernard Landry. [Parti Québécois leader] Jacques Parizeau was actively on the phone to Quebec members of the Conservative caucus trying to persuade them to resign because they said the Anglos would never let Meech go through. Because if Meech Lake went through, they would have lost their argument that they got screwed in 1982.

Mulroney, on Quebec if Bouchard's Bloc Québécois won the day:
An independent Quebec, first of all, would use the Canadian dollar, his independent Quebec would use the Canadian economic union, and his independent Quebec would use Canadian citizenship. The only thing that would be authentically Québécois would be the taxes, which would go up by $5 billion a year. I mean, this is crazy. If this is what an independent Quebec is going to give you, plus $5 billion in new taxes, it would be cheaper to remain Canadian.

Bouchard's newly expressed affection for Jacques Parizeau left Mulroney dumbfounded:
He's now in the arms of Jacques Parizeau. Both of them say they get along famously. Parizeau, who openly denounced Bouchard when he was Canadian ambassador in France, who refused to support him when he ran for Parliament and who attacked him on everything. Bouchard attacked Parizeau everywhere, called him a slovenly old crapper, the most disparaging things. He calls him every goddamned name in the book.

I've heard it a million times, his attacks on everybody, his vulgarities. I'm not criticizing him—I'm a profane guy myself—I'm just saying how far removed he is from reality. He hated Parizeau with a passion and now here they are arm in arm, walking down the Champs Elysées of Quebec towards the new republic.

Stanley Hartt wished Mulroney could sometimes see the worst in his friends:
Bouchard is one of those people Mulroney created. This isn't a unique phenomenon to the prime minister. A lot of people who are open and giving and friendly will fix on what is good in people, rather than what is bad, exposing themselves in that way.

I once had an incident with Brian, which is really funny. It was during the days when Lucien Bouchard had first resigned and every day some other Quebec Conservative was joining him. Mulroney had just run into one guy on the stairs on the way up to his office, and asked, "Are you going to stay with me?" And the guy said, "I'll stay with you forever, Prime Minister." Mulroney came into the office and he said to me, "Is he going to leave? I heard he's going to leave." And I said, "I honestly don't know."

He picked up the phone and phoned Marjory LeBreton and said, "Marjory, is this guy going to leave?" And she said, "Turn on your TV. He's standing in the House right now, and he's saying he's leaving."

Mulroney pooh-poohed Bouchard's reputation as an "idealistic intellectual":
This is all bullshit; this is stuff for the English media. The fact of the matter is, Bouchard would write my speeches sometimes because he wrote very well. But you know what was evident to me after maybe five or six of them? Always the same stuff, same phrases, same quotes. This is not a widely read man. This is a hard-working guy and a

disciplined guy, but not a widely read man at all.

I would never have thought him capable of this kind of stuff, or he would have never been around. And apart from the disloyalty, there is also an erratic dimension to his personality, driven by such vanity. His role, his looks, his life, the press attention given to him—he had his teeth redone. He's an extraordinarily vain man.

The day after Bouchard announced the founding of the Bloc, with himself as leader, Mulroney was still trying to figure out how he'd been bamboozled:
On July 27, I phoned Marcel Danis [a Quebec MP, and youth, fitness and amateur sport minister] and asked him about the situation with Bouchard. He said, "Yeah. Well, I knew about it." I said, "Well, why in the name didn't you phone me?" He said, "Prime Minister, what in the hell did you want me to do? I'm here, as a junior minister from Quebec. I'm dealing with the leader of the Quebec caucus, who it is widely known you've helped all his life—you've made him ambassador, cabinet minister, Quebec leader, you gave the reception for his wedding and he was supposed to be your best friend. Christ, I couldn't pick up the telephone. You'd have thought I was crazy."

He was absolutely right.

And he said, "It never crossed my mind that a betrayal this horrendous could be going on. I was afraid you'd kick me out of the cabinet."

Now, should I have known about Lucien Bouchard? I know the answer to that was no. I think there's no way I could have known about Bouchard. No way. I trusted him too much. You've got to understand, I had his goddamned wedding reception in my house. That's how close he was.

David Peterson:
It was obvious that bringing in Lucien Bouchard was a goddamned mistake. To give this guy, a four-flusher, a forum and then turn him into a hero is naïveté in the

extreme. I predicted all of this long before it happened—
I told Mulroney, I told others. The goddamned thing was
absolutely predictable.

Trudeau advisor Michael Pitfield:
Bouchard is a very daunting figure, but believe me, if you
talk to him at length, you find out that he's neither a
Trudeau nor a Lévesque. Still, superficially he has the
intellectual glibness of a Trudeau and the populist appeal
of a Lévesque. Bouchard's intellectualism is skin-deep, his
reading is far more narrow than he lets on—it's a little bit
like Kim Campbell. And his populism hasn't got the sincerity of a Lévesque.

Mulroney's friend Arthur Campeau:
If you promote the breakup of Canada, you're a traitor.
Had Lucien Bouchard done what he did in the 1970s,
there's no question that the RCMP would have been called
in to conduct a full investigation. I mean, this is traitorous;
this is treasonous. I said to Brian, "Jesus Christ, Brian, if
this had happened then, they would have called out the
horsemen." He said, "You're absolutely right." I told him,
"I'm convinced that this is not something that happened
accidentally. This is something that was planned. The only
thing that was not clear was where, when and how, but
that you had ceased to be in his mind the ticket to ride,
that he saw no further opportunities for himself by riding
your ticket, essentially by slipstreaming you. You weren't
going to hand the mantle over to him, and if you were, he
wasn't prepared to wait until you did."

**As the 1995 referendum approached, Mulroney vowed to
play his part in keeping Quebec within Canada:**
I am going to take part in the referendum. We're losing
every day. You should hear what's being said on the
streets of Montreal. I tell you that when the battle begins
here, it is going to be awful. The outreach that you see

from the PQ—I mean, they're applying the old principle, you get more bees with honey. Every time you turn around, Parizeau is on the phone, they're trying to get you to do something.

We have names too. People who can fill a hall are Daniel Johnson, Jean Charest, Jean Chrétien, Robert Bourassa, Pierre Trudeau, Brian Mulroney. Now if you can think of anybody else, you add it to your own list. That's a handful. That's six who can fill a hall in Trois-Rivières simply by putting out a poster saying they're coming. Now, here you've got a situation where Jean Charest, Daniel Johnson, Robert Bourassa and Brian Mulroney would be saying the same thing, right? And Pierre Trudeau and Jean Chrétien would be saying something entirely different.

Bouchard was a wound that would not heal:
Bouchard now says, "I was never a Conservative." That's true. He can also say, "I was never a friend, I was never an ally, I was never trustworthy, I was always deceitful."

Look, this is a guy who is actually convinced that he had a mission in life and that, as it turns out, if the price that had to be paid for him to move along in the mission was the betrayal of someone who did more for him than anybody else in his life, with the exception of his parents, so be it. If betrayal was the price that he had to pay to move along, he paid it gladly.

NEWMAN: His ultimate ambition is to be the first president of Quebec.

MULRONEY: Yes, his ultimate ambition is that.

Was Mulroney a fool, or just fooled?
My point is, that if you're prime minister, you are always making decisions, even if you don't make too many for your own good. That's why my government became

unpopular. The quote-unquote "unpopularity" is not the result of any goddamned character flaw, it's related to somebody else's character flaw. It then becomes a question of mediocre leadership, if something like this is going on and the prime minister or the leader doesn't know about it.

So the legitimate question is, should I have known that Lucien Bouchard was actively conspiring to bring about the destruction of his own government? In normal circumstances, I would say that the prime minister and the party leader should know about these things. I must say in my defence, as Marcel Danis said, "Prime Minister, this would have been like me telling you your brother was betraying you." So I say to myself, there was a character flaw, but it wasn't mine. It wasn't mine.

9.

"When Irish Eyes Are Smiling"

The Free Trade Crusade

THE CONSERVATIVE GOVERNMENT'S chief claim to fame was its free trade deal with the United States. The agreement had many fathers, all anxious to claim their paternity, who contributed to the DNA of the historic pact, but Brian Mulroney was not one of them.

Before he was elected, Mulroney had unequivocally dismissed the idea. Speaking on a windswept day in Thunder Bay during his 1983 leadership campaign, he declared, "Now, there's a real *beaut* for you. Now, there's a real honey—free trade with the Americans! Free trade with the United States is like sleeping with an elephant. It's terrific until the elephant twitches, and if the elephant rolls over, you're a dead man. I'll tell you when he's going to roll over—he's going to roll over in times of economic depression and they're going to crank up the plants in Georgia and North Carolina and Ohio and they're going to be shutting them down here. That's why free trade was decided on in the election of 1911. It affects Canadian sovereignty, and we'll have none of it, not during leadership campaigns, nor at any other times."

As prime minister in the fall of 1984, he added a dash of vinegar to his condemnation, speaking into my tape recorder: "It's such horseshit, the *Toronto Star* trying to get me to talk about free trade. I told them, listen, that thing was resolved in 1911. I don't want to fight those crazy imaginary wars anymore. This notion of a great comprehensive free trade agreement is crazy; I never spoke about anything like that in my life. There's not a single place on the goddamn record where I've even once mentioned free trade, not once. Ah, these crazy, indolent journalists . . ."

Still, Canada's business community recognized Mulroney as our very own Margaret Thatcher or Ronald Reagan, and promptly attempted to set Ottawa's political agenda, co-opting a compliant head of state in the subtlest coup d'état in history. The animating agent of that silent takeover was Tom d'Aquino, the messianic president and chief executive officer of the Business Council on National Issues (BCNI). For years, free trade with the United States had been his wet dream. D'Aquino was not a one-man show. The 150 CEOs who were members of his organization controlled $1.7 trillion in business assets, earned annual revenues of more than $500 billion and had 1.5 million employees. A tall, humourless gent, d'Aquino once told me that he didn't really mind being called a lobbyist, since "the Pope is a lobbyist too." It was a valid comparison: both men behaved as though they had missions, not jobs, and it was a toss-up whether d'Aquino or the Pope was the most dedicated.

"After Brian was elected but just before he moved into Sussex, and while he was still living in the Opposition leader's house at Stornoway, I was walking along Acacia Avenue and ran into him," d'Aquino told me, recalling when he had first raised the free trade issue with the new PM.

"Lookit," Mulroney said, "I know you people have been promoting this idea and I've read your most recent paper. It's got a lot of appeal and I'm really looking at it with great interest."

"That was within ten days of the election," d'Aquino exulted. "Brian had sufficiently high regard for the BCNI that if we thought it was a really important issue, he should at least take a good hard look at it. And he did. By the end of that autumn, he had bought the argument. The Shamrock Summit followed in April, and the rest is history. The free trade idea didn't start among the senior civil servants at External Affairs, as they contend. It was ours."[1]

Well, maybe, but I don't think so. The idea of free trade was in the air after the 1984 election, but it took a year or more to land. Several others offered similar advice to d'Aquino's. In his royal commission report, Donald Macdonald, a former Liberal finance minister, recommended that Canada risk "a leap of faith" through the window of opportunity by negotiating free trade with the Americans.

The most obtrusive presence in the debate was the uninhibited Paul Robinson Jr., the American ambassador to Canada who took Ottawa by storm following his accreditation in the summer of 1981. Allan Fotheringham justifiably described Robinson as "the only bull that carries his own china shop around with him." A former U.S. naval officer in the Korean War who raised $700,000 for Ronald Reagan's 1980 election, Robinson exercised extraordinary influence in both national capitals. At a briefing before Reagan and Mulroney met at the 1985

---

1. Free trade certainly turned out to be a bonanza for d'Aquino's members. According to the Canadian Centre for Policy Alternatives, thirty-three BCNI affiliates used the Free Trade Agreement as an excuse to slash 216,004 jobs, while eleven members increased their payrolls by only 28,073.

Shamrock Summit in Quebec City, for example, U.S. secretary of state George Shultz was having problems communicating with Erik Nielsen, then deputy prime minister and minister of national defence. Nielsen, who was not known as Velcro-lips for nothing, had used up his weekly quota of a hundred words. Finally, Shultz leaned across the table and said to Robinson, "This fellow doesn't say much." To which Neilsen deadpanned, "I only talk to Paul."

That exchange neatly summed up how Robinson had wormed himself into the confidence of the Ottawa administration, acting less like a diplomat than a crusader for the newest version of manifest destiny: hemispheric free trade. He also imagined himself influencing what passed for Canada's defence policy. Robinson became so vehement on the subject of our maritime vulnerability that at a Rideau Club dinner convened to discuss the issue, a senior civil servant jokingly suggested one of the Canadian navy's new patrol frigates ought to be christened the HMCS *Robinson*. The ambassador thought this would be a grand idea. Realizing to his horror that he was being taken seriously, the bureaucrat quickly pointed out that the vessels in that class were all being named after Canadian cities. Even that didn't faze Robinson. "Hell," he said, not missing a beat, "rename one of your cities."

Robinson had top-level connections in the Reagan White House, where he kept the free trade issue in play.[2] The first and most public indication that something unusual was afoot took place during the St. Patrick's Day Summit held in Quebec City in 1985, when Reagan and Mulroney met ostensibly to reach an understanding about reducing acid rain, which was causing hazardous pollu-

---

2. The only other presidential reference to North American free trade came up during the Nixon years. When the subject of such a deal with Canada was mentioned, Nixon stiffened and said, "Oh yeah, then we could let that fucking Trudeau grow a beard and go play with Castro."

tion in both countries. Reagan was actually convinced that pollution was caused not by industrial emissions but by trees. No matter how many experts patiently explained that trees actually helped the earth breathe, Ronnie held fast, publicly stating that "trees cause more pollution than automobiles."[3] At the Quebec City meeting, the acid rain problem was put off for further study, but a protocol was signed that called for "a more secure climate for bilateral trade."

As I watched the two political leaders pirouette through the weekend's festivities, it was nearly impossible not to be affected by the infectious good spirits that pervaded their every encounter. Their contented aides basked in the residuals of all that *bonne entente*. Except for the nearsighted Nancy Reagan, who nodded to every pillar in the Château Frontenac dining room, possibly thinking they were Mounties, the occasion was genuine enough. Brian and Mila displayed a finely honed sense of choreography, moving through the crowds with disarming charm.

This was Mulroney's most poignant moment. He had been an indifferent, insolvent student in this town, and now he was hosting the world's most powerful politician. I quietly did a round of the bars where we used to meet, drank a toast to how far he had come and even ventured to his boarding house at 71 Rue St. Louis. No one was home.

It was amusing to watch the spectators surrounding the hotel, swaying to get a better look at the celebrities, their heads ruffled by Quebec City's strong March winds. The tuxedoed men at the Sunday-night musical gala clutched their magnificently gowned wives and partners as if they had invented them to enhance the hard-sell glory of the spectacle. Few realized that the summit ran

---

3. Aware of his bizarre views, a group of students at a northern Californian university being visited by Reagan hung a sign on a large oak at the gate that read, "CUT ME DOWN BEFORE I KILL AGAIN."

on double tracks. Alongside the international diplomacy, Mulroney undertook some highly effective parish pump priming. The presidents of the twenty-two ridings held by the Tories east of Quebec City were given four tickets to distribute to their key poll captains. While Reagan was building his dream of a Fortress America, Mulroney was consolidating his Fortress Quebec.

That evening, my wife Camilla and I attended Le Grand Théâtre for the concluding spectacle of the summit. Its highlight, forever etched on the national consciousness, was the musical finale. Arms linked, the Reagans and the Mulroneys sang Ireland's unofficial national anthem, "When Irish Eyes Are Smiling." The prime minister took the solo on the penultimate and final lines (an A in the key of C). The sun came up the next morning anyway.[4]

In the months that followed, so many high-level players were busy creating a consensus on the free trade issue that an agreement of some sort became inevitable. But in terms of its timing, I remain convinced that free trade was conceived on a bed of rancid tuna—the fish from a New Brunswick cannery that government inspectors had declared unfit for human consumption. As the destruction of so many cans would have closed the plant, the owners lobbied Fisheries Minister John Fraser, who decided the tuna should be allowed on store shelves after all. Although no one suffered from the tainted fish, it was recalled six days later. In the process, the government's internal communications broke down, so that Fraser and Mulroney were releasing different versions of why the fisheries minister had to resign. "Tunagate" became the code word for several subsequent ministerial departures. No one seemed to be in charge. Only months

---

4. Not for Mordecai Richler, who later confessed that as he watched the quartet perform what must have ranked as a diplomatic first, he wanted to "take a shotgun to the TV."

after being elected with an overwhelming mandate, the government was falling apart.

Afloat in a sea of mounting troubles, Mulroney searched for an initiative that would take commentators' minds off ministerial resignations and would get them gnawing at a substantive issue instead of at him. To regain respect—or at least divert attention—he realized that he had to come up with a macho position on something big, and soon. Thus, free trade with the Yanks.

That's an oversimplification, of course. But whether free trade was an economic panacea or a diversionary tactic, Mulroney recognized the issue as key to his political survival. Who could worry about his half dozen nameless ministers who had jumped or been pushed overboard when the ship of state's destiny was in play? Mulroney had correctly interpreted his 1984 election results as a mandate for change, and the most daring gambit he could imagine was free trade. Sir Wilfrid Laurier's government fell on the issue in 1911. Only a gutsy leader would bet the farm in 1985.

On the surface, free trade was about removing tariffs on items crossing the forty-ninth parallel. But since 80 per cent of goods were already duty-free, the debate quickly turned into a clash of values, with each side claiming its cadre of true believers. Along with most of the country's cultural community, I came out strongly against the agreement, and to Mulroney's credit, though we met often during that turbulent interval, he never tried to dissuade me. As I wrote back then, "Fond as we are of Americans individually, collectively they scare the hell out of us. We can see in our country, but not theirs, the possibility of realizing our potential as Canadians. We are a people with little talent for excess. Most of us dream of being Clark Kent instead of Superman. The element in the free trade mix that causes us the most trouble is fear. Not fear of economic competition or vestiges of traditional feelings of inferiority, but an innate sense of alarm that somehow the disturbing verities of American society would expropriate our daily lives. A closer analysis of the pact revealed that it had its own agenda—agreed to but never discussed by our negotiators. It had less to do with trade than with harmonizing the economies and regulatory frameworks of the two countries."

My peeve was that we gave away—lock, stock and oil barrel—unhindered access to our energy resources without gaining any compensating advantages. One paragraph of the treaty even committed us to provide "proportional access to the diminished supply" if we started to run out of oil for our own use. It was madness. The most apt comment came from inside the Mulroney administration. Ray Hnatyshyn, then energy minister and later governor general, quipped that "free trade in energy with the Americans is like wife-swapping with a bachelor."

That was traumatic enough, but there was a wider, cultural dimension that Mulroney's business-oriented initiative never considered. While Canadians continued to fuss about individual (and collective) survival, as enshrined in Pierre Trudeau's legalistic Charter, Americans identified their past and future with greater ideals, spelled out in their founding documents: the Declaration of Independence, the Constitution and the Bill of Rights. These daring proclamations shattered feudal land laws and gave individuals supreme sanction to pursue the lively and inspiring notions of life, liberty and the pursuit of happiness. We were stuck with having to obey the bland recipe of peace, order and good government.

Thomas Jefferson, the greatest of the American presidents, believed in the freedom of each generation to rediscover itself, and that gospel catapulted the U.S. into a state of perpetual revolution. While Brian Mulroney insisted he was merely negotiating a free trade treaty, he was really asking us to become the unprotected citizens of a brave new world we never made, with a partner that was a fierce and unforgiving competitor. "Free trade," wrote the commentator David Frum, with unusual insight, "broke the elite consensus by which Canada is normally governed."

In the brooding winter of 1988 when Ronald Reagan and Brian Mulroney signed the free trade agreement, I found myself mourning for my country. We seemed to be left with little more than the fugitive souvenirs of our exalted past. "We've signed a stunning new pact with Canada," gloated Clayton Yeutter, the chief U.S. trade representative, in an off-the-record comment that soon became public. "The Canadians don't know what they've signed. In twenty years they'll be sucked into the American economy!"

Mr. Yeutter was wrong. It didn't take twenty years.

—

During his first months as prime minister in the autumn of 1984, Mulroney dismissed media reports that a comprehensive free trade deal with the United States was in the works:

NEWMAN: There's much informed speculation about free trade.

MULRONEY: Free trade was never in the cards.

Ten years later, Mulroney remembered his position very differently:

I was against unfettered free trade—*unfettered* free trade. I was in favour of free trade, but against unfettered free trade. A very important distinction.

NEWMAN: What does "unfettered" mean?

MULRONEY: Well, free trade for Canada. The key to the Free Trade Agreement was an independent dispute-settlement mechanism. The U.S. Congress insisted that it should retain supreme and unalloyed power. I couldn't see how any trade agreement could work if you didn't have something removed from the traditional trade tribunals and courts that would allow you to settle disputes because of the imbalance in size and economies. I was very strongly in favour of greater trade, but I was against unmanaged trade because I knew damn well that free trade without some safeguards would cause us great problems.

At first, American politicians were hostile to the idea:
MULRONEY: People like [Democratic senator and 1988 vice-presidential nominee] Lloyd Bentsen and [Ronald Reagan's chief of staff and later George H. Bush's secretary of state] Jimmy Baker told me personally, this could have been interpreted as a surrender of sovereignty, and that the U.S. Congress wouldn't do it. But what were the alternatives? Well, one alternative was sectoral trade, and the Americans said, "We don't want to touch it." The other alternative was managed trade. The General Agreement on Tariffs and Trade [GATT] said, "You do that and you're dead." This was antithetical to the GATT, so we were looking at something that had to be GATT-able.

Mulroney became a true believer:
If not free trade, what? What is the alternative for Canada in ten, fifteen years? What position are we going to be in? Europe will have 450 million people. The United States by itself internally has a trading bloc of probably $10 billion, and here we are off by ourselves with no world product mandates, with antiquated plants and equipment, with marketing methods that went out with the horse and buggy. If not free trade, what for Canada? What are the great currents of history going to be? Remember, we are a trading nation whose wealth depends more on international trade than any other country in the world except Germany. So you think it through and you say, this is it,

this is the way it's got to be. This is what the world is going to look like in twenty-five, thirty-five, forty years. So if the world is going to look like that, then this is my vision of the future of globalization, of increasing competitiveness, of the requirements for value-added, of all of these things. I've got to do something. If not free trade, what? And as you look at the alternatives, they're worse. So you do this because you think it's right for Canada, that's all.

Free trade and the 1988 election:
MULRONEY: The Free Trade Agreement was so huge and so challenging it required an election, and that election was probably the most bitter campaign in Canadian history. There was violence in that election. We had a hugely difficult time in 1988. I mean, every time we brought about change, we had a difficult time, right? At a crucial moment during the 1988 campaign, my campaign chairman, Norman Atkins, tried to get me to abandon free trade completely.

Mulroney felt opponents of free trade had an easier time:
Try and get up in the morning and devise a free trade agreement with the United States and then try and sell it. Try selling these policies through the prism of an unbalanced, biased and malicious press gallery. And before you can get on TV, [Canadian Labour Congress president] Bob White, [National Action Committee on the Status of Women president] Judy Rebick and every other socialist in town is on the goddamned tube before you, and you come on about ninth. Try and do that—it's pretty tough going.

On January 1, 1989, Mulroney's trade deal with the United States came into effect. Four years later, the North American Free Trade Agreement included Mexico:
I looked at the currents developing in Europe, protectionist pressures developing in Washington, and realized the

solution to the whole thing was a free trade agreement where we've got to have an independent dispute-settling mechanism, because if we've got that, we're going to win nine times out of ten. What you're talking about is a free trading agreement that Sir John A. Macdonald himself tried to get. It's a lot of crock that Sir John was against free trade; he turned against free trade when he couldn't get it. Wilfrid Laurier tried to get it, Mackenzie King nibbled at the edges.

Stanley Hartt worried about the simplicity of Mulroney's pitch:
If you're going to trade with a country that doesn't believe in your social contract, which doesn't believe that the state should look after people—that if you get sick, you better have private insurance; that if you want to retire, you better contribute to Social Security—if you have a free trade agreement with a country that doesn't believe that the state should accumulate additional revenues, then there's only one tax that can help you keep your sovereignty to do those different things while not injuring your competitors, and that's a tax on consumption. By the time that you are consuming, the article has been in trade, it's been sold maybe by an American, but it's still taxed, even if it's sold by the Americans, so it gives no advantage to an American or a Canadian. It's a self-assessment the way you assess yourself in a golf club if you want new furniture in the clubhouse—you pay for things you hold dear. That's what the GST is. That's why a consumer tax is a condition for membership in the European Community, because it's the only way two countries can have a fund out of which to make different decisions than their neighbours make.

But Mulroney was never able to sell it that way. All of his initiatives he sold as one-off. His skills as a political pro made him think that way. We've got to get free trade through, and to get free trade through, we've got to concentrate on selling it, so don't put too much else on the agenda. If you mix that issue up with a million things, people won't vote for it, so let's make it really simple. Do you want free trade? Yes or no. It's a chance for the future, that's going to be the issue; it's me versus Turner, our visions of Canada—openness versus protectionism, government intervention versus small government or private sector.

In so doing, Mulroney de-linked the GST from the income tax reductions because he didn't want to have the GST as an election issue at the same time he had free trade.

Senator Michael Pitfield didn't question the need for free trade, just the way Mulroney went about it:
It was inevitable that we would have free trade, but not that we would come at it that way. The real problem is that we don't have a view of our own country and therefore a sense of what our priorities are of things to be secured, things that mustn't be dealt away. In a purely ad hoc negotiation, you make it more difficult to exercise any national view in the country. Brian didn't seem to have impressed Canadians as having a view of the country.

One could say the only view of the country that is now widely accepted is the Trudeau view, which has the following of about 30 per cent of the population. You don't have to go out and organize, and Mr. Trudeau doesn't have to make speeches—it sort of comes to the fore by simply blowing on it like an ember. It's quite strongly held. It means a country in which we share a national capital, in which the French Canadians are attracted to it because it's a larger stage and it opens outward rather than being a smaller stage and opens narrowly, a country in which French Canadians can feel at home from one sea to the other, as Trudeau used to say.

Trudeau takes great pride in not being a nationalist, but in fact his view of the country is very close to a nationalistic view. He doesn't like nationalism because he doesn't like to see the passion let loose. He wants it to be reasoned, but the fact of the matter is that what registered with most Canadians about Trudeau is that he did have a view of the country.

Canada emerged from its economic slump during Jean Chrétien's first term, and Mulroney felt his policies had cleared the way:
How can the Liberals be given credit for anything? Let me put it this way. We bring in a free trade agreement, and today the entire world is out of the recession. Canada was plunged deeply in a recession, and they say the reason was clearly because of the policies of my government. Well, Christ almighty, I'd like to think I was right, but obviously I was wrong, right? But that's not what is happening. What's happening is a lean and modernized and productive Canadian economy is being driven by exports to reach brand-new heights and job creation, with its manufacturing base strengthened and the largest productivity gains since the Second World War. That's what's happening.

The fight of John Turner's life became the life raft of Chrétien's Liberals, according to Mulroney:
The Liberals said it was the wrong thing to have done and we have to cancel it. But [Finance Minister] Paul Martin never had to make that speech, saying everything about the FTA and NAFTA has gone wrong. Our exports to the United States are up almost 100 per cent in five years, with Canada having the largest and most favourable trade balance in the world in history. You measure success or failure by the manner in which your successor government treats your heritage. If it was right, they keep it. If it was wrong, they throw it out. Just look at the building blocks of the revolution that we brought in. Every one of them has been maintained.

Mulroney on free trade as his contribution to Canadian history:

Look, when I did the Free Trade Agreement, I didn't know how it was going to turn out. I thought it was the right thing to do. I believed that it was the way of the future. If you looked at it in the new millennium, you would say this was so obvious that it had to be done. Without it, Canada would be small and atrophied. The Free Trade Agreement and NAFTA will be regarded one hundred years from now as a major defining moment in the evolution of Canada. The *New York Times* did a big article in the financial section on NAFTA and they basically said, the United States and Mexico may have a little trouble with this but, boy, Canada doesn't. Canada has emerged the true winner on everything.

Twenty-five years from now there's going to be the biggest goddamned banquet you ever saw to celebrate the Free Trade Agreement, but I'm not going to be able to get into the room because Bob White and Judy Rebick are going to be chairing it and saying it was their idea. That's the way history works. If it works out, they're all there to claim credit, and nobody remembers that they were the same people trying to undermine it.

10.

"A really sick place"

———

Life in Ottawa

Late in his tenure, Mulroney felt like a stranger in a strange land in the nation's capital:
This place is sick. They're all married to one another. They're shacked up with one another. Their wives are on the payroll of CBC. It's just awful, the goddamned incest here. Ottawa is really a sick place. This is really a sick town. A sense of loyalty and friendship and devotion and mutual respect in some cases is non-existent, and there's something in the air here that transforms people from supplicants to sinners overnight. You appoint them to the position and they forget completely not only who appointed them, they forget that they sought the appointment on bended knee. Ingratitude is the only thing they understand.

Paul Tellier, the clerk of the Privy Council, said

Mulroney and his new Conservative regime started out being highly suspicious of the place:

When this government came to power, I don't have to tell you that they had never worked with a bureaucracy. They had been cut out of power, as the prime minister says, for twenty-five years. Therefore, they came in with a great many suspicions that the echelon of public service were a bunch of Grits.

The prime minister decided to beef up ministerial offices with the political chiefs of staff and what have you. He is quite frustrated by the attitude too often of the bureaucracy producing seventeen reasons why something can't be done. There was something with the Progressive Conservative Party, which was perhaps more obvious but also existed with the Liberals—a love-hate relationship between politicians and public servants.

For the average taxpayer, the average Canadian, public servants are a necessary evil, so nobody ever gets up in the morning and says the public service is great. The world doesn't work like this. Therefore, it is very easy for politicians to pick on the public service—very, very easy, because they are easy targets.

Still, after the initial, rightly founded suspicions or to-be-expected suspicions of the Conservative politicians in 1984 vis-à-vis the public service, the relationship became good quite quickly. The prime minister started to realize after six months in power that he needed the public service perhaps more than they needed him. And he realized that his attempt to strengthen ministerial offices with chiefs of staff was not that successful, not to say it was a mistake.

He became frustrated by the fact that too many of his ministers were becoming super deputy ministers and were not worrying enough about their ministerial duties and their political duties. The public service played as large a role if not a larger role under the Mulroney government than they had under a Liberal government. I have seen some ministers, Mr. Mazankowski being one, putting in writing his views about his deputy minister of the day. I've never seen letters full of praise like this, and he was not unique. You ask Michael Wilson about Finance, the quality of human resources in the department. Ask Flora MacDonald about her relationship with some key people in the Department of Employment and Immigration. Ask Perrin Beatty about the key people that he worked with in National Defence, or in Health and Welfare and so on. They would be full of praise.

But their criticism of the collectivity of the public service as a whole was perhaps louder and more frequent than under the Liberals. And the prime minister on occasion would meet with all the deputy ministers and say, "I rely on you to run these departments. Listen, these people are professional administrators. You let them run these departments and you provide the policy direction. I don't want you as a super deputy minister. I want you to be members of my staff or my government." So, in many ways, he was expressing his personal confidence in the professional public service.

Hugh Segal did not have such a sunny view of Tellier, who was kept in his key job until 1992:
This is something that I put on record because I worry about it. I don't think Brian is being well served by the civil service. I have several incidents where the prime minister asked Paul Tellier to do something and Tellier pursued the order in a fashion so as to dilute what the prime minister really wanted.

For policy advisor Geoff Norquay, part of the problem was Mulroney's own team:
Bill Fox, the press officer, provided a set of judgments and a set of street smarts that nobody else had. On the other hand, the reality was that Bill Fox pissed a lot of people off. And that contributed to some of the difficulties in office.

You know there are some funny, funny people in this party. Jeffrey Simpson was not at all wrong when he wrote that a lot of the same problems associated with the discipline of power are still here. You know, it's very frustrating to me as a bit of a bystander to notice that Norm Atkins and Bernard Roy can sit in splendid isolation, one in that building and the other in this building, saying, "The fucker never calls me." Now, this is crazy. This is absolute lunacy. These are grown-up men. One is the chairman of the campaign, the other is the principal secretary to the prime minister, and they're playing little boys' ego games. It's frustrating to see that kind of thing happening and it's so bloody unnecessary. These guys should be thinking about one thing: what can I do to help the prime minister and this government succeed? Not "So-and-so won't call me, I didn't get invited to the meeting. He never calls, he never writes." Well, hell.

Charley McMillan:
I'm appalled at the lack of creativity, the fucking around and the gamesmanship. And the patronage bureaucracy, it appalls me. Let's say the Liberals came into power tomorrow, and John Doe is the new chief of staff. What would be the one piece of advice I would give him? "Get the hell out of Ottawa." The place is teeming with people who are tired and worn out and haven't come up with a new idea, and they're forty years old.

Frank Moores agreed:
People ask me how I like it here, and I hate Ottawa. I can't find anyone in this town with any roots, whether it's embassies or the politicians or even the bureaucrats— they're all transients. Everyone here is a transient. And as transients, there's only one thing they're interested in, and that's impressing other people of how damned important they are. It's a very artificial lifestyle. If you don't get the hell out of it and go back to the real world fairly regularly,

you can get caught up in this comfortable pew awfully fast, whether as a minister in a department or the prime minister or just someone doing business.

Mulroney needed a clearer sense of how to earn the public's trust, according to Moores:
I told Brian the other day he's got to switch the pitch and forget that he was the coattail that elected everybody. People want a team approach now, and he has great difficulty getting his mind on that. The communications out of the PMO have been an absolute disaster. I don't care, there's even friends of mine involved in it. The lack of public relations in this government is almost incredible. I mean, they're naïve to the point of incredulity. Not one of them has ever held elected office, including Brian, Bernard Roy, Fred Doucet and Foxy. Not one has ever had any experience in the artificiality of politics, for lack of a better word.

Brian's whole background in politics was as a backroom operator in Quebec. A backroom Tory operator in Quebec wasn't in a very crowded room. I mean, Christ, there was no one there. Whether it was setting up a trust fund for Claude Wagner or whatever deal had to be done, Brian was the dealmaker. He was extraordinarily good, but to go from that to leader of the party in an elected capacity is not an easy transition.

Bill Pristanski recalled how the Tories literally had to shovel the manure:
When Don Mazankowski was elevated to deputy prime minister, he left his East Block office after the swearing-in and was walking up to meet somebody in the West Block. As he was coming along, he saw this enormous pile of shit on the sidewalk down by the eternal flame. He got almost to the East Block and there was this Mountie on the horse. He said, "Excuse me, I'm the deputy prime minister of Canada, and I think your horse just left a whole pile of

shit on the sidewalk, and I want you to have it cleaned up." The Mountie said, "Yes, sir. Right away." As he walked over to the West Block, Maz thought to himself, "Well, Mulroney said I was here to clean up the shit."

II.

The Mila factor

—

Brian's Greatest Asset

COMPASSIONATE, CHARMING AND FUNNY, Mila Mulroney was Brian's sanctuary. She understood more intuitively than he did the rebellious political mood that gripped the land, becoming his resident diviner of moods and character, spotting the plotters among the favour-seekers. She set the boundaries on his rhetorical excesses and diverse impulses—she alone could contradict him without bruising his ego.

Mulroney was a loner who couldn't stand being alone. Like most loners, he needed a strong compadre to keep the world at bay. Enter Mila. She was the only one he totally trusted. She grounded him and levelled out his mood swings. It was Mila who endowed their life together with the patina of normalcy, as if every husband spent more time on the phone than eating and sleeping.

Her smile could have been auctioned at Sotheby's.

With her natural beauty, crinkly nose, gregarious manner and impeccable taste, she played the role of Canada's glamorous First Lady to the presidential prime minister. "You want to know the measure of Mila's charisma?" asked David Foster, the Canadian-born Hollywood composer who was a friend of the family. "Everyone knows the moment she's left the room." She gave the Mulroney administration its human face, and gave her husband his closest shot at fulfilling his fascination with the Kennedy mystique—a hard sell in a country crippled by regional wars and economic recessions. London's *Daily Express* described Mila as "the most glamorous political star since the early Jackie Kennedy." Whenever she was welcomed at a public occasion with a bouquet of flowers, she would snap off one of the blooms and smiling, hand it back to its blushing presenter. The audiences loved her.

Brian first caught sight of her in a red bikini at the Mount Royal Tennis Club in 1972, when she was only eighteen (and he was thirty-three). He decided on the spot that she would be his wife. This took some persuasion. Milica was the eldest daughter of Serbian psychiatrist Dimitrije Pivnickl and his devoutly Catholic wife, Bogdanka.[1] The woman he instantly anointed as the love of his life was in reality a precocious teenager, busily studying for her civil engineering degree. The family took its time validating his martial brief, but there came a moment, well into the courtship, when it was decided that the couple could finally be left alone at home. The story was best told by Mila's younger sister, Ivana: "My parents whisked my brother and me off to the Fairview Mall so the young couple could, at last, be alone together. We no sooner left them in the house for this intimate moment than the phone rings. It's a neighbour who says,

---

1. Ironically, Dr. Pivnicki treated Margaret Trudeau in the late 1970s, when the position of being the prime minister's wife grew so frustrating that she sought solace with the Rolling Stones.

'I hate to disturb you, but your cat has just been hit by a car.' Brian checks it out, and sure enough, there is a dead cat on the road. He has to go out onto the street with a shovel and pick up the cat and put it into a box in the backyard. Mila is hysterical and crying. When we return, I'm sent immediately to my room because at the age of eleven, I'm too young to hear bad things like this. I tear upstairs and, being the snoop that I am, listen to the conversation from the stairtop. I race into my room to get something and there was our own cat sleeping on my bed. I scooped it up, ran down the stairs, and said, 'Is this why Mila is crying?' Brian had been consoling Mila for three hours, and to this day he's convinced that some poor strange cat was sacrificed for Mila's chastity."

Several of Brian's friends, myself included, were introduced to Mila with the aim of imagining her as his political wife. The verdict was unanimous: he was the luckiest guy in the universe and had better grab her quick. Except for the stressful interlude after he lost the 1976 leadership campaign, they were an inseparable couple, profoundly in love and lost without each other.

But once her husband became prime minister and the press started to use them both for target practice, Mila shared Brian's resentment of journalists; she was put off by the cockiness of columnists and stunned at how often the country's media gurus used the gutter distortions of *Frank* magazine to source their stories. "I eventually learned to take their coverage with a grain of salt," she once told me. "But initially, it was almost like being raped and pillaged in full view." While she commiserated with her man's obsessive loathing of the media, she went well beyond merely despising individual journalists. She placed them in the same category as the Ottoman Turkish raiders who slaughtered the Serbian army on the bloody battlefield of Kosovo on June 28, 1389. Serbs do not live by half measures. One of my best buddies is Vlad Plavsic, a Serb who defected to Canada in 1951, became a

signature architect, played in Stan Kenton's trumpet section and is a champion bluewater sailor. "You're my
friend. I would kill for you. You cross me, I kill you," he
once calmly explained when we were discussing the
boundaries of our friendship. Then he added, "But don't
worry, I'd say the same to my mother." That would roughly
define the limits of Mila's love for Brian.

I felt her sting after I wrote what several members of
the Mulroney entourage thought was a fair but critical
assessment of Brian's first term. She promptly returned the
antique wooden candlesticks I had sent them as gift for
their first Christmas in Ottawa. The candleholders were
one of the very few objects my family had managed to rescue when we fled Czechoslovakia in 1939. Her accompany-
ing note was curt and to the point: "PETER—Under the
circumstances, your mother's candlesticks should reside in
a more appropriate place—Mila Mulroney." She neither
forgot nor forgave any slights to her husband and measured her reactions to people according to the countless
nuances of hurt and criticism nurtured in her elephant-
like memory. Of the high-velocity bazooka shots aimed at
the PM, she told me, "There's no doubt that he likes to be
liked, but many of us are that way. It's human nature. As I
see it, sometimes he's almost too good to be true, so people
just assume he's not."

During the stormy decade he was prime minister, Mila
Mulroney won respect from the party's insiders for her
unerring instincts about people. Her internal radar was
tuned not to what they said or did, but to the aura they
projected. She was suspicious of Lucien Bouchard years
before he defected. She equally distrusted Clyde Wells
long before he pulled the plug on the Meech Lake agreement, having promised in writing that he wouldn't. As
they were being driven from the conference centre where
the accord was finalized, Mulroney said to his wife that
he was glad it was all over. "It's not over yet," she told
him. "When you were speaking and your attention was

diverted, I was watching Clyde Wells. I watched him very closely and saw such a degree of deceit . . . There's something in his eyes that I don't like, that doesn't ring true."

"Honey, for Christ's sake," Brian replied, "he just signed a constitutional document in front of the entire nation. It's the future of the country, and he's undertaken to take this to a vote."

"Well, you may be right, but I think he's going to betray you all, betray the country."

Later, after recounting that conversation, Mulroney said, "Guess who was right? Mila's judgment about people is unerring. It's amazing. I think she was born with it."

Not surprisingly, her qualities drew criticism. Conrad Winn, an Ottawa pollster, made the point: "She became the prime minister's wife in the heyday of feminism, when the litmus tests of an adult woman were, are you successful as a professional? What about the amount of makeup you wear? Do you make sure you're only averagely attractive? And here we had a woman who was obviously brainy yet had quit her engineering program. On top of that, she's not only gorgeous but is probably more charismatic than her husband, though as prime minister he could grant favours, and she couldn't. Most people still preferred to be under her umbrella than his."

Her husband had infinite admiration for Mila's ability to bridge the gap between motherhood and feminism. "She's not afraid to be her own self," Mulroney told me. "She doesn't go around being a roaring feminist to prove that she's feminine. She does her own thing, looks after our kids, does all kinds of other stuff, more things than feminists do." Mila took mothering seriously, and since she had an office inside the PMO, she occasionally found herself extending her maternal instincts at work. "Combining politics with a young family is not easy," she complained. "Feeding, hugging, counselling, wiping away tears, cleaning up the messes—and then you had to leave the PMO staff behind and start all over again with the children."

She didn't have children so that they would be raised by other people, and the Mulroney offspring—Caroline, Benedict, Mark and Nicolas—did their parents proud. "Those four kids, they were unbelievable," recalled Stanley Hartt. "I don't know where she found the time to raise such presentable, self-assured, intelligent youngsters." Hartt also recalled going on, much too long, about the charms of his favourite among them, Mark, who was intellectually the most curious. He told Mila that he thought Mark would be the best candidate for a future prime minister. To which she replied coldly, "Oh you do, do you?" Only then did Hartt realize he had picked one of her children over the others, and that was not allowed.

Mila's influence on her husband was potent, but she was careful not to be seen openly influencing government policies. There were exceptions. Health Minister Jake Epp found it surprisingly easy to get approval for increases in medical research funding, and everyone involved knew who was talking up that spending priority. She was opposed to Via Rail cutting its passenger services. When I asked Derek Burney, the toughest of Mulroney's chiefs of staff, whether Mila influenced government policies, he flatly denied that such a thing could happen, then added, looking heavenward, "How do you say no to an angel?"

In fact, Brian sought Mila's counsel on almost everything. But as she rightly pointed out, it was more corroboration he wanted than criticism. The exception was her role in the administration's many cabinet shuffles, when her comments on the candidates were seriously weighed as Brian drew on his confidence in her reading of people's natures. "When he was shuffling cabinet, he would make a list, balance Quebec and Ontario, read it to the missus, then send me to the shredder with it. Then he'd start over, wake her up to read her the new list, and after a few times at about 3 a.m. or so, she'd say, 'If you read that list to me one more time, I'm gonna kill you!'" recalled Bill Pristanski. "Brian used to try cabinet changes out on me three months ahead of time," said Mila. "He didn't need to remind me not to tell anyone, that was just an assumption. Then I'd read about it in the paper and wonder if I was the only one he'd told. Sometimes it was quite a responsibility."

Under the pressures of high office, they grew so close that there came a point when Brian seemed unable to face controversial occasions without her presence. During election campaigns, the only phrase he repeated more often than describing his policies as sacred trusts was his urgent plea, "Where's Mila?" Early in 1984, I asked Mulroney about her impact on the election and whether he thought she should run a campaign on her own in order to double their efforts. "No way," he shot back, laughing. "She'd get more votes than me." Unlike her husband, Mila appreciated the difference between being liked and respected, and she was both. Her mantra, which she picked as her favourite saying in the 1970 Westmount High School yearbook, was a telling choice, "We were all born originals, let us not die as copies."

"Her influence on him is incredibly strong," Sally Armstrong concluded after completing Mila's biography. "I'd be very worried if anything altered that, and I certainly would worry about him. At the beginning, when they used to do those funny clips of him going whistle stop to whistle stop and people would shout, 'Mila! Where's Mila?' I thought it was rather endearing, but having seen it for longer, I felt the balance of power was shifting. He needs her beside him, he really does. I think it's charming except in terms of the balance of powering the country, needing his partner like that. It's not my issue, but I guess I get nervous when I see one person so dependent on another. Mind you, he thinks she's everything. I mean, I would love to live with a man like that. He's forever showering her with compliments—you look gorgeous, you did a great job, I'm so proud of you—all the time."

Mila provided another secret bonus to her husband during their Ottawa stint. Should anyone question any pertinent details of their reign, she is the keeper of private journals exceeding a thousand pages of handwritten notes on the Mulroney years. Brian refers to these diaries as his "ultimate protection—there is nothing like the revenge of a prime minister writing his own memoirs."

The relationship was not without its tensions, especially during his drinking days after his aborted run for the Tory leadership in 1976. At one point Mila packed up the kids and temporarily moved back to her parents' house. Another point of contention was her compulsive shopping, criticized as a self-indulgent excess in a country where being successful in politics demands a certain measure of drabness. When the prime minister pulled in to his favourite downtown Montreal hangout, better known as the Ritz Hotel, he asked Gilbert Lavoie, his press secretary, if he had seen Mila. "Don't worry, sir," was the reply. "It's six o'clock on a Saturday, and the stores are closed."

"Gilbert," Mila's husband replied, "even on a mere rumour that Mila's in town, all the stores in Place Ville Marie stay open till ten." (That was a variation on Mulroney's joke that his credit cards had been stolen but that he didn't bother reporting it because he was sure the thieves would spend less than Mila.) She bought about a dozen new outfits a year, favouring Canadian designers Leo Chevalier and Michel Robichaud, also slipping into Escada sportswear, Linda Lang sweaters and more precious labels. Her favourite jewellery depot is Bulgari. "She's the bargain hunter from hell," Sally Armstrong told me. "She can cut a deal even at those chains that carry designer clothes at deep discounts. That's not to say that she won't buy an Yves Saint Laurent jacket, or have one given to her."

But how much did Mila love politics? Mulroney's closest social, as opposed to political, friends privately speculated that in 1983, when Brian went back into politics, he made an unspoken pact with his wife that went something like this: despite all the grief and personal aggravation of his previous leadership foray, he would run again; if he succeeded and won the election that followed, Mila would become his active political partner, campaigning at his side, entertaining at the official residence, taking on a public role that, no matter how well she fitted it, went against her natural preference for luxury and privacy; in return, once they were back in civilian life, she could live in a splendour of her own choosing and buy anything, no questions asked. That has indeed been the case. Since they left government, she has vanished from the news, except for occasional sightings at their winter mansion in Palm Beach, at the large stone family home in Westmount or during her occasional jaunts to stay at Peter and Melanie Munk's or Helen and George Vari's apartments in Paris.

The Mulroneys' term in office wasn't the Camelot-on-the-Rideau they imagined it would be. It turned out to be an interregnum to the life that Mila really wanted.

—

Mila was the first child born to Dr. Dimitrije and Bogdanka Pivnicki, who had immigrated to Canada from Yugoslavia in 1958 after Mila's father accepted an offer to carry on with his research as a clinical psychiatrist. Mila's mother—a nurse in her homeland—had a tougher time adjusting to life in North America. In February 1985, just months after their son-in-law had become prime minister, the Pivnickis offered their views on their daughter's life, choices and future:

DIMITRIJE: One afternoon in 1972, Mila arrived home with Brian, who requested her hand in marriage. Brian was sitting over there, and I was sitting here, we were sitting somehow diagonally. She was nineteen when she met this gentleman, and we really did have mixed feelings. I could not object to the age difference, because I am twelve or thirteen years older than my wife.

BOGDANKA: Brian came on very strong, and I was the one who objected, but not to the age. I voiced my objection to Mila—which I will not reveal—before she married, and I never said anything again. I told her, "You're marrying a grown-up man, you will stop seeing your friends, you will have to grow up overnight." I certainly knew that he would have demands on her politically, because he asked her if she would be able to keep up in the same steps with him, in case he decided to run for the Conservative leadership.

DIMITRIJE: Mila had three semesters, at Concordia and later at McGill. At the end of the second year—actually before the semester was over in May—she married. We insisted from the beginning that she should try to finish her studies. I believe she was always an assertive girl, if I can say so. Always an assertive girl and, like all Bosnians, hard-headed. Even now, from time to time, I ask Mila when she's coming back to finish her degree, but being Mrs. Mulroney is a full-time job.

BOGDANKA: That was a difficult time after Brian's 1976 leadership loss. I told Mila, "Handle this lovingly."

NEWMAN: I remember his drinking and especially his bitterness with Lowell Murray, who had supported Flora MacDonald for the leadership. He was a hard case for a few years.

Years later, Mila reflected on that harsh defeat:
1976 was a good thump for him. I don't mean that in a bad way, and I was terribly sorry it happened—I wish it hadn't, but he got a chance to retrench, to think about what he

wanted with his life, whether he wanted to stay in law, go into business or go up north and write a book. That was probably the best thing that could have happened to him.

I had very little input that time; we had been married for three years. We're much closer now. In 1976, he didn't come to me and say, "Mila, what do you think?" as often as he does now.

The Pivnickis, as was the custom of most new Canadians in the 1950s and 1960s, originally leaned to the Liberals and admired Pierre Trudeau:
BOGDANKA: We are not politically minded, so our opinion doesn't really count, but we were Liberals before Mila met Brian.

DIMITRIJE: At least we were voting Liberal. When we came here, the Yugoslavs, the Serbian group here, which we joined, they were all Liberals.

BOGDANKA: And we really liked Trudeau. He's an intellectual. He's a man. We have admiration for him.

DIMITRIJE: Sure, and we have here somewhere a photograph where the three—Mila, Brian and Trudeau—are standing together.

Mila said her parents became Tory supporters almost overnight:
My father had a sort of quasi-love for the word "liberal," as most immigrants do. Sounds good, "Liberal." He came to Canada, and Trudeau was his age. We never really spoke about it, but I think they always voted for Trudeau until I decided to get involved with helping Michael Meighen [who ran for the Tories in Montreal and lost], and then they voted for Michael. I was a gofer. I answered the phone. I did all kinds of things.

Mila was driven into the arms of the Progressive Conservatives by Liberal cabinet minister Bud Drury:
I purposely went to hear Bud Drury speak—he gave a speech at McGill—and he had his fly down the entire speech. I thought, "My God, I can't vote for this man! He can't even zip up his fly, and doesn't have anybody there to tell him to zip it up."

Mila's mother believed that history would not be kind to her new son-in-law:
BOGDANKA: He likes to please people and he does please people, but I'm afraid he will not get anything in return. It's a tough world. Brian is a very smart man. He tries, hoping that if you do good it will come back. Maybe it will, but I am afraid for him.

DIMITRIJE: No, but we cannot influence that.

During the courtship, Mulroney told a disbelieving Mila that he intended to live at 24 Sussex Drive:
We never really discussed politics. On the third or fourth date, Brian told me he was the vice-president of the Conservative Party of Quebec. He told me one day that he would run for prime minister, and I said, "That's really nice." I sort of put it on the same page as, you know, "I'd like to be an astronaut and go to the moon."

That's not what he told Mila's biographer, Sally Armstrong:
They were not engaged yet, and he said, "I want to be prime minister." Mila told me that, but when I talked to him about it, because I wanted everything to be correct, he denied it. He said, "No, that's not true. I never said I wanted to be prime minister." God, they said that all over the place. The problem is, why does he tell stories that are not true? Why does he feel that he has to present himself as a perfect person?

Mulroney used to tease Mila about what would have happened if she had wed one of her other boyfriends:
BOGDANKA: He would say, "Mila, if you had married Andy, you would be pumping gas." And she would reply, "No, if I had married Andy, he would be prime minister."

As the 1983 Conservative leadership campaign was set to begin, Mila intended to keep a low profile:
My friend Janis Moores was the one who got me campaigning. On March 21, 1983, Brian announced he was running for the leadership. The day before, which was Brian's birthday, we'd had dinner with Janis and Allan Fotheringham. Brian told them, "We announce our candidacy tomorrow, and Mila goes back to Montreal with the kids." Janis said, "Mila, are you crazy doing that?" She was very right about that.

Mila looked out for Brian's interests fiercely:
If the minister is not in the House of Commons, Brian will pick up the question and that's why he becomes a target. I have a problem with that, because I don't find there's enough times that Brian Mulroney's name comes up when a minister is interviewed.

She regularly tried to take him away from the Parliament Hill frame of mind:
He doesn't have a mean bone in his body, there's just no malicious intent on his part anywhere that I've seen yet, and I've known him for a long time. He's loyal to friends, which some people see as negative. I don't. There's just no—I guess the colloquialism would be "ego-tripping." He just isn't that way. Having been exposed to the atmosphere out here, I know what enormous egos there are here in Ottawa. People who should never have them, have them. People think we go to Florida for the sake of Florida. It could be anywhere as long as he can be out of

the Ottawa mentality and the government mentality. He has to decompress a little, so I encourage trips.

Mila hated suck-ups:
It's not that I'm influential, it's that we think alike. There's a bond on the human issues of the country that I feel very, very much. We're on the same page. I won't hide anything, but I don't like being used as a tool. It happens a lot.

And Trudeau was not her pin-up boy:
All his ministers eulogized him; much of the Trudeau myth came from the people around him who built him up into this incredible messiah of the Liberal Party, endlessly repeating, "Oh, he was brilliant, the man is just so in touch." Pierre Trudeau, this short little ugly man, all of a sudden became a sex symbol.

And here's Brian, with this wonderful deep voice, these beautiful blue eyes, this generous nature and this wonderful sense of humour and his warmth. He's so warm, and there was Trudeau, cold as a cucumber.

I've met so many people in this way and I'm totally horrified. I met Placido Domingo in Paris, and he's not particularly tall, kind of a pyramid, big bulge in his stomach and kind of goofy. But when I saw him in *Othello*, I mean, he was just this unbelievable sex symbol with this voice.

She couldn't understand why voters and the media tagged Brian with the "sleaze" factor:
I have to be honest with you; there are very, very few people that I confide in totally. Brian and I really trust each other 100 per cent, and I don't know if that's very nice to say, but there's nothing that he can't say to me and there's nothing that I can't say to him, good, bad or indifferent, and it never gets repeated. There's no need to say, "Oh, don't tell anyone." There's just an assumption. I don't always like that because he would try the cabinet changes out on

me for three months and tell me not to tell anyone and everybody was pumping me. So I had to stay calm. A week is all right, but don't start three months ahead of time.

On what people said were her own profligate ways with the public purse:
John and Geills Turner did nothing to 24 Sussex the three months they were there. There was very little organization and a lot of strange people in there. There was a household co-ordinator who was very much like an ambassador in the house. The houses [Stornoway as well as 24 Sussex] do not come furnished. And when I had the rugs taken off the floors, there was no hardwood floor, it was just plywood because in 1949 when they redid the house, wall-to-wall was the in thing and it was the new rage and they had obviously worried about money and so they just laid carpet right on plywood floors. So faced with that, what am I going to do? I laid hardwood floors down. So I was faced with curtains and flooring and making it livable for six people, or at this time it was five. And that's what we did.

Other prime ministers spent more:
We put a lot of our own money into it and we put a lot of our own furniture into it, but because there was no access to information prior to [our tenure], any amount that we spent was too much. And it was a shock to me because we were really very careful, but Giovanni [Mowinckel] had been once through the revolving door of bureaucracy and he knew how it worked, how the system worked. He sent the money to the party and then the party paid for it and then Brian reimbursed the party. [Mulroney personally spent $211,796.68 for most of the interior decorating and furnishings at 24 Sussex Drive, as documented by the exchange of letters reproduced as Appendix D.]
So we were hurt by that scandal. But we have proved that we are not spendthrifts, because if we had been, there

would have been more stories about us. And every year reporters access us and they find that it was a one-time deal—we moved ourselves in, and we've tried to live within the confines. Now that they have this access to information, they just put down what we spent, what Turner spent and what Chrétien spent, and already our figure is much lower. Time will settle many of these questions.

Mila and Mulroney explain "Nanny-gate":
MILA: Tell Peter that story about Fred Doucet . . . You put your foot in it one day when you said, "I'll be damned if I'm going to let the public pay for my nanny."

MULRONEY: On that day Tom Charrington was asking me about the expenses in Ottawa—this was on his program in Hamilton. He said, "This guy Trudeau, the government pays for everything, he never puts his hand in his pocket for anything. There's a story that he's flying in these nannies from Scotland. What are you going to do if you're prime minister?" And I said, "I'll pay for my own nanny."

MILA: So Fred Doucet is now called upon to bail us out because they've caught us, you see—our so-called nanny that I call the "mother's helper" is being paid by the public. I thought there's nothing wrong in it, I'm there, and she is a mother's helper. So Fred's statement is, she's not a nanny, she's . . .

MULRONEY: She's an employee who interfaces with the children.

MILA: In a habitual way!

MULRONEY: It's bad enough that we were in deep trouble, this ruined us forever.

But overall the media spotlight was nothing to joke about:
MILA: You know when it hurts? It hurts when it's the children. I said it once on television. It was a really hot Canada Day, and we were sitting on the ground, you know how the set-up is—the shell in front of Parliament Hill. It was hot and my children were little and they had to behave for a whole hour and then they had to watch us for an hour, we have to shake hands. And they were so good. They put up with all this stuff.

Mark was wearing a little jacket and he had a drip of perspiration, so I took my finger and I was wiping it, and then there's a photo of me wiping his face and under the picture it says, "Mila Mulroney scolding one of her children." I mean, that made me so mad. Why would I scold him? He's just sitting there. But you see, people would read that and say, why would she be scolding this poor little angel? But those are the kinds of things that really anger me, and that's why I chose to appear less often.

If they could have seen into the future:
MILA: Brian was never terribly analytical as far as his own personality went. He was very rational and very reasonable, but never analytical. In a large measure, he was more spontaneous at the start. Then he learned that even a body motion or a gesture signified God knows what in this city. I always say ignorance was bliss. Look at the two of us on election night in 1984 with the blue background. If only we knew what was in store for us, we wouldn't be smiling.

Friend and babysitter Michael McSweeney on the Mila factor:
Derek Burney treats Mila as though he was talking to Brian because he knows how close they are. It really is a true partnership. And Brian seeks her counsel on almost everything, and so it was very refreshing to see that Mila's needs were being responded to equally with Brian's, because if she's down, then he's down, and he

needs her so much, especially at public functions. It's just incredible. He hesitates to go out to public functions without Mila. Brian needs that softening. If Mila is there, the tough questions don't get asked by journalists or by people who are just plain rude.

She put her own stamp on things, and constantly worked to be an asset to the prime minister:
MULRONEY: Mila's Christmas dinner takes place in the hall of the House of Commons. It used to be everybody gathered for drinks in the [House] leader's boardroom. When Mila came here, she said, absolutely not—this is going to be for spouses and it's going to be black tie, none of this junk about people in sports jackets coming for drinks. It's black tie, and we bring in an orchestra from Montreal. She hired a choir from Ottawa, and it's in the Hall of Honour of the Parliament Buildings. She doesn't even let the parliamentary restaurant cater it; the catering is done by the National Arts Centre restaurant. It's absolutely gorgeous. All of the spouses get a little gift from Mila, which is like a decoration for your Christmas tree. No one is allowed to come unless you're an MP or a senator, and your spouse or guest. It's the most sought-after occasion of the year. The women, the wives come in from the Prairies and from across the country, from British Columbia and Newfoundland. And then after the dinner and the sing-along and so on, there's an open bar with two dance bands. This is the night. Nothing like this ever took place before. It's part of forming a family. It's part of leadership. Leadership skills are not just picking up a phone and telling somebody to go screw off. I mean, nobody works for you anymore. They either work *with* you or they don't work at all.

Mila's assistant Bonnie Brownlee:
There's not a situation I've ever seen her go into that she couldn't handle. And she's quick—quick on her feet,

quick to think, sees a problem, knows what to do and never looks like she's stumbling. And he's an expert at that. I don't know whether it's through osmosis, or if she's just as good as he is, but I'll tell you, as a team they're unbelievable. They never miss a beat. They never stop. They're in stride. They see a problem and they just keep on moving. And as for staff people, it sure makes our jobs easier. There's a lot more that she can get herself involved in, but Mila herself will tell you it's a job with no point of reference.

NEWMAN: She's not really the First Lady.

BROWNLEE: No, she's not. Mr. Sauvé is.

NEWMAN: I'll quote you.

BROWNLEE: He probably wouldn't like that.

Frank Moores:
Mila's not only attractive, she's not only a fashion plate, she is bright. I'll tell you how bright. Mila stood right next to Brian for the last month of the 1984 campaign, and she could spot the audience when he was starting to get in his "one of the boys" moods, and every time he'd start to get carried away, she would tug on his jacket and he'd come right back. She was the best political analyst on the bloody tour. That's a fact. She is fantastic. I mean, they really are a terrific couple.

Stanley Hartt figured Mila had a tough time when Mulroney switched from private enterprise to public service:
She misunderstood the standard of living that a prime minister is entitled to in the Canadian culture. The people of France would find nothing wrong with the style of her furnishings or her dresses. There is an elegance

demanded of the head of government in a sophisticated country like that. I mean, no one would dream of criticizing Mitterrand for the cost of a couch in his house. That was the kind of model she was looking at.

Mila knew what a lawyer at Ogilvy earns and what a president of the Iron Ore earns. She knew how a house is obtained when one really can't afford a house—the device of an interest-free or low-interest loan for corporate executives is built right into the Tax Act. It's considered a legitimate business expense by a company because you entertain there.

But when the time came to be in Ottawa, she ceased to have any conception. The house is provided, it's free, and so we're talking about upgrades: how is that financed, how is clothing financed, how are private schools financed? The prime minister gets $185,000 before tax and pays for his own food and the total expenditure nut. She sort of thought that someone would provide.

He acknowledged how important Mulroney's wife was to his performance and demeanour:
I remember this was at the summit in France in 1989, seeing him come to the door of the room, which had two hundred journalists there, and he whispered, "Where's Mila?" I mean, he was literally physically unable to go into the room without her there. I think that's great. What she does for him is support of the kind that every man would want in a relationship with a woman. Mila is magnificent.

Bill Pristanski:
For a while, there were as many press requests for interviews with her as there were for the boss. It was a constant struggle, and a tough, tough situation. Nobody ever had to deal with someone as dynamic as Mila. The campaign strategists and the RCMP originally treated her as second fiddle, and that was the best way to motivate her to do even more work.

Shirley Corn on her friend Mila's sense of style:
You put Mila in a Marks & Spencer, she goes in, bang, bang, bang. She puts it all together and looks like she stepped out of *Vogue*. Mila's not a snob. How many people can you say that about today? Look at anybody who has "made it." They don't have the humility that this girl has, and the voters felt it. Mila is a very special person. It's almost like walking down the street and meeting a friendly puppy. You're sort of taken with its friendliness, and then your second question is, "Why is this puppy so friendly? Is it lost?"

Corn recalled their first encounter:
When I met her, she was so warm and delicious that you really had to step back, because, you know, we're a little more leery as we grow older, and we sort of wonder, what is it? She said, "You must come over and meet my husband, you'll absolutely love him." So when my husband got home from the office I told him.

At about 8:30, the phone rang and it was Mila, saying, "Why aren't you here? I'm coming right over to get you." And there she was, taking her apron off at the time she was walking around to get us.

She was always like that. People tend to think that she's this way because of Brian. I'm sure that it's accentuated what she had, but it was there to begin with. She wants to get to know people. She gets into you. She won't let you be superficial. She'll have nothing to do with you if you are—she has no time for people like that. She wants to know all about you, and I'm that way too, so we really hit it off.

At first I felt crushed that I was never going to live up to what this girl can do with a bat of her eyelash. On the other hand, she gave me the courage to do things that I thought I could never possibly do. I love being next to people who are that positive and that aggressive, because it washes off on you. That's very true for most people.

Arthur Campeau was less enthused:
A large part of his problem was Mila. I mean, at a time when the entire country had the highest rate of unemployment and was in the throes of a recession, people being thrown out of work and God knows what else, and everybody was pulling in his belt, Mila was out shopping at Holt Renfrew. Jesus.

By the same token, I know how enamoured Brian is of the Kennedys—that aura, that mystery. He had hoped that somehow we could overcome our inferiority complex and could have black-tie dinners in Ottawa and invite leading Canadian artists, and create this sort of aura of our own. It didn't work.

Hartt begged to differ:
She stayed out of Hillary Rodham Clinton territory, trying to be prime minister in bed, which she never did. I witnessed only one exception in all the time I was there, five whole years—there was this one occasion where she made one off-handed remark on policy. Everything else was pure support. Everything else was kids, and she's done a magnificent job.

I mean, those four kids—they were unbelievable when they first came to Ottawa, and they're more unbelievable now. I don't know where she found the time to take care of them and raise them to be such presentable, self-assured, intelligent youngsters.

No one would loathe her husband, Mila thought, if they could see him at home:
He's a person who really has a good heart. I've seen the hours he puts in and the stress that he's under, and he always comes back, he always makes time for the children and for his mother and for me, and even if the country is in crisis, he makes time for that too. So he thinks of himself very little, and people are not used to selfless people. They're not; they're used to an ego society.

But where were all the people who supposedly hated him, Mila wondered:

This past year we've done six or seven fundraising dinners across the country. Brian does his speech, more of a lecture, saying, "This is what we're doing, this is why we're doing it and if you have any questions I'd like to respond to them." That was the format. After that, he does half the room and I do half the room. I didn't get one negative comment. Basically, the companies buy the tables and then they fill them, so it's not necessarily our supporters who are there. And many of the people were business-oriented, but they were also there to learn. Why is this man so disliked? Why is he doing this? Most of them left quite impressed. They didn't hit me up on what I call the single issues. They didn't hit me on abortion. They didn't hit me on any of the ones that they felt the government had erred on. And that was the same case throughout the country. I felt that what was good about it was that everybody was going to go home and talk to a person.

Blaming Trudeau:

When you ask where the breakdown comes from [between the man she knew and the public figure], and maybe this is totally foolhardy on my part, but I think it comes from people who really do not want to know him any better. They have lived with that political attitude of public life and private life—Trudeau certainly had it for sixteen years—you're going to get what I'm going to give you and that's it. Brian is not like that.

Mila on Chrétien:

The one thing that I know about Chrétien is that he's a really good family man and I know his daughter very well, France, and I like her a lot—a bright girl, really bright and a really good mother. You could see how intelligent she is with her children—she has three boys and one girl—married to Andy Desmarais, who is a very talented young man who is a really good thinker, and I like Aline Chrétien, what I know of her, very well.

But where Jean Chrétien is not good is that he thought that history would carry him and that his reputation would carry him. But he also thought that he could do it without any work. John Turner did that too. Neither of them were workers. Brian's success is that he's a worker. He never leaves anything to chance. If there's a good speech, it's because he worked on it for many hours. He never gets a speech ten minutes before and reads it, ever. It's always been worked on and the French has been worked on.

On the charge of cronyism:
Brian is very loyal to his friends—his friends have been very, very important to him. And you know it's a bit of a sticky wicket, because people assume that Canada is very large and that the political arena just beckons to everyone and that no one turns it down. Well, there are a lot of people who don't want to have anything to do with politics, so you find yourself in a position of leadership and you need to entice people to come to work for you. You can search out and many of the people that you search out are your friends.

Mila refused to attend Lucien Bouchard's wedding:
When Brian made Bouchard ambassador, I assumed he knew exactly what he was doing, and since I didn't know enough about Lucien, I didn't question it all that much. Personally, I was not overly impressed with him. I always had a bad feeling about him. As a matter of fact, when Bouchard left his first wife, Jocelyne, and married Audrey, Brian held a little reception for the family in Sussex and I chose not to be there. Brian had them without me. I just had other things to do. I don't do that very often, but I just didn't like the way everything was handled.

Sam Wakim, on the other hand:

MILA: Sam Wakim is my buddy. I have to tell you, I always put Sam into perspective. He has eight sisters, he was the baby. The fact that he's walking and talking in a normal way is to me a total surprise. I mean, I see my three boys and they have one sister and she is in charge and has to know what they're up to every minute. I mean, imagine, here's the baby of a Lebanese family, the son is born and the sisters play a dominant role in his life. Then he meets a man that's like his brother, Brian Mulroney—just like his brother—and he watches the evolution of this man and probably does things in business with Brian's consent. He's a loner, and he is sort of hooked onto Brian and lives vicariously through him. It's a long, long friendship.

Bouchard and Trudeau were "peas in a pod" according to Mila:

I put what Lucien did in the league of Trudeau coming out against Meech Lake. Trudeau was with us in Toronto at Cardinal Carter's the night before he went public with his opposition. I think it was the Cardinal's seventieth birthday, and Trudeau was on the dais and we were on the dais and Peterson was there, and Trudeau shook Brian's hand, and that night he could have said, "I'm coming out against you tomorrow on Meech Lake." But he never did—he went out and he laid out his own platform the following morning, I think it was on *Canada AM*.

And it's the same—you see, a gentleman or a person who truly believes in what they're doing can look you in the eye and say, "Look, you've been very nice, you've been very fair, but I don't believe in it and I have to go my way and I won't hurt you and I respect you but I want, for the record, to tell you where I stand." That to me is somebody with some kind of backbone.

Trudeau and Lucien are two peas in a pod. They think of themselves first, everything else second. Because you see, the policies of the previous government, none of the policies would have turned out this way had the man not only thought of himself. He didn't care much for the economy so he didn't meddle in it. Let's build up the deficit. He cared about the Constitution but not enough to negotiate, not cnough to stroke, not enough to work with it. He wanted to bring this constitution home at any cost. It's just never happened before, where a prime minister that has left has come back to haunt you.

Bouchard's were sins of commission:
I remember there was this article in the newspaper which said that the PQ were recruiting from the Tory caucus— it was a headline in either *Le Devoir* or *La Presse,* it was one of the French papers, saying they had infiltrated the party. Brian was quite perturbed about the whole thing, so there was a meeting. Often for me the best thing to do is to step back and observe, so I did. He called in Lucien because he was his Quebec lieutenant, and it was an interesting scene, because I was upstairs getting dressed and there was a balcony so I could look down and see what was going on. Lucien was saying, "Oh, Brian, there's nothing to worry about, you have nothing to worry about, just relax." I mean, he was saying to Brian, "Oh, there's no truth to this." Now you have the proof that he was part of the whole set-up to shaft his friend.

Mila disapproved of the way Bouchard used his second wife:
Audrey is terrific. First of all, she's very beautiful, she's bubbly, she's bright, but after he left and broke off with the Conservative Party and Brian, she would go to my hairdresser in Ottawa. I never thought very much of it— still, it was funny how we were scheduled. I had not seen her once prior to that, and then the next two appointments that she had were scheduled at the same time as my two appointments. So I go into this little private room and I have my hair coloured, she came in and she had tears in

her eyes and she said, "I'm really sorry about what happened." I said, "Audrey, I have no problem with you and I wish you and the baby all the best, but as far as I'm concerned, Lucien Bouchard does not exist. I will have nothing to do with him."

And I know for a fact that he had her make phone calls because he wanted to get out of his lease and Camille Guilbault—who works for us in the office—her husband, Michael, owns the building. So Lucien had Audrey phone Camille and say, "Will it be all right if we got out of it?" And they said, absolutely not, this is a business transaction and business is business and friendship is friendship. Lucien used her like that, he tried to.

Bouchard's betrayal on top of the loss of Meech Lake were the worst moments for Brian:
MILA: I've never seen him as hurt or as sad. I've never seen him as devastated—at least, I thought it was devastating—as when Meech Lake died. For him it was one of the most important things because he really felt that Quebec had been misunderstood in all of this. He genuinely felt that if Quebec was in the fold and it could be just laid to rest, that everything would go on as normal, so that Lucien just compounded it. The amending formula that was put in front of him that he had to use was so faulty.

Mila on her husband's naïveté:
I don't blame Brian. That's what makes him good, that's what makes him who he is, and I really don't want him to change. If more people were like him, we'd have a much better system. But if you're going to assume that everybody is evil, he's just not like that. I'm much more suspicious, much more suspicious. He's not suspicious—it's just not in his nature. He really thinks the best of people and I don't think you're going to meet one person who is going to tell you otherwise. His mother is like that, his mother is

really genuinely a nice person. She raised him in an atmosphere of trust and hard work and that's the way he is and it has served him so well to this point that he had no reason to be otherwise. In business, in labour negotiations, he was who he was because of what he exuded on those one-to-one meetings, and so you can't take that away. And it only doesn't work in an environment where the people are in that "gotcha" frame of mind.

Mila prohibited TV news in the bedroom:
My sleep is better, I'm better off if I don't watch the news. Will life change if I don't know exactly what's going on at eleven o'clock at night? My life doesn't. So if Brian wants to stay with me, there won't be any news on. And often he does—for example, he did not follow the news through the holidays. Brian said, I want to stay here, and the rule of thumb is that we don't watch the news. You can read the morning papers, I won't take that away from you. The one thing about Florida is that we don't get Canadian news—he gets the clippings, but you get away from all the nonsense, the gossip, who is saying what, and that's really why I go. I love it here, but I go and then I worry about what Farrah Fawcett is doing with Ryan O'Neal. I mean, this is my biggest crisis of the holiday and it's totally irrelevant.

After the failure of Meech:
Now the weight of the job is certainly on his shoulders. This constitutional thing has been very important to him—very, very important to him. He wants to right this wrong more than he wants to do anything. And it is a question of the right time, and as a negotiator he knows what is necessary.

On her husband's political beliefs:
He believes we have riches, we have resources, we have manpower, we have a country that's not as productive as

it should be, and so if we go on our past history, there's a lot of changes that have to be made and these are the changes as he sees them. He's also very interested in international affairs. He wants the country to be respected and from that standpoint he's been very successful. I think that by virtue of the fact that [George H.] Bush phones him weekly . . .

NEWMAN: He does?

MILA: Oh yeah, Bush. So Brian really doesn't have sort of an entrenched conservative philosophy, and he believes that the economy is the only thing that could keep the country strong and that a productive society can keep the country strong. When he says a job is the best social policy, he believes in that.

Stanley Hartt credits Mila for a wonderful decompression job after Mulroney retired:
She's extremely admirable for what she's done for him. Just look at what happened when he left office. The first thing she did was she got him out of the country for four weeks—brilliant. There's a guy who works the phone, but the government was not paying for the phone calls anymore. You could have a million-dollar phone bill very fast with that guy. She took him to a place where he couldn't get a Canadian newspaper, couldn't find out what the fuck was happening.

The dirty dozen

———

Some People Who Really Bugged Him

"NAZIS": THE RAT PACK

Mulroney's nemesis in the House of Commons was the Rat Pack, a loose assembly of young Liberal MPs who relied on shock tactics. The group—which included Sheila Copps, Brian Tobin, Don Boudria and John Nunziata—capitalized on John Turner's shaky leadership and the indulgence of the Speaker of the House, John Bosley, to savage Mulroney at every opportunity.

Mulroney minced no words:
The Rat Pack? These are Nazis. They deal in lies and calumnies. They are the worst kind. The Liberals developed this Nazi-style caliper—tell a lie often enough about somebody and people will believe it.

Copps and the F-word:
MULRONEY: I'm in Question Period and to my absolute

horror, I'm getting the shaft for being the co-chairman of the UN Summit on Children. Then finally this guy from Winnipeg gets up and accuses me of bringing in these children from across the country to have a photo op. And I said in a very loud voice—very loud voice—"That vulgar bastard. What a vulgar bastard to say something like that before Christmas on an event that involves children, I can't believe it." I could care less who heard me, what do I care? Then Sheila Copps comes out and said I used the words "fucking bastard," which of course I never did.

It was a lie, but to show you the hypocrisy and the cant and the unprincipled nature of the House of Commons and its members, when I went back upstairs to my office on the second floor, there were about fifty reporters and they were not interested in the children— all they were interested in is whether I used the words "fucking bastard" . . .

That night on television they led with Sheila Copps fabricating a falsehood. So what happened? The media should have been after Sheila Copps to apologize to me, but not a word. The case we made for children, gone down the sewer because the media were chasing around the House of Commons asking me whether I used those words. They weren't interested in the word "bastard." No one is interested in that. It was the "fucking," and I had never used it. Sheila is a partisan but she's also her own worst enemy and she'll never be a leader because she has no judgment. She never knows when to stop.

Chief press secretary Bill Fox thought Mulroney made matters worse:
I don't think the prime minister should take questions from anybody except the leaders of the two opposition parties. You get the short fuse because Sheila Copps is just egging him on, egging him on. If he doesn't get up, Sheila Copps is nobody; she doesn't make *The National*. Let them hoot and holler. Nunziata is a psycho—he makes the

wildest accusations, completely unsubstantiated. If the prime minister gets up, he gives them legitimacy.

I like Bosley a lot, but he's completely ineffective. Jim McGrath told the prime minister the other day that in his estimation—and this is a guy who's been around since 1957—80 per cent of the questions put to the prime minister are out of order and should be ruled out.

Pat MacAdam, caucus liaison at the time, agreed with Fox about the role of the Speaker:
People are totally dismayed with the man's performance. Bosley would allow a member like the NDP's Raymond Skelly or Lorne Nystrom to call the prime minister a phony. Liberals like George Baker and Brian Tobin were allowed these long preambles as well.

Charley McMillan had another suggestion:
What we should have is a deputy prime minister, like Erik Nielsen, with no other responsibilities. He takes the crap in the House, sits on committees, rides herd on a whole bunch of things and allows Brian to perceive the big picture. Erik can turn it on with the best of them. You can't have the prime minister going after Sheila Copps, or saying, "I will resign if . . ." He's a role model for a lot of young people.

Sam Wakim took a cue from his old friend and blamed the media:
The media have Sheila Copps and Nunziata as stars who can shout "fuck off" the loudest and who can say the most vulgar, wild things. When you couple that with the fact that what you've got is the *Ottawa Sun,* the *Toronto Star,* the CBC giving everybody who wants to call Mulroney a liar, a crook and a fraud the front page. It's theirs. I mean, they can go to the bag lady down the street to call Mulroney a cocksucker or something, and it's all on the front page.

The agenda of the Opposition is based on going into the House and applying a new type of terrorism with the Speaker's complacency. Mulroney only has to go there a couple of times and maintain civility, maintain a sense of decorum. It may cost you a little bit of your sense of humour and you'd have to bite your tongue a little more. I mean, my instinct, we would just call them a bunch of rotten whores, and kiss my ass and don't bother me.

"A ROTTEN SON OF A BITCH": PATRICK WATSON

Mulroney spent months pondering whom to appoint as chair of the Canadian Broadcasting Corporation. Names like Barbara Frum and Adrienne Clarkson were thrown about, but in 1989 he finally picked Patrick Watson, of This Hour Has Seven Days *fame.*

At first, Mulroney was all excuses:
I'm getting criticized for holding up some appointments, but I would rather take a little more time—these people are really hard to find. It's hard to believe the negativism and the cynicism, but the jobs that have to be filled will be filled. I'm getting an awful lot of negativism about Watson, and you'd think I'd be talking from the right-wing conservatives, but not a bit! I'm getting this from people that I would have instinctively associated with his friends. I'm just astonished that I was his only defender. I was really astonished. I'm thinking, why not Barbara Frum? How is she regarded? Is she a Meech Lake supporter? I suppose she could run the CBC as well as anybody else.

NEWMAN: But would she move to Ottawa?

MULRONEY: That is the big question. The answer, I suppose, is no. She's rich. But Patrick Watson is a good man.

Under Watson, the CBC was put on housecleaning mode. Mulroney thought the problems at the public broadcaster were brought about by former president Pierre Juneau:

Juneau went out of his way. As soon as you've said we have to cut back, he'd rush out and cut regional programming. He was blackmailing the government. One of the reasons I wanted Watson in there is I thought that Watson would play ball in the best sense of the word. And he knows the government is going through tough times. It's not that we want to hurt the CBC, but they know there's fat all over the place.

Then Watson began to criticize the government:
MULRONEY: Watson is an unrelieved disaster. And I really overrode my whole cabinet. Every single one of them said Patrick Watson would be a disaster, the worst thing that ever happened to public broadcasting. And I put him in there. His failure is kind of universally acknowledged today, inside as well, because I do have a few friends in the CBC, and people say Patrick has been a disaster. That's what they tell me, from inside the CBC.

Mulroney felt as if he had been stabbed in the back:
It's quite true that I said to Watson that I would consult with him before appointing directors to the CBC board. And then he denounced me, when all I did was quote quite accurately what he had said. And for that, Watson crapped all over me. I may cancel his appointment, because of his mean-spirited calling of the press in to denounce me for something I never said. Watson is a rotten son of a bitch. I said to Roy Faibish [a Diefenbaker Tory who was a good friend and advisor to Mulroney], "You tell Watson to stay the fuck out of my way." He begged for the CBC job for twenty years. He lobbied for it, got it from me and, without any provocation, turned and attacked me.

There's something in the air in Ottawa that some of them take in. Watson is asking to be bought out, but we'll be cruel and let him stay in his job. He hates it. We've surrounded him with commissioners who hate him. This is making his life miserable and he'll have to leave within a year, but without any buyout. I was trying to protect him against being fired by the Liberals, but he asked to be bought out. I wouldn't buy him out, fuck him. He will go this coming fall—he's through—with no compensation, that's why I'm not going to buy him out.

"BITTER, MALICIOUS": ERIK NIELSEN

Mulroney's former deputy prime minister publicly alleged that he quit politics because of his aversion to patronage.

There seemed no way to keep the guy happy:
MULRONEY: One thing I've heard, and it's quite disturbing, is that Erik Nielsen in his book is really bitter, malicious throughout. Particularly nasty about me. First, Nielsen believes I jettisoned him in the Sinclair Stevens thing, and therefore he left under a cloud, humiliated and so on. Second, because I came in promising to get rid of patronage and to his dismay it was patronage as usual. The real problem with Erik's chairmanship was that he was so partisan that I had to remove him, but one of his first requests was that Chris Pearson—the defeated government leader—be made consul general in Dallas, which I had to turn down for obvious reasons. And then I gave Erik one of the finest patronage jobs that exist; he's the chairman of the National Transportation Agency. He's making around $150,000 a year with a chauffeur and a limousine, and will be able to leave with a second pension because of the biggest patronage plum available. This job, which he has now, is the highest patronage appointment I can give. Erik feels that I apparently abandoned him

because he was left to defend Sinclair Stevens in the House of Commons. That is the price you pay when you're deputy prime minister. If Erik hadn't done it, I would have done it, but I was not here. I was with Prince Charles opening Expo '86 and then the Tokyo Summit and a state visit to China and Korea.

He says the reason he didn't run for leader in 1983 was because I knew that he had fathered an illegitimate child. I did know, but I didn't even tell my wife—I respected his privacy and confidentiality.

So I spoke to Erik again and he said to me, do you think I could be ambassador to Washington? And I said, "Erik, look, let me talk to Joe, but I doubt it." And I talked to Joe and he said—you know the answer to that, the answer of course is no . . . I didn't know that Erik was getting angry. And he came to feel that I was dragging my feet and I wasn't promoting his interests enough.

Ray Hnatyshyn believed he knew what was behind Nielsen's criticism of the prime minister:
MULRONEY: Ray said, "The real story is that Nielsen wanted to be named chief justice of the Yukon." At the time, Ray went to the Canadian Bar Association Committee on Judicial Appointments [on Nielsen's behalf] and they turned him down. They rejected Nielsen as being unqualified. And Nielsen started to berate Hnatyshyn, for not having it done. Nielsen said to Ray, "The prime minister owes this to me, and I want him to override the selection committee of the Canadian Bar Association and appoint me to the bench."

And Nielsen writes about how badly his heart was breaking, and all he wanted to do was to get rid of patronage. I mean, Christ, if the CBC knew what really happened, they'd have the biggest story of the year. Even the press who don't like me would say, "Jesus Christ, the guy's making a quarter of a million dollars a year."

Marjory LeBreton on dealing with Nielsen:
I was never an Erik Nielsen fan. As a matter of fact, I quite disliked him. I thought, "Oh, geez, don't tell me we've got to put up with that jerk again." A mean, mean man. I once took on Erik Nielsen and called him a self-serving male chauvinist for criticizing patronage. In his book, he wrote, "I thought it would be different, we wouldn't be as tolerant about patronage." And then he took the biggest appointment of them all.

We eventually got rid of him. That meeting I was telling you about on November 30, 1992? Remember I told you? I was drinking coffee with Brian and I said, "We should be raising a toast today, we should be celebrating something." And he said, "What's that?" I told him, "Today is the day Erik Nielsen's appointment to the National Transportation Commission runs out!"

"NOT A RATIONAL PERSON": PAT CARNEY

An economist and former journalist, Carney was Mulroney's energy minister, charged with deconstructing the National Energy Program. Then, in the international trade portfolio, she was a key player in the free trade negotiations in Washington. She lobbied hard for her Senate seat but promised to relinquish it in return for being appointed chairman of Canada Place in Vancouver. She never submitted her resignation.

When told that the former international trade minister was writing a tell-all book about her years in cabinet, Mulroney chuckled:
She ain't going to get the time of day, and let me just tell you this, if she wrote a book—I mean, if it sold five thousand copies that would be a huge, huge success. I'd be surprised if it sold two thousand or three thousand. Who the hell is Pat Carney?

I want to point out that when Norman Atkins was campaign chairman for Bill Davis, he demanded total loyalty from the Ontario caucus for Davis. Finlay MacDonald, when he was campaign chairman for Bob Stanfield, demanded the same thing. Janis Johnson, who worked for the Conservative Party and who has been a child of the Conservative Party, demanded the same thing. And now they don't give it to me. Carney, by doing what she did— by not stepping down when I asked her—Carney deprived me of the opportunity of somebody like Lyall Knott [a Vancouver lawyer and Mulroney loyalist]. She told me she was going to give me the appointment and she never did. She fooled around like she always does. Her conduct has not been the conduct of a rational person. Lyall was supposed to have her seat.

LeBreton said Carney played hard-to-get during important debates in the Senate:
I called Pat Carney and they said she wasn't in the office yet. I left an urgent message for her to call back. I called her again; they said she was in the office but on the phone, that she would call me back as soon as she was off the phone. She didn't call me back. I called her again, they said she'd gone to the washroom; they would have her call me. So I called her again, and they said she'd gone to the Chamber. This is kind of over the course of a morning and lunch. I phoned the whip's office and I asked them to take a note into Pat in the Chamber, which they did. She didn't call me back. That was Pat Carney.

Of all the Senate appointments we made, that the prime minister made, Pat Carney's appointment brought forth more outrage from the party and non-party people than any other. This idea that she speaks only for women, give me a break. She'll use stereotypical arguments, and all she did in my view, she substantiated in many people's minds, particularly in men, that women expected special treatment.

As far as LeBreton was concerned, Carney was no feminist: Carney called Mulroney and said, "There's rumours around that you're going to resign—don't do it. You're the only person who can keep the coalition together; we'll lose all the Quebec caucus. I know Kim Campbell. She's shallow, she's only interested in herself, she's only in it for herself, she'll destroy the party." Pat was a "great defender of women," and here she was, attacking Kim. Pat once asked me if she could be a senator and chairman of the Asia Pacific Foundation at the same time.

"PROMOTED BEYOND HIS COMPETENCE":
RAYMOND CHRÉTIEN

Jean's nephew was a mid-level diplomat when Mulroney was elected, and Mulroney took him under his wing. Then a scandal over preferential treatment of an Iraqi national, Mohammed al-Mashat, led to the end of several political careers.

Mulroney, on the Chrétien family's conflicting allegiances: When I got here, Raymond Chrétien's highest-ranking position was ambassador to Zaire. I'm the one who made Raymond Chrétien, which he will acknowledge and has acknowledged to everybody. I made Raymond Chrétien. I appointed him ambassador to Mexico. Then I offered him Rome, and he asked for the associate deputy minister's job instead, and I gave him the job. Everyone told me that I had promoted him much beyond his competence, but I did it because I felt that he was a good guy and that there was a role for a younger francophone in the department in that area.

What do I know about the al-Mashat thing? Well the answer is, I know absolutely nothing. All I know is that Allan Gotlieb phoned up Raymond Chrétien privately and asked Chrétien to do something for this guy al-Mashat and apparently in some way something was done. Chrétien's way of expressing his gratitude to me for what I had done for him was this: his daughter, Caroline, who lived at his house, joined the staff of the leader of the Opposition and was in charge of the Opposition's attack on Barbara McDougall in the al-Mashat hearings.

So you had the following situation: Raymond Chrétien's daughter leaves his home in the morning to work for the leader of the Opposition to undermine my government. When the al-Mashat thing was over, Lloyd Axworthy gave a cocktail party for the Liberals—and this was reported in the *Ottawa Citizen*—where he paid a particular tribute to Caroline Chrétien, thanking her for her indispensable contribution to hurting Barbara McDougall's career—Barbara McDougall being, incidentally, the minister to whom Raymond Chrétien was the deputy. Can you believe it? I gave Raymond the two biggest promotions of his life.

"TREATED ME VERY SHABBILY": STEPHEN LEWIS

Mulroney appointed the former Ontario NDP leader as Canada's ambassador to the United Nations.

When Mulroney assessed which politicians inexplicably abandoned him, Lewis was near the top of the list: My first ambassadorial appointment was Stephen Lewis. I feel that someday, if I have nothing to do, I will write a couple of paragraphs about people who had accepted my friendship and support and for no reason that I could discern, quite frankly, turned around and treated my wife and me and my government very shabbily.

Just one of many ingrates:
MARJORY LeBRETON: There are people that took the positions but also were recipients of some very personal

kindness from the prime minister. Stephen Lewis. After Lewis said all the things he said, he falls off the stage and breaks his hip, and there is the prime minister calling him and consoling him. Why won't they say these things? Would they be tainted if it was ever thought that they were treated kindly by the prime minister?

"A MAN OF NO HONOUR": KEITH SPICER

Mulroney had fought many Tories over his choice of Spicer for the top job at the Canadian Radio-television and Telecommunications Commission.

Mulroney:
I appointed Spicer to the CRTC job, and the only communication that I had with him came when he was under very serious personal attack from the Liberals and the NDP in the House. The Rat Pack was in full cry about everything, from his morals to his administrative skills, and they wanted the whole thing folded because he had ruined it. I defended him for three or four days in the House. I was told through the grapevine that Spicer was pretty depressed by everything. So I gave him a call, told him to hang in there.

In 1991, Spicer acted as chair of the Citizens' Forum on Canada's Future, which collected the opinions of more than 75,000 Canadians across the country. The findings demonstrated a growing aversion to politicians, a patent objection to bilingualism and the rejection of special status for Quebec. The group was supposed to issue a report to the prime minister on Canada Day but instead released a scathing preliminary brief in April:
MULRONEY: The morning I accepted the Citizens' Forum report, none of the other commissioners knew that Spicer had written this addendum to the report. He betrayed his

own colleagues on the commission. Politicians are duplicitous in the extreme, but this one takes the cake. Spicer was getting heat from Roy MacGregor of the *Ottawa Citizen,* one of the leading Mulroney-haters here. To buy his peace with him, Spicer engaged in this little secret, denouncing me for all the country's problems. Now nobody wants him back.

Spicer spoke to Glen Shortliffe, begging for the CRTC job back, and Shortliffe said, "Well, Christ, nobody in the country wants you, Keith." I imagine least of all the broadcasters. Spicer is a man of no honour, and now you know why the country's in trouble.

According to LeBreton, once again Mulroney had miscalculated:
Keith Spicer said to an acquaintance of Derek Burney when the prime minister put him as head of the Citizens' Forum, "If that son of a bitch thinks that I'm going to be the front and make him look good, he's got another think coming because I hate his guts and I'll stab him in the back." And by God, isn't that exactly what he did do? Spicer, through the Meech Lake process, wrote some very, very positive columns and editorials. It was almost as though the prime minister, by reading those editorials, kind of interpreted that this person would be onside with him. Some people would say that that's a character flaw, whereas it's very understandable because he just kind of takes people sort of at face value in what they say.

"THE BLESSED VIRGIN MARY": PRESTON MANNING AND THE REFORM PARTY

The birth of the Reform Party did not affect Mulroney personally as much as had the emergence of the Bloc Québécois. Mulroney considered Manning and his allies to be chauvinists, and claimed that there could be no plausible justification for purported "western alienation" when he had scrapped damaging Liberal legislation and three Albertans held key posts in his cabinet.

Mulroney on Manning's baby:
The Reform Party is anti-everything. There's a really deep, deep-seated racism there. I still don't know what to make of Reform. I know that for the moment it's growing, but these are one-trick ponies. They're not standing on a whole lot of sound ground—it's all negative.

He wondered where Reform was finding its foothold:
I went out there quite often and I sat down and talked to Albertans, and they were very clear. They wanted more influence in the federal cabinet, in the decision-making process. So today you have Don Mazankowski in Finance, Joe Clark in Constitutional Affairs and Harvie Andre as government leader. They said that they wanted the National Energy Program scrapped. We did that. They said they wanted the Foreign Investment Review Agency scrapped. We did that. They said they wanted deregulation of the industry and the transportation system. We did that. They said they wanted free trade with the United States. We did that. We've done it all. I know that no Canadian government can or ever will do as much for Western Canada as my government did. That I know. More than Diefenbaker. Oh, by a long shot.

We increased grants to western agriculture by 650 per cent in six years. We moved the head office of the National Energy Board to Calgary. We moved the Western Diversification Office to Edmonton. No government in history has ever, ever given Western Canada this kind of attention and this kind of results.

One of the reasons why I'm quite calm about it all is that I know that it's just a matter of time before they'd be saying, "Boy, we were better off with Mulroney." But now people propose to vote Reform? All you're going to do is elect the NDP. A vote for Reform is a vote for the extreme left wing.

Preston Manning attacked the Charlottetown deal as the "Mulroney Accord":
MULRONEY: Manning painted himself as being different from the rest of us lowlife—he was like the Blessed Virgin Mary and the rest of us were a bunch of pretty bad actors. The Canadian people are capable of great acts of stupidity, but even when they are being stupid, they know what's going on. They know that the Charlottetown agreement is not the Mulroney deal.

In the lead-up to the 1993 election, Mulroney could not understand why Albertans weren't thanking the Tories for all his government did for the west, and why they weren't supporting Kim Campbell:
MULRONEY: The psychos are not loose on the streets of Quebec. They're elsewhere. Kim Campbell is not some frog from Baie-Comeau, even though the frog from Baie-Comeau gave the west more power and more money and more prosperity. I gave them everything they said they wanted. But I'm a frog from Baie-Comeau—this had to be done by some pure westerner. The fact that so many ministers came from the west was not good enough.

After Campbell's resounding defeat, Mulroney still believed Manning was no national alternative:
There are serious reasons for thoughtful people to conclude that Jean Charest will, in a reasonable period of time—not tomorrow or next year—be prime minister of Canada. I have great confidence in him and great confidence in his capacity to lead. What you need now is a good man or a good woman with some refreshing ideas, an articulate young person with access to a television camera, and you can go from 2 seats to 152 seats overnight. It's a brand-new dynamic.

"SHE'S RUINED HERSELF IN THE PARTY":
MAUREEN McTEER

*John Crosbie, the Newfoundland court jester who was
finance minister in Joe Clark's brief government, kept a
Dali reproduction of Christ's crucifixion above his desk in
St. John's—a draped female figure looking up at Christ
with stoic concern. When John Fraser, then with the* Globe
and Mail, *asked him about the painting, Crosbie replied as
sarcastically as he knew how: "That's my beloved leader
Joe Clark, up on that cross."*

"It is? Then who's the female figure?" Fraser asked.

"Ah, that's Maureen. She put him there."

*Anybody who knew her or heard of her had a Maureen
McTeer story. Brian Mulroney was no exception.*

Mulroney thought he gave McTeer what she wanted:
Joe's wife hates me, but then again, she hates most people.
She asked for an appointment to the Royal Commission on
New Reproductive Technology, and I appointed her over
the objections of a lot of people. And she became a royal
commissioner and made a lot of money at it and then tried to
organize a coup. To say that she was unfriendly is to under-
state the case. But we had no relationship with her at all.

Stanley Hartt, on McTeer's effect on Clark:
When Mulroney appointed her to the Royal Commission
on New Reproductive Technologies, he sent me to ask Joe
if she would behave. Joe told me, "She's her own person.
I can't give you a guarantee." Eventually, she had to get
fired. She could have handled her objections so differently,
without embarrassing the government and making herself
persona non grata for any kind of future appointment.

Clark was like the little girl in the nursery rhyme.
Eighty per cent of the time his judgment and his leadership ability were astounding, and 20 per cent of the time,
utter, absolute foolishness would come out of his mouth.

Sometimes his instincts didn't work that day, it was as if he was having his period. Maybe the key to his good versus bad days was Maureen. Was she friendly or nasty? Who knows. She's so totally fucking nuts.

Flora MacDonald, on how most Tories regarded McTeer:
They dislike Maureen terribly. The prime minister respects Joe in a way that he respects few others. From 1980 to 1984, Joe went through the most humiliating experience that any public figure could go through—from the media, from his peers, from everybody. He never once complained about it or blamed anybody, and he seemed to rise to another level of tolerance and magnanimity. You can't help but respect that, but Maureen doesn't exactly attract people and she has a very cutting way of expressing herself and she's never hesitated to do so about Brian or anyone else.

Bill Pristanski remembered McTeer badmouthing Mulroney:
I guess one of the times that she created a real problem for us was that women's conference, Initiatives '84. Maureen had made some statement saying that the party had taken a step backward by electing Brian as leader because of all of the good things Joe had done for women, and that she wasn't sure whether Mulroney would do the same. I remember Brian saying, "She's ruined herself in the party, and caused Joe all sorts of embarrassments." She wasn't doing Joe any favour at all, and yet she thought she was.

Clark himself believed both wives—Maureen and Mila—were put in unpleasant positions:
In any conflict, the principals accept the result more easily than the spouses do. It's difficult for Mila to allow Maureen space, and it's difficult for Maureen to allow Mila space. That's just there. That's just a reality.

Ontario Tory operative Paul Curley recalled how Maureen became active before the 1980 election, but not in Canada:
Maureen was trying to resolve the Iran hostage issue with President Jimmy Carter. I can still remember saying to Clark, "I have a lot of volunteers who are giving eight weeks of their time to help you get re-elected. They want to work with you—they don't want to work for your wife."

Marjory LeBreton, on McTeer as her own woman:
Joe Clark always performed much better when Maureen wasn't around. There is no question. He was not really a strong-looking individual in terms of his physique. I mean, if Mila Mulroney had used the name Mila Pivnicki, that would not cause one bit of problem for the image of the prime minister, but because of Joe Clark's image and the fact that she used her own maiden name, it was.

I used to defend Maureen, but I will no longer do so because she's not a feminist, she's claiming to be a feminist. She hides behind Joe Clark's name when it suits her and she treated people in the party terribly when he was leader. I spent half my time talking to volunteers into not quitting because they had suffered terrible tongue-lashings from Maureen McTeer.

13.

"Even fucking Hitler got better press"

———

Mulroney on the Fourth Estate

FOR MOST OF A DECADE, the public's perceptions of Brian Mulroney were filtered through the chroniclers of Ottawa's press gallery, whose suspicion of his character was matched by his distrust of their motives. Most reporters just plain didn't like him. They resented the fact that, unlike them, he had not come up through the appropriate apprenticeship. This uppity backwoods-Irish climber, who had never been elected to any previous office, didn't share their cozy paradigm. He didn't fit in. His wife was too beautiful, his kids too perfect, and he had arrived in town accompanied by his own roughneck retinue, who had never sipped sherry and chomped those stale cashews at the Rideau Club.

For sixteen long years, most gallery members had shared the sensibilities and prejudices of Pierre Trudeau's Ottawa, even if they felt exasperated by the man himself.

The capital's mandarins behaved as though they were aspiring to be Renaissance men, even if they were mostly dilettantes. They had never visited a Rimouski beer parlour, yet they could parse John Maynard Keynes's general theory. If you were to ask the Mulroney Brigade about general theory, they'd look puzzled then cite their leader's seminal thought: "You dance with the one who brung you." The land beyond the Perrier belt, where Mulroney had originated, was as alien to the Ottawa-cocooned journalists as life on another planet. Because Mulroney had appeared out of nowhere, they thought he was a nobody and treated him as shabbily as they habitually treated one another. Unlike Trudeau, whom the media claimed with good reason to have created, Mulroney had won office with no help from them, which doubled their fury.

Much as he might have been a creation of the press, Lucky Pierre not merely affected but genuinely felt disdain for journalists "and their ilk," as he would so elegantly add. Mulroney lacked such distance. He was as fragile as the mythical playwright who read his putrid opening-night reviews and lashed back at his critics by threatening to shoot his dog. Mulroney didn't have the gonads of a Lyndon Johnson. The U.S. president once silenced a reporter who had bothered him with a trivial query, demanding, "Why do you come and ask me, the leader of the Western world, a chicken-shit question like that?" Instead, Mulroney's trepidation over what reporters wrote and broadcast led him to believe that every other head of government enjoyed a more impartial press. He was certain that journalists made up in conviction what they lacked in evidence and that they suffered from collective dementia aimed directly at him.

My own view, based on a dozen years in the gallery, was that the Ottawa press corps had gone through three distinct periods: the lapdog epoch when journalists formed a propaganda arm of government, which lasted into the 1950s; the watchdog era of the next two decades, when investigative and advocacy journalism thrived; and the attack-dog journalism of the Mulroney years, when reporters lusted for celebrity status by trying to tear their subject into confetti. They didn't set out to treat Mulroney worse than any other prime minister, but because he reacted so emotionally to criticism—both valid and vengeful—he turned himself into a target. The process fed on itself, until both press and government became armed camps.

I spent the Mulroney period interviewing him and his intimates, often about newsworthy events, for my book. Since my intention was to write a full-scale biography of the man and his period, I published not a word intended for that magnum opus, including the contents of this much slimmer volume. There were, of course, complaints among my colleagues about my unique access, but since I took no advantage of it in print, they soon petered out. Meanwhile, I wrote favourably about the Tory initiatives I supported, such as the Meech and Charlottetown accords, and attacked those I thought were ill conceived, such as the GST and the Free Trade Agreement.

Still, I subscribed to the harsh criticism of Claire Hoy's Mulroney biography, and agreed with Patrick O'Callaghan, publisher of the *Calgary Herald,* who wrote of *Friends in High Places,* "Every time Mulroney sneezes, you wait for Hoy to somehow suggest that he is the first prime minister to catch a cold while drinking the blood of infants." More serious was the relative absence of thoughtful analysis of Mulroney's radical policies, always with the exception of Jeffrey Simpson, Doug Fisher, Richard Gwyn, Hugh Windsor, Gordon Gibson, Lorne Gunther and Anthony Westell.

Once his heart was broken by his press coverage, Mulroney treated even the thoughtful members of the media like creatures as void of dignity as a slew of wild monkeys. He once got so flustered in the attempt to answer a reporter's abrupt question at a press conference that he shot back, "I'm not denying anything I didn't say." Asked to comment on his government's achievements, Mulroney would go into a zen state and start listing the 354 most recent bills passed by the Commons. That didn't turn anybody's crank. Voters never cast ballots for what they already have; they want a vision that promises a better future, and this Mulroney seldom provided.

After the scandals of the first few months, the media paid more attention to the dimensions of Mulroney's shoe closet than to the size of the national debt. That set the stage for the demonization of the man and his politics of opportunity. Perception was reality, and the messengers became the message. News morphed into entertainment, its objective less to inform than to titillate. Ottawa journalists appointed themselves Mulroney's character police.

After the first few run-ins, Mulroney rarely made himself available. At one point, he didn't hold a news conference in Ottawa for three years, a record equalled only by President Ramiz Alia of Albania at the height of the Cold War. When Pat MacAdam suggested he defuse the hostility by inviting journalists to Sussex for off-the-record breakfasts, Mulroney agreed. But the *Toronto Star* got wind of the idea and published a satiric piece titled "Breakfast with Brian." He went berserk and ordered a witch hunt to find the culprit who had leaked the story. (It turned out that Mulroney had discussed the idea with his caucus.) After that, the Tories tried to control the flow of information by appointing $80,000-a-year political commissars in ministerial offices, who were the only ones authorized to talk to the media. At the same time the PMO press office was transformed into a booking agency for Mulroney photo ops.

These gimmicks were quickly laughed out of contention, but they still cost him. Gallery members felt empowered by Mulroney's tacit admission that only a favourably disposed press could save his government. They would show him. We were back to 1962, when the *Toronto Star*'s Val Sears climbed aboard the Diefenbaker campaign plane announcing, "To work, gentlemen. We have a government to overthrow!"

Mulroney periodically announced to his inner circle that he would never again look at a newspaper or watch television news. He regularly read seven dailies before breakfast and listened to half a dozen radio and TV newscasts every day, as well as leafing through six-day-old papers from Halifax and Vancouver in the evenings. His resolve to boycott the media occasionally lasted an entire day, but it wasn't just a daytime activity. Unknown to all but Mila, he slept on a special speaker-equipped pillow that allowed him to listen to shortwave radio news (Voice of America, the BBC's overseas service and France's ORTF) long into the night. "It's a little flat plastic thing which tucks under, so the whole pillow talks to you," Mila explained to me. "I rued the day he got it, but I had to eat my words because once or twice that stupid little radio saved the day. We were at the Commonwealth Conference in Kuala Lumpur when Brian happened to tune into a BBC press conference that Margaret Thatcher was giving, in which she retracted her backing of the sanctions against South Africa she had previously supported in Brian's presence, which helped him deal with the issue the next day."

Only very occasionally did he crack jokes about his relations with the media. "Actually, I think of the press gallery as family," he once told me, recalling a conversation with his press secretary at the time. "Just the other day I said to Gilbert, 'What are those mothers saying about me now?'" It was an inside joke among his advisors, however, that if they wanted to change his mind on an issue, they just had to hint that television pundits Craig Oliver and Mike Duffy had been overheard discussing it and that they both thought the government ought to reconsider its policy—in the direction the advisors preferred.

Mulroney's press office, manned by Bill Fox, Bruce Phillips, Gilbert Lavoie, Marc Lortie and Michel Gratton, valiantly tried to stem the tide of destructive comment, occasionally resorting to elaborate ploys of their own. Gratton, who never fit into the Mulroney (or any other) crowd, wrote in his memoirs, "After six years of Brian Mulroney, Canadians have sized him up as a scheming, conniving politician, who comes out with the truth only when he gets caught"—not your usual valediction from a public relations advisor. "Why don't we ever consider the truth as an option?" an exasperated Charley McMillan once asked a gathering of dispirited and befuddled Tory press office factotums. They had no reply.

Among the many journalists Mulroney loathed the most was Don McGillivray, a columnist for Southam News. Their relationship had a peculiar subtext. Mulroney loved to wax eloquent about francophone contributions to Canada, and would frequently invoke "the Honourable Pierre Sévigny, who left his leg for his country on the shores of Normandy during the Second World War." What Mulroney never knew was that Sévigny's leg was actually in McGillivray's living room. After the war, Sévigny used an artificial limb that eventually wore out and had to be replaced. The McGillivrays lived down the street from him, and Don's daughter found it in the garbage. She dragged the prosthesis home, where her father used it to stoke his fireplace.

Among Mulroney's severest critics was Allan Fotheringham, the *Maclean's* columnist, who had once been a close friend and had used his column to first nominate Mulroney for the Tory leadership. One noonish Sunday when Fotheringham was at a private cottage up the shore from Harrington Lake, the PM's summer residence, a waiter arrived in a speedboat dispatched by the Mulroneys, bearing chilled champagne, smoked salmon and eggs Benedict. As he was munching the prime ministerial brunch, Dr. Foth realized he was too tight with the reigning power, and asked for a transfer to Washington. While in voluntary exile, he reassessed his view of Mulroney, mainly because of his patronage excesses, and returned to Canada as one of the PM's severest critics. He had previously given Mila a croquet set, which was now out of bounds. "Sometimes," she confessed to me, "I feel like giving the goddamn croquet hammers right back to him."

The most agonizing example of the savagery of Mulroney's press coverage occurred in the fall of 1991 when *Frank,* the guttersnipe satirical magazine, featured on its cover a contest to "deflower" his seventeen-year-old daughter, Caroline. This incitement to rape an innocent girl raised not a word of protest from any feminist organization in the country, presumably because she happened to be this particular prime minister's daughter.

What little comfort Mulroney found among journalists came from Marjorie Nichols and from William Thorsell, editor-in-chief of the *Globe.* John Fraser, who had worked for Thorsell before becoming editor of *Saturday Night* and later master of Massey College, described the *Globe* editor as "someone who identified with power so much, who admired strong leaders and who took an essentially conservative view of economics, that Thorsell must have found access to the prime minister irresistible, and he resisted it not a jot. All he got in return was venom and distrust, both inside the *Globe* and outside."

Marjorie Nichols of the *Ottawa Citizen,* Mulroney's most vocal defender in the press gallery, became terminally ill with lung cancer. Eight weeks before she died, she wrote, "The whole world has turned on its axis in the last five years. The only way to describe the political culture is that everyone has become mean and ugly. It's not journalism, it's scandal-mongering. What this country really needs is a psychiatrist to analyze the hate and verbal violence that permeate national debate. Prime Minister Brian Mulroney has been a lightning rod for this rising tide of incivility. But clearly he is its victim, not a perpetrator."

Mulroney had the bad luck to arrive in office as an increasingly competitive television industry was keeping the country on constant alert. Every Canadian living room became a whispering gallery, with political events flashed from coast to coast as they happened— well, not quite as they happened, since each tightly edited item was squished between reporters' commentaries with little time devoted to subtlety or nuance. News bites were reduced from an average of one minute in the early 1970s to twenty seconds by the 1990s. Voice-overs and fade-outs often reduced even that minimal first-hand coverage.

Over the tube, Mulroney transmitted the unfortunate impression that the glass television eye turned the prime minister of Canada back into the small-town boy awed by having won a raffle at the Baie-Comeau fall fair. His eyes darted like minnows from one camera to another; his mouth formed a tight loop that betrayed his fear of flying in the face of a medium that he regarded as witness for the prosecution. Anyone ever touched by his humour and decency had trouble recognizing him on TV, yet that was how most of the country observed him. On daily exhibition in the nation's living rooms, Canadians gradually felt they could see right through the man.

While Trudeau, ever the cool dude, had mastered the knack of staring down the glass eye, Mulroney acted as if cameras were X-ray machines taking the measure of his character. To survive such intrusive exposure required a rock-solid sense of self, which was not Mulroney's long suit. Television works best for those who speak in languid, passionless tones, and is not the ideal arena for a fiery orator. Gradually Mulroney found that a highly regionalized democracy, mobilized by television, was almost impossible to govern.

Mulroney was a tough hombre. But he had a soft underbelly; he depended on the kindness of strangers to validate his self-worth. That vulnerability left him exposed to being got. He ruled nervously, as if awaiting the commutation of a death sentence, a reprieve that never came.

"LAZY, CYNICAL AND SELF-SERVING": THE NATIONAL PRESS GALLERY

Only a few days into the 1984 electoral campaign, Mulroney started to complain about the press:
I believe the Canadian people are saying that the Conservatives have lots of promise, but the media pick up the Liberal line. They keep repeating that the Conservatives have no policy, and the indolence of the press in this country is such that unless they're careful, they become unwittingly servants of that message. The press doesn't know anything. The same way the press didn't know I was going to run for the Conservative leadership and win. The same way [*Toronto Star* columnist] Richard Gwyn and [*Toronto Sun* columnist] Douglas Fisher are sort of goddamned glad to have Turner, because they think Turner's going to win. Turner can't win, but they don't know that because they spend all their time sitting there, holding hands with each other.

I have a policy for offshore development in Atlantic Canada, economic equality for women, Crown corporation accountability, Revenue Canada and youth unemployment. It's all there, right on the desk of Bob Hepburn of the *Toronto Star,* and he won't read it. If you look at the elections of 1968, 1974 and 1980, those were won by the Liberals on issues we ran. They were won on Conservative policy proposals. What we're trying to do now is not to give the Liberals an issue. They are best when distorting someone else's position.

Even the Mulroney honeymoon after he was first elected didn't seem to extend to the press gallery:
MULRONEY: The recent Gallup poll was very encouraging, but I think that some people—like the Barbara Frums of this world—are not impressed and are still always bitching about us. The press basically amputates any favourable reference to me. I came to the House of Commons and I succeeded in facing overwhelming hostility from the press gallery, but I won the goddamn election. Why should I worry about them?

I'm not giving them the time of day. Not one of them I've let into this office, not one. They're lazy—lazy and cynical—self-serving, so goddamn indolent. Everything is cynicism. They have no sense of history and they have no understanding of economics. There are very few of them who do. There's a lot of malice. It's mindless and you kind of wonder what to do about it, but there's not a hell of a lot you can do.

Strategist Lowell Murray on Mulroney's thin skin:
One of Brian's bad habits is that he scarcely lets a caucus go by without a real, sometimes caustic attack on the media or certain sections of it. The thing is, there are impressionable guys there, and he sets a tone. Sometimes he's quite personal, like, "Barbara Frum and others, who shall remain nameless." It's a problem; he shouldn't sound off too much in caucus. He does that a lot in the privacy of his office.

During the first months of his tenure, Mulroney looked to the example of another Tory prime minister who became one of the country's longest-serving heads of government:
There's a quote from a leading *Globe* editorialist in 1873, something to the effect of "Thank God the country has seen the last of that drunken bum Macdonald, thank God this wretched man is taking his leave of the nation." Eighteen years later, Sir John was still prime minister. You can't go by media returns.

Mila's take on the situation:
MULRONEY: Mila said, "You have been confronted by a hostile media from the day you got here." If you look back to the 1983 leadership convention, I was an outsider and the press was supporting either Joe Clark or John Crosbie. If you look at it subliminally, reporters are sent to Ottawa to cover national politics, and it doesn't take them long to be overtaken by their own sense of superiority in this town. It doesn't do much, however, for their sense of superiority with their children and with their friends back home if covering national politics means that a guy like me, who has never been elected church warden, can come in and become prime minister. What does that say about the importance of this place? So I think there was a lot of antagonism because of that.

Press secretary Bruce Phillips—a veteran of the Ottawa press gallery—had a different spin:
There used to be much more objectivity, there was much less bloodthirstiness, there was a kind of an attempt to put forward things as they happened, rather than as the press gallery thought they should have happened or shouldn't have happened. The competitive pressure of the very large electronic component was not there when you and I first came here, Peter, and has made a big difference. The television clip is now an important factor—ten seconds of the most dramatic part of a statement are used and the reporter fills in the blank spots.

The age of the press gallery has gone substantially down, and I think there's an absence of the kind of maturity that was here twenty years ago. The competitive race has made the major difference, plus perhaps some backwash from the Woodward-Bernstein business. I notice that the unnamed source has now become a far more important factor than it ever was in my time. When I worked at Canadian Press, it was a matter of practice that no quote could ever be put in a story that did not have a name attached to it. Now the unidentified quote has become the standard. Nowadays, a reader has no way to know whether a quote is imaginary or real.

I don't think reporters dislike the prime minister particularly, but there is a general sense that established institutions are the natural prey of the journalist, and since the prime minister happens to represent the largest and most visible institution in the country, he is a victim of that.

That attitude has been accentuated by the introduction of the Access to Information Act, which is a new feature in Canadian political reportage in which all the expenses and the lives of politicians are laid bare in a financial sense. Things that have been normal for years, and which previously were not reported upon, are now reported upon in what I—if you forgive the word—call a *discontextualized* setting. A paper will report that a minister has gone abroad and spent several thousand dollars of public money. With no attempt to put that in a framework, it suggests extravagance. It's just Mr. Mulroney's bad luck that he happened to be the first prime minister who had to live with it.

Mulroney thought his bad press was more personal than that:
You know, Canada is as Conrad Black always says, "a country nurtured on envy." So rather than say, "We've got two nice, reasonable people," they say, "No. They are Ken and Barbie, some kind of plastic people." That's point number one.

Point number two is that there was not very much support for me in 1984; they were all for Turner. The best evidence of this was Peter Desbarats's study for the University of Western Ontario's School of Journalism when they surveyed the press gallery after the 1984 election and they found 91 per cent of the members of the gallery had voted Liberal or NDP. When I was winning the largest majority in Canadian history, I got 9 per cent of the press gallery. So you can fairly assume from that that they were not big supporters of mine.

Then there was the unintended consequence of his big majority to factor in:
MULRONEY: Because the Opposition was so weak and ineffective, the press became the opposition, abandoning the objectivity of the media and acquiring the malice of the Opposition. In the beginning of year three, we had the infection of [*Toronto Sun* columnist] Claire Hoy and people like that, and the moral collapse of people like [*Globe and Mail* managing editor] Geoffrey Stevens and [CBC reporter] David Halton, who should have been providing some moral leadership in the country and in the gallery. If you ever said anything nice about me, you got attacked personally and so everybody shut up because they were fearful.

I can't do anything about the mediocrity in the gallery. These people are galvanized by Question Period. They think it's important, because it makes *them* important. They interview one another on television and on radio, and it gives them a sense of self-importance.

His jokes backfired with the media:
I was giving a scrum and a guy asked me a question about the official plane and I said, "Well, you'll have to be careful of that because these aircraft are sacred instruments of travel." I said this with a big grin on my face. And the guy put it down as if I were serious. He never said, "The prime minister said it with a grin" or "with a chuckle." It's unbelievable.

I tell jokes all the time. I have the cabinet laughing and the caucus laughing, but if you do it with the reporters, they put it down as if you're just saying it. There's no context . . . This plane was so broken down that when we would take off, water would come out onto my papers while I was working with deputy ministers and ministers. The aircraft of the prime minister of Canada could not land at any metropolitan airport in the world unless I was on it because it violated all of the environmental laws and standards. It was twenty-nine years old. It was a rustbucket.

For nine years, I travelled the globe as prime minister of Canada in an aircraft so old and decrepit that I never once was able to make or receive a telephone call, because we didn't have proper communications. The gallery used to pass resolutions asking me, begging me, to get rid of the goddamned thing, to trade it in, not because they were concerned about my going down but because they always travelled with me. The chances were, if it went down, we'd all get killed and they didn't mind me but they didn't want it happening to them. The only thing that we agreed on was that!

I mean it's terrible, every African despot has a brand-new plane and here this thing was twenty-nine years old.

Pat MacAdam remembered one of the last events held for the press at 24 Sussex:
The only knee-capper who wasn't there was Claire Hoy. Everybody else was there in force with their wives, kids and husbands. They were all anxious to get their photograph taken with Brian. It was interesting to see how obsequious some of these people had become, having spent three years kicking the shit out of the prime minister. They were down there drinking his booze, and eating his hamburgers and hot dogs.

When the press began to publish secret facts about his government, Mulroney blamed his old friend:
MACADAM: Brian has an obsession with malicious leaks. Somebody was feeding stories about staff members to the press. That infuriated him. He didn't have a press conference for months. In caucus we actually discussed

whether we should stop talking to the press altogether. Fortunately, it was defeated.

But somebody says something to the press and the goddamn witch hunt begins. Track it down. Staff is suspect. It's not very pleasant. Some leaks were coming right out of the caucus—the goddamn place is like a sieve.

Brian was very quick to point a finger at me, and it really hurt. It hurt when he questioned someone who's loyal to him. He wrote me this nasty note. I was so shaken by it. I shredded it.

I think he panicked. He was hit where it hurts most, right in his vanity. He's down in the polls, and there's the spate of cartoons. People are laughing at him, and that's the one thing he can't stand. You're prime minister of Canada, you're king of the mountain, you should enjoy your job. And he's not enjoying his job. He's grumpy.

After the 1988 leader's debate, Mulroney counted those he considered unbiased media voices:
John Godfrey says in the *Globe and Mail,* "Mulroney walks away with this thing." Bill Gold in the *Calgary Herald* says, "The leaders all did well, but Mulroney won." He was persuasive, he was prime ministerial and so on. I'm actually starting to get a little credit.

Now, I'll name good ones for you. I'll name 'em. There was never anything wrong with [*Financial Post* columnist] Hy Solomon. There was never really any malice in [CBC television reporter] Jason Moscovitz. There was never anything wrong with [CBC reporter and anchor] Don Newman. The French guys were always on a higher level, on a different level; don't ask me why, that's the way it was.

Norman Atkins, the prime minister's campaign advisor:
Mulroney's so obsessed by what the reporters are saying, what the press is saying, that the media becomes the priority. He tends on television to put on a performance, rather than be a natural respondent to whatever challenge

he has. It doesn't work . . . I remember just after Meech Lake, the interview with Barbara Frum—it was an awful interview because he wanted to be aggressive; he wanted to be provocative in terms of what he saw as the failure in relation to Meech rather than just being honest about the problem. He took it all too personally and as a result he was too defensive. And when he becomes defensive, he loses credibility. People don't believe him.

Press secretary Bill Fox wanted to get his guy out of the line of fire as much as possible:
There's a mischievous, downright malicious approach. It's just awful. They will write stories about our guy and his credibility problem, but they're not interested in the truth. It's kind of *People* magazine journalism gone awry. I would really rather that the prime minister didn't do scrums, frankly. The media gets a snippet and it's just not reflective. And even visually, I'm a great believer in the message that you get out to people without any words necessarily. How can anybody concentrate on what somebody has to say when the visual is an individual standing there with all these microphones shoved up their nostrils?

Policy advisor Keith Hamilton opted for a more direct solution:
All we've got to do now is get the prime minister to keep his mouth closed. Especially when he's tired and he's been successful on something, he starts getting smartass, and he gets in trouble. We've done a lot of good things, but we don't do the groundwork before we make the announcement, so we haven't answered all the negative items about something. We're attacked, and we spend the next three months defending what we've just announced.

Days after achieving a second majority, Mulroney laughed at the expense of a columnist who prematurely predicted his defeat:

Roy MacGregor from Southam wrote a column in early November about being on the Conservative bus, saying that all the journalists knew that Mulroney was finished. He wrote, "We knew all along that this lousy mediocre guy from Montreal who had no right to lead the Conservative Party was a one-termer and we knew he was possessed by the Americans. I fall asleep on this bus tonight knowing full well that this is the end of the Mulroney government."

Stanley Hartt thought television was the problem:
Brian's better when he's with people. We've only put him on to address the nation on television once. When that glass eye comes at him with the little red light above it, he looks at a piece of glass, and a piece of glass does nothing for Brian Mulroney. He's a hot personality, and when he gets angry or builds to an oratorical crescendo, television doesn't like it. He comes across as pushy. Sometimes he writes into his own speeches what he calls "poetry" and it doesn't sell. It might sell if he was in a crowd of people who were on an emotional high. Then you have tears in everybody's eyes. But when he does it on television, they say, "Who are you trying to kid?" They think he's a bastard, you know.

Paul Tellier:
His so-called advisors, turn him loose for God's sake! Don't give him a script. In some of the interviews, it's just godawful. This is not the kind of guy that we see day in and day out, a normal human being like you and I . . . Canadians never had a chance to see him *au naturel*.

Mulroney marvelled at the disconnect:
How many times have you heard people say, "Geez, you know, I met Mulroney or his wife—holy smokes are they nice people." So then, how could a man whose character was conveyed by the Canadian media as flawed,

dishonest, corrupt, venal, unprincipled, unintelligent, thoughtless, arrogant, vain, rude, imbecilic . . . How could a man like this become the leader of a great political party, hold a very, very difficult caucus together, survive more ups and downs than any other prime minister since Sir John, deal rationally with important events, and have these people support him? Unless you assume that the caucus and cabinet, that every single one of them was an idiot—they would be the first to see that they were dealing with a fool or a knave, and they'd do something about it.

Business is booming, our jobs are up and everything is going fine. But the *Toronto Star* says Brian Mulroney is a shit. So I changed newspapers. I went to the *Globe and Mail,* which says I'm a spendthrift and an asshole. So I decided to go to the *Sun,* a real conservative paper run by Paul Godfrey. I read Claire Hoy's column, and I'm a thief and a murderer.

Former Newfoundland premier Frank Moores on what that disconnect was all about:
Brian is too much "one of the boys." No mystique at all, it's all off the cuff. People who have met the real Mulroney privately know he's a very, very enjoyable person. But out in public he's got this library of clichés that, Jesus, if he'd only get them out of his vocabulary . . . But he can't help himself. When he said, "My neck is on the line on free trade," he doesn't need to say that. Nobody's forcing him to say that. All he had to say was, "We're going to have free trade and it's good for the country." Very simple, everybody understands that. When he does things like that, he comes off as a terrible politician. He comes off as desperate.

Or maybe it was the whole world hating a winner:
MULRONEY: If I had been a failure like—and I don't mean this cruelly—if I had been a Conservative leader who lost like Stanfield, they'd have thought I was terrific.

Clark managed to win, but then he blew it so quickly and became an object of scorn and derision. But because he lost and was out of it, they liked him, too. If you were a Conservative leader who won, different story. And look, I was a big, brassy guy who won and won big and I did what I wanted. I did what I thought was right. But even in the good times they were opposed to me.

He was astonished that even his voice became a point of debate:
You can't even be yourself. You can't even speak with the voice that you were born with. Now you watch and see what will happen if my successor came in here with a high, tinny voice. They'll say, "Well shit, at least when Mulroney was around, we knew we had a virile guy running the show."

Even Adolf Hitler . . . :
MULRONEY: If you go to the Montreal *Gazette,* you can push a button and call up things on me written by their reporters, you will not find one favourable adjective in ten years. Even fucking Hitler . . .

NEWMAN: Even what?

MULRONEY: Even Hitler had somebody writing one good adjective in ten years. Maybe one day he said hello to somebody, and it was recorded, I don't know.

CBC reporter Christopher Walmsley had an unusual take on Mulroney as the author of his own misfortunes:
How many reporters were in the press gallery in the 1980s who got sucked up by Mulroney into the system? Anybody who was the least bit friendly all of a sudden got offered a huge job. Keith Spicer, Bruce Phillips, Luc Lavoie. Mulroney decimated the people who were legitimately friendly to him, and cut his own throat. And who

did he leave out there? He should have made Claire Hoy a senator. Dalton Camp said once that there was at one point serious consideration to make Pamella Wallin a senator just to get her off the air.

Both Trudeau and Mulroney were obsessed with the media, but only one of them cared, Walmsley contended:
Mulroney reacted to everything that the press said. You'd never get a call from Trudeau; you'd get a call from Mulroney. Christ almighty, in the dying days of his administration, the *Toronto Star* printed something unfavourable about his trip to see Bush. Not only did Mulroney phone Honderich [the publisher], he got Bush to phone the publisher and say, "Linda Diebel's story on Mulroney isn't true."

Mila retained no illusions:
One thing is constant in the case of the press: they are not our friends . . . I understand it and I've accepted it and I'm not even angry about it anymore. I do think, though, that history will set the record straight. Reporters unfortunately go for the weakest link, they fabricate false stories, so you can't fight. How do you fight fabrication? If somebody says you're a liar because you said X, Y and Z, you could bring up the transcript and correct it. But this is the old, "When did you stop beating your wife?" That's their approach.

I have learned so much since we've been in Ottawa, so much, but also a lot of positive things. It's made me stronger, it's made us stronger, it's made my children stronger. The lies hurt—don't get me wrong—but I think my children have their priorities, and their judgment is so good.

In the end, Mulroney is convinced that English Canadians ended up despising him because of the press:
Nobody can explain the hatred, because it's been fed to

Canadians by the Ottawa media, the English media. It doesn't exist at all in Quebec. The English-speaking media fed this caricature of me to the people every day, and so a guy says, "I hate that son of a bitch." Yeah, why? "Geez, I don't know." Trudeau had it sporadically, but in my case it seemed to be unremitting . . .

Our press gallery was comparing our situation to Watergate, to Iran-Contra, to the problems in the United Kingdom or former prime minister Pierre Bérégovoy committing suicide in France. Is it just me that has to be responsible and professional and objective and unbiased? Am I the only one? What about *their* obligation to fairness and objectivity and the truth? What about their honourable obligations to convey to millions of Canadians something that resembles fair treatment? Do you agree with Claire Hoy and Derek Hodgson and Don McGillivray, who say I am a corrupt, venal, deceitful, unprincipled man and my government is no good? Or do you say, piss on them, I'm not going to get a break from a bunch of unprincipled, corrupt failures.

Then of course I committed the ultimate sin. I won the 1988 election on an issue that drove them bananas. Let me ask you. Do you go down the street and people say, "I want to lynch Mulroney"?

NEWMAN: No, but you can read that suggestion.

MULRONEY: That's key. That's absolutely key. I mean, after a while reading the coverage you start to say, "Well, Christ. There is something wrong with the guy. I mean, shit, we voted for him big-time. He's been there for nine or ten years." For the press, it was just pile on, pile on. Who can pound the piss out of the guy? And what was his crime? Well, gee, you know what? He spent a lot of money on furniture. Oh yeah? He paid for it. Oh, gee. What was his crime? He made patronage appointments. Anything compared to what's going on

now? Did he ever appoint his family? Did he ever appoint
his relatives? Did he ever appoint his brother-in-law? Did
he intervene on behalf of his son-in-law? Did he override
the CRTC? Did Mulroney take money from Jack and Don
Matthews, advising them on privatization of Pearson
Airport, and then cancel the deal? What did I do? Well, I
was a Conservative, who won. And as [New Brunswick
premier] Frank McKenna once said about me, "He looked
good and he sounded good and he didn't give a shit and
they couldn't stand him."

THE GLOBE AND MAIL

**Mulroney had a soft spot for *Globe and Mail* editor-in-
chief William Thorsell:**
I can't complain about the editorial support I got from
the *Globe*—they put me on the front page. They supported us tremendously, both Thorsell and [previous
editor-in-chief] Norman Webster. But [columnist] Hugh
Winsor is useless, absolutely useless. One of the big
enemies I had at the *Globe* was Geoffrey Stevens, the
managing editor. He's just awful; he's the one who hired
Stevie Cameron.

**Mulroney claimed that *Globe and Mail* columnist
Jeffrey Simpson perpetrated the wrong impression of
Lucien Bouchard:**
Bouchard got the story out, helped by Simpson, that he
was an honourable man. Why would Simpson come to
that conclusion? Because he spoke to Bouchard and
because he didn't speak to me. And why would he not
have spoken to me? Because there was no communication
between us. His unprofessional misconduct had taken
him out of play.

Mila had her own take on Simpson's motivation:

MULRONEY: As Mila pointed out one night, "What do you think is going on here? Don't you understand that Jeffrey Simpson, a WASP from Toronto and Queen's University, is beside himself at the thought that a poor broken-down electrician's son, Irish Catholic from Baie-Comeau, Quebec, via St. FX, could come forward and take over the leadership of the Conservative Party right under his nose, though he opposed him every step of the way, and win a huge majority government? Why do you think he hates you?" She said, "I'm amazed that you pay any attention to it. Jeffrey's view is that he should be leading the government and you should be writing a column about him, preferably one that would be favourable." And so I had to laugh.

Mulroney says that other heads of state critiqued the *Globe*'s coverage:
Margaret Thatcher showed Reagan a copy of the *Globe and Mail* at a luncheon, saying, "This is what Brian has to put up with. Look at this disgrace. This is Canadian journalism. Look at this disgraceful, putrid newspaper."

Mulroney's version of his infamous "roll the dice" remark:
Thorsell was a new editor; he didn't have control over anything and it got out of hand. The expression was actually the opposite of a gamble because we couldn't gamble in terms of time. We couldn't gamble in terms of people coming onside because it was irrelevant. The people who had come onside were going offside, namely Clyde Wells. Look, the philologists would say this was an infelicitous turn of phrase. For me, the expression "roll the dice" means that I'll goddamn well do everything I can humanly possible for my country, and that's what it meant.

Mila had warned Mulroney that the *Globe* interview could backfire:

I was against that. I told him, but Brian felt that William Thorsell was a credible person. I said, "Honey, any time you put three people in a room and you just let yourself be you, they'll screw you." Excuse me.

THE CBC

Mulroney felt like he pulled out all the stops to support the Canadian Broadcasting Corporation, only to see it become a vehicle to discredit him and his government.

He claimed the drubbing started early:
The unemployment numbers came out like ten days after I got sworn in, and the CBC reporter who covered it—a guy by the name of Christopher Walmsley—actually did the following piece. He took a clip of somebody talking about the unemployment—29,000 more people unemployed in Canada or something like that—and then he took a clip of me in the campaign saying, "I'm campaigning on jobs, jobs, jobs, and when we get elected you're going to see that there's going to be a new climate of investment." He did that, and he concluded by saying, "Mulroney has failed his first test!" I knew right then it was going to be lethal and that they wouldn't give us a break, and they never did.

Walmsley explained his side of the unemployment story years later:
Prior to the campaign, we were up in Prince Albert at a meeting of the Conservative caucus, and Mulroney, in his typical hyperbolic way, said there would be tens of thousands of jobs created in Canada with a Conservative government.

Later, I was chatting with other reporters, and told them I was going to ask Mulroney about this unemployment figure, about the tens of thousands of jobs. When I did, I expected him to turn around and say, we've been in power for two weeks, the Liberals left us in a mess, give us a chance, we're working on it, something like that. Instead, he turns around and he said, "I never said that—check the clip."

Now, we didn't quote him out of context, we quoted his hyperbole. The story I ran at noon—the one I had control over—questioned his credibility: the prime minister said he didn't say it, but he did say it. For *The National* that night, the editors in Toronto thought the story was not the credibility, but the actual unemployment figures. It became formula television; they were trying to link things that weren't linkable. For me, the story wasn't that he hadn't lived up to his promise, it was that he had denied making that quote. There's a subtle but important difference. The editors seemed to have a desire to kick him on policy, when they really should have kicked him on credibility.

Walmsley remembered one off-putting attempt at camaraderie from the PM:
David Halton and Don Newman were there, and the prime minister came down late at night as we were shooting the final pieces for *The National*. He stopped on his way to his car and he was genuinely trying to communicate with them, but for some reason he decided to use the most foul language. He started with fuck this, and goddamn, and son of a bitch and all that. Everybody just sort of shut up. An occasional swear word by a prime minister or anyone is appropriate, but when all of a sudden you hear a string of the most awful expletives, you're taken aback, because it's that same barrel-chested sonorous tone that used the most antiquated words of the English language. You go, what the hell was that all about? What is he trying to do? I'm not a mineworker from Baie-Comeau.

At the 1986 G-7 Tokyo Summit, Canada and Italy were finally invited to partake in the group's discussions on

economic policy. Italian reporters openly celebrated the feat, but Mulroney vividly remembers the first Canadian accounts on the CBC:

The first report was from David Halton: "The prime minister arrived in Tokyo earlier this evening and true to his imperial fashion he insisted on . . ." And the camera pans this big jet from Air Canada. Here's the jet and anchor Peter Mansbridge says, "Is there anything wrong with that?" And Halton replies, "Well it's a private jet—it's chartered at extra expense. You know, Mulroney's imperial tendency." Then he said, "But there's a larger question: the question is what are we really doing here? Why is Canada at the G-7? We're really quite a mediocre little country, our economy is tiny comparatively, we're the smallest of the G-7 countries, we have no influence, we have nothing to do or say, we're kind of like an add-on here, and really I have to tell you, I don't know what we're doing here—I feel quite ashamed." And that was it.

Here we get Canada into the G-7 monetary thing. The headlines in Italy? "Bettino Craxi victorious." In Canada? Zero.

Mulroney couldn't help thinking in tit-for-tat terms:

Believe it or not, I'm a supporter of public broadcasting; witness what I did giving rise to Newsworld, building that new headquarters for the CBC in Toronto and all of these things. However, you've got to be right out of your mind to think that the CBC is a public broadcaster. This is not a public broadcaster—this is a private broadcaster, and it's being broadcast for the benefit of the CBC. It's conducted for the benefit of the employees of the CBC, not for Canadians.

If the CBC's new headquarters were burned to the ground tonight by a group of CBC employees, the union would grieve to prevent the police from making an enquiry of any of the employees, lest it violate their professional integrity under the collective agreement. You'd never find out who burned the goddamned place down because nobody is responsible for anything in the CBC.

In Mulroney's view, the CBC started falling ever further down on the job when it began to rely on pundits instead of reporters to fill its twenty-four-hour news channel:
With the advent of Newsworld, everybody and his brother was on television every day. We became a nation of gossips and instantaneous experts. I remember going out and making an important speech to begin the Charlottetown referendum campaign in 1992, and Mila was in bed recovering from an ankle injury. I said, "Well, how did I do?" She said, "Well, I have to tell you, I thought that your speech was great, but the bad news is that [Mulroney critic] Deborah Coyne has been on Newsworld nine minutes for every minute you've been shown."

In a way it came down to hurt feelings:
MULRONEY: The only thing you hear about me, every night, is that the "unpopular Mulroney government" is cutting back on the CBC, which is all bullshit. I never cut. I saved the goddamned thing. I'm the one who kept the money going for the CBC. They increased their grant from $800 million to $1.1 billion when I was there.

THE TORONTO SUN

The newspaper provided Mulroney with more examples to bolster his views on Canada's highly partisan press. He identified columnist Claire Hoy as the main accomplice in a plot to damage his reputation, which also involved reporters and Liberal politicians. The Sun *was also home to Allan Fotheringham, who had been one of Mulroney's staunchest boosters during his brief time as leader of the Opposition but became highly critical of him in office.*

Sam Wakim on Claire Hoy's psychological state:
At the *Sun,* they know in their hearts that Hoy is a very unstable guy. He hates politicians and thinks they're all liars and cheats and frauds and crooks—there's gotta be something undesirable about that.

Allan Fotheringham's musings got Mulroney's goat:
Fotheringham suggested that I was at home green with envy over Trudeau having a child with Deborah Coyne. Unbelievable.

Mulroney mused about Fotheringham:
What I think happened to him was this—he was a friend of mine, and because he was a friend of mine, and could have been an insider, they transferred him to Washington. In Washington he failed. He had no contacts. He wasn't a player. None of the Americans knew him. They didn't care about him. So he became unfunny and embittered in Washington. I think as a person he felt diminished because he was used to being a big shot and all of a sudden he was a nobody. He plagiarized that stuff, and he got into a rut and he became an anti-American because he was knocked down fifteen pegs by the Americans. He didn't like the Free Trade Agreement. And when he came back, he left Southam.

The *Sun* organization sent him to Toronto, where he was plunged into the literati left-wing, anti–free trade, anti-military, anti-NATO, anti-NORAD crowd. So you go from Washington to the sewer in Toronto. And there he became an active member of the crowd trying to stop free trade and becoming part and parcel of that left-wing *Toronto Star, Saturday Night,* CBC crowd, who take great pride in all of the failures in town, come together at their cocktail parties in Cabbagetown and crap all over the leader of the Conservative Party, namely me, the prime minister.

I mean, when Fotheringham was in his prime, it was different. He was funny and entertaining, he was fresh and so on. But now he's jaded. Fotheringham—piss on him.

SOUTHAM PRESS

One more link in the chain of vilification, as far as the prime minister was concerned.

A Southam journalist was on his case within twenty-four hours of his 1988 election victory:
MULRONEY: Les Whittington gets up in my first press conference—I had been re-elected the night before—and his question was, "When are you going to resign?" I apparently said years ago that I would only serve two terms. But at least you give the guy one day. People say, "Well, all the politicians get a honeymoon." I didn't get twenty minutes after I had a cup of coffee in the morning. I go to a press conference, Les Whittington—this is the guy who is covering my press conference for fourteen newspapers—and his question on television was, "When are you going to resign?" I said, "Les, I just won an election last night. Give me a break. Give me a couple of days."

Some would say that Mulroney protested too much:
Look, we all grow, eh? You grow in this business or you fail. I came in looking for the approval of the press gallery, right? And I am now the person in Canadian history who has (a) received less of it and (b) couldn't give a good goddamn. I genuinely couldn't care. I genuinely don't care what they say.

I'm a student of Canadian history and I do not know of a period in the history of Canada where a prime minister has been under such a constant, unremitting and bitter attack.

Mulroney didn't hold the views expressed in Conrad Black's newspapers against him, exactly:
Look, Conrad has never done anything for me. His newspapers are the shittiest. In fact, Conrad is not a very generous guy . . . But what I like about him is that he's himself—he accomplished a great deal by himself. He has a sense of history and he's got a sense of humour. And he doesn't have the insecurities of the typical Canadian . . . There are all kinds of things that he does that I disagree with. So what else is new?

FRANK MAGAZINE

The satirical publication poked fun at Mulroney and his family on a weekly basis. Frank *gave Mila the nickname "Imelda" in reference to the wife of long-time Filipino dictator Ferdinand Marcos, who owned thousands of shoes. But then it crossed the line.*

Frank featured Mulroney's daughter in a "Deflower Caroline Contest" hoax:
MULRONEY: When *Frank* magazine did that about Caroline, it was just the end. Nobody came to her defence. The great leaders of the gallery, the Jeffrey Simpsons and such, were totally mute, not a word.

I picked up the *Globe and Mail* and there was a big column on the *Frank* thing by Michael Valpy. And I called Valpy up; he just about had a heart attack when he heard me on the phone. I said, "Look, you've taken a pretty good swing at me over the years. I just want you to know you've got a free pass forever, you say whatever you want about me, you'll never hear a word of complaint. The column that you did today about Caroline was the only thing that mattered."

The *Frank* magazine thing represented the absolute gutter, and only one journalist defended my daughter against an invitation to gang rape. And you know why? Because the ethos of the day required that if they had defended me, they would have been attacked by *Frank*. So they chose to remain silent when a magazine invited the gang rape of a seventeen-year-old child. They did not want to be attacked by the knee-cappers. You don't have to teach me four or five times, I understand it. That event explained the corruption of the Fotheringhams and the silence of the Simpsons, these bullshitters who pass for journalists, spending their time moralizing about the failings of others when their careers in fact are now essentially marked by pusillanimous personal conduct and fear of attack from other journalists. So to keep their skirts clean they say nothing.

Frank theorized about Mulroney's visit to a detoxification centre:
MULRONEY: Apparently—and I say "apparently" because I don't read it myself—*Frank* came out with a story saying that I was in the Betty Ford Clinic, that I was on the bottle. Of course, I knew nothing about it because it's in the garbage pail, but to show you how bad the media is, Julian Beltrame from Southam wrote a story saying, "*Frank* magazine has made this allegation about the prime minister. *Frank* is known as an irreverent, quite trashy little magazine, therefore not everybody believes that he's either in the Betty Ford Clinic because of drugs or drunk up at Harrington Lake. But inasmuch as we haven't seen him, we're kind of wondering." He set this up in fourteen Southam papers.

This is what kicked off the rumours about everything, from a divorce between Mila and me, to drunkenness to drugs—the fact that Southam Press would use *Frank* as a hook, knowing it was false.

Mila remembered how a Frank story sparked another little frenzy among the mainstream media:

I had made no public appearances [for a time], and that story just kept feeding and feeding on itself. *Frank* has a story saying that I've left Brian—it was on the cover. And then Craig Oliver called and Pamela Wallin phoned to find out, saying, "We know it's not true, but . . ."

I finally thought, enough, I'm just going to pick Brian up at the office. So I went to pick him up and those bureau chiefs finally got off our backs.

Have you ever heard anything so stupid?

Somebody else phoned me once and said, "I know you've got a lover in New York City." I said, "Could you send me a photo? Just in case I run into him, I'll know who he is." It was so silly.

THE MULRONEY AUTEURS

CLAIRE HOY AND *FRIENDS IN HIGH PLACES*

Anna Porter, through Key Porter Books, published Hoy's 1987 book on lobbying and patronage in Mulroney's Ottawa. Her husband, Julian Porter, was the libel lawyer.

Mulroney says he never read the book, but it influenced at least two of his patronage decisions:
I heard that the Hoy thing was awful bad stuff, but in fact I should tell you that in the month that followed the publication, we gained seven points.

All that is left of the Hoy thing is that it cost Julian Porter the chief justiceship of Ontario. They came forward with him for chief justice of Ontario, and I killed it right on the spot. I killed that. And then he tried to get back in as one of the Ontario candidates for the Senate, and I killed that too. I hope that Julian and Anna Porter made a lot on that book. That's what it cost them.

MICHEL GRATTON AND
SO WHAT ARE THE BOYS SAYING?

*After he resigned in March 1987, Mulroney's one-time
press secretary wrote a tell-all book on his experience in the
prime minister's inner circle.*

Mulroney was not amused:
Gratton's a joke, you know. He's back on his worst problems again. He won't be around for long.

Hartt pondered one of Gratton's points:
Gratton has this wonderful thing that he says, that the
prime minister always refers to so-and-so as "I appointed
him, he's a judge" or "I appointed him, he's an ambassador" or "I appointed him, he's a deputy minister." The
implication is that none of these people had any value of
their own life before they encountered Brian Mulroney.

And the funny part of it is that I consider I was a person of value before I was appointed by Brian, but if you
said to me, were you underemployed? I would say,
absolutely. If you said, would anybody else have given
you the chance to have those jobs? No. Did anything happen to you when you got those two jobs? Well, in terms
of personal development, it was like going back for four
PhDs. It was unbelievable. Did it help in my subsequent
career in terms of who I am in the business community?
Absolutely. And so, his gift was not meant to prove that
he could give it, but it was genuinely intended to help you.

JOHN SAWATSKY AND *THE POLITICS OF AMBITION*

*Sawatsky's 1991 unauthorized biography chronicled
Mulroney's youth, his resentment over the 1976 Tory
leadership defeat, and some pitfalls in his academic life.*

Mulroney insisted that most of it was untrue, and wanted the author to take a polygraph test:
The whole thing is a goddamned falsehood and it's a disgrace that as prime minister I would have to put up with it. I'd like to hear from the goddamned publisher. The book had me in a hotel room at the Pierre Hotel, with girlfriends down in New York City. All false. You know, I've never been convicted of rape, never robbed a bank, never done a goddamned thing that 5 or 25 million people haven't done, except be prime minister. If somebody wants to take a lie detector test, tell them to come on down.

Mulroney was particularly critical of the fact that researching him became a class project at Carleton University, where Sawatsky taught journalism:
I find it interesting that the guy wouldn't even pick up the phone. He didn't even do the interviews himself—the interviews were done by kids in the middle of the night. There is no substance, none, no evidence. And in fact, if all of this salacious stuff was taken out of the book, you couldn't justify putting it back in by his editors. Sawatsky's researchers even phoned [Southam political columnist] Charlie Lynch. He slammed the phone down and did a column on it, on their disgraceful behaviour, on being called by a couple of kids in the middle of the night for negative things on Mulroney.

Mulroney's opinion:
The book is a dud and it's poorly written. It's like I said to Mila, "What the hell am I supposed to do, take a billboard and say that I haven't screwed fifty good-looking blondes?" Now why would I say that, for God's sakes? Why would I say that and ruin my reputation?

But they're not going to hear a beep out of me. They can say whatever they want. I've never commented on Sawatsky's stuff because every piece that I saw in the *Ottawa Citizen* excerpt was false . . . I have never seen the

Sawatsky book. I have never read it. I've never looked at it, ever . . . They can say whatever they want, they're not going to find me on the front page of the *New York Times* fighting this book.

The book's "Missing Year" chapter suggested Mulroney was hospitalized in Halifax during his time as a student in Dalhousie:
MULRONEY: I was never in the hospital in Halifax in my life. He has no medical record, nothing, no evidence. I could prove that I was never in the hospital.

NEWMAN: He says venereal disease was one of the possibilities.

MULRONEY: Well, I guess another one would be leprosy. I was hospitalized once in Baie-Comeau, once in Quebec City and once in Montreal. I asked my mother, "Do you have any recollection of the time I was hospitalized in the Maritimes?" She said, "No, and if there's anybody who would know it would be me." She didn't know why I was asking, and I never told her. Then I had my lawyer in Halifax search the hospital records with a proxy from me. No records. I would guess that even my enemies are going to find a lot of this stuff hard to believe.

It was not much of a lost year. I flunked an exam, that's all. I passed all the tough exams and, as usual, I flunked an easy one. I think it was six of the Supreme Court justices in the United States at a given point flunked the bar exam.

Weeks after the book was published, Mulroney remained angry. Still, he poked fun at the situation during his traditional Wednesday caucus:
Look, I discussed this with my caucus. I discussed this stuff openly. I said, "Now listen, did you read that I took a shower with my landlady's daughter? This is the latest

thing from our friend Sawatsky. Do you know what pisses me off? I get the blame without any of the god-damned pleasure." The caucus, they're all roaring on the floor with laughter.

Sawatsky contended that Mulroney sought help to deal with his alcohol problem:
MULRONEY: Never went to an Alcoholics Anonymous meeting in my life, ever. I woke up one morning and thought, you know what? I'm drinking too much and I'm going to stop. I've never had a drink since. Just that simple. I did the same thing with smoking. My wife didn't even know I had stopped smoking. She didn't even know. I didn't want to tell anybody. I had just decided. And finally about a day later she said, "Oh, you've given up smoking." That was it.

Hartt thought his boss had lost perspective:
I'm not saying that Mulroney should have urged all of his friends to read it and sent people copies for Christmas. But if you said to me, would you like a book like that written about you, I would say yes. Leaving aside Sawatsky's method, which I didn't admire, I would say yes. If you painted me as having three or four human foibles—I like booze, I like women—and then painted my achievements in such a glowing light, I'd be very happy.

   Brian did overreact . . . He believes that to govern he has to be revered, and if he shows any human frailties, he can't be revered. I think it hurts him to give off this aura of perfection. People don't want him to be perfect. They don't believe he's perfect, and therefore they start look-ing for what he's hiding from them. He does want to be loved, but he also believes that he cannot have a flaw and be loved. Whereas we all have flaws and the people who love us, love us in spite of our flaws and sometimes because of them.

You would hurt this man more than insulting his wife to admit that you read Sawatsky's book, but every one of his friends has read it. The conclusion of the book is that this guy can do anything he sets his mind to and that he's overcome all kinds of adversity and he came to this position from the most unlikely origin and he's fantastic. And so along the way maybe there was an unexplained visit to a hospital, and who the fuck cares? But the insecurity says, if I catch anybody reading the book, he's out. Everybody understood they could never admit having read it.

MICHAEL BLISS AND *RIGHT HONOURABLE MEN*

The historian's 1994 volume ranked the importance and legacy of Canadian prime ministers.

Mulroney seethed:
Look, if you're a historian and you can say that Pierre Trudeau was the greatest prime minister in the history of Canada, you've got a problem. You've got a real, serious problem. I'll match my record against any prime minister in the history of Canada and come out a winner. But Michael Bliss thinks that Meech Lake was a catastrophe. He thinks that the 1982 constitution was a work of magic and art and that Meech Lake was an absolute disaster, so anybody associated with it, namely me, is a disaster. For that to be right, you have to assume that a constitutional deal without Quebec is the way Canada is going to go forever, and you know that's eventually the end of the country.

—

STEVIE CAMERON AND *ON THE TAKE*

THE NEMESIS WHO WALKED into Brian Mulroney's life when he became prime minister, Stevie Cameron, turned hating him from a spectator sport into a full-time obsession. Her 1994 book, *On the Take: Crime, Corruption and Greed in the Mulroney Years,* was a smashing bestseller even if the text did not pin any such accusations on its major target. Later Canadians learned that she had exchanged juicy bits of info with the RCMP.

The RCMP tried for most of a decade, but neither they nor Cameron could document any substantial allegations of corruption against the big guy. Most of the government's "bad guys," such as Roch LaSalle, were operating on their own account rather than on the government's. As David Frum pointed out, *On the Take* contained much that was damning and much that was well documented, but what was damning was not well documented, and what was documented was not that damning.

Stevie never let up. She broke the Gucci-gate story, ran savagely critical articles every time a new patronage list was published and wrote two other books, indirectly condemning Mulroney for everything except plagues of locusts that descended on prairie wheat fields. Mulroney never publicly commented on Cameron's attacks, but during one of our interviews, when I asked him directly about *On the Take*, his verdict on Cameron, then still promoting her book, was short but not sweet. "She's on the road like a horny pirate," he said, "because she's trying to whip up interest in a book that implies that the prime minister is a thug and a crook and a killer."

—

Mulroney knew it was coming:
What would you say is the most serious accusation made against me in the Cameron book? What would you surmise I personally did wrong? I mean, if I have to answer something, what do I answer? What is the charge against me? What is this extraordinary lifestyle? I don't drink. I don't smoke. I don't run around. What's it about?

Mulroney downplayed the book's success:
Note Conrad Black's review of the book where he said it was just absolute trash, there's no evidence of anything, just innuendo everywhere. Conrad Black was on television talking about her. He said, "She's a total failure, and the book was a disgrace. She's like a dying vampire trying to suck blood from the Mulroneys for her own financial gain." He said, "The goddamned book is not worth five cents, there's nothing in it. The book is a disgrace." I mean, this is as clean a government as Canada has ever seen, if you put our stuff in perspective.

Yet Mulroney never contemplated legal action against Cameron, not even when his picture in a black tuxedo was used on the cover alongside the title, *On the Take*:
What am I going to sue on? She told the Montreal *Gazette*, "I have no evidence that Mr. Mulroney ever did anything wrong and I have no evidence that he ever condoned wrongdoing." The cover is suable, but then all I do is sell books; that's all I do. I'm told by the people who have examined it for me that there's not the slightest direct allegation of wrongdoing by me or by my wife, not one. And it's all a tissue of smear, I mean, as if I had anything to do with Roch LaSalle or Sinclair Stevens . . . I thought on a scale of one to ten, this book had the potential of being a ten. In my assessment, it's less than a one.

David Angus, who worked as a reporter before becoming a lawyer and later a senator, on the book:

I was just a guy that Brian recruited to keep party finances honest and do a good job, but Stevie Cameron wrote horrible things about me. I was doing a public service. My mother would say, "If I ever see your name in the paper as a bagman or anything like that again, you're going to be disowned."

I had a three-and-a-half hour interview with Stevie— it's all on tape and I had a lawyer present. I asked her if she was engaging in her favourite sport. She said, "What's that?" I said, "Character assassination. Why do you hate the Mulroneys?" She said, "I hate them with a passion because they act like millionaires." She admitted that, right on my tape, and that's when I said, "What do you mean, *like* millionaires? They *are* millionaires." Brian was a substantial millionaire after the Iron Ore Company settlement and he had a successful stock portfolio. I mean, this guy Jonathan Deitcher, who was his broker, did wonders for him and a whole lot of guys ended up as his clients.

I mean, what do you have to do? Inherit your money like Trudeau to be legitimate? I thought that if you make it the old-fashioned way in Canada, it ain't all bad. There is a tendency in our media to assassinate characters first without checking. I saw a lot of that. I saw a lot of good people dissuaded away from public life.

Marjory LeBreton thought Cameron was jealous:
Well, apparently early on she wasn't included in Mila's circle, which is really dumb, but she just decided that she would get in with some journalists who had a rat-pack mentality.

A friend of mine sent me a speech she gave in Winnipeg to the Women's Canadian Club, and it was an insulting speech. It's insulting to women first of all because she talks about meeting all her very best friends at parties, parties, parties, all about the Gotliebs and how they throw wonderful parties, and about her wonderful husband, David.

To me, I read that as a woman and think, yeech.

Then she started talking about how Ottawa threw out the Tories because Ottawa people knew they were all corrupt and dishonest, and she talked about unsolved murders. I mean, just sick stuff. She was talking about that guy who used to work for Roch LaSalle and had been employed at a strip club in Toronto, all kind of tied in a neat little package. I mean, she's driven.

THE FRIENDLY U.S. PRESS

After the 1988 election, Mulroney compared editorials from American newspapers with the homegrown response:
We just got the *Washington Post* and *Baltimore Sun,* and they basically say, well, what the Canadians got is a great prime minister. The proof of that, he's unpopular. We couldn't get a favourable review out of these rinky-dink Canadians, and the *New York Times, Washington Post* and *Le Figaro* were giving us—*Time* magazine, too—tremendous reviews.

If it isn't Trudeau doing it, it isn't good for the Canadian press. Canadians must be perplexed by the reaction of the international media. They say, "Mulroney has always been a great prime minister—it's about time those Canadians smartened up and realized what's going on."

The prime minister's friendship with the *Washington Post*'s publisher, Katharine Graham, began after a speech he gave to American publishers meeting in Montreal, said Bill Pristanski:
That's where he came out with his famous line, "If I was president of the United States, I'd wake up every morning and thank God that my neighbour is Canada." He challenged the publishers, saying, "If it's not Wayne Gretzky or a snowstorm, you don't report anything about Canada.

It's a unique relationship, yet you don't have any news about us." Kay Graham fought her way through the crowd to tell him it was a great speech.

Senator Edward Kennedy's praise of Mulroney, during a 1992 visit to Massachusetts, never made it into Canadian newspapers:
MULRONEY: The Canadian press gallery just about collapsed when Ted Kennedy said, "My brother, the president, had people like Prime Minister Mulroney in mind when he wrote *Profiles in Courage*." And he said, "This is a guy that's done more and taken on more than any other leader."

Mulroney, on his last tour of the U.S. as prime minister, in 1993:
I just got back from Washington and I had quite a time. I did an hour and twenty minutes one on one with President Clinton this morning, and then Kay Graham had lunch for me at the *Washington Post*. Then I did an hour on [political affairs cable channel] C-SPAN, which is going to be shown on their network Sunday night. And then I did the MacNeil/Lehrer newscast on PBS. And so we had a very good go of that, a wonderful final trip down there.

In 1995 he reflected that his legacy and policies made Jean Chrétien's Liberal government look good in American eyes:
Does popularity mean that the Liberals are a bunch of geniuses? Do you think looking at that front bench that this is a bunch of geniuses? Or has the mood changed? And why has the mood changed? The mood has changed because the recession is over and Canada has emerged, as the *New York Times* points out, as the strongest nation in the world because of Brian Mulroney's policies. We took advantage of the recession to do tough, difficult things

that have strengthened the nation immeasurably economically. So I mean, people are happier today.

**One of Mulroney's favourite reviews was published in
the Baltimore Sun:**
I'll read to you. "Brian Mulroney fell from power in
Canada after doing everything right. What Mr.
Mulroney did right is cut spending, increase revenues
through an unpopular sales tax to reduce the deficit,
lower import barriers to spur trade, de-regulate much of
the economy and hold down inflation. His great monument is the free trade agreement with the United States.
Mr. Mulroney's achievements didn't help him in the
polls. He has won two elections and has served nearly
eight years, roughly what the U.S. constitution allows the
president. It is long enough. As a bilingual Quebecker of
Irish ancestry, he seemed the ideal choice to bring
Canadians together. He certainly tried, offered Quebec
more than previous agreements. Yet his approach was
rejected. Canada is back to square one on the constitution. In the U.S. it is fair to say the economy determines
who will be president but foreign policy is the most
important thing the president does. In Canada, the economy chooses the Prime Ministers, the constitution making his or her most important challenge. As for Mr.
Mulroney, he is stepping down at age 53 after successes
that will hold his reputation extremely high with future
historians. He is one of those remarkable Conservatives in
English-speaking countries who defined the 1980s, along
with Ronald Reagan and Margaret Thatcher and he made
a much more lasting imprint on the nation than most
predicted when he rushed in from private life to rescue
his sagging party in 1983."

Mulroney loved to cite another op-ed on his tenure:
Well, I'll show you another one, it was a profile from
Washington, by the diplomatic affairs editor of the

St. Petersburg Times. His name is Jack Payton and he writes, "Mulroney seemed the ideal politician, movie-star handsome, obviously bright and a bureaucratic infighter second to none. He could also deliver a speech in English or French so smoothly and so persuasively that even the Great Communicator Ronald Reagan looked like a mere actor in comparison. Americans, those who paid any attention at all, noticed that when the Canadian leader visited Washington and when he and the President came out to talk with reporters, Mulroney usually looked like he ought to be the one running the White House, not the other guy. Finally, the bright young son of a rural electrician realized the Progressive Conservatives were doomed to defeat with him at the helm, and did the honorable thing. He decided to resign for the good of his party. The last American politician to do anything even close to that was Lyndon Johnson." That's the kind of stuff that's all over the place down there.

14.

"I Told You I Loved You, Now Get OUT!"

The Perils of People Power

IF THE SECRET OF GOVERNING Canada is deciding which touchy issues to leave alone, Brian Mulroney was a dud—and never more so than during his final attempt to set new rules of engagement between Quebec and the rest of the country. The Great Referendum, held under his feverish sponsorship on October 26, 1992, was supposed to decide the country's constitutional future. Instead, it decided his.

The popular vote against the Charlottetown Accord set the stage for his exit from politics a few months later. Charlottetown faced the handicap of being the third in a series of constitutional showdowns, following the Trudeau patriation pageant of 1982 (which most voters had forgotten) and the fiasco of the Meech Lake agreement (which they didn't want to remember). At a time when unemployment was running at a devastating

11 per cent and the economy was ravaged by uncertainty, tinkering with the constitution didn't rank on anybody's list of high-priority items. When one provincial premier warned that if the accord wasn't passed the economy would be devastated, I remember wondering, "How will he be able to tell?"

Unlike Meech, which all but two provincial premiers regarded as a mutual triumph they shared with the prime minister, the Charlottetown meetings had an air of desperation from the very beginning. The eventual accord was the compromise of many compromises, with seventeen designated negotiating chefs concocting a brew that contained only those ingredients on which they could all agree. At one point, a Saskatchewan cabinet minister named Robert Mitchell spoke for most of the delegates to the Prince Edward Island capital where the final version of the accord was negotiated when he sourly commented, "My friend George Peacock, who is in our delegation, leaned over to me yesterday, and said, 'The truth of the matter is that we were all killed in a huge car accident. And this is Hell.' And he was right."

In the referendum campaign that followed, the "Yes" side was never able to demonstrate that the accord delivered the proper balance between individual and collective rights and that the courts could be counted on to protect both. On the contrary, Charlottetown's "distinct society" Quebec clause and the self-government provisions for Aboriginal Canadians made it appear that Canada was developing into a multinational state with more than one class of citizenship. This was particularly true of Quebec, which was guaranteed a perpetual 25 per cent of the seats in the Commons.

There were good reasons for both supporting and rejecting the accord, but they were so complicated that most Canadians shifted their attention to reviling the deal's author. (My own position was that I preferred Meech to Charlottetown, but I actively supported the latter, to the point of organizing fellow members of the Order of Canada.)

Any voters Mulroney had failed to alienate with his recently passed and highly unpopular goods and services tax and the still negatively perceived Free Trade Agreement were now granted a chance to vote against him, and they lined up to seize the opportunity. "In the course of a referendum, people do not answer a government's question," French president François Mitterrand had pointed out, having learned that lesson the hard way in his own run-off. "They answer the questions they are asking themselves."

Four years after endowing Brian Mulroney with a second majority mandate, voters were desperate to send him a message, echoing the heartbreak Chicago blues, "I Told You I Loved You, Now Get OUT!" Mulroney had characteristically claimed too much for the accord's acceptance (2.5 million new jobs) and exaggerated the effect of its failure (a busted country). The defining image of the referendum debate, which raged across the boardrooms and the taverns of the nation, was of the PM afire at a hall in Sherbrooke, Quebec, where he had been listing thirty-one benefits that that province had achieved through Confederation. He interrupted himself, picked up his speaking notes and tore them in half, then declared, his mouth twisted in anger, "If we vote 'no' we rip up these historic gains!" In the same speech he predicted that a vote against the accord would mean "the beginning of the process of the dismantling of Canada."

The real meaning of the referendum became clear only when people realized that they didn't have to use their ballots to pass judgment on a legalistic arrangement they could barely comprehend. By voting "no!" they could legitimize their mistrust of the politicians who acted as their surrogates in constitutional decisions. This pushed the "yes" side into appearing to defend the status quo, which put its supporters in an increasingly untenable position. They were actually fronting revolutionary and creative reforms of the Constitution, but they were cornered into appearing to defend the status quo because of their support of its sponsor.[1]

Referendum night in Canada, 1992, signalled open season on incumbents. The "yes" faction, which included nearly every head of anything that mattered (except the Reform Party) and just about every opinion leader in the country, spent $14 million on its campaign; it had nine hundred professional organizers in the field and the best polling brains money could buy. The "no" side raised much less than a million dollars and campaigned through radio phone-in shows (notably Rafe Mair's passionate invocations on CKNW in Vancouver), fax machines, church basements and leaflets dropped in mailboxes. They became the equivalent of the guerrilla fighters in black pyjamas who won the Vietnam War against the might of the high-tech American killing machine. "The trouble was," Jeffrey Simpson noted in the *Globe*, "that tolerance and compromise had long since yielded to a seething mass of regional, class, ethnic and linguistic passions, usually directed against other parts of Canada."

At the end of that long and agonizing process, both Canada and Brian Mulroney took on some of the characteristics of a beached whale: immobile and beginning to stink a little.

—

Mulroney, on why he tried:
After the Bélanger-Campeau report [recommending a referendum on Quebec sovereignty], there was a lot of

---

1. Previous Canadian prime ministers had avoided referenda, with only two exceptions: in 1889 on prohibition and in 1942 on wartime conscription. Both proved inconclusive.

uncertainty about the future of the country. There was pressure on Robert Bourassa, and he gave in with this undertaking that there was going to be a referendum of some kind on sovereignty before October 26, 1992. So this psychologically was the litmus point.

With the economy the way it was, I became very pre-occupied by this. I didn't mind a referendum on Canada, but if there was going to be a referendum on Canada, I wanted it to be with Canada having an opportunity to put its best face forward. You don't want people voting against Canada because they can't get a job or because the recession has impacted their family and their kids can't find summer employment and therefore they can't go to junior college. This happens in a recession. So there were a number of reasons why it was important to seek a resolution.

Mulroney shuffled his cabinet, placing Joe Clark in charge of dealing with the provinces:
I put Clark in Constitutional Affairs because I needed somebody at this point in time who was bilingual, who had not been sullied by the attacks and counterattacks of Meech and post-Meech. Clark had been totally out of the fray for seven years. It was almost as if Clark weren't a Canadian because [as minister of external affairs] he wasn't part of the everyday fighting. When he took a position on something, it was generally a position that the nation supported.

While preparing to lead the "Yes" side in the referendum, Mulroney reflected on what Canada might become without a new constitutional deal:
I might do a speech where I refer to these predictions by futurologists that the Canadian fragments would be swept up by the United States. To put things in perspective, California has a larger economy than that of Canada in terms of influence. So there would be no discussions or

bargaining—provinces would enter on a take-it-or-leave-it basis.

So you've got the nine provinces of English Canada coming in with the equivalent of about 22 million people, and that's substantially less than the population of one state. You'd eventually find yourself with the same kinds of crime rates and the right to bear arms in your new constitution. You wouldn't have to worry about western alienation. The concept would disappear from our vocabulary, because you'd be a member of the melting pot. And Albertans, seeking to do business with their fellow Americans in California by mid next century, will probably have to deal in Spanish, and may—horror of horrors—find Spanish on the side of their cornflakes box.

Mulroney thought the Charlottetown agreement confirmed the original contents of the Meech Lake Accord:
The only memorable quote I ever heard from my father was, "You can never go wrong doing the right thing." And what I was doing with Meech was the right thing. Now the proof of that, if you ever wanted proof, is that, aside from a couple of little changes, every single item and word of Meech Lake was in the Charlottetown document.

He worried about how to get the terms across to Quebec:
René Lévesque's politicization of the teachers' union left them much more interested in propagating separatism than in teaching their students how to write French. If these people can't read, what do we do so they get the message? . . . We've got to put our message on television in a very simple, straightforward way. No use putting dancing girls on, trumpets and so on, just put it on in black and white: here are the gains Bourassa achieved at Charlottetown. And then have a voice-over as it rolls, one, two, three, four, five, six, seven . . . Just as if you were

speaking to functional illiterates, because according to this, you are.

On the west coast, Mulroney envisioned a different publicity strategy:
In British Columbia, I suggested to our people not just to assemble but also to do direct advertising. Say something like, "Ladies and gentlemen, you may not have known— may we introduce you to the leaders of the 'No' side in Quebec?" And flash on a picture of Jacques Parizeau and Lucien Bouchard. "Do you know how they are going to interpret a 'No' win in Quebec? They say as soon as they get a 'No' vote, they're going to take Quebec out and destroy Canada. You may not have known this, but these are the people who are working for the 'No' side."

Mulroney, on the unlikely coalition that came together to reject the deal:
Look at the "No" side. Can you imagine being associated with a group that involved people like Trudeau and Judy Rebick—a Trotskyite—and [Parti Québécois leader] Jacques Parizeau and Danny Cameron, the leader of the Confederation of Regions Party in New Brunswick? And Preston Manning? The malice of a Sharon Carstairs in full flight, when she is not complaining of nervous breakdowns and her possible imminent withdrawals from politics because of stress, is a sight to behold.

This campaign is tough, because if you say anything, they say it's fear-mongering. If you say nothing, they say, "Jesus! Hey, Prime Minister, why didn't you warn us?" I fully expected all the rats to come out, and they have. The press, the wimps like Manning, the haters like Trudeau, the destroyers like Parizeau and his gang. Canadians are going to have to decide very, very soon whether they want to keep the country together. Just that simple.

Some pundits thought he should step aside and let someone else lead the constitutional battle:
MULRONEY: When this thing started, I could have gone to Harrington Lake or Florida and said, "Look, if you need me, give me a call." And then they would say, what a coward, he does this deal and he's not even ready to fight for it, what kind of a leader is this?

I'm out there fighting away, which is what I should be doing. And I get these stupid, sophomoric editorials from [pollster] Angus Reid saying that I'm dragging the cause down and that Joe Clark should be leading the fight. But it never occurs to Angus to ask himself, if Joe Clark is so popular, how come we're way behind in Alberta, where I haven't set foot?

The other thing I find quite funny, just between us, is that everybody is gearing up all the so-called experts to blame me. But you know the fact of the matter is that by the time I got to British Columbia on the first leg of the campaign, they were calling this guy Mike Harcourt "Premier Bonehead." By the time we get to Alberta, Don Getty has resigned, thereby ensuring that the Conservative Party is not supporting the "Yes" side— they're all running for leader. When I get to Manitoba, Filmon is still in Europe. In Newfoundland, Clyde Wells spends the first three weeks arguing about the legal text, deciding whether or not he's going to come. And in Quebec, Robert Bourassa has been betrayed and blind-sided by everybody from the tapes in *L'actualité* [in which two renegade bureaucrats blamed Bourassa for caving to English Canada] to a stab in the back by Pierre Trudeau, who calls him a blackmailer.

And a simplistic mind like Angus Reid is saying the "Yes" side didn't plan its campaign. How was I supposed to plan for this?

Mulroney believed Charlottetown was a crossroads:
Fifty years later, people will say, you know, how did these

people manage to lose Canada? How did they do something like that?

The answer is that when confronted with a challenge, Canadians failed to respond. And what was the challenge? Were they challenged to find a cure for cancer? No. Were they challenged to end poverty in the world? No. Were they challenged to put a man on Mars? No, nothing that dramatic.

Canadians failed to agree on language that would have enabled the country to survive while, for example, building a new Senate like the Germans and the Australians did, or redistributing powers between the federal and provincial levels, as goes on all the time, or strengthening the constitutional position and distinctiveness of its French-speaking minority in Quebec, or innovating a defined and appropriate degree of justice and fairness in constitutional and economic terms for our Native people.

He couldn't help resenting the fact that the media downplayed his efforts to make the accord work:
I brought Bourassa back, just through personal relationships . . . He didn't want to come back and then I got him to come back to Harrington Lake and we just kept working it through and finally we got the deal, right?

In the seven weeks since I've been involved, I think most people—and I certainly know what they're saying privately—agree that I salvaged the whole thing. In fact, Clark is saying it quite openly; he's saying it very openly. We were dead and this guy walked in and he resurrected the whole goddamned thing. All the premiers are saying it, but not a single solitary person in Ottawa has written it. This is what I'm up against.

Seven weeks after the prime minister for the first time since Sir John A. Macdonald does this—this is my third time, but this time even the Aboriginal peoples are in there, and the territorial leaders. I do it, and there's not a goddamned word. My name is not mentioned except to disparage me.

Public opinion polls began to suggest a defeat for the "Yes" side:
MULRONEY: I got off the plane the other day in Winnipeg and I said to Jake Epp, "How are we doing?" He said, "We're doing fine, we're working hard. It's a very, very tough fight. The enemy is anti-French, anti-Quebec." You know what could happen? We could have a repeat of the John Major phenomenon, where all of these highly respected polling organizations the day before the UK election predicted that Labour leader Neil Kinnock would win, and the next day the Tories won a majority. At the last second, people went for Major. If that were to happen, we could wind up certainly winning the popular vote in Canada and most provinces.

On October 26, 1992, six provinces rejected the deal, with the highest rejection rate coming from British Columbia:
We did the right thing with Charlottetown. We did the right thing by putting it to a referendum, no question about that. I have no trouble with Charlottetown—they voted on it. I don't care what people decide as long as they vote. I haven't the slightest regret about the referendum, not one. It was a great opportunity missed. A great opportunity missed . . .

Trudeau advisor Michael Pitfield on why Canadians rejected it:
Charlottetown was overworked. Nobody could understand it. If there ever was a case of Jeffersonian justification, the people spoke against what it was. With $7 million funding on the "Yes" side and about $190,000 on the other, they went with the $190,000. It doesn't really matter that it was an unholy coalition—various interest

groups were each unhappy for different reasons, some of which were contradictory.

Mulroney later rationalized the referendum defeat:
We had to deal, quite properly, with Aboriginal concerns and institutional reform, as a result of which a fairly complicated package had to be put together. The referendum was interesting and beneficial, because it took the poison out of the system for Quebec. It laid something out; the Canadian people had a chance to say yes or no to it. They said no to it, but not in overwhelming terms.

Generally speaking this thing was 45–55 across the country—four or five provinces in favour, four or five provinces against it. But it was rejected. And having rejected it, Canadians moved on. The package had to be put democratically to the people. It was, and they said No. I don't think there are any winners or losers in that. When the people speak, they are always right. They have spoken on this.

15

"I led a revolution"

Mulroney on the World Stage

As often as he could, Brian Mulroney escaped domestic criticism by incarnating himself as an international states- man. His relationships with U.S. presidents Ronald Reagan and George H. Bush set new boundaries for coziness. He cherished his fiery exchanges with British prime minister Margaret Thatcher on South Africa, and developed a genuine friendship with French president François Mitterrand. German chancellor Helmut Kohl credited him with helping tear down the Berlin Wall. Mulroney's biggest disappointment on the international stage was his inability to pursue the offer to become secretary-general of the United Nations in 1991.

"MY PAL BRIAN WANTS THIS, AND THAT'S THAT": RONALD REAGAN

Pierre Trudeau was called "an asshole" and worse by Richard Nixon, while Ronald Reagan relied on the Pentagon to ridicule Trudeau's peace initiatives. Mulroney steered his government in precisely the opposite direction, becoming a surrogate—and often a propagandist—for Washington's good intentions.

A few weeks after becoming leader of the Opposition in 1983, Mulroney met with Reagan for the first time:
I told him I was going to get lynched by a lot of people who think it's unconstitutional to get along with American presidents, but that this country was fed up to the goddamned teeth with people going around saying the United States is our enemy. They know the United States is our friend, and they elected us because they thought I was going to do something about it, because of the credible relationship between Reagan and me.

It's the only thing that'll move mountains around here, when the president gets up in the morning and says, "I want this done. My pal Brian wants this, and that's that." George Mitchell, a Democratic senator from Maine, said everybody in Washington knows that Reagan's special relationship now is with me. Canada has gone right to the top of the hit parade.

A hidden message in the March 1985 Shamrock Summit in Quebec City:
MULRONEY: I chose Quebec first because it's not Ottawa, and secondly, it has historic significance, and great security for Reagan at the governor general's La Citadelle summer residence. We won twenty-two seats in eastern Quebec, and all of a sudden, this big bird will arrive out of the sky, and two people are going to get together: the president of the United States and the prime minister of

Canada. The premier of Quebec ain't going to be there. Quebeckers are going to say, "Mulroney is in the big leagues, he's the guy we've got to keep our eye on, he's our boy."

I've got Lévesque going crazy. He's turning himself inside out. My original thought was to have President Reagan stop at the little boarding house where I lived when I was going to Laval and take a look at it. It wasn't that the thought was too corny; it was just that we couldn't do it with all his Secret Service and what have you.

The sing-song that made history:
MULRONEY: Here you have on St. Patrick's Day two pure Irish people, mothers and fathers 100 per cent Irish, singing "When Irish Eyes Are Smiling" on the feast of all Irish people. This is supposed to be a signal of friendship, but becomes in the eyes of the media a signal of servility.

Do you remember when [Soviet leader Mikhail] Gorbachev went to the White House in 1989 and one of the famous Russian pianists showed up and began to play Russian popular songs for Gorbachev, and Reagan got up and started to sing? Nobody thought this was anything other than normal, fun and appropriate.

Only the inadequacies and insecurities of the Canadian media vis-à-vis the United States, and their overwhelming self-doubt, would allow them to transform a warm, senti-mental little occasion into a piece of footage conveying ser-vility. There's something wrong with this. Just the last verse, we sang the last verse, that's all. It was nothing more than that. But this is the kind of country you deal with. Now, if I would have said to Reagan, "Look, why don't you go home, you imperialistic old fool?"—this would have been a declaration of independence!

Paul Robinson, who served as the U.S. ambassador to Canada from 1981 to 1985:
These two men get on like long-lost fraternity brothers. The president likes Brian personally, and wants to help

him. They really like each other. Brian has no fear of America gobbling up Canada or any such thing. He sees our closeness as an asset, and he's right. Who wouldn't like to be anchored next to the world's greatest market?

They're both conservatives and that's important. There isn't anything those two men couldn't solve or at least get to the point of maximum return. I'm seeing now that the government and the official bodies in Canada are accurately reflecting what the people have felt all along, namely a positive and friendly attitude towards the United States.

Mulroney on the benefits of American influence:
Canada was successful at the 1986 Tokyo Summit, in ensuring that decisions on monetary policy and exchange rates take place within all G-7 members, and not just the original G-5 [which excluded Canada and Italy]. When the Europeans tried to keep us out, Reagan said, "This is all very interesting, but I've listened to Brian Mulroney, and how can he be a second-class citizen? How can he be a member of the G-7 when we have a private club off on the side deciding monetary policy? It doesn't make any sense. So I'll tell you what, either Canada gets in or we're getting out." That was the end of the debate.

Mulroney always headed straight for the top:
BILL PRISTANSKI: As the boss said, he always waits to deal with the big boy. He'll wait to deal with the President. He's not going to deal with anybody else. He said, "The U.S. never paid attention to the Grits because they were always petulant in the House of Commons. Trudeau used to deal with Reagan's staff and go through six pipsqueaks in the Pentagon."

Mulroney didn't think that Reagan or his policies were always right for Canada:
I don't think Star Wars [missile defence] is a big deal. I've

never been impressed with the whole concept. I can't see how we'd gain anything from it. I don't think we'd participate. It doesn't make any sense to me. As far as defence, we need some changes. We're building these goddamn frigates that are useful for NATO, but I think the Navy's wrong the way it's building huge World War II convoy vessels.

Fred Doucet, during his time as chief of staff, remembered how Mulroney influenced Reagan at one lunch meeting:
I carried a reduction of the National Film Board map of North America into the lunch, and the prime minister— always with a nose for how to impress another person and sensing that Reagan reacted better to what he could see—took the map out. In the middle of the lunch, he said to the president, "Could I show you something?" We put a yellow line all across the Northwest Passage— because Artic sovereignty was on our agenda—and he said to Reagan, "Now look, Ron. This is what we call the Northwest Passage, that's the Polar Sea, where one of your ships went last year without my knowledge, and dare I say without your knowledge. Now, we have stated publicly that all of this is ours—Canada. Now see this white stuff here, Ron? That's ice. Not water, ice. You can walk across from here to there, see? Walk across. That's different from any other so-called waterway anywhere in the world."

Reagan said, "Or march across?"

The prime minister said, "Yeah, whatever. Now look, some of your people are telling you that this is an international waterway and that you want to preserve the right of passage. Look, Ron, if it were an international waterway, which we can question whether it is or not, that means that everybody else has rights to it. So how about this? We own it and we have an agreement that gives you certain exclusivity because of our allied relationship." Reagan just said, "Well, we'll have to look into that." That was it, a map of Canada with a yellow line.

Mulroney says it was Reagan who began to experiment with the thought of a free trade zone encompassing the United States and Canada:
Reagan was very much a free trader. What I liked about him, quite frankly, was the position he took in 1980 against [fellow Republican presidential hopeful] John Connally. Reagan's argument was, if you start this protectionist American stuff, you're going to bring on the greatest goddamned depression we've had in fifty years. You've got to be a free trader.

If the Japanese make money selling into the American market, it's because American consumers want to buy their Toyotas. The answer is not to keep the Toyotas out; the answer is to make a better Chrysler in Detroit. These were his fundamental views. People kind of laugh at Reagan. They can laugh all they want—there were five or six things that he believed in, and he bloody well pounded them home all the time. Free trade was one of them.

Despite his reputation as the Great Communicator, Reagan was never regarded as particularly bright:
MULRONEY: He once said, "Brian, did you read that article in the *Reader's Digest* that trees cause pollution?" I knew him and liked him well enough that I didn't get into an argument. I just said, "I gave up reading *Reader's Digest,* Ron."

Reagan was very different, very warm and considerate and thoughtful. He had very simple principles. He believed in free trade. He believed in a strong United States. He believed in the free enterprise system, anticommunism. He believed in 100 per cent support for Israel. Just that simple. That was it.

Still, there was a touch of jealousy in Mulroney's feelings about how Reagan was treated by journalists:
Look, Harry Truman had the worst press of any president in modern history. Most historians today will say he was a great president. Ronald Reagan has had marvellous press. I don't know how well Ron is going to be treated by history. He got the supine press, but history is going to be tough on him, though he will do well internationally because he did some great things.

Fred Doucet, on the relationship between president and prime minister:
Brian treated Reagan to some degree as a father. Reagan in no way treated him as a son. If you saw them publicly, you wouldn't sense a father-son relationship because Brian can still be blunt, if you know what I mean. It was the proximity; it was the case of, "Well, finally we have a prime minister of Canada who wants to be a friend."

"THE AMERICANS DIDN'T WANT US IN":
GEORGE H. BUSH

Reagan's vice-president, George Herbert Walker Bush, easily defeated Democrat Michael Dukakis in the 1988 presidential election. Bush had approached Mexican president Carlos Salinas—also elected in 1988—to pursue a bilateral trade accord.

Mulroney said he fought hard to join what eventually became NAFTA:
I'm telling you, George Bush was trying to do a deal with Salinas. The United States is here—they've got a free trade deal with Canada. Then they get a free trade deal with Mexico. Then they get a free trade agreement with Chile, and guess what, they're the hub and we're the spokes. What Canadians don't understand, because we've never

told them, is that we had to fight to get into the negotiations. The Americans didn't want us in. I had to insist that we be part of the NAFTA. They were going to drive a separate deal with the Mexicans, so they would be the new Rome, sitting in the middle.

I said, no, no, no. We're going to be right in the centre, we're going to be right in the hub of this. That's why we got in. And I had to fight like hell. I had to use a lot of influence with George Bush and others to get in.

Michael Wilson recalled how U.S. secretary of state James Baker tried not to disturb Bush as the free trade negotiations were near completion:
We were discussing the dispute settlement mechanism, and we thought it wasn't nearly as effective as it could be. The prime minister wanted to call the president, and Baker said, "I don't think that's appropriate at this point—let's get the lawyers in and see what we can do. Besides, it's after eight o'clock, the president is watching a movie."

We were very close to losing the deal right there, but the prime minister didn't lose his nerve on it. That was on a Saturday night. Baker finally did call the president, there was a pause, and Bush said, "I want to speak to him—don't give me that nonsense, I know he's there—put him on the phone."

Bush shunned the spotlight, and was more comfortable one on one:
MULRONEY: I was sitting with Bush in the backyard of his house for four hours in Kennebunkport, and he was complaining because he didn't like summits because they force expectations, and on that one he's right. But I said, "Why don't you have the same kind of conversation with Gorbachev as you're having with me? Here we are, just the two of us sitting in the backyard, there's not an advisor in sight, nobody taking notes, and you don't have to

size me up because you know me, and I don't have to size you up, but you don't know the other guy."

The Bush and Mulroney friendship evolved rapidly after Saddam Hussein invaded Kuwait in 1990. Mulroney quickly ordered the cessation of bilateral trade with Iraq and deployed three Canadian warships to the Persian Gulf:
MULRONEY: Bush just called me. I've got it right in front of me, he called me at 1:05 p.m. and he had just had a report from Defence Secretary Dick Cheney, which said, "Kuwait is province 19 of Iraq, and it looks bad."

NEWMAN: The prestige of the United Nations is on the line.

MULRONEY: Well, that's my argument against all these left-wingers. What do you want to do, for God's sake? This guy Hussein is a Nazi and you can't let him just sit there and ruin the United Nations. We had a tough decision to make, but we went in there and said where we stood and committed the resources with the two opposition parties dead set against us, all the peaceniks and so on.

Mulroney on his influence during the Gulf War crisis:
The *Wall Street Journal* and the *New York Times* wrote that in the preparations leading up to the war in the summer of 1990, Bush was in the Pentagon, and he stood up before the generals and left to place a call to me. They said, "He's calling Brian Mulroney four or five times a day." The Gulf War was obviously a huge thing.

Bush's domestic approval ratings skyrocketed after the Gulf War. Then came allegations about possible love affairs. Mulroney offered this advice:
Bush said, "Isn't that the goddamnest bit of trash you've

ever seen? Can you goddamn well believe it?" This is the way he talks, you know.

I said, "I can, George. By our standards, this is normal up here in Canada. Let me tell you something before you get too worked up. I've got a guy [John Sawatsky] up here who wrote, among other things, that I took a shower with some beautiful blonde that I had never met in my goddamned life. It wasn't even true at all."

And he said, "What's that got to do with it?"

I said, "Well, a month later my popularity jumped seven points. So whatever you do, don't deny a goddamned thing!" He laughed so hard and he said, "Can I tell Barbara?"

You know, sometimes they say this must be very sensitive stuff, when the prime minister is talking to the president. Well, that was the way the conversation on the North American Free Trade Agreement ended.

Mulroney saw some personal parallels in Bush's resounding defeat in 1992 at the hands of Bill Clinton:
All of a sudden the economy goes and a guy who had the vision to put together the greatest coalition in the history of the world, wins the war, has the vision to put together the NAFTA, and a 91 per cent approval rating, goes down the chute. Horrific defeat, and all of his qualities are weaknesses.

People don't like him. They don't want the vision thing, he's mediocre, he's tongue-tied, he's dishonest, he's sleeping with his secretary, they don't like the look of him on TV, he looks terrible. All of the qualities of naturalness and good nature that made George Bush were swept asunder by a bad economy. The most popular president in American history lost his election because of the recession.

He called me on an unrelated matter during the election campaign and I was trying to pep him up, and he said, "Brian, I'm in California, it's in a state of depression and I don't see how I can win with this attitude. There's an attitude, it's morose, it's sad. It's depressed." That's what happens. People get down on themselves, they get down on their country and they get down on their leaders. Well, that's the way it is and that's what happened to me too.

"IF I DON'T, I'M A THIRD-RATE PLAYER":
BILL CLINTON

Just as the former Arkansas governor replaced Bush at the White House, Mulroney's days at 24 Sussex Drive were about to end.

Mulroney says that Clinton used the Canadian prime minister's accomplishments as a yardstick:
Clinton told me in a telephone call that everybody knows about the structural changes I've made. The tax structure, consumption tax, free trade, NAFTA, privatization and cutting down the deficit. It was amazing. And he said, "Now if I make structural changes like that, I will have made a difference. If I don't, I'm a third-rate player." I told cabinet about it. I was very impressed—not that he told me, but that he knew about it.

"THEY THOUGHT SHE WAS ARROGANT, SMARMY":
MARGARET THATCHER

Mulroney's relationship with Margaret Thatcher was one of extremes.

He was proud of the fact that he stood up to the British prime minister:
I fought Margaret to a damn standstill on apartheid, but that's because if I hadn't taken her on, I would have had to take a lot of crap from Canadians. I like Margaret

Thatcher. I think she's terrific, provided that she doesn't put one goddamned toe in the Canadian pool. If she sticks her toe in the Canadian pool, she's going to get clobbered.

Mulroney believed television was to blame for Thatcher's fall:

I was the first prime minister ever to be re-elected with television in the House of Commons. Trudeau was defeated. Then Clark got defeated fast. And then Trudeau left before he was going to be defeated by me. I survived for nine years.

I said to Margaret Thatcher once, "Margaret, do not allow television in the British House. It's going to defeat you." And it defeated her, because Margaret's great qualities of leadership came when you heard them on the radio. Remember the way the British used to do it? The picture of the prime minister with her voice—the debates were broadcast but not telecast—so you had this nice picture of Margaret properly coiffed, looking elegant with her beautiful blue dress and diamonds on, and her very stern voice kicking the bejesus out of the Opposition. It just was a perfect combination.

When television came in, she came across as *schoolmarmish,* hectoring and sweating. All of a sudden she wasn't the same person, and it caused enormous damage to her image.

The recession also played its part:

MULRONEY: The recession was going to drag everything else down with it. Countries became morose and people wanted a scapegoat. And so, qualities that they may have approved for months and a few years before all of a sudden became character flaws. That's the way it was and that's what happened to me, and many more.

The socialists were thrown out of office in France at exactly the same time because of the recession, and the conservatives in Greece. Why did Margaret go? Because of the recession, because they didn't think they could win an election with her. She was the lightning rod. All of her qualities were transformed. They thought she was arrogant, smarmy. All of the things they liked about her they didn't like anymore.

Mulroney appreciated Thatcher's take on Pierre Trudeau's economic management skills:
In a G-7 meeting, you walk into the room and they know what your bankbook is. The prime minister of England, the president of France and the president of the United States all know how much money you've got in the bank because they've just been briefed by their people, who are saying Canada is in real bad shape. Margaret Thatcher said at a G-7 meeting, "Brian Mulroney has been left an extremely serious situation—Pierre Trudeau single-handedly ruined the public finances of one of the greatest countries in the world."

NEWMAN: She said that?

MULRONEY: Absolutely.

When Thatcher published her memoir, *The Downing Street Years*, in 1993, Mulroney looked for his name in the index:
Mrs. Thatcher didn't have much to say that was very nice about either Trudeau or myself and quoted a reference about me where she and I disagreed so vigorously on South Africa. I thought it was a little strange because of my relationship with Margaret. You never expect to be quoted extensively in somebody else's memoirs—that's not the object of the exercise—and moreover, Margaret's orientation was completely European and British. In the great scheme of things, the prime minister of Canada, his role is what it is—important at home and much less important abroad, eh? And you have to be realistic about that.

But I was kind of surprised. Somebody sent me a copy of her memoirs and so I look up that passage, and sure enough she says, "Brian Mulroney and I disagreed very strongly over South Africa." And then another thing, something like, Brian Mulroney was a charismatic and an attractive leader with whom I became very close friends, and he did this and he did that and so on, three or four pictures of us together in the book. I guess you know what the point is.

Bill Pristanksi recalled the 1987 meeting of Commonwealth leaders in Vancouver, where Thatcher became irate over South Africa:
Indian prime minister Rajiv Ghandi and Mulroney were telling Thatcher she's full of shit and she'd better budge on the South Africa issue, for the sake of the Commonwealth. Mulroney really went at her. "What do you mean, you don't believe in sanctions? Of course you believe in sanctions—you have sanctions, you've used them before." He went at her so hard that she cancelled a scheduled CBC interview afterwards for their Sunday night show. She told Deputy Minister of Foreign Affairs Reid Morden three times to quit taking notes on our side, saying, "I don't want this all over Ottawa." The atmosphere in the room was just terrible, and the boss gave a very tough speech—he went right at Thatcher and pointed at Zimbabwe president Robert Mugabe, saying, "This guy was in the slammer for ten years because he believed in this stuff. We're not kidding around. This guy was in jail!"

After this, Mugabe came and corrected him, saying, "Prime Minister, your speech was very eloquent. I just wanted to correct you on one thing. I was in jail for ten years, three months and four days."

Fred Doucet recalled a particularly nasty Thatcher meeting:

Let me tell you about the bilateral between the prime minister and Margaret Thatcher. This occurred on Monday afternoon, October 12, 1987. Mrs. Thatcher arrived in the morning and we were forewarned that she wasn't feeling well, that she had the flu and that as a result, the bilateral might be brief or briefer because she wanted to go to bed early that evening to be in shape for the next morning.

She arrived in the prime minister's office as if driven by a force that needn't be explained and all of us quickly concluded that she wanted to come in and out because of what we had been told before. She plunked herself down on a seat and before the prime minister could welcome her to Canada, she had launched into a tirade on why sanctions had not worked, how she had been duped into giving this little bit of agreement in Nassau and in London subsequently and how she and the world were convinced of the foolishness of it all.

And the prime minister initially thought that . . . she wasn't feeling well; she's going to make her point and go. Not so. She pressed the analysis to limits beyond the reasonable and then some, and every time the prime minister tried to insert something balanced on the management of the issue, let alone the substance, she would have none of it. She was there for an hour, and she was supposed to have been there for ten minutes. It was like a football game, and the percentage of the time with one team having the ball for that one hour was about 95 per cent.

She sat on the edge of her seat throughout the piece and lectured the prime minister in ways that civility was injured if not downright demolished, particularly when at least she ought to have had the decency of acknowledging that he was the host, quite apart from being a colleague Conservative. She just lambasted him.

First he tried to insert substantive elements, saying, "Now look, Margaret, one of the things Joe Clark tells me is that there is possibly here an opportunity for us not to let the eminent persons approach die off." No sir. She would have none of that, absolutely not. I mean, it was just bang, bang and bang. Fire broadside. When the prime minister said, for instance, "Maybe the sanctions have worked psychologically. Maybe they haven't worked economically, but they've had a lot to do with sensitizing the world to the reality of apartheid." She said, wrong, wrong, wrong, surely you wouldn't say that at the meeting. You might want to say that to me, not that I'm going to be taken in by it, but surely you wouldn't say it publicly. What kind of analysis is that . . . This was mild compared to everything else she said.

So at the end of the hour, the prime minister was moving away from it for obvious reasons because she was not to be moved. She said, "There's only one way to manage this issue and that's to be done with it, be done with it. Forget it. Be done with it. I was pushed, cajoled, last time. This time I tell you I will have no part of it!" And she stuck to her word.

But we didn't know that what was going on behind the scenes was a massive British media operation led by their main briefer to discredit Canada, and they started, as you recall, by quoting statistics that were two years old. In other words, they were making the case that sanctions had not worked. Not even for Canada, because our trade had increased. Those statistics were, in fact, from a year before the sanctions were applied, and even when confronted with that evidence, they didn't move away from it. Now, I spoke with the acting high commissioner about that quickly after we found out that this was so, and his case was that they were using our own publications. I told him, "That's not the point. You're using a publication that is twelve months behind." They never acknowledged that.

"NEVER REPORTED IN CANADA": HELMUT KOHL

Mulroney on his leading role in the fall of communism:
I led a revolution. I never thought I would, but I did, because this was a revolutionary time.

Let me put it this way. You go from March of 1985, sitting in the Kremlin with Gorbachev, and five years later he is sitting in your house talking about the fact that the Soviet Union has collapsed. Germany is being reunited, the Warsaw Pact is gone and communism is over. When Helmut Kohl made his speech to the German parliament, he said, "There are three leaders in the world we want to thank for German reunification: George Bush, Mikhail Gorbachev and Brian Mulroney"—I knew I'd been part of a revolution.

That's never been reported in Canada. Now we have a united Germany in NATO and the Warsaw Pact and so on. During the Meech Lake discussions, I was brokering this with Bush and Gorbachev right in Ottawa. I was very actively involved in things like that, working directly with Kohl.

"OUR FRIEND FOREVER": FRANÇOIS MITTERRAND

The French president—an ally on many fronts.

Mulroney, on the personal connection:
François Mitterrand had Mila and me and the kids, the only heads of state who ever went to his summer place, twice. After we left office he called me and said, "Of course, Brian, you're our friend forever."

Fred Doucet, on exclusive access, following a summit in France:
After the dinner finally ended, Mitterrand said to the prime minister, "I understand that you have a real sense

of history and a deep appreciation for the forces that came together. Follow me." So a little group of seven people followed him—Paul Desmarais and his wife, his son and his wife, myself, Mr. Mulroney and Mrs. Mulroney. We went through a long corridor at the Palace Elysée and then into a little rotunda where there was a huge door. Of course, in these high ceiling areas, the doors were all huge. Mitterrand opened the door, and there was a little dark corridor inside. Finally another door, and then the office where Napoleon resigned after Waterloo.

He told us that he had never brought any other leader into that room. Napoleon's letter of resignation was still on the desk. Obviously, that room isn't cared for in terms of being dusted very often, because when he lifted the letter to show it to the prime minister, you could see its outline. And Mitterrand relived for us the manner by which Napoleon had summoned the clerk to give him his letter, and the trauma of it all.

"NO OPPOSITION THAT I CAN SEE":
MIKHAIL GORBACHEV

In 1989, Mulroney thought the young general secretary of the Communist Party would be the Soviet Union's leader for the long haul.

Only financial problems might drag him down:
MULRONEY: He has no opposition that I can see. There's no question that the guy is in control, but his economy is such a basket case and, like all of us, he's in the business of expectations.

Bill Pristanski, on Mulroney's visit to Moscow for former leader Konstantin Chernenko's funeral in 1985:
We got into the motorcade and ended up in their largest hotel, right across from Red Square. So we got up to this

quote-unquote "suite," which was decorated in the most bizarre fashion. Brian took one look at the suite and said, "Well, Fernand Roberge has nothing to worry about, 'cause this hotel's got nothing on the Ritz."

We had word from the Kremlin, and they said Gorbachev was very busy taking over, but Nikolai Tikhonov, his number two man, would see the prime minister. So the prime minister kind of looks at the chandelier, knowing that the room is bugged, and says, "Look, you go back to Tikhonov and tell him that Canada let this guy Gorbachev do a major visit when no other NATO country was entertaining Soviet officials because of Afghanistan. You tell him that, of all Western leaders, I've travelled the farthest. You go tell him that if he won't see me, I ain't seeing Tikhonov. I'm going to get into my little plane and fly home and he can fuck himself." He says this right into the chandelier, and one hour later, we had the meeting with Gorbachev.

The funny thing is the people at the Canadian embassy got a call from [Soviet press agency] TASS saying, "Your meeting is on for tomorrow." TASS always knows before the Foreign Office. We were scheduled for twenty minutes and saw him for forty-five.

"IT WOULD HAVE BEEN A GREAT JOB": THE UNITED NATIONS

In 1991, Mulroney's name was briefly thrown into the mix as a potential replacement for United Nations secretary-general Javier Pérez de Cuéllar.

Mulroney was fighting a recession at home:
Timing was the problem. The procedure is a mandated one—it has to begin—and once it begins you have to try and kind of play it out until the end. So that was it. I just had to do what I thought was right. It would have been a

great job, a fun job. I mean, look at all the problems they've got. By the way, I saw that my former friend Fotheringham, who savages me every day now for reasons I don't understand, had this piece saying that I promoted myself for the job.

"HE NEVER MISSED!": DENG XIAOPING

Reminiscences of a swing through Asia . . .

Lost in translation:

BILL PRISTANSKI: In South Korea, the problem we had was our translator, who was born in Korea and emigrated to Canada, and he froze, because all of a sudden Mulroney was yelling in English at Chun Doo-hwan, and there's no way this guy could yell at the president of Korea. He couldn't handle doing it in an animated sort of way. Chun's translator would have yelled out to us. It wasn't a successful meeting. Mulroney saw China's Deng Xiaoping for an hour and ten minutes, and the meeting was scheduled for fifteen minutes. Fortunately, we were warned about the spittoon. In the middle of the room, Deng hawks, and right in the spittoon! That would have thrown me off, but not the prime minister.

Fred Doucet:

The spittoon was located right by the edge of Deng's seat, and they were sitting kitty-corner to each other with their feet dangling about the spittoon fairly closely. Deng never missed! Every time he aimed for the spittoon, it went right in. After the meeting, Brian told me that one spit passed dangerously close to his tassels.

16

"What did they achieve?"

———

Mulroney Rates His Peers

SHRUGGING TO ETERNITY: RT. HON. PIERRE ELLIOTT TRUDEAU

Throughout the Mulroney years, Pierre Trudeau lingered in the wings to rattle his successor's chain at every opportunity. Even if he was no longer running the country, he could still sway its perceptions and dominate its headlines. Although he was far removed from power, and old age had set his face into the carved alabaster mask of some distant crusader, this exquisitely stubborn man never yielded an inch in his determination to undermine the Tory prime minister's initiatives.

During the Meech Lake and Charlottetown debates, Trudeau adopted Che Guevara's guerrilla tactic of husbanding his resources for a single dramatic putsch; his ability to manoeuvre the media made up for his non-existent constituency. His most forceful intervention took the form of a vintage, hour-long rant on October 1, 1992, to a gathering of Liberal cronies, in which he attacked the Charlottetown constitutional provisions. The venue he chose was La Maison Egg Roll, in Montreal's working-class Saint-Henri district, which offered an all-you-can-eat buffet for $6.95. It was the perfect joint to launch a militant call for a grassroots rejection of the elitist accord. Trudeau called down Mulroney as "a sniveller, a constitutional pyromaniac." His call to arms prompted nearly half of undecided Canadians to vote against the deal. Trudeau was the Great Spoiler of any constitutional revision that wasn't his own.

His performance was a reminder that Lucky Pierre's much-heralded arrival in Ottawa during the 1960s had introduced a new political paradigm: just showing up guaranteed ecstatic receptions. (Reporter to writhing teenybopper: "Why do you like him so much?" Writhing teenybopper to reporter: "Oh, I don't know . . . Just love his pockmarks!") Such hokey-pokey left Brian Mulroney angry and dismayed. He believed that a highly partisan media had collaborated in creating a Trudeau mythology that had no basis in his record as either a citizen or politician. Blindsided by his devil-may-care shrugs, journalists had inexplicably declined to deconstruct Trudeau—for example, seldom mentioning the fact that during the Second World War he had cruised around Montreal on a motorcycle wearing a German helmet. Not the garb of a patriot, or even the mask of a future philosopher-king.

Mulroney believed, not without reason, that Quebec separatism, provincial inequalities and the Americanization of Canada were encouraged by Trudeau's constitutional narcissism, namely his Charter of Rights and Freedoms, passed into law in 1982. Unlike Mulroney, I saw the Charter as a necessary reform but also recognized that it prompted citizens to contemplate their past dues, re-examine their existing entitlements and set out their future aspirations. This they did with a vengeance. From being passive voters, citizens started demanding instant consultation followed by immediate results. These unrealistic expectations contributed mightily to Mulroney's unpopularity and to Trudeau's ability to influence events from beyond his political grave.

In fact, Trudeau operated a virtual government-in-exile out of his Montreal law firm. He daily briefed his former deputy prime minister, Senator Allan MacEachen, who would bring parliamentary business to a halt by rallying the seventy-three Trudeau-appointed senators to vote against Tory legislation. (MacEachen was characterized by Mulroney as "someone who brought a new dimension to political duplicity, a whole new richness to the term.") The Red Chamber became Trudeau's countervailing force inside the Parliament buildings, where such Liberal warlocks as Jack Austin, Keith Davey, Jerahmiel Grafstein, Michael Kirby, Leo Kolber, Colin Kenny, Joyce Fairbairn and Royce Frith obstructed pivotal Tory legislation.

At the same time, nearly every move Mulroney made was restricted by Trudeau's fiscal legacy. During his sixteen years in power, Trudeau turned the balanced books he had inherited from his predecessor in 1968 into a $38.5 billion annual deficit and increased the national debt by 1,200 per cent, from $17 billion to more than $200 billion. By the time Mulroney took over, less than 15 per cent of the government's annual budget could be classified as discretionary spending. He was thus robbed of manoeuvring room to finance his numerous promises.

Mulroney was perplexed by the fact that a politician who had never achieved back-to-back majorities as he had done or won nearly as many ridings could be celebrated as a political wizard. In 1972 Trudeau had squeezed out only a two-seat margin running against the comatose Robert Stanfield (whose idea of animated behaviour was to raise an eyebrow).[1] Seven years later, he was actually defeated by Joe Clark. They didn't run against one another, but Trudeau was never able to come anywhere near Mulroney's popular appeal. In his first outing, Mulroney won fifty-six more seats than the Liberal leader had at the height of Trudeaumania in 1968. Mulroney's worst showing, in 1988, yielded fourteen more seats than Trudeau had delivered at his best.

In terms of scandal, there wasn't that much to choose between them. During Trudeau's sixteen years in power, twenty-one ministers resigned in various degrees of shame, while twelve departed the Mulroney cabinet in nine years. Their patronage record smelled about the same, too, especially in their last months in power, when they both named hundreds of hardcore partisans to government jobs, not to forget the nineteen hacks Trudeau pushed Turner to reward *after* he left office. While campaigning, Trudeau had declared, "Patronage is incompatible with modern government—appointments must go to the most qualified people." Yet his first Senate appointment went to Louis "Bob" Giguere, his personal bagman, whose daughter he was squiring at the time. Of the original twenty-five members of his cabinet, two died and eighteen received patronage positions; the other five continued in active politics.

It was difficult to compare their spending habits because Trudeau had set things up to absolve himself and condemn his successor. He timed implementation of the Access to Information Act, which allowed journalists to examine politicians' expense accounts to take effect just as he was leaving office. Mulroney and his ministers thus became its first victims, while Trudeau's spending habits remained exempt from scrutiny.

---

1. My favourite Stanfield moment occurred at a rally in a small Manitoba town, where he was marched into a hall behind a bagpipe band. He had to be grabbed and stopped from following the Highland musicians on out through the rear stage exit.

Considering that Trudeau was prime minister almost twice as long as Mulroney, he certainly did not leave behind double the accomplishments—not nearly. (I once described his governing style as despotism tempered by epigrams.) "What was the Trudeau legacy?" demanded Senator Marjory LeBreton, the keeper of Mulroney's political flame. "He left no legacy. It was Mulroney who left a legacy, made all those radical changes. He was the one who stopped this country from becoming another Sweden—he really did."

Mulroney felt that he had been sentenced to walk permanently in his predecessor's shadow. Few bothered comparing the two men, since they were so obviously different, but he did. I talked to him right after he returned from a historic visit to Moscow, which happened to coincide with implementation of Mikhail Gorbachev's radical reforms. "I just came from a meeting with Gorbachev," he informed me breathlessly. "I was with him forty-five minutes on the busiest day of his life. When Trudeau was in Moscow, they left him hanging around a hotel lobby for two days, waiting for old Konstantin Chernenko," [Gorbachev's ineffective predecessor as chairman of the Communist Party].

Particularly galling to Mulroney were the public opinion polls from 1988 onwards, which showed Trudeau consistently running ahead of him in voter approval (55 per cent to 14 per cent in April of 1991, for example), though Pierre was long retired and seldom budged from his art nouveau mansion on Montreal's Pine Avenue. Mulroney comforted himself with sarcasm. "I suppose if you're Pierre Trudeau," he said, "it must be kind of difficult to get up in the morning and look in the mirror and know you've seen perfection for the last time all day."

Mila was even less forgiving. "I want to know," she once told me, "why people keep saying Trudeau is such a great intellect. Because he quotes Nietzsche? I could train Nicolas to quote Nietzsche if I wanted to. This doesn't make someone brilliant. The two keys that can unlock any door are intelligence and good judgment. Trudeau had no judgment. In sixteen years he took a strong country and damaged it."

The last time I saw Trudeau in the flesh was at a Montreal reception in the spring of 1995. I recalled having stood near a Liberal matron nearly three decades earlier in Ottawa's Château Laurier hotel, during his leadership campaign. Just before he came through the door, she turned to her multi-chinned husband and urgently whispered, "What if I faint when he comes in?" The husband cut her in two with a look of disgust, his eyes rolling heavenward. Then Trudeau loped by and happened to shake the husband's hand. The man looked bewildered, then hugged his wife and started quietly to cry. It was a brief encounter, and yet it summed up for me the difference between the two leaders: Trudeau magicked us, and Mulroney didn't.

—

Mulroney marvelled at the cultural amnesia that kept the halo shining over Trudeau's head:
I'm surprised at how much we all forget what the country was like when he left office in 1984. Imagine him talking about me causing regional problems—Trudeau, the architect of regional disintegration in Canada. He was elected in June of 1968. At that time René Lévesque had left the Liberal Party, and by 1976 he was in power as a separatist. And who was prime minister? Mr. Trudeau. So separatism went from not existing, to a movement, to a party, to opposition in 1970, to power in 1976. They were still in power in 1985, and he was saying that I had created separatism! The beauty of it is he has got people like [Montreal *Gazette* columnist] William Johnson and those phonies at Southam repeating this, and there are people out there who should be saying, this is a lie, this is false.

Trudeau gets away with it because of an abdication of responsibility by the Canadian media. Am I wrong, or did I miss something? When Trudeau left office June 30, 1984, was not René Lévesque the premier of Quebec? Did I miss something here?

The majority of Quebeckers believe that federal-provincial relations would vastly improve with Bourassa-Mulroney than with Bourassa-Trudeau. I remember those days when everyone treated Bourassa like a pariah, and Trudeau was calling him a hot-dog eater while Lalonde, André Ouellette and Chrétien were abusing him every day. I used to take Bourassa out to lunch at the Mount Royal Club, before he went off to Brussels in 1976. Trudeau says today that the separatists were gone and that only I, with my foolish haste to reopen the constitutional file, resurrected them.

After he did his constitutional matter, the PQ, the separatists, did not vanish—they were re-elected with a massive majority government.

Bill Pristanski on the one piece of advice Trudeau gave the incoming prime minister:
He said, "Don't trust the premiers, even though they are all Tories. Don't trust them. It just doesn't work that way; they're out to get you. Don't trust those cunts."

Though they sat across from each other in the House of Commons for only a few months, Mulroney vividly remembered his reaction to Trudeau:
I saw the less attractive dimension of him every day in the House of Commons. I think he'll be regarded with some affection for the 1980 referendum stuff, but he'll be unquestionably regarded as a very inept fellow on the economic side. Very, very inept, and very bad for our relations around the world.

He has an unbecoming habit of distorting the truth and he has a streak of vindictiveness to him. He's infinitely more partisan than I ever thought possible. He has a streak of malice in him that is most unbecoming. This was all new to me, this dimension of verbal brutality. In the Throne Speech he said, "If you're sick, don't depend on the Conservatives." He conducted himself on the floor of the House and elsewhere like a cruel dictator.

NEWMAN: How do you get along on a personal level?

MULRONEY: I never call him Pierre, but he always calls me Brian. We always speak French anyway. As far as our interaction, let me put it this way: he has always been very civil and very cordial with me, and I have been the same way.

Peter Lougheed, the long-time Alberta premier, comparing Mulroney and Trudeau:
It has nothing to do with the fact that we're both Conservatives. Brian was a great chairman. Mr. Trudeau . . . his nature was adversarial. Mulroney's nature was consensus-building, and that was the difference.

In an initial inspection of his Parliament Hill office, Mulroney noticed armoured glass in the windows facing south:
Go bang the window, Peter, and see what happens—just go test it. See that? Trudeau had the office bulletproofed. I always contended that the reason he did it was because the American embassy is right outside. They probably wanted to shoot him.

Michael Pitfield remembered how hostilities began between the two politicians:
Mr. Mulroney, very soon after he became prime minister, invited Mr. Trudeau to come and see him, and they had a discussion. Following the discussion, Mr. Mulroney went out and said that Mr. Trudeau had agreed to act as his

advisor and tried to push Mr. Trudeau in front of the cameras to say this. Trudeau was furious; he went back and told all his friends that he had been gulled. The relationship became soured.

Mulroney on Trudeau's reputation as a statesman:
Did you see the *New York Times* the day before yesterday? They had a big piece in the financial pages by Andrew Malcolm. He wrote, "Mulroney is the first Canadian Prime Minister not to conduct himself with the President of the United States as a troublesome younger brother. Mulroney treats Americans like equals, and he gets treated the same way in return."

I mean, God almighty, you've seen the notes that I made on what Margaret Thatcher, Helmut Kohl and François Mitterrand said about my predecessor. It is unbelievable. Trudeau, point of fact, was always treated with absolute contempt and derision by all of our allies. They had no time for him. It was almost a joke. The only people who thought Trudeau had any influence in world affairs were the *Toronto Star.* God bless them for their ignorance.

Let's deal with Trudeau's foreign policy record—tell me what he did. Just tell me what he did. That's point number one. Then let us go see what the others say about him. Right? Read what Reagan says about him. Read what Thatcher says about him. Well, the answer is nothing. He's not mentioned at all or he's mentioned once in a footnote in book after book after book. You kind of wonder what was going on here.

Where was Trudeau's voice, for instance, during the U.S.-backed invasion of Grenada in 1983?
MULRONEY: Canada is planning $350 million worth of aid to Caribbean countries—we're supposed to be the most influential member of the Commonwealth in this hemisphere, and the United States is supposed to be our

closest friend and ally. And yet this kind of operation is contemplated without seeking advice from someone who's supposed to be the senior statesman of the Western world. This is a serious matter, a very troubling matter which should be concerning Canadians as to why our government in many cases—most recently this one—has been excluded.

Where was Trudeau when the country was burying former House of Commons Speaker and governor general Jeanne Sauvé in 1993?:
MULRONEY: Today, Jeanne Sauvé was buried, 30 below zero, everybody was there, but Pierre Trudeau didn't show up, didn't even interrupt his holidays. I can remember at Peter Curry's eightieth birthday party in October, I was there at the Ritz with Mila, and he was there and he left at one o'clock in the morning. And the next day was Paul Martin's funeral in Windsor, Ontario, and he never even showed up. It's Jeanne Sauvé, for God's sake! Jacques Parizeau was there, Lucien Bouchard was there, Marcel Pépin was there, but Pierre Trudeau didn't even bother interrupting a holiday.

Paul Tellier on how each man behaved during cabinet meetings:
Mr. Trudeau would very much join the issue and say, why do you say this, why do you say that, or I cannot agree with what you're saying, or this is a phony argument and so on. Mr. Mulroney would use other people around the table to disagree with him on a given subject matter. Most of the time, the prime minister would leave it to somebody else to take part in the argument. Very seldom were there fights and aggressive exchanges in the Mulroney cabinet. He would use Lowell Murray as a go-between; he [Murray] played a major role on abortion, for instance, trying to bring the left and the right wings of the party together.

Mulroney dismissed Trudeau's electoral appeal:
There never was popular support for the Liberals in Quebec—it was just Pierre Trudeau and the provincial machine. The Liberal Quebec constituencies were always privileged with money. They put up big billboards with big coloured pictures of themselves. Whether the projects got completed or not, they didn't care. This concept of Trudeaumania was so compelling and so powerful a political force in Canada that at its apogee he won 20 seats fewer than I did in my worst election. Trudeaumania won [in 1968] 155 seats, the most he ever won. The least I ever won was 169, in 1988. At my best in 1984, I won 56 seats more than he did. And he was defeated by Joe Clark! You see, there's an intoxication that can come. You keep winning elections, you're fighting off the infidels, and you can do pretty well. And that's what he did because he had this Quebec base, and because he had no opponent. He started with all the French seats in Canada—all he had to do was win 10 in Toronto, and he had a minority, which wasn't very hard.

NEWMAN: Well then, what was this hold that he had over us?

MULRONEY: The media.

Stanley Hartt says Trudeau shrugged his way onto a pedestal:
Trudeau floundered through his first three terms, lost to Clark briefly and then won again. Up until that time, if someone had said, "So, what did he do?" you would have said, "Absolutely nothing." He came back and that's when the NEP, FIRA, the Charter and the spending happened. And everybody loved him because he's sort of an intellectual Socrates or Plato of Canada.

The Charter was the excuse, but the real reason was that Canadians just loved Trudeau's personality, they loved him. And Mulroney was resentful, because he said, "I'm doing all the hard things to fix what he did wrong, and I'm called the bastard who's tearing down the national institutions as we know them."

Pat MacAdam, on Liberal hegemony in Ottawa:
Otto Jelinek inherited a situation in multiculturalism, when he took over as minister in August 1985, where they were still sending out brochures with Trudeau's picture on them even though the Tories had been in office almost a year. They wanted to send a form letter that they gave Otto to sign, which said, "As the great Canadian Pierre Elliott Trudeau once said . . ." Otto said, "I'm not signing that. Do you think I'm crazy?" People in there were saying, "There's going to be a Liberal government again in 1988 or 1989. Why change the brochure?"

The year after Mulroney left office, Michael Pitfield reflected on the key difference between the two governments:
There was no smoking gun in the sixteen years of the Trudeau government—there was not a single scandal that is linked directly to Trudeau. There was no evidence of an organized racket in terms of fundraising, and I warn you, we will encounter them all in the next few years. You cannot be ignorant of the instances in terms of factories being built in Quebec, in terms of aircraft contracts being let, and even the helicopter thing and the airport thing—we shall see where these lead.

Mulroney on the Trudeau government's economic record:
NEWMAN: How flawed do you regard the Liberal legacy? Remembering this is going to be published years from now.

MULRONEY: It was overwhelmingly bad. We had an $18 billion national debt in 1968 when he arrived, and a

$200 billion debt in 1984 when he left. And we got nothing for it. No productivity growth, and a loss in our international trade. I believe they will be judged quite harshly. From the days of Sir John as prime minister until the first of July 1967—that's a hundred years having fought two world wars, fought off the Nazis, gone into Korea, built an infrastructure across the country—on that day, Canada owed a net debt of $18 billion. Enter Trudeau as prime minister, and fifteen years later he leaves a net debt of $200 billion. We got nothing for that money—nothing for saying yes and yes and yes to every interest group, every left-wing idea that came about. We have the worst situation in public finances of the industrialized world. That's another bit of Trudeau's "great heritage." Trudeau left the single worst record of any country in the history of an industrialized nation. They accuse me of cutting back on the CBC and Via Rail. That's because Trudeau left me with no money to fund the infrastructure of the programs that he put in, and he spent so much goddamned money. I've got 65 cents left to meet a dollar's worth of obligations . . .

Sometimes I feel when I'm talking to people about it that they just don't understand the gravity of where we were, and how close to irretrievable decline the country was. Had we not made radical changes, the number today would be 58 cents on the dollar and Canada would be run by the International Monetary Fund. The thing that I find most offensive was that for a man who talked about sovereignty, his policies placed us on the road to servitude under the IMF. Now, why would Trudeau not have done the GST when the nation clearly needed it?

Trudeau remained a hot button for Mulroney:
Pierre Trudeau was a coward and a weakling because when Guy Charbonneau, Pierre Sévigny and Paul Sauvé were fighting off Nazis on the battlefields of France, Pierre Trudeau was fighting off blackflies in Outremont.

This guy was a bully with people when he became prime minister, he was dishonest intellectually, he moved from party to party for opportunistic reasons and his record as a prime minister is absolutely mediocre.

The media have made of him, for the moment, a hero. But it ain't going to last. He knows it's not going to last. So what he's doing is suckering people into producing television films about him, which he controls so he can deify himself. He is smart and he knows that his record is totally mediocre. He had failed in his first eleven years, and when Joe Clark miraculously resurrected him, he was determined to put his mark on history and he did it with the National Energy Program, for Christ's sake, which crucified Western Canada, the patriation of the Constitution that drove Quebec to the brink of separation, government spending programs that took the country to the brink of bankruptcy, and quixotic left-wing foreign policy attitudes that dismayed our allies and eroded our influence in world council. Trudeau is the first one to know that it was a fraud and so what he's trying to do is sustain it on videotape.

NEWMAN: What about his "Just Society" measures? Surely they were necessary reforms. Also, how could a one-time justice minister who refused to take action against war criminals still be regarded as a humanist?

MULRONEY: The Just Society? Let me give you a small illustration. Pierre Trudeau was minister of justice and prime minister for twenty years. During that time, he had access to the most sensitive information of the government of Canada dealing with the Nazi war crimes, and he personally killed the idea of an inquiry for twenty years.

You know why we couldn't get the Nazi war criminals? Because that son of a bitch Trudeau, as minister of justice and prime minister, personally vetoed the idea of a royal commission into the Nazi war crimes. He personally

vetoed it because he didn't want to upset social peace in
Canada. He said it would be disruptive to other communities. I couldn't think of anything more repugnant to a so-
called just or civilized society than to allow war criminals
to live side by side with other Canadians in an untroubled
fashion. This was a moral commitment from me. I was
going to smoke the bastards out . . .

NEWMAN: Do you ever see him, now that you both live
in Montreal, nor far from each other?

MULRONEY: I ran into him once—he was having lunch
with Pitfield. As a former prime minister you have to be
civil, that's all . . .
    The way he used to run things was fairly abusive—I
never commented on it. He stayed too long. The damage
that he did in his last term may turn out to be irreparable.
That's our "Defender of Canada" . . . Who else could bankrupt a nation, split the federation, exclude Quebec, bring
about the rise of separatism, get us known as an unreliable
ally among all our friends around the world, a peace mission
that made us the laughing stock of every single person in
the world, and then become a hero to the *Toronto Star*?

"POOR JOE": THE RT. HON. JOE CLARK

**A few days after becoming leader of the Opposition,
Mulroney was claiming that Clark was the divisive one:**
As I look back on our party's history, our problems were
a result of our fractiousness. People perceived us as
unworthy. The most important thing in a job like this is
the quality of judgment that you can bring to people and
problems. You have to understand people. You have to like
people. You would fail as a leader if you allowed vindictiveness or mean-spiritedness to enter your judgment or
your personality. This is for the book, right?

NEWMAN: Yeah, this will be in the book.

Mulroney claimed the Clarks shunned him and Mila:
Here we are, at Stornoway, a pretty nice place. It's some kind of comment on Clark that in seven years in this house, he never once invited Mila and me for lunch, breakfast or dinner. It may have been insecurity, or maybe the guy just profoundly disliked me. In seven years, my wife and I were never invited to any social occasion by the Clarks.

After he became prime minister, Mulroney spun several theories on why the previous Tory government collapsed after just a few months:
Poor Joe. Poor guy. No wonder our goddamn government fell apart in 1979, no wonder. Holy smokes. I try to look for people with business experience, people who know what the hell is going on. Sinclair Stevens—for instance—is a big hitter, he's terrific. He's smart as hell and he knows what's going on. If you don't have the caucus, you can't govern, it's just that way. That's what Clark found out. Because the argument is quite obvious: you have to control your own caucus and manage your own caucus. The problem was Clark's caucus. He never knew how to manage men and women. I'm not so sure that he does today, although if he hasn't learned anything over the last seven or eight years, he'd be a very stupid man, and he's not stupid.

Mulroney believed Clark was responsible for his own fate:
Clark's people started out with what I've referred to as a scorched-earth policy. They just proceeded with overwhelming brutality towards us. I mean it was godawful. They thought they were going to scare us off. I often wondered, why the hell it was that Clark, with almost 70 per cent of the vote, did what he did in Winnipeg? Well

the answer is very clear: he might have had 67 per cent of the delegates, but he had about 25 per cent of the caucus.

Mulroney claimed Parti Québécois leader René Lévesque wanted Clark to remain as Tory leader:
René Lévesque never had a kind word to say for me, not one. He made snarky remarks, called me a "mini-Trudeau." Christ, he was openly supporting Clark in the leadership campaign. That was the kiss of death for Clark. Lévesque later figured, why only be onside? Why not try and take some credit for this? That's when he eventually started to make some nice sounds about me. And so this is nonsense about Lévesque helping us—that's crazy. Lévesque thought Turner was going to win, right? Wrong. In comes a guy who supplants Trudeau as the leading French Canadian.

After Mulroney became prime minister, other Tories found it difficult to deal with Clark:
MacADAM: I don't know how long it's going to take some of these guys to sanitize themselves. They've still got blood on their hands from Winnipeg. We all do. I still feel a little guilty when I see Joe Clark in the parliamentary restaurant.

Mulroney denied having anything to do with Clark's defeat:
I had a full-time job running the Iron Ore Company of Canada. Most of the time I was out of the country, Clark was the leader and he had control of the party, the PC Canada Fund and the caucus. But the Jeffrey Simpson myth is that I deposed Joe Clark. The truth is he deposed himself, helped by John Crosbie, Michael Wilson, David Crombie and all of the people in his caucus who didn't want to serve under him anymore. That was the issue.

The whole thing about 1983—it's all a crock about me unseating Clark and all that stuff. It's a total crock. He knew he had lost his caucus. It didn't matter if he had the editorial backing of the *Toronto Star*. He failed to understand that in a parliamentary system you can't lead without your caucus, and the caucus didn't want him. The whole thing about Clark and me is an absolute bloody myth. Sure, when he called a leadership convention, I ran, because at this point in time I was convinced of what his caucus already knew: that his leadership skills were weak and that he just couldn't command their support into the next election.

Clark and his own behaviour toward him were still a sore spot for Mulroney in the early 1990s:
MULRONEY: Stop giving me the goddamned gears about Joe Clark. Who do you think the prime minister of Israel is today? And guess where the former leader is. Well, the prime minister is Yitzhak Rabin, because he overthrew Shimon Peres and he won the election. Now, this goes on all the goddamned time in democracies. But I had nothing to do with the defeat of the government in 1979 in the House of Commons. I had nothing to do with the defeat of the government in the election in 1980. I contested the leadership when Clark threw it open and won it fair and square.

On September 17, 1984, Mulroney appointed Clark as secretary of state for external affairs:
PAT MACADAM: Mulroney told me he offered him Paris, and Clark wouldn't budge. Brian says, "Why would anybody want to be external affairs minister when your position would be subservient to the prime minister? Traditionally in this country, the prime minister is the chief spokesman in external affairs, and carries that portfolio in his hip pocket."

Mulroney on having a former prime minister in his cabinet:
After Thatcher overthrew Conservative leader Ted Heath

and then won a government, Heath wanted to serve in her government, and she said, "Over my dead body." Christ, he just about fell off the chair. Then the Canadian press says in 1984, "Wasn't Joe Clark a nice guy to serve in Brian Mulroney's cabinet?" The only reason he served in my cabinet is that I invited him. I had 209 other members, and the only reason that he's there is because I asked him to be. So we'd better get a few things straight.

Joe Clark:
There's no question that I had special status in the cabinet and the party. I make it a joke that no one is more popular than a former Conservative leader, but it's true, and you acquire a constituency in this party *after* you leave the leadership, never at another time. And Brian recognized that and he knew it was an asset and I could kid about it.

After Mulroney's record win, former chief of staff Hugh Segal spoke about the way he handled Clark's supporters:
It's fascinating what Mulroney has done. He's taken the Clark faction and given them high-profile roles, but in areas that are essentially peripheral to the core of our policy. Joe had been led to believe by his friends that travelling, getting out of the country and not brooding was the best way to preserve his future, rather than sitting around and wondering about all the maybe's and what-if's. The Clark faction has been peripheralized and happy. They are doing what they think are important things. It doesn't matter a shit in terms of domestic politics. They're out of the way. They're being co-opted on a regular basis . . . I don't know what Joe's deep, dark, innermost aspirations are, but it doesn't really matter. If Brian can win the country, he can lead this party for twenty years.

As far as Mulroney was concerned, he always behaved impeccably around Clark:
I always treated Joe Clark with the greatest of respect. He was the only one I treated differently in cabinet. I always gave him more accord. He was the only one I deferred to, because he was a former leader, former prime minister, and indeed I kept it going right to the end. I'm the one who got him a job at the United Nations. I went to see [United Nations secretary-general] Boutros Boutros-Ghali and I got him in the corner and I said, "Canada wants something for Mr. Clark, we've been supporting this place now forever. You've got these mandates going . . ." And he said that Hans-Dietrich Genscher had just turned down the Cyprus assignment. Genscher had resigned as foreign minister of Germany and the UN had tried to give him the Cyprus mandate, but because of his heart problems he turned it down. I said, "I've got the right guy for you—his name is Clark." When I told Clark about it, he turned it down.

Geoff Norquay, comparing Clark and Mulroney:
One of the similarities between Brian Mulroney and Joe Clark is that they are both horrendously bad managers in that they will go to any length to avoid having to make any harsh personnel decision. I know from first hand having worked with both of them. A positive similarity is that both of them are incredible writers. The more important the message that either of them has to deliver, the more likely they are to take up pen, or typewriter, in Joe's case, and do it themselves. I know again by trying to approximate what's in their minds, on occasion, when it gets really important they just shout, "Give me all your stuff and leave me alone. I'm going to go home and write it tonight."

Stanley Hartt, on Mulroney's attitude:
Not only did Mulroney extend uncommon courtesy to Clark on every single occasion, even when Clark would

tell Mulroney that nobody trusted him or believed a word he said. He would never show chagrin or shut him out or cut him off. He was very careful not to be seen to be continuing his knifing of Clark.

Bill Pristanski, on incompetent public servants at External Affairs:
Clark's problem, my analysis of it, is that his department lets him down constantly. Stephen Lewis has told us, Bernard Roy has told us, and even Joe. It's evident time after time after time that the department just isn't up to snuff. The advice they give you is Mickey Mouse that the ambassadors send back over the cables. They get it by reading the *Economist* and the *New York Times*.

Charley McMillan was convinced the Tories would not take another chance on Clark:
My own belief is that if Brian were hit today by a beer truck, Joe wouldn't get two votes in caucus. Brian could fly to Timbuktu and lose every goddamn piece of luggage, and people wouldn't hold it against him.

Mulroney, on Clark as steward of the Charlottetown process:
The guy wanted a deal so badly—he wanted to be associated with a winner. I mean, how else do you explain it? They showed me the transcript of his statement [prematurely issued], saying, "We have just produced the most historic constitutional arrangement since Confederation." It's a real, real mess. I tell you, if Clark walked the streets of Montreal, they'd throw tomatoes at him. And these are the federalists, not the separatists—"Get rid of this son of a bitch."

I have to conclude that Clark saw himself in a position as a nation builder, doing something that I couldn't do. Jesus, it's hard to put even the most charitable construction on this. Clark fancied himself, believed all this crap in the newspapers about how much Canadians loved him and trusted him and all of this stuff, and he was going to be Sir John A. Macdonald. Lookit, if you think that it was the Quebeckers against Clark at the cabinet meeting, you're dead wrong. It was everybody against Clark, saying, "What in the name of God? Whatever possessed you?" He's accident-prone—I say that with no malice. Happens to some people I guess.

As the Charlottetown referendum got closer and the "Yes" side remained confident of victory, Mulroney changed his tune on Clark:
Clark softened up the premiers a lot over fourteen months—he wore them out. Clark's process built up a lot of goodwill, no question. But in 1992, you cannot club provincial premiers to death, you can't. I tell you, there were about ten times this thing could have gone off the rails just like that. And sometimes it was a premier with a timely remark, sometimes it was just a timely adjournment, and sometimes I had to take them right to the woodshed.

Maybe some day it's going to dawn on these dummies in the press gallery what's going on here, although I'm doing fine without their credit. I don't need it.

Marjory LeBreton blamed Clark:
The referendum was probably the toughest, most difficult time the prime minister has had in his entire period as leader of this party because, all of a sudden, the coalition that he had so carefully stitched together and held together—the Quebeckers, the Albertans and the people from the west generally—Joe Clark had turned them into two solitudes. I just couldn't believe it, but yet I could, because this is just the kind of thing that Joe Clark would have put together. There comes a point when you have to say enough is enough.

In the wake of the Charlottetown failure, prospective leaders began to show their colours. Mulroney, on Clark's intention to become a leadership candidate:
I don't know how it will all shake down, but Clark now is counting on the fact that because he is well known, Angus Reid will go out and do some polling and that after I step down, polls will show that he could defeat Chrétien and therefore the party will kind of draft him. He actually thinks he's going to be drafted! But you see, I've got half a dozen people who dream of nothing else. There's no way that they're getting out of the way for Joe Clark, no way: Jean Charest, Kim Campbell, Bernard Valcourt, Michael Wilson, Perrin Beatty. They're not getting out of the way for anybody, nor should they, nor should they.

Once at the convention, in Mulroney's view, Clark backed the wrong candidate:
Quite frankly, I once thought that Joe Clark would be a good successor, and he blew the whole goddamned thing with his stupidity. I mean, look at what the poor bastard did. Oh God, it was a terrible performance. A former prime minister of Canada in a sweaty T-shirt looking not like a senior statesman, but like a ward boss . . . berating Jim Edwards. Many people now think that he cost Charest the leadership. Edwards, who normally would have gone to Charest, went to Kim Campbell in substantial part because he was so pissed off at Clark for trying to strong-arm his delegates.

This is Clark's greatest act of political stupidity since he threw away the government. How can you urge Edwards not to support a fellow westerner and the first woman? They had trouble with Clark all week at the convention—he grumbled and complained and bitched all week about Campbell. Clark's just not a player anymore.

As he prepared for his own retirement, Mulroney reflected on Clark's career:

In ten years, I've come full circle on Clark. I thought for a while that he had learned. I gave him all those good jobs, gave him all this flexibility. And you know what? He was a good minister, but his greatest success was in persuading the Ottawa press gallery that he's a humble, modest guy. He's anything but. I don't say this with malice. I say it with regret. It's now very clear to me how he blew his own leadership, how he blew his own government after a few days in the House of Commons, and then how he managed to so alienate his own caucus. His judgment is fatally flawed. I really didn't understand how Clark ever managed to do what he did. It's a judgment flaw. Otherwise, he's got many fine qualities.

"THE POOR BUGGER": THE RT. HON. JOHN TURNER

When John Napier Turner succeeded Pierre Trudeau as prime minister on June 30, 1984, Mulroney had already developed his views of the man who would twice become his electoral opponent. Benefiting from media accounts of Turner's tactless behaviour—and from Turner's pathetic performance during the 1984 English-language TV debate—Mulroney won the largest majority in Canadian history, putting an end to Turner's ten-week tenure at 24 Sussex Drive. Mulroney referred to his rival with condescension, pointing out that Turner lost his influence after allowing his party to succumb to a wave of anti-Americanism. In 1988, Mulroney's second majority victory precipitated Turner's political retirement.

As the Liberals were about to elect a new leader in 1984, Mulroney rated his chances:
The prime minister [Trudeau] has clearly indicated that he considers himself to be the best of that lot, and I can't disagree with that assessment, as I look across the aisle and see what he's got there. He's clearly a cut above the rest.

347

The funniest thing about the Liberal leadership convention was watching Jean Chrétien producing Goldfarb polls to show that I would defeat Turner in the election, while Turner was producing Angus Reid polls to show that I would defeat Chrétien.

Now, Chrétien would have been more dangerous. The guy is a loose cannon. He'll say anything and do anything. Turner will be no trouble. Lookit, the poor bugger's going to wake up today and he's finally where he wants to be, except he ain't there yet. He's got to earn it. The polls show the Liberal hold in Ottawa is 26 per cent. That's the high. The guys are goners. They're fucking goners.

When the writ was dropped, Mulroney made a point of comparing his humble beginnings with Turner's:
I don't think it's just a difference in attitude. It's also background and accomplishment. It's the difference between—at similar ages—driving a truck, and being home and having steaks flown over to you. There's a pretty fundamental difference. I don't want to dwell on it, but to me it's so obvious. It's the difference between inheriting a seat when he was thirty and going through the usual Quebec Liberal routine, getting to be parliamentary secretary automatically, then minister and so on. I had hands-on management responsibilities. I have run a shop. Corporate things are irrelevant, the directorships and what have you. That comes from being a perceived success. It's what you do that counts. As a lawyer, I built my own practice. I wasn't a PR man.

As the 1984 campaign began, Mulroney radiated contempt for his opponent, at least in private:
As far as I'm concerned, the guy is very unpleasant. He's involved in a double shuffle, first repudiating what the Liberal Party has stood for, and then attempting

to adopt our positions. You won't find a single solitary thing that Turner has said this year that I haven't been saying for four or five years. Even the words are the same.

After his victory, Mulroney couldn't help but crow over Turner's fate:
That guy, God bless him. There's a fellow who really, really is only trying—he just wasn't as good as he thought he was. See, I had to get him on TV. The Liberals probably counted on Turner either winning or losing; they didn't expect a rout, in English and French. "I had no option." That was my campaign right there. "The devil made me do it." They would yell at me in the back of the hall, "Tell us about the devil." So I'd have to go through the routine. No wonder the goddamn thing went poof. Poor Conrad. [Black had supported the Liberals.]

NEWMAN: Don't let Black tell you that he backed you. He didn't.

MULRONEY: He couldn't convince me of that. I'd just laugh. The word flowing around is that there was a big chunk of dough for Turner from Conrad, which surprised me, because he's fundamentally ungenerous, tight as a drum.

Mulroney recalled one of his first visits to 24 Sussex, to discuss the transition with Turner:
We both sat in here. I ordered coffee and he ordered Perrier, in the morning. He was in pretty bad shape, the poor bugger. He was pretty hungover. He said, "I know you think that I shouldn't have called the election when I did, but I had no choice." And I said, "John, if I can give you any advice, it would be don't do what I did—don't spend your time wondering what if."

NEWMAN: Was he emotional?

MULRONEY: Oh, yeah. We provided him with an automobile and chauffeur, which the leader of the Opposition never had, though the Conservative Party provided one for me. So we talked about the transition, and I said, "At your convenience." We agreed on the seventeenth of September, which suited him to be sworn in as an MP from Quadra.

Mulroney believed that Turner was ineffective as leader of the Opposition:
I have trouble figuring him out. He's off to a strange start. It's not that he's unlikable, but he's even worse than he appears to be as a leader. He always performs under expectations, and that's the greatest secret of politics and life: always outperform expectations. If you're very, very lucky, they continue to underestimate you. And so what I do is encourage that as best I can. Any time anybody for the Liberals or the NDP says, "Mulroney's not too smart" or "Mulroney's really quite dumb," I don't disagree with that. I encourage them to think that. I'll say, "It's true. I didn't have all that much grounding and I really don't understand politics."

Turner has done nothing to attract any support. We know what the Liberals are against. They're against a productive relationship with the United States. They're against the western accord. They're against western strength in the federal government. They're against all of these things. What are they for? They're for character assassination. But it'll be another year, year and a half before the press starts asking Turner what he's for. The job of opposition leader is not easy, eh? It's a pain in the ass.

He blamed some of Turner's troubles on Lloyd Axworthy:
The Liberals are not a very impressive bunch of people. I think they have persuaded Turner to rebuild from the extreme left. I don't see how they'd do that, but that's clearly what they're doing. I think the Lloyd Axworthy school of politics has won that one. Axworthy has sucked Turner into taking anti-American positions, so now Turner is associated in the public mind with Axworthy's negativism and bitterness. The polls are 80–20 in favour of what we're doing. Ronald Reagan would win an election in Canada. The Liberals had it all wrong. They thought everybody hated Reagan, everybody hated the United States and Trudeau was doing the right thing.

In *Reign of Error: The Inside Story of John Turner's Troubled Leadership,* Greg Weston had revealed the existence of a semi-secret trust fund. Mulroney defended Weston's research unreservedly, a first when it came to the country's political writers:
Turner was the most astonished person in the country when we caught him with his hand in the till. He'll pay for that forever. He'll pay for that in Quebec with his life. The word going around is that this is not a Claire Hoy book kind of thing, where somebody told somebody, whose first cousin heard from the executive assistant to the prime minister. That was gossip, vital distortions. The Turner story is not that at all.

If you said to me, "Brian, do you have a trust fund?"— my answer to you is no. There's not one directly, there's not one indirectly, there's not one for my kids. But to have one—and God knows it's not that I couldn't stand the money—would be the highest form of stupidity.

Before the 1988 election, Mulroney was so delighted by a study comparing the contenders on leadership

questions that he took time away from running the country to read me the following results:

I've got this study. There are seventeen questions, all right? I won't read them all to you, and I won't even give you Broadbent's numbers because they're of a modest degree of relevance. Here's the stuff.

Who do you think will do what he thinks is right, even though it's unpopular? Mulroney, 42 per cent; Turner, 22 per cent.

Who has a vision of Canada that best reflects the needs of the nation? Mulroney 41, Turner 20.

Who shows human feelings? Mulroney 27, Turner 19.

Who is easy to relate to on a human basis? Mulroney 31, Turner 15.

Who admits human error when he believes he is wrong? Mulroney 32, Turner 24.

Who is more careful with taxpayer money? Mulroney 28, Turner 16.

Who is the best negotiator to defend the interests of Canadians? Mulroney 54, Turner 19.

Who can best represent Canada abroad as prime minister, of whom you can be proud? Mulroney 60, Turner 18.

Who is the most competent of the leaders to be prime minister of Canada? Mulroney 42, Turner 17.

Who best understands Quebec and its vital role in national unity? Mulroney 63, Turner 19.

Who is the best communicator on behalf of the nation? Mulroney 47, Turner 14.

Who is most respected by his own political party, whether you support that party or not? Mulroney 34, Turner 8.

Who best understands the nation? Mulroney 47, Turner 23.

Who is the most decisive? Mulroney 40, Turner 21.

Who is most caring? Mulroney 28, Turner 16.

Who is the most trustworthy? Mulroney 29, Turner 16.

Who makes me proud as leader and possible prime minister? Mulroney 38, Turner 16.

What you've got there are seventeen components of leadership, and John Turner is dead last in all seventeen. It's a national survey. They've never seen numbers this bad for national leaders since they began polling, and Broadbent wins a couple of the personality things, but all of the tough ones are mine.

Mulroney was thrilled to watch Turner offering the perennial loser's quote:
You know, I watched Turner on the television reviews in the House, saying he "won the hearts and minds of Canadians." I love it, because that's what we used to say. Remember how old Dief used to say that? So it's nice to have the other guy saying that.

As the Liberal Party was about to pick a new leader, Mulroney offered one last thought on the man he had succeeded:
I think Turner is in bad shape psychologically—there's more bitterness and malice in him that I've ever seen in anybody. He's having private dinners for members of the business community, having ignored them and crapped all over them for five years, apparently because he's trying to get a job.

"A MEAN, DIRTY BASTARD":
THE RT. HON. JEAN CHRÉTIEN

Before Jean Chrétien became a significant contender for the Liberal leadership, Mulroney was quick to praise his sense of humour. Over the years, his views of the man who would eventually earn three Liberal majority governments changed dramatically. For Mulroney, Chrétien was an intellectual greenhorn—subjugated by his spouse—who built his political career by failing to commit to issues or ideas and by changing his mind according to the polls.

Mulroney claimed very few politicians were as unqualified as Chrétien to lead a national political party, and was convinced that the "Little Guy from Shawinigan" would shame Canadians. When Chrétien took over from Kim Campbell in 1993, Mulroney was dismayed at the way the press gave him a free ride.

Mulroney recalled a joke told by Jean Chrétien about John Turner during a memorial service in 1985:
Chrétien can be very funny. He said, "You know, my leader he's like Doug Wickenheiser." Now, for an old hockey buff like me, I started to laugh like hell. Chrétien then continued by saying, "You dress him up, put skates on him and he looks terrific. He looks just fantastic. Skates up and down the sidelines and the game starts."

Wickenheiser isn't anywhere to be found—he was the guy who was brought into the NHL as a number-one draft pick and bombed everywhere. He just looked sensational; he looked like the greatest thing since bottled beer. I had to laugh, because only at a Quebec political funeral would the boys be discussing things like that. He didn't say it with malice; he was sort of kidding around.

Frank Moores on the tempestuous relationship between the top two Liberals:
I was down fishing with Chrétien last week, and he really hates Turner with a passion. He might be interested in joining the Tories if Turner is re-elected as Liberal leader, although it would take a lot of discussion.

In 1990, Chrétien—who had finished second to Turner in 1984—and a young Paul Martin were regarded as the front-runners for leader:
MULRONEY: I hope they select Chrétien and the spotlight goes on him. His first press conference will be fine—he's going to have the English-speaking journalists in Ottawa eating right out of his hand. The second one,

well, not so good. By the third one, Chrétien's going to be in serious trouble. I'm waiting to see what Paul Martin can do, but I'm afraid that there's not much hope for him.

Bill Pristanski rated his guy's chances against either Chrétien or Martin:
There's no other mythical candidate, and the convention will be a bore. Chrétien running against Chrétien, I mean, who else is going to run? Paul Martin is not stupid enough to run now, because (a) his business won't allow it, and (b) he's playing with his own money. Why would he run against Mulroney? He knows Mulroney will run again and then retire, and that's the time he'll run for the Liberal leadership.

Mulroney's not afraid of Chrétien at all because he feels that under public scrutiny for the top job in the country, he won't make it in English Canada and probably not in French Canada, because outside of Shawinigan, a lot of people are offended by the act he puts on. He's an asshole. He's very shallow. Under the spotlight, he would melt and the boss could beat him in a debate in either language.

Mitchell Sharp, Chrétien's mentor and advisor, on Chrétien's qualities:
Jean is not accustomed to reading as much as I am or you are, and therefore we tend to judge him on that sort of basis. We read all sorts of things; Chrétien doesn't. Chrétien's reading is limited. He has an instinctive approach, and faced with a problem, he always comes out with sensible answers, and that's why I say that he never has had to eat his words. What other Canadian politician do you know who hasn't had to go back and say, well, that was not what I meant?

After Chrétien was officially anointed, he was no longer amusing:

MULRONEY: When we get to 1993, the Liberals will have reached back to a guy who came into politics in 1963 and hasn't had a new idea since. He's not an impressive guy at all. Imagine those guys winning an election!

He thinks he's a stand-up comedian; well, at least Crosbie was funny. Chrétien is just vulgar, with these phony old ministerial jokes. I was out of politics for seven years, reading and working and thinking and learning new things, and new approaches. Chrétien hasn't done a goddamn thing; the only thing the guy reads is the Montreal *Gazette;* he hasn't read a book in twenty years. He's not going to make any appeal in Western Canada without me cutting his throat in French Canada. He got emasculated by both sides. I'm sure a lot of young people looking at this for the first time will want to look again before they consider giving this guy their vote.

Mulroney harked back to Chrétien's view of the Meech Lake Accord:
Can you believe Chrétien? He won't say if he's for or against . . . He wants to be prime minister, and on the greatest moral issue confronting the country he's neither for nor against. By the time Jean Chrétien gets finished sabotaging the Meech Lake Accord, he isn't even going to win his own seat.

At the time, Mulroney thought Chrétien should have distanced himself from Trudeau, and stopped listening to his wife:
He should have disowned Trudeau before and done Meech Lake and said, "Lookit, Meech Lake is done—I didn't like it but it's done, and now let's get rid of Mulroney on economic issues." He could have had the whole thing!

In fact, if you look at it from my perspective, in 1993 with the GST done, the free trade agreement done and Meech Lake, what am I doing hanging around? I'd be gone and I'd have been succeeded by an English-speaking Canadian and therefore he'd get a free ride in Quebec.

But his wife wouldn't let him change his mind on Meech. His wife is the dominant figure in the marriage. She is the one who said he would look wishy-washy. She didn't understand the implications. She thought that no matter what he did, her beautiful Jean would come back and put the frogs in their place because the two of them now view Quebec as a plantation after living in Ottawa for twenty-five years. They move in a different society, no roots whatsoever, none in Quebec.

Mulroney underestimating the enemy:
The fact of the matter is Chrétien will not run in Quebec because he cannot get elected. You know that press conference I did with Bush, carried live on CNN, in Kennebunkport a couple of days ago? I heard somebody on radio saying, "I'm starting to get a little worried because I wasn't a Mulroney supporter until I saw that press conference and then it occurred to me, I try to imagine Jean Chrétien there representing Canada and, Jesus, a cold sweat came over me."

The disparities are worse than they were with Turner, and Turner was the worst we had seen. Now we've seen worse. The numbers go like this: who do you think could best represent Canada internationally? Mulroney, 64 per cent. Chrétien, 2 per cent. *"Dis and dat and I'm going to do dis . . . And I'm a frog, and all dese tings . . ."*

Mulroney on what would happen if he led the Progressive Conservatives into the 1993 election:
I have the total support of my caucus, total support of my cabinet, total support of the party, and I think I could win a minority government. If we can't put Chrétien away in a fifty-one-day campaign, we don't even deserve to be sitting around the caucus table. He's a disaster. I can win a minority.

But what can I do with a minority? I don't think I can win a majority, but I may be able to win it in a campaign. I think you're going to see Chrétien really begin to sink.

But I don't have the enthusiasm. I have spent my enthusiasm in some reasonably exciting causes, and I've spent my energy. I don't have any bright ideas anymore. I had some good ideas, but most of them have already been enacted into law.

Chrétien was simply too old and unfit to be prime minister, in Mulroney's view:
Lookit, if the guy had grown commensurate with the world, then you'd be confronted today by a towering public policy intellect. I have never in my whole life seen anybody less well equipped to lead a great national party or to become prime minister of Canada than this guy. I mean, the sight and spectacle of this guy across the floor of the House of Commons is a danger to behold.

Only a few days into his tenure, Chrétien was already getting rave reviews:
MULRONEY: They've got a Canadian Press story today in the Montreal *Gazette*—to show you how it never changes—about Chrétien paying for his own vacation in a hotel and saying that's contrary to me, who stayed at Paul Desmarais's all the time and went out to these fancy dinners. Well, I never stayed at Paul Desmarais's once, never. I rented places. When I went down to Montreal, I never went out once.

I don't go to fancy dinners. I don't go anywhere. I go to movies, I'd go to the baseball game with the baby and I'd do things like that. I was there for a rest, played tennis. I never ever went out to any dinners or anything like that. It never changes, never changes for me. They've got a total double standard.

Mulroney argued that his tough policies benefited Chrétien:

The heart of the problem is Canadian sovereignty. That's what it was all about. I can see the William Johnsons, the Trudeaus and the Jeffrey Simpsons saying, isn't that Jean Chrétien smart? Boy, he was really smart where Mulroney was stupid. He managed to sneak that tax and he's hidden the tax and the Canadians, boy, oh boy, the poor old stupid Canadians, they don't even know they're paying it anymore. And isn't he a wonderful politician. Isn't that leadership? It is deceit. It's not leadership. And this is a country that has been deceived for so long, particularly in this important area of public finance.

I'm not saying we were perfect, but if you look at what we tried to do, the areas that we tried to take this, I mean unless you assume that everybody was entirely stupid and we didn't know what we were doing and we had no vision at all and we were all dishonest—just give us a modicum of credit.

Publicly, Mulroney wanted to keep things smooth:

Quite frankly, I wish him well. It's not easy—it's a tough job and it's going to get tougher as the months unfold. I don't believe in the theory that a prime minister should leave office and then try and seek to undermine their successor. I believe more in the American tradition where they tend to work together on important national or international issues, where the former presidents are called in and they're consulted and they kind of give the benefit of their advice.

I mean, if I have some disagreements I'll spell them out privately or I'll write to him or I'll speak to him on the phone or I might even make a speech from time to time, but there won't be any animosity. Chrétien and I have always gotten along very well on a personal level. I know his family very well. I have affection for members of the family I know and so there's no problem.

Still, it burned Mulroney that Chrétien's patronage appointments were going unchallenged by the same people who had made his life a misery:
They were just on the tube, Hugh Winsor and all those fat slobs, they were right on the tube saying, "Well, this is entirely appropriate, Raymond Chrétien is a great professional public servant."

Can you imagine where I'd be, trying to do that? Hugh Winsor would have been right there saying, "In point of fact, Mulroney's nephew—I mean, I didn't want to say this—but he was really a mediocre son of a bitch and he never should have risen to where he was, and now for the prime minister to elevate him is a disgrace for the country. Well, either Mulroney should resign or his nephew should go jump into the Potomac." That's the double standard.

What about the skeletons in Chrétien's closet:
When I came to office, I took Mr. Trudeau's house and we spruced it up. I took his old plane. I took his old cars. I took his office. I never did anything. I never changed anything. I took the swimming pool that he had built. I took Harrington Lake. I mean, what is this they say about my extraordinary lifestyle?

You tell me, talk about a lifestyle, how does a guy like Chrétien wind up owning a golf course? And a house in Ottawa, and all of these other things. His son gets charged and convicted of rape, yet he's never been sentenced. His daughter is married to Andy Desmarais, one of the richest people in Canada, and he's supposed to be a poor boy. And I'm supposed to be some rich spender.

Mulroney wondered how Chrétien could so effortlessly go back on his campaign promises to repeal the Goods and Services Tax and the North American Free Trade Agreement:
All this nonsense going on, the guy just swallows himself whole on NAFTA, nobody says a word. It's just been

an awful bloody piece of business. Only a mean, dirty bastard would do something like that, or a fucking stupid one. And you know what? He's both. And he's sucking in this bunch of assholes in the press gallery in Ottawa.

Look, if what we were doing was so wrong, how come they're endorsing everything we did? I mean, Christ almighty—I had to fight an election on the Free Trade Agreement. I mean the then leader of the Liberal Party, endorsed by Jean Chrétien, said that if we had the Free Trade Agreement, we were going to lose our social programs, we were going to lose our cultural identity, we were going to lose our regional development, we were going to lose the country. And now they are saying, this same Liberal Party is saying five years later that they're kicking the United States around because they're not committing to NAFTA fast enough for the countries in Latin America.

And the GST? For that I got pilloried personally.

So the Canadian people, they're sitting there and they're watching the Liberals do exactly what I did and they're going to start to wonder after a while, how come they pilloried Mulroney for this, now they're doing it themselves. And we're supposed to think Chrétien is a great guy?

Two years into Chrétien's first term, Mulroney was still mulling his chances if he'd fought the 1993 election:
I came from fourteen points behind in 1984 to win big, the biggest in Canadian history. I came from twenty-three points behind in 1988 to win another huge majority. And I was going to come from behind again had I run. If I couldn't defeat Jean Chrétien, this guy, I'll jump out that window right now.

17

"Keep your pecker up, Kim!"

———

Severing Her Own Jugular

As he stepped down from public life, Mulroney was unwilling to concede voter hostility toward him, preferring to blame it on a weak-willed electorate. Although his party stood at a pathetic 18 per cent in the polls and was about to suffer the most humiliating defeat in Canadian history, Mulroney believed he had left a strong legacy for his successor, the Rt. Hon. Kim Campbell.

According to her version, she was a multilingual cellist with talent to burn who held a graduate degree in Soviet strategy and could conduct the nation's business while baking a cake and speaking Yiddish.

Mulroney was aware of Campbell's inexperience:
I mean, Christ—she only got here in 1988. She'll grow. We all grow. If you're smart, you'll grow into it. Some prime

THE SECRET MULRONEY TAPES

ministers have not. Dief, I think it's probably fair to say, did not. Dief was too old. Turner was there too brief a time. But most of us tend to grow in this job, and if she's given an opportunity, she could do that.

Only the overwhelming stupidity of Southam News and the Vancouver *Province* could ever write an editorial saying that I was trying to penalize her by giving her these departments [Justice and Defence]. Look at all of the stuff going on in Yugoslavia and Somalia. It takes knowing that stuff if you're going to run for leader.

Although he claimed publicly that he was removed from the Tory leadership race, he said something different in private:
I've been manoeuvring this thing for two years, to be succeeded by Campbell. Twenty-five years of Quebeckers is enough. The country needs somebody from the west—preferably a woman.

It's not that she's going to do anything different. She's not going to do any miracles. The important points are who she is and where she's from. She's a woman from British Columbia. This changes the perspective of Canadians about how they see themselves. It's so goddamned hilarious. We got this Gallup poll out this morning, which showed that if Campbell were leading the party she'd be defeating the Liberals. Panic has totally taken over the Liberal Party.

Preston Manning has been badly hurt, and he hurt himself. I think you can safely assume that Reform is going to elect nobody and the NDP are going to elect nobody. This is going to be a collision between the Liberals and the Conservatives with a three-party fight in Quebec.

He believed Campbell's selection as leader would single-handedly reverse the deep antipathy toward the Tories in Western Canada:
Not a goddamned thing will have changed, but the

Conservatives will sweep every seat in British Columbia. And British Columbians will see themselves differently— they will see themselves as being in power. But it will be different because it will be one of their own and, more importantly, it won't be a Quebecker.

I see a situation where she can win the leadership and she can become prime minister. She's going to attract extraordinary publicity; she would be the only woman prime minister of an important industrialized country in the world. Right after the convention, she can benefit from all this publicity, and then go to Japan for the G-7 summit. That summit is going to be fascinating. It's [U.S. president Bill] Clinton's first and she would be the only woman at the table.

As soon as she becomes prime minister, you would have an English-speaking woman, who happens to speak French, from British Columbia. Okay? The first thing that happens: goodbye, Reform Party in Western Canada. Goodbye! Canadians don't like the frog from Baie-Comeau, because he's from Quebec and as everybody from Jack Webster to Rafe Mair [British Columbia's leading broadcasters] will tell you, everybody from Quebec is a sleazy, slimy, dishonest, corrupt, venal Union Nationale phony politician. So let's get rid of him, let's get rid of this guy, and now, let's turn to a nice, pure, forty-six-year-old person from British Columbia, born in Campbell River. What could be better than that?

If they don't vote for her, I hope somebody will have the decency to tell them to go stuff it. If they won't support a young woman from British Columbia to be prime minister of Canada, I hope they stop talking about western alienation.

As the leadership convention approached, Mulroney became increasingly concerned about Kim:
She's sinking, Jean Charest is rising and this will all be decided by public opinion polls on the two days leading

up to the vote. If the polls indicate that only he can win and beat the Liberals, then they'll vote for him. If the polls indicate that it's anybody's game, she's going to win because she's far enough ahead now to maintain her lead.

I have never in my life seen such a lack of enthusiasm for a front-running candidate. Not only did the bloom go off the rose, the rose is wilted. What they're saying to me is that there is not a whole hell of a lot there and what we see, we don't particularly like. And I say to them, "Well look, she's a good woman. She's got this. She's got that." And so then they say, "Well, you may be right, but look, we're not very thrilled by all of this." The kind of enthusiasm we saw at the beginning is completely gone.

On the eve of the vote, Jean Charest captivated the leadership convention audience with his passionate oratory, while Kim Campbell lectured the Tory delegates like a schoolteacher. Mulroney took credit for grooming Charest, too:
That Charest speech last night was better than mine in 1983. It hit the same notes, sort of. "My name is Jean Charest and I'm goddamned well going to win for you." That's what they wanted to hear. This is not a Rotary Club speech or a political science class. Hers was not even a good election speech; it was a lecture to the Kennedy School of Government.

I'm the one who kept Charest in the race. He would have never gotten in. He said, "It's all over. Campbell has got it won." I said, "You're out of your goddamned mind; you don't know what you're talking about. If you don't run, Jean, you can be a has-been. If you run, you can become the leader and the prime minister."

I made them both, so I can't have a favourite. In these circumstances, Charest would do better, but who knows. I'm a happy man. I know that the verdict of history is going to be favourable. I know that already.

In the aftermath of the leadership vote, Mulroney wanted to ensure party unity at any cost:
Campbell won this goddamned thing fair and square, and we're all behind her and we're going to make sure we're all behind her. She cannot win the next election if there's a split in Quebec. If there's a perception of a split in Quebec, she cannot win. I said to Michel Cogger—one of Charest's supporters—"You tell him that if he's not there standing up saluting Kim Campbell when I walk in with her tomorrow morning at nine o'clock, he doesn't have to worry about his political career, because I will have terminated it by noon." When I walked in there the next morning, Charest was standing up cheering.

Mulroney anticipated a triumphal return to Parliament with Campbell on his arm, and her subsequent electoral victory:
Kim Campbell called me and asked me if I'd remain an MP until the election. I had planned to resign as soon as she gave us an indication whether she was going to call the House back. I thought she should have a Throne Speech and a platform. I also thought the visuals of her being in the House as prime minister for a week would be positive. At her first meeting with the federal cabinet, she said, "If John Turner had one-tenth of 1 per cent of the support from Pierre Trudeau that I've got from Brian Mulroney, he might still be prime minister."

She will inherit a party with $5.7 million in cash and an untouched $12.5 million line of credit, the best organization this country will have ever seen, with John Tory in charge, a united party and an economy growing strongly. At the G-7 summit, Canada will receive the report card as the world's leader in economic growth, employment growth, productivity growth, and the lowest inflation.

Mulroney and Campbell were dismayed by the reaction to her leadership victory:

MULRONEY: She got a little bit paranoid listening to some of these crackpots in British Columbia who don't understand how important certain things are. I said to Kim, "If you think that the media are mad at me because I'm Brian Mulroney and because I wear nice suits, you're crazy. The media don't like me because I'm a successful Conservative leader. All you've got to do to find out if I'm telling you the truth is run for leader, and you'll quickly find out exactly what will happen to you."

You couldn't blame her for not anticipating the total distortion that was in that *Toronto Star* article on the front page, which gave rise to the CBC coverage.

It was shocking even by my standards, and the low regard I have for the Ottawa press gallery. But I've come to expect nothing less from [*Toronto Star* publisher] John Honderich and the Southam sewer. She came to see me in the House the other day and I told her, "Remember what Dief said—keep your pecker up, Kim! What can you do? This is the way it is, and it gets a hell of a lot worse. I told you and you didn't believe me. Now you do. You're dealing with a sewer."

In the ramp-up to the federal campaign, Mulroney expressed concern over her campaign team, even though most had fought elections with him in the past: Perrin Beatty, Jodi White, Denis Boucher, Allan Gregg, Marcel Danis, Patrick Kinsella, Tom Trbovich, John Tory, Ray Castelli, David Camp. He maintained his generous interpretation of her qualities:
She's doing very well on relatively little so far—nothing wrong with that. She has no ideas, and there's nothing wrong with that. Her program is more of the same. I understand she can't say that—she's got to try and differentiate herself from me and my government—but Perrin Beatty is in charge of her idea bank and it's just going to be "Spend money." That's all.

But now people are saying, "We were told she could speak eighty-nine languages, and now we find out that she can't speak Russian and she's not fluent in French." Her people have been doing a powerful hard sell, and nobody can meet those expectations. That's her biggest problem.

Her campaign team wanted Campbell to distance herself from his regime:
MULRONEY: It's a lot of bullshit what she's been saying, and you really have to wonder whether she has her mind around the main issues. I mean it's crazy to be worrying about moving into 24 Sussex or selling off the Department of Defence plane. Can you imagine her going to a G-7 summit on a commercial flight? What does she think? What does she believe in? That's what the country is kind of uneasy about.

Pretty soon he was calling her ungrateful in private:
The caucus just about threw her out. I'd have to pick her up off the floor and say, "Here's how we're going to do things." She's tempting fate. Not only did she not do things differently, but she couldn't even do them. The prime minister had to get them done for her. I wouldn't say that myself, but her opponents may. I retired the whole front bench so she could put a fresh face on it. I declined to do the restructuring of government to give her a better opportunity, and then I spent the week patching this thing together when it came a lot closer to disaster than most people know.

His feelings were clearly wounded:
Her campaign began in a strange, almost defiant way. She was not only going to separate herself from me and my government, she was never going to mention my name.

What you should do is pay homage to the out-going guy. She went from city to city and managed to avoid mentioning my name. There's nothing wrong with saying,

"I'm in favour of what Mulroney did but now I'm going to do this differently, and this the same." Or, "I'm in favour of what he did, but I'm going to change such-and-such." Your policy has to make sense—but you've got to have one, and she doesn't have one. She doesn't have a policy on the Constitution, on national unity, on the economy, on international affairs.

Then Campbell flubbed an important meeting with the editorial board of the *Globe and Mail*:
MULRONEY: During her visit with the editorial board of the *Globe*, she showed up with her press secretary, Paul Frazer, and the board began questioning her on the deficit. She started to give them wrong answers and they told her so. In front of the whole group, she excused herself and went to the end of the table and sat there with Paul going through flip charts to find out where she was wrong on her own speech.

The most tragic thing is that in anticipation of that meeting, John Tory had dispatched two senior people from the Privy Council Office and the Prime Minister's Office out to Vancouver to get her ready for this thing. They went back to Ottawa without getting in to see her.

Mulroney's disenchantment took on a personal tone, as he declared that she should be concentrating on the campaign instead of having sexual adventures with her boyfriend, Russian-born Montreal entrepreneur Gregory Lekhtman, inventor of a spring-loaded exercise shoe known as the Exerloper:
Throughout the whole goddamned thing, she's been screwing around with this Russian guy. The guy was sneaking into hotel rooms and the campaign bus. If I'm in an election campaign and you bring Marilyn Monroe and fifteen others into my hotel room, I'd throw them out. You have no time for that stuff. If you have fifteen minutes, you phone some of your candidates.

Christ, she'd arrive in Montreal and the Mounties would drive like hell over to her boyfriend's house. She'd spend the whole goddamned afternoon and night there, then make a quick speech and come back. They prepared really good briefing papers and she disappeared. She never even opened them. She was with the boyfriend.

Soon Mulroney felt like he'd been had, on several fronts:
During the campaign, Sam Wakim called me and said, "I saw a Russian interviewer on television here in Toronto ask her a question in Russian today, and she didn't know what he was talking about." He turned out to be right—she doesn't speak Russian, and she never had a degree. She turned out to be a very vain person. She told someone after one of the debates that everyone else in the race was a pygmy. In this business, if you don't have respect for your opponents, you can't win.

Mulroney started to remember some earlier incidents with Kim:
Remember the time [in Justice when] she threw all the Jewish groups out of her office because they had said something to the press? Or the way she was so cool with Mrs. Joyce Milgaard? I was forever stepping in behind the scenes, but not in any dramatic way. Nothing caused me to say this woman was crazy. There were some unsettling things. The people she wanted to put on the Supreme Court were nuts.

Then Campbell told a reporter querying her stance on social spending that an election campaign "is not the time to get involved in a debate on very, very serious issues." And she authorized a televised ad campaign that mocked Jean Chrétien's partial facial paralysis. Mulroney was in despair:
It doesn't look too hot. I don't know what's going to

happen if Kim loses this. This will be the most destructive and the most incompetent campaign I've seen in my life.

On October 25, 1993, the Conservative majority of 169 seats was reduced to a rump of merely 2: Jean Charest and Elsie Wayne. The Liberals won 178 seats and formed the government; the Bloc Québécois gained 54 seats and official opposition status. The Reform Party also made a strong showing, with 52 seats. It was the most crippling defeat for a governing party in Canadian history:
MULRONEY: Kim Campbell giving away the campaign is the only thing that pissed Mila and me off. It was all given away. That's what irritated us. We had spent so much time and energy in building it all up and she threw it away. Nobody minds losing an election if you fight hard and lose. It's different when you give it away.

What Mulroney would have done in Kim's shoes:
She began this silly distancing in the campaign—didn't even know my name, didn't know our record. Can you imagine going into a television debate and not telling Chrétien, "Mr. Chrétien, you're attacking me for my government doubling the national debt in nine years. Well, you know this morning inflation is at 1.4 per cent; when you left office it was 12.9 per cent. Interest rates are five and three-quarters, and when you were in office they were twenty-two and three-quarters, and if a government doubling the national debt in nine years offends you, what would you say about a government that increased the national debt eleven times in fifteen years, like yours did?" But you know, she didn't.

Here we've got record exports, record high productivity. What she should have been saying was, "Look at the Mulroney government. He made the fundamental and painful structural changes that have placed Canada on a brand-new course. He's laid the foundation; I'm going to build the mansion, and here's what it's going to be."

In the inevitable post-mortems, her chief of staff and transition advisor, Bill Neville, shared with Mulroney an interesting anecdote, which he was only too pleased to pass on:
She just had no political instincts whatsoever, none. Can you imagine doing something like going into a campaign without a platform? Bill Neville attended a meeting where it was decided that they would have no platform. It was a formal decision, approved by the leader.

Can you imagine how goddamned vain you've got to be to think that in 1993, with all the difficulties we have, you can go to a great pluralistic democracy and ask them to vote for you without telling them what you're going to do?

Mulroney had left her with a perfectly good platform to take to the electorate:
She implied that there had been no Throne Speech and no policy documents given to her. I asked the Privy Council to send me a copy. Jean Charest came to see me and he just about cried. It's by far the best Throne Speech that my government put together in nine years. We saved the best for her, but she didn't even read the goddamned thing. Charest, the deputy prime minister, had never heard of it.

But Mulroney distanced himself from the Tory eclipse:
The election campaign is a necessary piece of brutality. Canadians expect you to perform a certain way during the campaign because it is a test of leadership. They want to know what you're like under pressure, under attack, under fire. That's what an election campaign is all about, and that's why some people succeed in politics and some fail. Some people are political leaders and some are followers.

I was out of the country for most of the campaign, so I truly don't know what happened. The results are profoundly regrettable, but as far as I'm concerned, I've turned the page on that completely. My focus is on the future and rebuilding the Conservative Party.

None of it was his fault, he insisted:
If Kim Campbell had thought the election was impossible
to win, she would not have run for the leadership. She ran
because she thought she could win the election. It's like
the press asking me, "Mr. Mulroney, how much blame do
you think you should take for Kim Campbell's defeat?"
Well, the desired answer is, "I'm fully responsible." But if
I had led the party and we'd come back with only one
seat, then I would apologize.

On September 1, Miss Campbell was in first place.
She had a twenty-point lead on Chrétien and a twenty-
seven-point lead on the gender gap. Canadian women
really wanted her to win. Forty-seven days later, she was
in last place. I have to conclude that something happened
from day one.

I'm not offended by a loss. You go into a campaign,
nothing is perfect, you go up and you go down, and sometimes you come in second—but you don't come in fifth.

After Campbell's stunning defeat, Mulroney said:
She never phoned anybody, she never spoke to anybody.
I not only phoned our losing candidates, but a lot of the
key Liberals. [Deputy Prime Minister] Don Mazankowski
put it best of all. He said, "We were taken over by a
stranger." She didn't know anything about Canada, or
about the party, or about government. She was only in it
for herself.

**Looking back on events, Mulroney's faith in his own
judgment remained unshaken:**
There was a desire to promote a woman from Western
Canada. She was a good minister. She was bright. But it
turns out I saw her in a one-dimensional way. I was
happily sailing under the impression that she was a university professor, with a doctorate in strategic studies
from the Soviet Union. Her French was awful, too. We all
should have been arrested for misleading advertising. She

showed a lot of arrogance and a lot of incompetence. People wondered what she stood for, if she stood for anything.

The only thing I didn't do was physically carry her through the doorway of 24 Sussex Drive.

18

Keeping caucus happy

———

Walking Through Fire for Brian

IN THE SULLEN SPRING OF 1992, Brian and Mila Mulroney had just finished a gruelling, pre-referendum tour of eastern Quebec, when word reached them that Mona Darling had died. She was the wife of Stan Darling, the oldest member of the Conservative caucus. The prime ministerial couple immediately dragged themselves back onto the government jet and arrived, unannounced, during the funeral service at Burke's Falls in northern Ontario. Mulroney was genuinely fond of Darling, but he also knew that his surprise appearance would send a clear message to Tory backbenchers: "If Brian will take that much trouble to support old Stan, he'd do it for me. By God, I'd walk through fire for him." And they did.

It was nothing short of a miracle that during the decade-long toboggan slide in his popularity, Mulroney never faced a caucus revolt, or even the hint of one.

Nearly every backbencher had a story to tell. The late Bob Wenman, MP for Fraser Valley West, tried for years to reconstruct the events surrounding his mother's death in 1991. He had been away in Brandon, Manitoba, when his father called to tell him that she had suddenly passed away. Within the hour, while his father was still notifying other family members, Mulroney was on the phone to Wenman in Brandon, expressing his sympathy. That was typical. Even if such solicitude was blatantly political, no one doubted Brian's sincerity. In the face of concentrated firestorms by the opposition and the press, the loyalty of his troops never wavered. It may have been a miracle but it wasn't accidental. Mulroney had no higher political priority than to keep his caucus happy, and every Wednesday morning he proved it.

"Lookit, if you have a problem with a colleague or you have a personal problem that you want to discuss with me, come and see me. I'll solve it if I can and it will never go any further," he lectured his MPs early in his first term. "If you have a problem with your minister, with your deputy minister or whatever, you can discuss it here. But also as important, if you have a problem with me, with my style, with my staff, with my approach—I don't shoot messengers. I don't welcome bad news, but I know that bad news is going to come and so I look on it constructively. If you have anything to say to me, your criticisms may help me and thereby help the government. You can mention them here, but if you feel inhibited by saying it in front of a large group, come and see me in my office. I'd appreciate it. What wouldn't be helpful was if you were harbouring some views that could be constructively challenged, or if you're saving stuff for your memoirs. Then you're not helping me or helping the party and the government."

His bravura performances—occasionally rated by caucus pranksters holding up cardboard scorecards grading his "blarney index" from 1 to 10—kept his members contented and amused. His weekly consultations with MPs were a healthy two-way flow, with policies often altered on the spot. He asked that each MP write him an annual letter, listing complaints and recommendations; he read each missive and dictated personal replies. He invited caucus members for regular breakfasts at Sussex and tended to the welfare of his MPs as if they were an extended family. (While there were no rebellions, Patrick Nowlan resigned, and two Alberta MPs, David Kilgour—who switches parties with every full moon—and Alex Kindy, were expelled for refusing to support the GST.)

When he thought it was necessary, Mulroney could scold his MPs and ministers, even telling them how to dress. In 1985, Tom Siddon, then minister of fisheries, drew the PM's ire when he walked into the Commons while Michael Wilson was retreating on his measure to de-index seniors' pensions. A grinning Siddon slid into a seat directly behind the finance minister, in full view of cross-Canada TV viewers. He was fresh from his son's graduation, still dressed like a peacock in his full-flowing, multi-hued academic gown, complete with the hood that marked his PhD in engineering. Mulroney came over and hissed, "Get that fucking thing off." Siddon did.

One of the PM's toughest admonitions was his insistence that the caucus sanction the right of homosexuals to serve in Canada's armed forces. "All right," he told his members, "statistics tell us that about 15 per cent of the population is homosexual, and since we in the Conservative Party are representative of the population, there are at least thirty gays in this room. Am I wrong? Is there a flaw in my logic? Are we going to deprive these people of their rights?" The vote carried handily.

"You can only weather the violent attacks to which I was subjected if your caucus keeps telling you that none of it is true," Mulroney once explained to me. "If you have to tell *them* it's not true, you're in big trouble. It doesn't matter a good goddamn what the *Toronto Star* thinks, what the press gallery thinks what the polls say, what Allan Fotheringham thinks, or even what the country thinks of you, so long as your caucus continues to support you, because then you have time to regroup. What happened to Joe Clark at the Winnipeg leadership review had nothing to do with the party vote. He might have had nearly 70 per cent of the delegates behind him, but he knew that his caucus wouldn't follow him. They saw him every week and figured he wasn't a leader. If you don't have the caucus behind you, you can't govern."

While the caucus strengthened Mulroney's hand internally, their lack of criticism left him largely ignorant of what was happening outside Ottawa's ramparts. This turned out to be a serious liability. Despite his success in forestalling revolts, his Wednesday-morning performances belonged to the world of theatre: dramatically satisfying but with little connection to the real world. By capturing the hearts and minds of his followers, he inadvertently formed a moat around himself, and few whispers of popular unrest made the leap across it. Mulroney was further protected from ordinary voters and their concerns by his personal staff, which at one point swelled past two hundred, nearly twice the size of Trudeau's.

Even his forays into the hinterland, designed to establish contact between the governor and the governed, were so minutely planned that the prime minister came close to becoming the Canadian equivalent of a pontiff, shunted around in his hermetically sealed Popemobile. Every event attended by either of the Mulroneys was scheduled to the nanosecond. A simple elevator ride three floors long required a printed passenger manifest with a vetted list in triplicate, showing who should be on board at each stop. These split-second itineraries—a day's timetable could run to sixty pages—made for orderly prime ministerial processions. But there was, literally, not a minute free to perform a spontaneous gesture, make an off-the-cuff comment or even blow their noses.

When Mulroney was on the move, he projected a mixture of attentive gravity and premeditated nonchalance. He behaved like the mayor of some ancient mountain village receiving distant tax collectors. Nothing was left to chance. His advance people were told he would never wear a hat of any kind, that he did not want to be touched, hugged or kissed in public, and that he should never, ever be seen jumping on a trampoline, handling a baseball bat or trying to catch a football. He felt that by not appearing vulnerable, he could reassure his subjects. (You got messy hair, you might legitimize polygamy.)

It was the ultimate paradox of the man that his public rigor mortis was so patently phony while his private self was so warm and amusing, especially when he trotted out his self-deprecating wit. "I try and avoid popularity like the plague," he told me several times during his second term, "and I've been reasonably successful at it."

If the Mulroney prime ministership seemed at times to be more like a presidency, it was also because he appeared to be governing by his lonesome. The weight of his presence was so overwhelming that in 1992—eight years after he assumed power—a Gallup poll showed that 34 per cent of Canadians (45 per cent in British Columbia) couldn't name a single Mulroney cabinet minister.

The prime minister's rapport with his MPs was unique, and didn't survive his departure, proving just how vital and dominating his presence had really been. Following the 1993 election, when the losers gathered one last time as a Tory caucus in Ottawa, Stan Darling was there, though he hadn't run again. Nearly alone among the lamenting politicians, he directly blamed the former prime minister for the slaughter. "It was the unpopularity of Brian Mulroney that defeated us," he declared. "A lot of people hated his guts. And our campaign certainly didn't set the world on fire. When those negative ads ridiculing Chrétien's contorted mouth came on, I just about died."

I had several spies inside the Tory caucus and very quickly realized from their reports that there was nothing magical about Mulroney's weekly performances. He simply addressed his MPs in exactly the same tone (including profanities and irreverent asides) as he talked to me, and as is recorded in this book. Whether or not Mulroney could have held the nation in his spell by just being himself—and not the artificial construct that appeared in public—is an open question. I tend to believe that it just might have worked.

Stanley Hartt was mesmerized by Mulroney's performance in caucus:
He walked into those sessions and entertained everybody for the first ten or fifteen minutes, a monologue, and what was amazing was his ability to take diverse sources, often newspaper clippings that he had clipped out and he'd put it in the file. As events sort of coalesced in his mind, he'd say to Rick Morgan, his executive assistant, I clipped out an article about four weeks ago from such-and-such paper and gave it to you and you put it away. He'd get this one and that one and do his show-and-tell with a string of things that were to all appearances unrelated. He'd tie them together in an absolutely magnificent way. He was spellbinding.

You know, some of the government officials are not necessarily partisan supporters of Mulroney and they just loved the show—it was a great show. When they say, if only people could see him the way he was in caucus, well, it wasn't just caucus: it was caucus, cabinet, planning and priorities, any meeting in which he felt safe from intruders, safe from hecklers, safe from the press, safe from the excesses of his own lips. In other words, God forbid he should engage in a small amount of hyperbole just to make a point and then they print it and say, ha, that is not literally true.

He comes from a tradition in Quebec where hyperbole is perfectly honourable, just like dressing up. Exaggeration is not a crime; it's fun. West of the Quebec-Ontario border, statements are parsed and dissected—that subordinate clause is not strictly accurate, the man is a liar. And he never, to this day, got used to that. He didn't understand that there are two different standards.

He ran the P&P committee as a forum in a way I've never seen before. I used to believe that sooner or later, when somebody is saying something that is very dumb, you'd say to them, all right, we've heard your point—everyone else wants to do the opposite, so we're going to do the opposite. But no one was ever made to look like a loser. You alone decided how long you would continue your fight. He would never say, you're being a horse's tail, get off it—the next meeting I want this through. Never—he would never do that. And that's one of the reasons he inspired such tremendous loyalty.

In fact, only once he imposed his will, and it was a really funny story. He wanted to invite Chaim Herzog, the president of Israel, to speak to the House, and one by one, people voiced their objections. At the end he said, "Well, it's decided. We're having him!" That was the only time I ever saw him impose his will, and it was on something that wasn't even policy. It was just an invitation that was basically within his gift; he didn't even have to ask them.

Mulroney gave a hint to Hartt as to how he pulled it off: He once called me into his office and said, "Do you hold meetings with your staff every morning?" I said, "Yes, I do." "How many people come?" "Oh, I don't know, whoever is there, but between seven and ten people. The idea is we've all read fifteen papers and the purpose of the meeting is to decide what's on Question Period so that we can use the maximum amount of the day for the legislative assistants with some researchers to go and develop answers for you."

And he says, "You shouldn't do that. Tell them to meet at 7 a.m., read the papers, and they should decide what they think should be done for the day and then come and tell you. They should appoint one spokesman, you shouldn't see the whole group—one person should come in and tell you what they've decided, and you keep a poker face. And then you keep all the credit. You haven't given yourself away, you haven't debated openly with them as an equal, including losing some points, which has to happen. So they haven't seen that you're not invincible, and you keep your authority that way, by distancing yourself."

Of course, he was talking about himself. He wasn't talking about me and my staff.

Peter White believed Mulroney was too dominating:
There was a British senior cabinet minister, unnamed, who had been interviewed, and in response to the question, he said, "Cabinet meetings? We don't have those anymore, we just have a lecture from Madame [Margaret Thatcher]." That sort of reminded me of the type of things that happen here. In any meeting, even if it's just a two-person meeting, Brian tends to monopolize the conversation, and that is a serious problem. I think it's a defence mechanism on his part, but it has become a habit.

Lowell Murray said sometimes caucus was one long session of prime ministerial self-indulgence:
This business of Brian making these very fulsome tributes to various people is a bit of a joke in caucus. Peter Elzinga got up and made a speech in his capacity as president of the national association, and Mulroney went on and on and on and on, what a marvellous person he was, how much the party owed such people, etcetera.

But Mulroney, Hugh Segal said, had it all over Joe Clark:
In 1979, my wife graduated with her MBA from Western, and before she started working, she went out as a volunteer advance person for Joe Clark's campaign. For nine

weeks, she hit the country, opening doors and doing all those things. I wouldn't let her take any money for it; I wouldn't even let her file an expense account. It was just good education for her about the world out there. She did great, but she has yet to get a thank-you letter.

My brother, Brian, [then] head of Ryerson, made only one minor contribution to the 1984 Mulroney campaign. He wrote a policy document on telecommunications, because that's his area of expertise, and he appeared in front of the caucus committee on manpower and training to make a presentation on some ideas they may want to consider. That's all he did—nothing else. He dropped Brian a short note saying, "Dear Prime Minister, splendid victory, every good wish, Brian Segal." He got a long note from Mulroney, noting specifically the contributions he had made, and then underneath it, written in the PM's handwriting, "Brian, if you see that fat guy who helped, give him my regards."

You know, my brother is not a very political guy. He's an academic. But for him . . . now the prime minister could call him, send him to Ethiopia, he would be delighted because he feels there's a guy there who really cares and understands. Clark was able to give even his closest friends the feeling that he didn't care. I don't know whether it's Joe's personality or coming from a small town in western Canada, or not coming from that kind of Irish French-Canadian mix where there's a lot of warmth on the table.

Perrin Beatty with further thoughts on why Mulroney inspired such loyalty:
He had my loyalty and the loyalty of most of us who were supporting Joe Clark the day he won, only because of the argument we had been making was that you support your leader. But very quickly, he won my enthusiastic support. A very minor thing, but it had a profound effect on me— I was sitting at home watching Elwy Yost on the TV one Saturday night with Julie, and the phone rang. It was

Brian Mulroney with nothing on his mind other than to chat on a Saturday night. I thought with all the responsibilities that he had, if he took the time out to call me where there was no brief, no question about my support, it really struck me. I had never had a call like that before. It was impressive because it was totally unnecessary.

That was the first thing.

Then I began to see the signs that he was much deeper as well, not only that he was good as a conciliator. I'm not sure that he accepts my thesis, but I've mentioned it to him on more than one occasion. My belief is that his great achievement was not winning two back-to-back majorities, but holding the caucus together. During my lifetime, every other Conservative leader has seen his caucus disintegrate under him.

Brian inspires an intense personal loyalty. I had thought that with the gang that we elected in 1984—sort of walked in without having had any political experience, never having been tested under fire—that when things got rough and we were at 22 per cent in the polls, everybody would break and run. Even under enormous pressure you found the intense personal loyalty there was to him. First, he's put caucus on his priority above everything else. He is always there. He attends caucus more frequently than any other member of caucus. He has an incredible magic when it comes to talking to people in a context like that. He makes everybody feel as if he's talking to them personally, and he's well informed, sensitive to individual needs. He takes time to just do little things, whether it's calling me or making reference to somebody.

On acid rain, for example, any time he deals with that issue he makes a point of saying, "It was Stan Darling from Muskoka who convinced me that acid rain was a problem. If it wasn't for Stan's effort, there would be no acid rain agreement." Just giving attention to individuals, he has a way of winning an intense personal loyalty.

Barbara McDougall said the PM respected all views but it was a little trickier to try to change his mind:
In cabinet, if it's something Brian's personally engaged in, then he's very central to the decision. There are some things that you just know it doesn't matter what you say, it's going to be decided by him. On the other stuff, he's very much a consensus-builder. He won't get in battles between ministers. He makes them solve it. I mean, Mazankowski has been the troubleshooter for him on that. I'm quite sure without any particular inside information on it that Maz would sometimes steer the debate because he knows the prime minister wants it. But on most issues, there is a consensus-building. But there are certainly some issues in which he's the boss and that's all there is to it.

I changed his mind once. Derek Burney told me that he had never seen the prime minister change his mind at the table before. It was on dealing with the backlog, the refugee backlog, but it had been dragging on, dragging on, and I was the only one who wanted to go through the determination process in cabinet. One by one I turned everybody around except the prime minister, who has a soft spot for all these people who are cluttering up our sidewalks. I do too, actually, in a personal way, but if you're going to have a system, then it's got to apply to everyone. I talked for twenty minutes and at the end of the day he said, "Derek, get out, get started, announce the policy."

So, it's hard to change his mind, but he will pay attention. It was inevitable after such a long period of one-party rule in this country that there would be a change in direction. I don't think that anybody would have contemplated the degree of difficulty in achieving that. You win a large mandate to change things, but people—actually people don't want change. They just want musical chairs, especially from a Conservative government. People like to feel when they wake up in the morning the world is going to be the same as when they went to bed, but Brian has made some very profound changes, partly through force of personality, partly through dealing with circumstances as they arise, or partly through having a strong view of what he wants to accomplish.

I tend to avoid the word "vision," which is probably the most overworked word in the political lexicon, but he came to office with some objectives. It has taken a great deal of strength to survive the kind of personal attacks he had in the first mandate, which I think are the worst I've ever seen a leader go through. He learned some very costly lessons—costly in emotional terms. Brian gets knocked for his loyalty to people. I think loyalty is a virtue, not a vice. But what happens is that he is loyal to people some of whom are disloyal back, and he doesn't know when to let go. So he continues to be loyal to people who have been disloyal, and in that way he is disloyal to those who are really loyal to him.

Marjory LeBreton, on her boss as the caucus glue:
I know this caucus of ours. We have men that hate women, women that hate men, French that hate the English, English that hate the French, westerners who think central Canadians are a bunch of fat cats, and we have right-wingers, left-wingers, pro-choice, anti-choice . . . He keeps them all together.

19.

"The best since Sir John A."

———

Mulroney Rates Himself

*Before assessing his place among Canadian prime ministers,
Brian Mulroney elaborated on the special situations he had
to face: rival politicians were dead set against his every idea,
the press constantly conveyed an image of mayhem and neg-
ligence on the part of the government—yet neither faction
really understood what Mulroney was trying to achieve. He
believed that financial recovery was the only plausible solution to Canada's woes, and the solution to the country's
future, even if it had to be initially painful and politically
divisive. The inevitable result of Mulroney's fiscal measures
was his abrupt loss of popularity. The Liberals later built
their budgets and plans on the structures Mulroney left
behind, affording Canada's eighteenth prime minister—after
he'd gained some perspective—a triumphant if retroactive
feeling of accomplishment.*

Just days after his first election in 1984, Mulroney offered a brief outline of what his eventual legacy would look like:

I think of two parameters: national reconciliation and economic renewal. When Pierre Trudeau became prime minister, he inherited a $700 million surplus. I inherited a $38 billion deficit, so that cramps your running room. It's pretty hard to dream great dreams when you're trying to pay the laundry bill, but we will. If things work our way, we can be reasonably austere for three years and see what it looks like in year four. In the short term, I've got to get a new energy deal. I've got to get Quebec into this constitutional thing. It's not going to be easy.

He did it his way:

MULRONEY: They keep talking about advisors and counsellors. It doesn't work like that. I do these things by instinct. I don't talk to [senior policy advisor] Charley McMillan, or any of them. I follow things myself; I don't run it past a bunch of civil servants. You have to know when to strike and when to sit, lie in the bushes. Charley plays a useful role, but he's not a strategist.

I even told Pat Carney how to proceed with oil and gas negotiations in Western Canada. I told her, "What you're going to do, Pat, is make a deal with Newfoundland, because Newfoundland is a poor province, it doesn't have any money and they need a deal. Then nobody in Alberta is going to be able to say that you can't negotiate. If you want to settle with Western Canada, negotiate in the east."

The strategy itself, from putting Stephen Lewis in the United Nations to Tommy Douglas in the Privy Council, that's me. The pundits were opposed to my trip to Washington, right off the bat. That's fine, I'm going. I don't give a damn who is opposed. The country is fed up with people who say the United States is our enemy.

And, as far as he was concerned, he had it tough:
I'm getting stung by the congruence of events. Clyde Wells refused to vote on Meech Lake, thereby sabotaging and throwing the country into chaos. Then we had an armed uprising with the Mohawk Indians in Oka. Then I had to deploy troops to the Persian Gulf. Then we were hit with a full-blown recession. Then interest rates and unemployment went sky high. Then I had to invoke an obscure constitutional provision to stack the Senate and get the Goods and Services Tax through, the most unpopular tax since the introduction of the personal income tax. And then we received a Bélanger-Campeau report recommending separation for Quebec. All of it is happening; there are pressures on us to change our policies. The cabinet got a little jumpy.

It doesn't bother me at all. In politics, you'll find it's hard to summon the will to dislike somebody, but the way these Liberals—Trudeau, [senators] Allan MacEachen and Royce Frith and so on—the way they've acted is just absolutely scandalous. What they did on Meech Lake, the way they tried to kill free trade, the way they tried to kill the GST. Look, I'm an old politician—I take my hits, I don't mind that—but boy oh boy, these are pretty low blows. Still, I'm absolutely satisfied that I'm going the right way, and that no matter what papers may say, history will look favourably on what I've done.

When things were not going his way, Mulroney invoked the image of Sir John A.:
The last few years have been breathtaking in the calumny and the smears and the bitterness and the malice directed against me. And so I had to decide, lookit, am I going to be influenced by it? Macdonald wasn't. Macdonald had some rough years and he took solace in the bottle, God love him, and he had a lot of family problems, as you know. But I got comfort from my family because I had no family problems. I've got a wonderful wife and magnificent kids.

In the last months of his tough second term, Mulroney looked forward to life away from Ottawa:
If I were to form another minority or form a minority next time or even a majority, I don't have the enthusiasm. Forget the mistakes that Bill Clinton is making in the U.S., and who knows, maybe he'll be a disaster. I suspect that's not the case, and I certainly don't want it to happen, but at least he's got the enthusiasm, at least he wants to put his ideas into effect. At least he's got all the hope and the vigour of a young man. And I was young when I came in, I was younger than he is, and I had all of that vigour and all of that strength and all of that enthusiasm and I generated all of that hope, but quite frankly, I don't have it anymore.

As his retirement drew closer, Mulroney counted his pleasures:
The main thing that I'm going to miss about this job is my Wednesday caucus. In ten years as party leader, I only missed nine caucuses. Secondly is Harrington Lake. Thirdly is the power of appointment. The PMO switchboard is great, but I won't have the need of it.

Mulroney entertained speaking offers and offers of positions on corporate boards:
The group from the United States—the Washington Speakers Bureau—has Reagan and Thatcher, and they want me as part of a package deal. They're offering me $50,000 U.S. a speech. I would expect that in Canada you'd get one-tenth of what you'd get in the United States, no doubt about that in my mind. So I think maybe I will do three or four or five a year and see how it goes and then keep going. Margaret Thatcher does speeches all the time. Hell, George Bush's first speaking engagement was at Jimmy Pattison's annual meeting.

NEWMAN: I assume that you've got all kinds of offers.

MULRONEY: Oh Christ, have I ever! I can tell you that it's like twenty-nine leading international directorships in writing, two offers of professorships at Harvard, offers of $50,000 a speech on a permanent basis, offers of international advisory boards around the world from Singapore to Paris, offers of every large law firm in Canada at huge salaries. You name it. And I've got Bill Safire's publisher calling me from New York offering me to do my memoirs! I said no. I don't want to do my memoirs. I'm too young. I may have another career left in me.

Mulroney took comfort from a column by Charles Krauthammer of the *Washington Post*:
Krauthammer talks about political capital and he says, "It should be a rule that any leader who leaves office with a high approval rating be automatically disqualified in considerations of greatness." He wrote that in reference to the former prime minister of Poland Tadeusz Mazowiecki, who set the country on a course towards free market and was thrown out of office for his efforts. Like somebody said to me, "How do you think you're going to be judged?" I said, "By serious historians? I am going to be judged very favourably. By the sports writers around Ottawa? Probably a hell of a lot less favourably." They'll look at the latest opinion polls and say, "He's only at 21 or 25 per cent, therefore he hasn't done well."

The fact of the matter is, if you're leaving office and your public opinion ratings are high, that means that you haven't expended your political capital in a good cause . . . Yes, I was the most popular. I won the most seats. I was the first prime minister in thirty-five years to win back-to-back majority governments. I was the first Conservative prime minister in one hundred years to win back-to-back majority governments. And I had huge approval ratings. But in the recession, we became unpopular. Nobody says that it was because of the recession; historians will say that because that's what it's all about.

Now, if you had come in with a 15 per cent approval rating and stayed at 15 per cent, you wouldn't have lasted very long. It's called leadership. It's not called *follower*ship.

I put the country up to a mirror and I said, "Here's what you look like and here's what we have to look like in ten or fifteen or twenty years." They couldn't swallow it; they couldn't take it. Now, does that mean that I was wrong? We'll have to see. I don't think so. That's what a leader has to do.

You see, if the political objective is simply to maintain popularity, if the object of the exercise is to do in office what Jean Chrétien is doing—namely, nothing—then I'm wrong politically. If, however, the object of the exercise is to use your time in office to effect deep changes in a nation that will benefit the country in the decades ahead, then what we did was right. And that's what leadership is all about. We stood the country on its head and said, "Here are the things that have to be done and we're going to do them."

Blowing his own horn:
I'd like you to point out to me who in Canadian history has a record of comparable achievement in terms of coming in the way I did, taking the Conservative Party from opposition, putting it in the government, keeping it there, keeping it together, running the government and winning again and keeping the government together for nine years, and then turning it over in very good shape—both the party and the government—to the point where Kim Campbell had the government back in first place on Labour Day, in spite of a recession, in spite of all of these things.

To have done all of that without the benefit of thirty years in Parliament and a rich father and well-connected friends—to start from nowhere, to start from Baie-Comeau, and to do that, this is a matter of some considerable achievement. At the end of the second term, I beat Robert Borden, even though his second term was a coalition. In fact, at the end of the second term, I was fifth in terms of longevity after Macdonald, Laurier, King and Trudeau. Not bad.

Contrary to what his critics believed, Mulroney described himself as a Canadian nationalist:
I was fighting for Canada's sovereignty because of what [the Liberals] had done by the profligate spending which was undermining our economic strength, and we were spending so much to repay our debt that we had compromised our sovereignty, our capacity to act as an independent nation. And you have people making speeches about sovereignty, all these phonies like Mel Hurtig who destroy Canada's sovereignty because they refuse to acknowledge that without economic strength, you don't have the capacity to assert your sovereign will.

The interesting irony is that one hundred years from now as they look back on it, the thing that they will be saying principally about me is that this guy was the greatest Canadian sovereignist, and he understood that (a) Canada's finances had to be cleaned up because of that to strengthen the nation, and (b) he had to put Canada in a new trading situation to enrich it so that it could assert its national sovereignty in a globalized economy.

He also stood up for independent Canadian foreign policy, and liked to point to his role in the battle to end apartheid in South Africa:
The leadership by Canada on the issue was a seven-year battle to galvanize and energize the Commonwealth and to provide it with a structural leadership. On apartheid, we really were in the driver's seat, because the United Kingdom was the odd man out. Thatcher went completely the other way. That made a difference on a great moral issue.

Nelson Mandela has acknowledged publicly Canada's role. Of all the countries in the world, Canada played the key role in what took place. The idea that because of my other policies we were following in lockstep with the United States is of course nonsense. Our policy on South Africa was at total variance with the policy of the Reagan administration. It was at total variance with the United States on Cuba. Total variance with the United States on Central America, Nicaragua and so on. At total variance with the United States on foreign aid tied to human rights—very significant differences with the United States. At the United Nations, Canada voted with the United States of America less frequently than all of the other industrialized nations in the world. Yes sir, *less frequently.*

Clarifying Canada's position on apartheid was one of the first tasks Mulroney assigned incoming External Affairs Secretary Joe Clark:
I called Clark into my office in the Langevin Building soon after I became prime minister and I said, "Joe, I don't know what we're going to hear from External Affairs—I don't know enough about it, we're all new here—but I'm telling you that I think you and I are going to agree this afternoon on this great issue: South Africa. We cannot nor will we take the compliant policy of the predecessor government. We are going to be an active leader in the fight against apartheid."

Mitchell Sharp, once the Liberal foreign affairs minister, attempted to deflate Mulroney's balloon:
The prime minister has a fault that causes him great difficulties and that is his exaggerated language. His hyperbole . . . When I was secretary of state for external affairs, we had the South African situation too, but we didn't project ourselves as the leader of the Commonwealth as Mulroney has done. When you do that, the responsibilities fall on your shoulders, and if you're not prepared to carry through, it doesn't help your image.

All things considered, Mulroney felt that only one previous head of government did more for Canada than him:
If you look at Canadian history, there was one great prime minister, Sir John A. Macdonald. There was one in terms of accomplishments who was great, and then there's all the rest of us.

Lester Pearson outshone Wilfrid Laurier many times in terms of accomplishments, but in those days you were in politics for life, and now we're dealing with an entirely different situation.

By the time history is done looking at this and you look at my achievements as opposed to any others, certainly no one will ever be in Sir John A.'s league—but my nose will be a little ahead of most in terms of achievements.

Nobody has achievements like this, Peter. I can say that to you objectively. You cannot name a Canadian prime minister who has done as many significant things as I did, because there are none . . .

I don't say this as a question of vanity; I say it as a question of what I believe to be fact. I'm not saying that everything was right—don't misunderstand me. But what I am finding is that as time goes on now, the economic policies have been vindicated. I think that's a fair statement. Meech Lake is going to be vindicated for sure as hell, but you still have to have Quebec's signature on the Constitution. You must have it, or you can't have a country. It's just an accident waiting to happen. And so eventually Meech will be signed and will be vindicated.

On his economic record, he figured he was number two:
You want to compare my record with Mr. Pearson, Mr. Diefenbaker and Mr. St. Laurent . . . My economic record has already been compared by outside experts with every prime minister since the Second World War, and only St. Laurent has a better record than me. And he just beats me by the skin of his teeth. St. Laurent inherited it because

395

the rest of the world was devastated after the Second World War, and only Canada and the United States were left standing. And so he inherited this; I had to earn it. But with that, I'll take the second place to St. Laurent.

Mila's take on his legacy:
MULRONEY: We came in with a lot of style, and we left with a lot of style, with a lot of fights in between, but this record is there and it's going to be hard to match. I'm more than willing to sit back and let history take its course. If I died tomorrow, I'd die a happy man. I did what I said I was going to try to do. And as Mila said, "You just let whomever the next guy is, have them look back to your predecessor, what he did in eight years, what you did and what your successor will do." And she said, "It will just stand out luminously in history." I couldn't have done it without her. She never lost faith you know, never, never. She always said, you can do it and you're the only one who can.

He did notice that Conrad Black's marquee London newspaper devoted no special attention to his retirement:
Isn't that typical? Conrad is the goddamned publisher! Isn't that awful? Not that it's the end of the world over there, but it would be nice to have something in the *Daily Telegraph* by somebody who is not a goddamned stringer, broken-down old fart of a guy who doesn't know his ass from his elbow, eh? Conrad is very selfish and very cheap, very cheap. I tell you, you wouldn't want to be sixty-five years of age without a pension and counting on Conrad.

After leaving Ottawa for private life in Montreal, Mulroney settled on his first post-PM directorships:
I took Archer Daniels Midland in the States, and I'm going to take Petrofina in Belgium, in Brussels. And I've taken American Barrick and Horsham, all small in terms

of the size of the boards. This is very simple; they pay you five times what they do in Canada. Five times.

He talked obsessively about keeping his perspective:
We've done all the tough things, all the brutal things that had to be done in the economy, and the big historic pay-out is going to come in the twenty-first century and they're going to look back and say, "Holy shit, how did we get here like this?" Well there's why. I insisted that we do things not for good headlines in ten days, but for a better Canada in ten years. And that's what it was all about. Somebody had to stop passing the buck and unfortunately it was me.

And then I had to take these decisions and insist upon them being implemented right in the middle of a recession. Within a short period, all of a sudden, a distinguished Canadian historian is going to say, "Holy Christ! The whole goddamned Ottawa press gallery was wrong!"

While powerless to achieve his dream of reforming the Constitution, Mulroney thought his government did deliver a better Canada:
Now the question is, was the revolution good for Canada or was it bad? Was it helpful to the nation or was it not? There are two things: there's a constitution and there's a country. I've always said—this constitution is imperfect but Canada is not. Canada is not an imperfect nation. Canada is about as close to being a perfect nation as you can find. The Constitution can be lousy—that we've got to try and fix. But all of this convulsive change, did it produce a more democratic, more participatory democracy, a more sensitive democracy, a more engaged democracy, a more competitive democracy, a more prosperous democracy, a more outward-looking democracy? Did it do all those things? The answer is yes. And so, my revolution succeeded.

20

"About as ideological as that coffee pot"

———

The Vision Thing

BRIAN MULRONEY'S GUCCI SMILE and the echo-chamber resonance of his voice made it difficult to take him seriously as a political thinker. But under his ambassadorial coiffure lurked a small-town boy with humble instincts, populist aspirations and real concern for the underprivileged. Neither rebel nor reactionary, Mulroney genuinely personified his party's oxymoronic Progressive Conservative label.

That is not to say that he spent any time or effort parsing political ideas of any stripe. During my roughly three decades of talking to and at him, I don't recall a single exchange devoted to his philosophical underpinnings. But what the hell—I became increasingly mellow as I prattled away, and finally gave up probing him on the topic. As I think back to our many conversations, I realize that he equated ideology not with ideas but with holding office: you exercise power not according to some fancy philosophy, but from the lessons you learned trying to grab it. His idea of governing was to swing like an acrobat between following his reason and listening to his heart, and then acting according to his instincts.

But certain casts of mind carried over from his life experience. Growing up in Baie-Comeau, he daily faced the dilemma of belonging to a triple minority: Catholic but not French; Anglo but not English; Canadian but Québécois. This was life on the margin. The family managed only one holiday each year: a trip to Quebec City in their 1938 Pontiac—the parents, six children, family dog, plus sixteen sandwiches and a six-pack—racing madly down unpaved roads to the ferry at Bersimis, "the children crying, the dog barking, my father grinding his teeth and my mother in the back seat saying the beads for the third time."

Enrolled as a pre-law student at St. Francis Xavier University, the youthful Mulroney came under the influence of Moses Coady, who described his ideal graduates this way: "We want them to look into the sun and the depths of the sea. We want them to explore the hearts of flowers and of fellow men. We want them to be eager to discover and develop their capacities for creation."

The other decisive formative influence on the future PM was his term as president of the Iron Ore Company of Canada, after his defeat in the race for party leader in 1976. The significance of that period of his life has always been downplayed because the firm's Montreal headquarters only had nine employees, though they administered a much larger field force. But as president of a subsidiary of Cleveland's mighty Hanna Mining Co., Mulroney had access to some of the most powerful families in the North American business firmament. After he turned the Canadian company around, his first decision was to double the pensions being paid to widows of employees. When he closed down Iron Ore's Schefferville operations, he allocated

$10 million to alleviate the shock to the community, even though declining markets meant that there were only 167 full-time employees left to be laid off at that point.

Still, during his time in the private sector, Mulroney became a sworn enemy of what he called the Swedenization of Canada. "There are no fancy-pants heroes any more with elegant theories and magic wands," he preached, "just overworked and harassed businessmen, labour leaders and ordinary Canadians who get their hands dirty every day dealing with the pedestrian problems of providing jobs, meeting payrolls, and producing products—only to come home at night to learn on TV that some brave new social artist has invented another government plan that will add to costs, increase paperwork and lessen competitiveness."

Despite such hardcore free enterprise views, Mulroney was a reactionary reformer determined to spread a large umbrella over the ideological centre of Canadian politics. That was his winning formula at the polls. Mulroney's legislative thrusts—free trade with the United States, reducing government services, privatizing Crown corporations and deregulating the economy's most competitive industries—were part of his private sector–driven agenda to make Canada more competitive. Mulroney's economic policies didn't work out as planned, partly due to unfortunate timing, with a deep recession and the short-term effects of free trade taking their toll. Equally destructive were the paradoxical attitudes of most Canadian business leaders: unfettered free enterprise was their religion, providing, of course, they could run to Ottawa for subsidies and bailouts whenever they got into trouble.

Reading his thoughts and listening to his rhetoric, I came to the conclusion that if Mulroney believed anything, it was that the highest state of grace for any individual was to become self-sufficient, as he himself always had to be. He felt that unearned handouts were deadly to the human spirit. His favourite quotation was from

Abraham Lincoln: "You cannot help the wage-earner by pulling down the wage-payer. You cannot help the poor by destroying the rich. You cannot establish sound security on borrowed money. You cannot build character and courage by taking away man's initiative and independence. You cannot help men permanently by doing for them what they could do for themselves." That was precariously close to the neo-con philosophy espoused by Reformers, and later by Harperites. But there was an essential difference: Mulroney may have been convinced that a competitive economy (and society) brought out the best in people, but he also believed in public safety nets. He insisted that it was "the vital responsibility of government to demonstrate compassion for the needy and assistance for the disadvantaged."

Essentially, Mulroney believed that Canada's political parties, his own included, existed not for the purpose of implementing coherent sets of ideas, but as instruments for the accommodation of individual, regional and national differences. He tried to appeal to a wide variety of special-interest groups—then tried to act as a broker among them. He expressed an almost gravitational pull toward compromise, conciliation and tolerance, and tended to subscribe to the Orwellian-sounding dogma of "strength through diversity." When CBC news anchor Peter Mansbridge once pressed him on his beliefs, he replied, "I'm not ideologically opposed to anything unless it doesn't work."

The best example of the Mulroney government's flexibility occurred in the Department of Finance, which ought to have been at the bleeding edge of ideological change. In 1984, Mickey Cohen, the deputy finance minister, had been asked by Prime Minister John Turner to draw up a national economic agenda for the Liberal government. Working for most of the summer, the department produced a multi-volume document too late to be presented to the defeated Grits. After the Tories won,

Michael Wilson ordered an economic agenda of his own. The brains trust at Finance read Mulroney's campaign speeches and decided that little had changed. Having no orders to the contrary, they slapped a new title and cover on their previous study. Thus *A New Direction for Canada: An Agenda for Economic Renewal* was immaculately conceived and triumphantly presented to the fresh minister. It became the cornerstone of the Conservatives' economic policy.[1]

Mulroney inhabited the barren land between pragmatism and opportunism. He held certain basic beliefs he would not compromise: his opposition to capital punishment, his commitment to having Quebec sign the Canadian constitution, his obsession with improving Canada-U.S. relations, his obdurate opposition to South Africa's apartheid policy, his support of Israel, his push for regional equalization, his encouragement of women in political life and his dedication to the principles of free enterprise. But most of the time, his mind was an open city, free of cant or dogma, committed to political functionalism instead of grand theories. When I asked Charley McMillan, the prime minister's policy chief and intellectual bodyguard, to define Mulroney's philosophy, he replied, "Oh, you know, Brian. He's about as ideological as that coffee pot."

Stanley Hartt believed Mulroney did have a fixed ideology, but had a tough time selling it:
He took power with a very profoundly held series of beliefs about the relative role of government and the private sector. It wasn't a poetic vision where he sees grand

---

1. Instant pragmatism was the order of the day. During the 1983 leadership campaign, Mulroney was under pressure from the media to explain where he stood on federal-provincial relations. Mulroney grabbed a Quebecair barf bag while on a flight to Mont-Joli, and wrote on the back of it the nine points that summed up his constitutional policy, from which he never wavered.

designs or the future in the sky. It was a vision that was practical but was nonetheless a vision. It's a vision that says we can't continue the old ways; we can't spend ourselves into feeling good. The government should do less and not more. If we have a private sector that's innovative and skilled and entrepreneurial, we'll succeed in the twenty-first century. And I describe that as a vision, not as the absence of vision.

But that being said, I think what destroyed him was his inability to integrate the elements of his vision and to sell them to Canadians as an integrated vision. Why did Mulroney fail to communicate his message? Partly because he saw every initiative as a one-off.

He never saw the system of his ideas as an integrated policy whole. And they were—the GST fits with free trade, it isn't just a way to be mean to Canadians. The deficit reduction is a manner to create jobs, it isn't just a way to cut valued institutions. But he always saw them as a one-off. In fact, he used to say, don't give me more than one thing to sell at a time, because people have to concentrate. And he'd be willing to use hyperbole to sell, but it never occurred to him that his last three initiatives were the best way to sell his fourth. Free trade and the GST are intimately related, but you couldn't find two Canadians who could tell you how.

Stanley Hartt wished his boss had been a little more open to other people's ideas:
He made decisions with his tummy, not with his head. It had to feel right. His insecurity made him not trust his own logic, which was very good, while also believing the worst gossip. He surrounded himself with people who abused his trust by gossiping a lot, and he insisted on having them there. I believe the right thing for an aide to do is, if you think somebody is badmouthing the prime minister, you get to him without involving the prime minister. Cut his nuts off is what you should do. But to go and

say, guess what I heard? It's like a little baby currying favour with daddy, and if daddy believes whatever tall tale you bring, you do it again and again and again.

Brian's a very nice guy, but his insecurities—when he projected them, he projected them onto other people. See, for a guy who showed up in university as a skinny, gangly kid, totally unsophisticated, who became the big man on campus before he was finished—for a man who did that, you wonder why he would still be insecure.

The staff was trained to believe that criticism of the prime minister was disloyal no matter how constructive. He actually believed that if you started a system where it was okay to criticize the prime minister, even in a very limited circle of people who wanted nothing but good for him, that before long the distinction between creative and constructive criticism and negative and destructive criticism would blur. He would not be seen as a god, and if he were not a god, he couldn't lead. His "prime ministeriality" didn't permit him to become criticized even by his top aides.

Here's one example. He gave the Singapore Lecture in 1989, a major achievement because if you look at who else had given the lecture, it's every major world leader. It's a very prestigious lecture. He did a very good job. His subject was why the world should not break into trading blocs and how free trade between Canada and the United States would be an example for the world, leading it to more open trade. He gave a really good speech which had been written very carefully for him, and he had practised and rehearsed it. Then came the questions, and the audience was below par—I mean, it was a Southeast Asian audience of mainly professors—you would not call the questions high-powered. And some of them were even hard to understand. So he had to punt—he didn't anticipate these questions, he hadn't prepared for them, but he did well.

I get in the van going back to the hotel and there's nobody there but us and his private secretary, Lisette. I told him, "I'm really glad that I negotiated the right to the transcript of the Q&A session before we publish, because there will be some stuff I'm going to have to fix." We get upstairs and Lisette takes me aside and says, "How dare you criticize the prime minister?" I said, "Are you kidding? I love this guy. I'm working body and soul for him; I gave up hundreds of thousands of dollars of income. I'm just saying he got caught with a lot of questions, he made up the answers and he did pretty well. With minimal editing, I'm going to make him look great." I edited the book, and if I changed more than 200 words, I'll eat the coffee cup. There was just the odd inaccuracy here and the odd exaggeration there. But that was the culture. No criticism. He really felt that any criticism was disloyal.

He told me a thousand times that famous story about Jim Coutts, who was travelling on a train after he ceased to hold office, and it was three o'clock in the morning. They were playing cards. They were drunk, smashed, and somebody said, "Aw, come on Jim, tell us what Trudeau is really like." And Coutts said, "No, I actually don't think I will." And he got up and went to bed.

I don't think I've told you anything that's disloyal. I start off from the premise that he's a fabulous guy and he did a fabulous job, but he had character flaws that made him very interesting, a Shakespearian character to this day. If you say to him that he wasn't perfect, he gets very upset. He calls Hugh Segal, who is writing a book, and says, "Hello, Hugh. How are you doing?" And Hugh's answer—he knows how to translate—is, "Prime Minister, you come off very well."

For Senator Norman Atkins, Mulroney really did do it his way:
He deals with people one on one and not as a group because he likes the singular input and then he wants to make up his own mind of how he's going to deal with whatever problem he's dealing with. I think saying to

people, "I know I'm unpopular, but I'm going to do what I think is right" is not a bad strategy. He's a very over-powering personality, and when you add the office to that, that's a tough thing for people to cope with, unless you have a relationship with him, like some of his cronies do. The one thing Brian has is a massive ego, and a tremendous pride about his accomplishments.

Bruce Phillips on the boss as an ideas man:
The bummest rap against Mulroney that I have heard is that he lacks vision. He has a very well-formed vision of where he wants this country to go and how to get there, and he's prepared to run big risks.

Geoff Norquay:
He is intensely pragmatic. On the other hand, he is also an incredible strategist and tactician. One of the frustrations of working with him is that he spends an awful lot of time thinking things through, and there are times when any one of us looking at a particular situation, not having as broad a picture as he does, may come to a certain conclusion and not really be able to understand why he won't take our advice. Sometimes he'll stop and take the time to give us the bigger picture, or sometimes he'll just say no. A couple of weeks or a couple of months later, you realize all too well that he figured the whole goddamn thing out and was six weeks ahead of everybody else, and was waiting for certain things to happen that he expected would, by which time either the crisis passed or his way prevailed.

National Progressive Conservative Director Janis Johnson felt Mulroney was not a thinker:
It was his total lack of judgment in terms of intellectual interaction that used to drive me crazy when I was there. In the last two years he realized it was too late, so he just started worrying about his future. God knows what he did in law school—he sure as hell didn't study very

much, or he wouldn't have done the Constitution. He's not a learned individual. He read, but I don't think he ever read a book from cover to cover. I don't think he's read Tolstoy or any of the great writers. He isn't interested in getting the perspective of history, or in reading any historians or anything like that. My ex-husband [Frank Moores] didn't either, so they got along well. They used to bore me to tears, those conversations, but then they both drank so much in those days.

It was like the 1960s never happened to Brian and Mila Mulroney. I mean, the 1960s changed the lives of everybody I know. It changed the whole bloody world, but it never happened to Brian, it was like he was still in the 1950s forever. He was still doing rock and roll when the Beatles were famous. He doesn't know anything about popular culture. This was the other thing that was just so amazing to me. They'd look at antiques and she would buy clothes.

Johnson also felt Mulroney did not embody the vision of the party:
I was naïve about Brian in some ways. I had such great expectations of him; that was so important to me. But he was not a real Conservative. I'm a red prairie Tory from the days of Duff Roblin. I mean, Christ, you couldn't find more diverse morals and ethics. The way Roblin, Lougheed and these guys ran a government, if you stepped one inch over the wire, you'd be dead in the water. You didn't dare do anything that wasn't totally upright or honourable. It was totally different back then.

Allan Gregg, on Mulroney's gut sense:
I was not his biggest fan, by any stretch of the imagination, and he's proved me wrong again and again, not just on the basis of his performance . . . On the basis of his judgment, consistently.

21

"He needs a bit of praise,
the poor bugger"

———

Mulroney as Others Saw Him

For nine years, Mulroney endeavoured to change Canada's political landscape and the way the federal government functioned. The people who were closest to him provided divergent views on the prime minister. Some say Mulroney wished to enjoy the infallibility of a pontiff, even after he made wrong choices when it came to his friends. Some of his collaborators—even some of his enemies—agreed with Mulroney's own assessment of his tenure.

John Crosbie, reflecting in 1991, said Mulroney often needed reassurance:
I've been through too much to bother kissing anyone's arse, so I don't kiss Brian's. But I feel like giving him praise and I do. He needs a bit of praise now and then, the poor bugger.

I've never seen anyone so maligned. He sounds too smooth, of course, too mellifluous . . . Is that the word?

That's one problem, a question of whether he's sincere or not, you know. He's as sincere as most politicians I know, but he has a tendency to exaggerate, which doesn't help, and sometimes he lacks a sensitive side.

He's got a sense of the ego, which can be harmful for him, which he has to watch. He pays too much attention to what people are saying. He likes to say he doesn't read the paper, but he's always telling you about something he saw in the press or something he heard on TV. Today everything's dominated by the TV, eh? So the difficulty that he has with the Canadian public is the difficulty caused by television, because he doesn't come across. All of these things, which are a part of his character and personality, are greatly exaggerated through television, so I think that's where the dislike comes from.

Another factor that affects Brian is the sort of sleaze and patronage factor, which now seems to be declining. Poor old Michel Cogger and his Quebec associates and so on give it a sort of gloss. They're all fixers. That's something that hasn't helped Brian Mulroney's image. It shows the frame of mind—that's been his weakness. He will fare very well in the history books and so will our government—much better than it is looked upon by contemporaries, in my opinion.

Liberal Deputy Finance Minister Mickey Cohen:
He is an underrated prime minister. I guess his personality was his greatest problem. He let his character, his desire to be loved, eat away at him too much. Brian's policies were very solid, but somehow his character prevented him from making that contact with the people. English Canada never got comfortable with Brian Mulroney. Despite the name they saw him as a francophone, and he saw himself as a French Canadian. He was never comfortable in Toronto.

I remember when he left government and became part of the business community. I spent most of the first year here in Toronto defending him, to my surprise. Somehow or other, he was a French Canadian in their eyes and in his eyes. Toronto was a strange place for him.

David Peterson, comparing Trudeau and Mulroney:
I don't dislike Mulroney—I like the guy. He's a hard guy to dislike, he's a charming rascal . . . He's good company. I'd much rather be marooned on a desert island with him than Trudeau. But to be perfectly honest, Peter, I would never trust him or respect him. He is a pathological liar. In fairness, I don't believe he knows he's lying. He will say one thing and then contradict it, and he'll take the umbrage and yell and scream and say, "I never said . . ."

Oh, God, you couldn't take anything he said at face value. His essential Achilles' heel is his baloney. Oh, I listened to him in the free trade stuff in endless meetings. And he's good and he's charming and he's got stamina, and he's charitable and he phones people—he's always on the phone. He stopped calling me, because we began to fight and disagreed on stuff, but he used to phone me every week. He'd sit there on the goddamned phone for half an hour, while I would try to have dinner with my kids and he just talked. Never listened, just talked. He'd be railing against the press and the polls and this and that, saying "We're all in this together." I could never figure what the hell he wanted.

Senator Jack Austin acknowledged Mulroney's successes:
I start with the incredible mandate he won, the largest mandate ever given by a Canadian electorate to a political leader. His first failure was that he came very quickly to power without a concept of what he would do with it if he got it. He had tactical ideas, but no strategic policy overview. He had the good fortune of the MacDonald report but only implemented parts of it. He left out the other wing to the trade relationship with the United States, which was a comprehensive adjustment process.

But the main point is that he had the inherent weakness of wanting power without having any solid idea of what he would do with it, except in terms of building his party.

But then there's another factor in his decline in Canada with the Canadian public, and that is what I might call his style of exaggeration and hyperbole. His "jobs, jobs, jobs!" or the whole nuclear submarine caper. The public quickly discovered that this government would say anything in its popularity period and then gradually finesse its way out of the commitment due to changed circumstances.

Archbishop Michael Peers:
Mulroney's was a Thatcherite/Reaganite agenda, which held up the value of accumulating wealth. I was the primate of the Anglican Church of Canada for seven years of the Mulroney era, and all of the church leaders together—all of us, Roman Catholic, Anglican, United—we never got to see the prime minister, not ever. Only twice did we ever get to see a cabinet minister in all those years, because the agenda was being set in a very different place, and access was determined in very, very different ways.

The Mulroney years taught us to forget about the homeless, and throw people in prison. If you want to see one of the greatest legacies of the Mulroney era, it's prisons. We incarcerated people at a ferocious clip and did almost nothing about rehabilitation in prisons. That's a sign of the hardening of the heart of a community. Get them out of sight, turn the key and forget it.

Michael Pitfield on Mulroney as a conciliator and negotiator:
He's very loyal to his friends and very loyal to the people he worked with and the group around him, but he doesn't reach out to people who disagree with him. As a result, he is not a consensus-builder. Let me put it this way: Trudeau may not have sought to secure consensus on sort of a daily

basis like Pearson and King did, but he benefited from it. He was able to reach out. One of the really, really striking things about the Mulroney years was what happened to the public service. We had built up a mythology based on the example of Norman Robertson and Bob Bryce, a sense of high mission and a belief in certain values, so that when a minister wanted to do this or that, there was a process of trying to gauge whether that was within the rules of the game. Sometimes the prime minister himself couldn't get things done the way he wanted—appointing a friend as an ambassador, for example.

But in the world of Brian Mulroney, even the most senior public servants were constantly being told, "If you're not prepared to do it, I've got half a dozen people who would like to have your job and we can put them in there tomorrow morning." All of a sudden people would do things as ordered and there was no rudder. The rules that had been built, the checks and balances, went out the window.

I don't think we've had as serious a failure in ethics in this century in federal government. As I've often said in the past, the extent to which this can be laid at the door of the prime minister . . . The vengefulness was extreme in the system—the favouritism. Personal alliances mattered a great deal more than merit. People had to choose between their pensions and their consciences, not to mention the prostitution of the Privy Council Office, and its use for political, partisan advantage. It's a very sad, sad story. They were told to either deliver what they had been told by their political masters or get out. I had one senior official come to me and say he had been told by one of the most senior members of the government, "If you can't take the heat, then step aside. I've got a dozen better than you to take your place."

Flora MacDonald wished Mulroney could have changed his mind about the civil service:

If there's one area where I would fault the prime minister, it's that instead of working with the civil service, he would work with individuals in it. The system to him was always going to be anti-Conservative, so whenever he wanted to get a round of applause or support or whatever, he'd launch into a major criticism of the public service and individuals within it. He would select certain individuals to hold up as examples, not publicly, but to rally the morale of the caucus. To bring the cabinet onside, he would often make outrageous statements. That didn't make for a good working relationship, and I felt very uncomfortable with it. It was sometimes done in the cabinet room with senior public servants right there.

Peter White thought Mulroney was too isolated by his team:
He talks all the time to Bernard Roy, constantly. What they talk about is not of the broad context at all, but about whatever files happen to be before them. Bernard goes to every P&P meeting and every cabinet meeting. He doesn't say anything at them, but he's there. So he knows what's going on, and that's what they talk about. He talks to Fred Doucet all the time, but Fred is the sort of personal management function—everything that relates to the family, or the residences, or Brian's personal affairs, or Brian's personal political interests. Fred calls me all the time and says the prime minister has asked me to tell you to get a job for so and so, that kind of thing. And so Fred talks to him all the time, but again it's not the broad context.

And then Bill Pristanski and Hubert Pichet talk to him all the time but about mundane things, except that I would say particularly Pristanski is fairly adept at slipping in messages. Geoff Norquay he sees all the time. Norquay's got a good sense, but he's not tough. And he isn't the guy who will say to the prime minister, you really have got to do this. One time, over the 1985 budget and the withdrawal of de-indexation, he entered a very slight demurral, saying something like, Prime Minister, do you really think so? And then he came out of that meeting, and for the rest of the day the whole back room around here was buzzing. "Geoff Norquay stood up to the PM."

Mila's biographer, Sally Armstrong, mulled about the prime minister's lost opportunities for leadership:
After the Montreal massacre [in which fourteen young female engineering students were shot dead in 1989], why didn't he say, "Damn it, how could this happen in our country?" When the troops left for the Gulf War, he didn't go to see them off. I said to his people, "How could this be?" and they said, "Don't be stupid, Sally. Don't be so naïve—the columnists would go crazy over the political opportunism." Then I asked, "Is he going to go to the Gulf and visit the troops?" They said they were worried about something happening to him. Bush was over there, everybody else was over there. I'm surprised that a man as astute as he seems to be believes such foolish, foolish advice on so many occasions. Those are the things that turned people against him. In 1986, I was disappointed that the man who was known as the great negotiator didn't negotiate when Senator Jacques Hébert was starving himself to death on Parliament Hill [to protest the government's decision to scrap the Katimavik program for unemployed youth]. I think he's probably a master manipulator rather than a negotiator.

Paul Tellier, on future analysis of Mulroney's tenure:
He was not tough enough in insisting that his cabinet would sell his policies. The majority of his ministers were lukewarm [on Meech] and he used to ask us to keep track of what they were saying when he was talking about it. But he didn't put his foot down as well as he should have. Was it possible for him to be tougher with them and force them to speak and to support his efforts and then Mr. Clark's efforts? I don't know. But he could have done it.

No doubt the government was not very good at promoting and selling and especially explaining and informing Canadians about their policies. The best example of that was free trade. Until that day in the November 1988 election, that deal was never explained to Canadians. When the dust has settled, historians will be inclined to say that he was a leader who had a vision. We've got to be very careful with this man because of the so-called scandals and bad stories and the bad press he got. The public perception has been totally distorted, and I feel sorry for him. I'm not partisan—I worked for Mr. Trudeau and I worked for this guy—but I deplore the fact that the average Canadian doesn't have a chance to see just who Brian Mulroney really is.

Mulroney tried to regard his unpopularity as a badge of honour:
I've concluded, Peter, that given the nature and the enormity of the problems, you cannot be an effective leader and be a popular one.

Mulroney Redux

———

*Out of the unguarded comments in this book
emerges the portrait of an elastic politician with
touches of grace and the balls of a canal horse.*

HIS EYES WERE SHINY that night in the fierce autumn
of 1992 when the Charlottetown Accord was relegated to
the ashcan of history. At first I mistook the gleam in
Brian Mulroney's eyes for excitement. Then I realized
they were brimming with tears that he hadn't allowed to
fall. His humiliations in the battles of Meech and
Charlottetown were the bitter beads of his rosary: the
death of his dream that he could best Trudeau in the constitutional wars.

It was October 26, 1992, and Mulroney had invited me
to his prime ministerial retreat at Harrington Lake so that I
could share with his innermost circle the results of the constitutional referendum. From the outside, the PM's rural
sanctuary is just another old farmhouse in the Gatineau hills;
on odd occasions, hikers, snowshoers and cross-country
skiers still stumble on the property to ask for directions.

Mila's deft decorating touches had created a cozy ambience, wrapping guests and residents in a warm, pine-scented and beeswaxed aura of serenity. The main floor's focal point was a stone fireplace that could accommodate entire tree trunks.

The guest list that evening was limited to Deputy Prime Minister Don Mazankowski, Health Minister Benoît Bouchard, Chief of Staff Hugh Segal, prime ministerial confidants Senator Lowell Murray and future senator Marjory LeBreton, PC strategist John Tory and the Mulroneys' personal assistant, Michael McSweeney.

"What's the difference between George Bush and God?" Mark, the second youngest of the Mulroney children, asked the assembled bigwigs. Then he answered his own question: "God doesn't think he's George Bush!"

"Now, now, Mark," Mulroney cautioned his son, then turned to the rest of us to announce, "Mark's the best slapshot in the business. I'm going to trade him to the Leafs." He was interrupted by the appearance on CBC-TV of Deborah Coyne, the mother of Trudeau's love child, who had become one of Mulroney's severest critics.

Benoît Bouchard shouted, "Turn it to *The Simpsons!*"

"I don't like them either," Mulroney glumly replied. He sat in a corner, wearing a green sweater, nervously picking at the palms of his hands. The most telling sign of internal stress was always the state of Mulroney's palms. At the start of every interview, I would glance at his hands to determine his mental state. Often bloodied by his nervous habit of picking them raw, that evening his palms resembled those of Mel Gibson's Christ.

He cautioned that it would be a bad omen for the rest of the country if the Yes side wasn't five points ahead in Halifax. When the early Nova Scotia results started coming in, swinging decisively against the accord, somebody said, "Do they realize it's hard to take them seriously?"—to which Mulroney replied, "There may have been an expensive buyout in Nova Scotia tonight." Referring to the government's bridge project to Prince Edward Island,

Hugh Segal sourly quipped, "The fixed link may have to stretch a little further. It will have to be extended."

Nicolas, the baby of the Mulroney family, arrived home just then from a karate lesson and did a quick demonstration, flattening his laughing father on the floor. As Mulroney got up again, the first indecisive Ontario results appeared on the screen. "There'll be no miracles, tonight," he predicted.

Unexpectedly, dinner (scampi and chicken) was announced and we sat down at a long table, Brian at one end, Mila at the other. By eight-thirty, the decidedly adverse results from Quebec began to show up. "The loss of Meech cost us 10 per cent," Mulroney speculated. "Trudeau's betrayal, another 10 per cent. That was why so many switched. My surveys show we will lose the province by 25 per cent."

Twenty-five minutes later, the TV was reporting a 50–50 split in the province. "It doesn't make you proud to be a Canadian," Mulroney lamented. "In 1984, we got the largest majority, yet half have now voted against us." After Quebec's polls had closed in a decisive renunciation of the Charlottetown agreement, Bloc Québécois Leader Lucien Bouchard came on to crow that the vote had really been about sovereignty and that his cause had been significantly advanced. To which an angry Benoît Bouchard retorted: "I can tell you, *les Québécois* are not separatists."

"They are now," Mila quietly replied.

Nobody said anything until the province's final results had been tabulated: 42.4% per cent in support; 55.4% per cent against.

"Forty-two to fifty-five—a big victory," Mulroney sarcastically observed.

"Aren't you sweet," Mila replied, not smiling. "You've been a Quebec Conservative too long."

As the bad news from Manitoba rolled in, Marjory LeBreton blurted out, "They haven't changed since they hanged Riel!"

"If I went to bed now," Mila glumly speculated, "perhaps when I wake up, we would have won." She was on a crutch with a badly sprained ankle.

"You know, it might be worth a try," John Tory chimed in.

Mulroney nixed the fantasy: "I don't think so."

By 10 p.m., nothing was slowing the slide. The only distinctive voice on the Yes side was the dignified statement by Aboriginal leader Ron George, saying the opportunity for self-government had been needlessly wasted. "You've kept apartheid alive and well in Canada," he warned.

The final referendum verdict was 44.6% per cent Yes and 54.4% per cent No. Nearly eight million Canadians had rejected the deal.

"I'd rather be with Ron George than Preston Manning, who is in the same camp as Doug Christie [the lawyer who defended most of Canada's Nazis], and Pierre Trudeau," Mulroney declared. Then he paused for a long moment before adding, "For that matter, I'd rather be back in Baie-Comeau, driving a truck. But Mila wouldn't like it."

Mila sat up and, in her sweetest sarcastic tone, asked, "Would that cover tuition costs at Harvard?"

"What is the heart of Canada?" Mulroney mused. "The amount of bigotry and hatred in this country is astonishing. I remember Bob Rae [then NDP premier of Ontario] saying that he would never forgive Trudeau for legitimizing the anti-French bigots. I've got a lot of time for that guy—he's very principled." In defeat, the prime minister's voice was flat, lacking its usual wit and cadence. Somewhere deep inside him the close-knit fabric of his life must have been coming apart.

Mark reappeared. "My dad is too good for Canadians," he announced. "They don't deserve him."

Mila nodded, then said to no one in particular, "I don't know how Brian does it. How he has the stomach for this."

As if by mutual telepathy, she and Brian moved toward each other, Mila managing to hobble on her crutch. She hugged her defeated husband with the ardour of pure enchantment. It was a magic moment in a night from hell.

THE CAVALCADE BACK to Ottawa, where Mulroney would face the press and public, took off just before 11 p.m. The Mulroneys rode alone, though I could glimpse the prime minister's silhouette, constantly on a cellphone. I was in the backup staff car with his assistant, Paul Smith. We didn't pass a single vehicle until we arrived in the city outskirts. It was as if we had become untouchables.

An old and entirely irrelevant quote from my favourite contemporary philosopher kept running through my mind. I heard the echo of Grace Slick, the sleaze queen of rock and roll, late of Jefferson Airplane, who had complained at a San Francisco concert, after butchering a number, "You know, it's not easy to sing and throw up at the same time." That was my mood. I had been enthusiastically in favour of both Meech and Charlottetown and now feared for the country's future. In a more rational corner of my mind I recalled my friend Allan Fotheringham's wise observation that "there is no such thing as Canada— only a collection of regional complaints." It was true. Politically we remained a commonwealth of provinces with little in common. The age of consent had ended; from now on, politicians could govern only on sufferance. The former B.C. premier, Dave Barrett, damned the lost accord with the faintest of praise. "Everybody was pissed off," he said. "It must have been a pretty good deal."

It had partly been a problem of timing, I decided as we passed the desecrated roadside signs pointing the way to Meech Lake. I was reminded that Canadians tend to act according to eleven commandments, the additional one being, "Thou shalt remain firmly undecided." Our so-called genius for compromise amounts to little more than the hesitation to choose.

Referendum Night in Canada had signalled open season on incumbents. Elitists like me, who had tried to buck the public's disdain for what the suits had decided in secret conclave, were eaten alive. The No vote crossed regions, languages, religions and backgrounds. For once, that opaque group of voters whom politicians had smugly dismissed as "ordinary Canadians" had their say. They promptly dispatched the Charlottetown Accord to that part of the politicians' anatomies where the sun don't shine.

AS OUR CARS CROSSED the bridge across the Ottawa River and swung onto Parliament Hill, I could imagine that Mulroney must have been thinking that the gods had dealt him the final karate chop. We pulled up to the Commons door and the cameras, as always, clicked like insects, but instead of being welcoming, they sounded off-key and menacing. The prime minister of Canada appeared stiff, holding himself together like a pane of shattered glass. It was a particularly dark night and his features were indistinct, appearing slowly like a developing Polaroid photo. He muttered something that no one remembers into the media microphones, and it sounded to me as if he was recalling a recent out-of-body experience, which I guess he was. This was the Requiem for a Heavyweight.

When he finally came into focus, Brian Mulroney turned to Mila, the love of his life, and they looked for a long moment into each others' eyes, then slow-marched out of that desolate hall, joined at the shoulder, each supporting the other—out of words, out of hope and out of power.

PRIME MINISTERS MUST BE JUDGED in the context of their times. Brian Mulroney had the bad luck to succeed Pierre Trudeau, the political wizard who charmed most of a generation, but he also benefited greatly by having as his successor Jean Chrétien, who turned out to be a political thug whose only original thought was the notion that he was fit to be prime minister. Chrétien was in turn followed by Paul Martin, who forfeited his great expectations by turning into the Inspector Clouseau of Canadian politics. In comparison to that duo of ineffectual hoofers, the memory of Brian Mulroney lost some of its sting. But only some. Eight years after he left office, Heather Mallick, the *Globe and Mail*'s Ideas columnist, still took time out to savage him. "I don't think that Jean Chrétien is dishonest," she wrote, "but even if I did, I would be more likely to forgive him than I would Brian Mulroney, whose very face, fingers, smirk and shoes were an affront to Canadians."

Mulroney's biggest mistake was not his determination to bring about fundamental changes within the Canadian polity, but his irresistible tendency to theatrically hype them as fundamental changes. For a people who took a full century to officially approve the words to their national anthem and nearly as long to pick their flag, Mulroney's radical reforms made Canadians nervous and suspicious. It was too much, too soon. Try as he might, Mulroney was baffled by the dysfunctional relationship between cause and effect in the country's politics. For instance, he never understood the impatience of Alberta's Conservatives, whose surrogate he imagined himself to be, to see the last of him. As far as he was concerned he had done everything they wanted, as conveyed to him by former Alberta premier Peter Lougheed, their patron saint. He had negotiated free trade with the U.S., deregulated financial institutions and gas exports, killed the National Energy Program, deballed the Foreign Investment Review Agency, imposed a consumer tax (the GST) instead of raising corporate taxes, moved the National Energy Board to Calgary and filled three of his cabinet's most influential portfolios with Albertans, including Don Mazankowski, who he promoted to deputy prime minister. Yet in the 1993 election, for the first time in fifty-three years, not a single Conservative was elected in Alberta. Gratitude was in short supply. Bill McCarthy, a PMO staff photographer, recalled the boss complaining, at the close of one busy end-of-summer day, "You know, Billy, Mila and I invited four thousand people to our home this summer, and we got only seven thank-you notes. That pretty much sums it up."

As one wise old Ottawa owl put it, Mulroney's sense of coalition-building was remote from the blending of ideas and long on the equations of power—in reality, the delivery of seats. He naïvely believed that the mere display of prime ministerial power automatically sanctioned his wishes. He realized too late that Canada's prime ministers are really Gullivers, immobilized by the Lilliputians of regional, ethnic and political pressure groups.

He felt particularly cheated that his magnificent handiwork in knitting together two constitutional accords—meant to be his chief entry points into the history books—received such short shrift from his peers.[1]

---

1. The provincial premiers tried Mulroney's patience. Outside their private conclaves, premiers strut about like regional power brokers who know the secrets of the deep. In fact, some would be well out of their depth as captains of tiddlywinks teams. My favourite example was Bill Vander Zalm, the screwball premier of British Columbia. During a warm-up session at one federal-provincial conference, he turned to Don Mazankowski and declared, "Maz, what are Pat Carney and Jake Epp doing with all this AIDS stuff? I was perfectly willing to let all those gay people die."

Mulroney's initial meeting with Vander Zalm, shortly after his election as premier in 1986, demonstrated the PM's brass-knuckle toughness. "Mr. Vander Zalm," he began (according to an aide who was present), "would you not agree that within your provincial Social Credit party, in excess of two-thirds are federal Tories?" When Vander Zalm concurred, Mulroney referred to the province's right-wing Liberal party, then trying to recruit

Mulroney had, after all, alone among the legion of past constitutional architects, found the formulas that would have granted Quebec considerable control over its destiny without wrecking Canada in the process. "The constitutional agenda failed because Canadians did not trust Mulroney enough to overcome their innate distrust of each other," wisely noted the political columnist Robert Mason Lee, in the *Ottawa Citizen*.

DURING HIS FINAL TERM IN OFFICE and for many years afterwards, an anti-Mulroney fury swept the land. Instead of earning praise for his daring initiatives, such as free trade, reform of the tax system and his many attempts at reconciling regional differences, Mulroney became the national fall guy. The prerequisites for Canadian citizenship—a sense of civility and emotional detachment—went by the boards. For a time, the once lovable Boyo from Baie-Comeau became the Canadian version of Luis Echeverría Álvarez, who had been president of Mexico from 1970 to 1976. Echeverría Álvarez was so unpopular that after he left office he couldn't enter a Mexico City restaurant without the patrons either booing him or getting up to leave. Lysiane Gagnon in *La Presse* noted that loathing of Mulroney had reached the point that people blamed him if their cars didn't start on winter mornings. Others sank to such generic insults as "the only

---

federal Tories, and calmly dropped the axe: "I haven't told my people to vote for the Grits but, if I ever do, you're a dead man. That doesn't mean I could elect Tories provincially, but if I were to pull my supporters away from you, you'd be finished and the NDP would win the next election by default." As the pale-faced premier sat there, dumbly nodding, the PM paused and delivered his real shot: "Well, you should know I'm prepared to do that. Now, let's have lunch." Even Vander Zalm, who, it was said, wore wooden shoes to keep the woodpeckers away from his head, understood that message. Come Meech Lake time, he was firmly on Mulroney's side.

good Tory is a supposiTory," or "I wouldn't believe 'Lyin'
Brian' if he had his tongue notarized."[2]

I remember arriving at Mulroney's official residence
on a rainy winter day in 1993, prepared for yet another
rant about how his bad rap was entirely the fault of misguided journalists who insisted on drawing him as a caricature of his charming and well-meaning self. Indeed, at
the time, the entire country seemed to have risen up
against him. But instead of a bitter and dispirited politician whining about how he had been robbed of his mandate, Mulroney all but waltzed in as if a great burden had
been lifted. Upon reflection it seemed that the act of having gambled all on Charlottetown had provided a cathar-
sis of no mean proportions. "Lookit, we're going through
tough times," he joked as I sat down. "I phoned my mother
the other day, and she put me on hold." As our laughter
died down, Mulroney paused for a moment, then silently
handed me a private letter from Clyde Wells, who had
been his nemesis on Meech and who had obviously
expected to be the object of the prime minister's revenge
for going back on his pledge to support the accord. "I am
not aware of any Prime Minister in the forty-three years
since Newfoundland has been a province of Canada," the
premier had written, "who has given a stronger commitment to the economic needs of Newfoundland, and for
that I express to you my personal appreciation."
Mulroney wasn't sure whether he should laugh or cry, so
he did a perfect imitation of a Trudeau shrug.

Effortless grace was never his strong suit, yet that
drizzly afternoon he was certainly touched by it, determined to leave his throne with pride instead of prejudice.
I never did turn on my tape recorder that day, but I recall
Mulroney speculating on the real lesson of history: in

---

2. The best reason for hating Mulroney was explained to me by Peter
Brown, the Vancouver investment guru. "If I was going to hate him, I'd
hate him for one reason only. He got Mila and I didn't. Isn't she something?"

order to attain the possible, you must reach for the impossible—which was exactly what he had tried to do. He also confided that he intended to spend the rest of his time in Ottawa being a giant poultice, drawing political poison to himself to protect his successor. "That shouldn't be a particularly tough assignment," I said, as I bid him adieu.

THE PREVAILING MYSTERY of the Mulroney years still abides. Why was its central figure so mercilessly pilloried as a political opportunist animated solely by partisan concerns when he spent most of his time and energy championing laws, pacts and causes that carried few political benefits—and many lethal, and ultimately fatal, short-term costs? Even Mulroney's most vocal critics gradually began to sense that there was another side to the man. Robert Fulford came down with a surprisingly favourable reading of his place in history. "If a politician's actions mean more than his words, as they usually do, Mulroney has turned out to be not at all the man we imagined him to be," Fulford wrote in the *Financial Times*. "He's not shallow; he's committed. He doesn't avoid the most important issues, he meets them head on. In fact, if we listen carefully enough, we may discover that he's defined his goals more clearly than most prime ministers. In history his government will stand or fall on three issues—the free trade agreement, the GST, and Meech Lake or its successor. Each of these has required from Mulroney certain qualities of character that most people, including his friends, seldom connect with him. Qualities such as courage, forthrightness and steadfastness." Diane Francis, then a columnist for *Maclean's,* described Mulroney as having been "a gutsy prime minister who deserved plaudits for the legacies he left behind." Even Jeffrey Simpson, who had questioned most of his tactics and policies, conceded that Mulroney had "been a better prime minister than his critics in the media, including this one at times, have suggested."

In his time, Mulroney stood up against capital punishment when public opinion pointed the other way; he
supported the protection of linguistic minorities outside
Quebec when that was such an unpopular position his
life was threatened. He liberalized the immigration laws,
officially apologized for the treatment of Japanese
Canadians during the Second World War and Ukrainians
during the First; and moved the country's ranking in economic competitiveness from eleventh in the world to
fourth. One object of universal anger was his substitu-
tion of the 7 per cent goods and services tax for the 13
per cent manufacturers' sales tax, which had been in-
visibly absorbed in the retail price of goods. This was
either the stupidest or bravest of Mulroney's initiatives,
since it was transparent but reminded everyone who
purchased anything of the punitive levy's author. He
campaigned effectively for Commonwealth sanctions
against South Africa's apartheid regime in the face of
Margaret Thatcher's furious objections. "As leader of the
Progressive Conservatives," the British prime minister
sniffed, "Mr. Mulroney puts too much emphasis on the
adjective, and not enough on the noun." His free trade
deal with the Yanks gave too much away but boosted the
country's economic potential, so that within a decade of
the deal Statistics Canada reported that we were selling
goods into the U.S. worth $1 billion a day.

The country was taken much more seriously in world
affairs when Mulroney was in charge. Under constant
attack at home, he became a useful go-between and coalition builder inside the (then) G-7, the Commonwealth and
other international venues. Ronald Reagan quipped that
"for a non-actor, Brian's done pretty well." George Bush
Sr. chose Brian and Mila as his designated companions to
share his farewell weekend at the presidential retreat in
Camp David in January 1993. Earlier Bush had recommended Mulroney to become secretary-general of the
United Nations. "Contrary to conventional demonology,

Mulroney was not an anti-Christ," wrote Brian Flemming, a former senior Trudeau aide, in the *Halifax Daily News*. "Recent attempts to rehabilitate his policy (as opposed to his personal) reputation are not misplaced. Canadians for years have wrongly tossed out the 1984–93 Tory policy babies with their dislike of Mulroney's bombastic blatherwater."

The only substantive charge against Mulroney—that he benefited financially from Air Canada's choice of Airbus passenger jets—remained unproven, despite an intensive investigation by the Royal Canadian Mounted Police that lasted most of a decade. The fact that the Liberals refused to drop the case, even after Mulroney sued and they had to issue an official apology and pay $2 million toward his legal fees, said more about Chrétien than about Mulroney. In the year after he left office (as reported by lawyer and author William Kaplan in his 2004 book, *A Secret Trial*), Mulroney received $300,000 from Karlheinz Schreiber—including an envelope containing $100,000 in cash passed to him in a Montreal hotel. Mulroney was being paid as a consultant to Schreiber in his venture as the operator of a chain of pasta restaurants, and later emphasized that he paid income tax on the payments. Prior to these transactions, few realized he was an expert on alfredo sauce. Even on patronage, which was Mulroney's most vulnerable flank, it was hard for any fair-minded political junkie to pretend that there was much to choose between the appointment practices of Mulroney and Chrétien, except that Brian was burned at the stake for scattering his favours, while Jean was barely criticized for playing the same shoddy game, as was established by the Gomery Commission, though only after the fact.

MY FINAL INTERVIEWS TOOK PLACE in the study of the Mulroneys' stone mansion on Forden Crescent, half way up Mount Royal in Montreal's most fashionable quarter. Overlooking the mega-dwellings of Paul Desmarais and Charles Bronfman, the house had been transformed by Mila from pretentious to gemütlich. We spent most of our time in Mulroney's elegant, walnut-lined study. Its leather couch was power-pointed by three embroidered pillows. One quoted Albert Einstein, GREAT SPIRITS HAVE ALWAYS ENCOUNTERED VIOLENT OPPOSITION FROM MEDIOCRE MINDS. The two others were gifts from Mila, reading, NAPOLEON LIVES: I MARRIED HIM and HAPPINESS IS BEING MARRIED TO YOUR BEST FRIEND.

As I sat there in the comfort of this luxurious retreat, it struck me that I had spent ten years listening to the most powerful man in the country lament his lack of power and his desire for beatification. The Right Honourable Brian Mulroney continues to count on history's benediction to salvage his record. But history's jury is still out, and history has a notoriously short memory.

Part of his legacy is beyond dispute: the most devastating aftermath of the Mulroney years was the demise of the Progressive Conservative Party. It was Mulroney's inability to absorb the discontents of Quebec and Western Canada within the political mainstream that allowed the regions' separatists and populists to establish their peculiar political movements. Thus vanished his great 1984 coalition, which had anointed him with the mightiest electoral plurality in the country's history. A decade later, the tectonic shift of political forces effectively ended Canada's two-party system and gave the Grits what Ottawa columnist Lawrence Martin called, "the gift of endless governance."

In the 1993 campaign that followed, two months after Mulroney's departure, Kim Campbell stumbled into the abattoir of federal politics. Her misbegotten campaign hit an all-time low in political sensitivity when she told a gathering of hungry street people on Vancouver's skid row, "I know that a lot of you have faced disappointment and loss in your lives. I have, too. I wanted more than anything to be a concert cellist." She led the once-mighty

Tories to a wipeout. It required no great leap of logic to speculate that the election had in reality been a devastating plebiscite on Mulroney's reign. In parliament, the Tories dropped from a solid majority of 169 seats to a pathetic deuce, and no longer qualified even as a cult. The historic party, which in its various guises had founded the country and fielded twelve prime ministers who had governed Canada for more than half a century, was eliminated from contention. Mulroney got the blame. In 2004, the tattered remnants of the Progressive Conservative Party slipped under the tight-ass command of Stephen Harper, who boasted the finest medieval mind in the Commons.

Having a fairly intimate knowledge of the man and his ways, I figured that what scuttled Mulroney's reputation was less what he did, than the way he did it. It may be impossible to differentiate between the man's image and his accomplishments, since one feeds on the other. When they became interchangeable, he suffered the consequences.

If nothing else, this book for the first time explores at length the dichotomy of the private and the public Mulroney, documenting an unexpectedly human side of the despised wax figurine who became the bruised punching bag of an angry populace. After several decades of interviewing, thinking and writing about this singular man, I have concluded that there are two Mulroneys: the anti-hero who Canadians loved to hate, and the hero who has yet to claim his legacy.

Out of the unguarded comments in this book emerges the portrait of an elastic politician who possesses both unexpected touches of grace and the balls of a canal horse. Mulroney was constantly being overwhelmed by events of his own making, so that some of his best-meant initiatives ended up as one more load of buckshot in his own foot. But in the process he created a new country. Instead of pretending that the twentieth century belonged to Canada, he made sure that Canada would belong to the twenty-first.

The Interviews

———

ANDERSON, Ian. *Senior policy advisor, director of communications and deputy chief of staff*
March 2, 1984; November 30, 1984; December 1984; August 29, 1985; October 10, 1985; November 15, 1985; July 10, 1986; October 15, 1986; January 16, 1987; April 28, 1987; June 23, 1988; July 25, 1988; August 5, 1988; August 26, 1988; September 8, 1988

ANGUS, Senator David. *Chief Tory fundraiser and Mulroney advisor*
October 31, 1994

ARMSTRONG, Sally. *Mila Mulroney's biographer*
April 19, 1993

ATKINS, Senator Norman. *Head of Ontario's electoral "Blue Machine" and Mulroney advisor*
January 16, 1989; October 24, 1990

AUSTIN, Senator Jack. *Liberal critic*
October 12, 1984; February 25, 1987; December 16, 1988

BEATTY, Hon. Perrin. *Minister of national defence*
October 30, 1986; June 13, 1990

BROWNLEE, Bonnie. *Executive assistant to Mila Mulroney*
November 30, 1984

CAMPEAU, Arthur. *Former Mulroney law partner and environmental advisor*
October 1994; October 31, 1994; April 25, 1995

CLARK, Edmund. *Architect of the National Energy Program (NEP)*
January 10, 1985

CLARK, Rt. Hon. Joseph. *Former prime minister and secretary of state for external affairs*
June 15, 1990

COHEN, Mickey. *Deputy minister of finance*
May 6, 1993

CORN, Shirley. *Mila Mulroney's friend*
February 26, 1985

COURCHENE, Tom. *Constitutional advisor*
February 25, 1992

CROSBIE, Hon. John. *Minister of justice and attorney general of Canada*
January 24, 1991

CURLEY, Paul. *Ontario Tory operative*
December 13, 1984

DEITCHER, Jonathan. *Mulroney's personal financial advisor*
October 21, 1994

DEVERELL, Dr. Rita Shelton. *Mulroney multicultural critic*
July 29, 1994

DOUCET, Gerry. *Former Nova Scotia cabinet minister and Ottawa lobbyist*
November 13, 1986; January 16, 1987

DOUCET, J.A. (Fred). *Chief of staff, chairman of Organizing Committee for International Summits*
August 1984; September 28, 1984; November 29, 1984; January 10, 1985; May 6, 1985; June 5, 1985; July 18, 1985; August 6, 1985; October 10, 1985; May 1, 1986; July 10, 1986; September 3, 1986; April 28, 1987; May 5, 1987; June 17, 1987; November 19, 1987; January 29, 1988; August 16, 1988; November 21, 1988; December 7, 1988; January 26, 1989

EDMONDS, Duncan. *Senior advisor to the PMO under Lester B. Pearson and senior advisor to defence minister Bob Coates*
March 19, 1985

EPP, Jake. *Minister of energy, mines and resources*
January 24, 1991

FORTIER, L. Yves. *Senior partner, Ogilvy Renault, and Mulroney confidant*
October 6, 1994

FOX, Bill. *Chief press secretary*
September 28, 1984; November 30, 1984; January 30, 1986; July 11, 1986; January 16, 1987

GOLDBLOOM, Michael. Publisher, Montreal *Gazette*
September 29, 1980

GOODMAN, Eddie. *Former PC Party national director*
October 10, 1989

GREGG, Allan. *Mulroney pollster, Decima Research*
December 5, 1984; September 1991

GUY, Gerrard. *Mulroney's friend from Baie-Comeau*
November 21, 1988

HAMILTON, Keith. *Policy advisor to Mulroney*
October 10, 1985; July 11, 1986

HARTT, Stanley H. *Principal secretary and chief of staff to Mulroney*
June 13, 1990; October 25, 1990; May 26, 1994

HEES, George. *Minister of veterans affairs*
January 26, 1989

HOLDEN, Richard. *Quebec MLA, personal friend of Mulroney*
July 18, 1985

JOHNSON, Al. *Secretary of the Treasury Board and CBC chairman*
July 10, 1986

JOHNSON, Senator Janis. *National director of the PC Party*
March 15, 1995

JOHNSON, Jon. B. *Policy advisor to the PM*
Personal correspondence with the author

KENNETT, Bill. *Federal regulator of banks*
January 10, 1993

KINSELLA, Pat. *Senior Tory advisor*
January 14, 1993

LAYTON, Irving. *Poet*
October 25, 1990

LeBRETON, Senator Marjory. *Mulroney confidante; deputy chief of staff, PMO; patronage advisor*
June 15, 1990; October 24, 1990; April 19, 1991; December 9, 1992; March 13, 1993

LeCHANCE, Gilles. *Mulroney's friend from Baie-Comeau*
November 21, 1988

LEOPOLD, Stephen S. *Mulroney's executive assistant during 1976 leadership run*
October 10, 1976

LONG, Tom. *Mulroney policy advisor*
January 31, 1986

LOUGHEED, Peter. *Former premier of Alberta*
April 20, 1985

MacADAM, Patrick. *Caucus liaison and chief Mulroney confidant*
September 16, 1984; September 28, 1984; November 29, 1984; January 11, 1985; May 6, 1985; July 18, 1985; August 6, 1985; November 15, 1985; January 30, 1986; July 10, 1986; September 3, 1986; October 15, 1986; January 16, 1987; April 28, 1987; July 15, 1987; April 15, 1991; January 30, 1993; June 10, 1993

MacDONALD, Flora. *Minister of employment and immigration, foreign affairs minister*
July 19, 1991

MAZANKOWSKI, Don. *Deputy prime minister*
June 13, 1990

McDOUGALL, Barbara. *Minister of employment and immigration, minister of foreign affairs*
June 13, 1990

McMILLAN, Charley. *Chief policy advisor*
March 9, 1984; April 10, 1984; September 28, 1984; November 29, 1984; January 10, 1985; June 1, 1985; October 10, 1985; November 29, 1985; January 30, 1986; May 2, 1986; July 10, 1986; October 15, 1986; February 25, 1987; May 5, 1987; October 1, 1989; June 11, 1990; October 25, 1990; May 5, 1992; May 6, 1992

McSWEENEY, Michael. *Ottawa alderman and Mulroney babysitter*
January 29, 1988; August 11, 1994

MOORES, Frank. *Former Newfoundland premier, Ottawa lobbyist*
October 1984; January 10, 1985; May 6, 1985; November 29, 1985;
September 3, 1986; February 1991

MORGAN, Gizelle. *Head of Mulroney's riding office*
July 11, 1986

MORGAN, Keith. *Mulroney advisor*
January 31, 1986

MULRONEY, Mila. *Wife of Brian Mulroney*
April 19, 1991; June 25, 1991; August 7, 1993

MULRONEY, Rt. Hon. Brian. *Leader of the Progressive
Conservative Party and prime minister of Canada from 1983 to 1993*
October 13, 1972; February 15, 1976; October 29, 1983; January 10,
1984; June 14, 1984; September 16, 1984; September 28, 1984;
November 30, 1984; January 10, 1985; February 10, 1985; March 16,
1985; August 7, 1985; February 13, 1987; July 23, 1987; July 20,
1988; September 4, 1988; October 2, 1988; October 10, 1988;
November 27, 1988; January 6, 1989; February 17, 1989; June 7,
1989; July 2, 1989; August 22, 1989; November 5, 1989; December 8,
1989; January 21, 1990; May 12, 1990; June 18, 1990; July 14, 1990;
September 2, 1990; December 24, 1990; December 30, 1990;
January 4, 1991; January 13, 1991; January 20, 1991; February 20,
1991; March 1991; June 29, 1991; July 4, 1991; August 3, 1991;
September 1, 1991; September 15, 1991; November 2, 1991; January 11,
1992; January 25, 1992; June 17, 1992; June 27, 1992; July 19, 1992;
August 8, 1992; August 23, 1992; August 25, 1992; September 18,
1992; September 19, 1992; September 30, 1992; October 18, 1992;
October 26, 1992; November 30, 1992; December 11, 1992;
December 12, 1992; January 4, 1993; January 30, 1993; February 19,
1993; February 26, 1993; February 27, 1993; March 14, 1993; April 19,
1993; May 31, 1993; June 3, 1993; June 13, 1993; June 20, 1993;
December 12, 1993; January 12, 1994; March 1, 1994; September 15,
1994; September 16, 1994; September 17, 1994; November 12, 1994;
December 10, 1994; January 19, 1995; March 15, 1995

MURRAY, Senator Lowell. *Chief Mulroney strategist*
March 13, 1984; August 24, 1984; January 10, 1985; May 6, 1985;
January 30, 1986; July 10, 1986; January 16, 1987; June 4, 1987;
October 7, 1987; April 20, 1988; October 24, 1990

NEAR, Harry. *Ottawa lobbyist*
June 14, 1990

NEVILLE, Bill. *Campaign consultant and Ottawa lobbyist*
August 10, 1988

NORQUAY, Geoff. *Policy co-ordinator*
January 30, 1986; July 9, 1986; July 10, 1986; October 15, 1986;
May 5, 1987; June 17, 1987

OSTRY, Sylvia. *Economic advisor to the prime minister*
January 16, 1985

PEERS, Archbishop Michael. *Head of the Anglican Church in Canada*
March 13, 1994

PETERSON, David. *Premier of Ontario*
November 29, 1990; May 11, 1992

PHILLIPS, Bruce. *Chief press secretary*
October 7, 1987

PICHET, Hubert. *Quebec personal assistant to Mulroney*
August 6, 1985

PITFIELD, Senator Michael. *Clerk of the Privy Council and advisor
to Pierre Trudeau*
January 24, 1991; November 15, 1991; March 4, 1994

PIVNICKI, Bogdanka; PIVNICKI, Dr. Dimitrije. *Mila Mulroney's
parents*
February 26, 1985

PRISTANSKI, Bill. *Mulroney executive assistant*
May 6, 1985; November 29, 1984; July 18, 1985; October 10, 1985;
January 30, 1986; May 2, 1986; August 6, 1985; September 3, 1986;
November 20, 1986; January 16, 1987; April 28, 1987; May 5, 1987;
April 20, 1988

ROBINSON, Paul H. *U.S. ambassador to Canada*
May 3, 1985

ROBLIN, Senator Duff. *Premier of Manitoba*
November 29, 1984

ROCQUE, Pierre. *Mulroney's friend from Baie-Comeau*
November 21, 1988

ROY, Senator Bernard. *Principal ssecretary and strategy advisor*
January 10, 1985; January 16, 1987

SEGAL, Hugh. *Chief of staff*
November 15, 1984; February 7, 1986

SHARP, Mitchell. *Liberal critic*
October 17, 1989

SPECTOR, Norman. *Senior advisor and chief of staff*
October 24, 1990

TELLIER, Paul. *Clerk of the Privy Council*
June 14, 1990; July 26, 1993

VARI, George. *Mulroney benefactor*
October 9, 1989

WADSWORTH, Page. *Chairman, CIBC*
May 21, 1992

WAKIM, Sam. *Closest personal friend of Mulroney*
February 3, 1986; October 29, 1984

WALMSLEY, Christopher. *Journalism professor and CBC TV reporter*
May 6, 1993

WELLS, Clyde. *Premier of Newfoundland*
March 15, 1992

WHITE, Peter. *1984 campaign strategist and chief patronage advisor*
September 28, 1984; January 10, 1985; May 6, 1985; June 14, 1985;
July 11, 1985; July 30, 1985; August 6, 1985; August 29, 1985;
October 10, 1985; November 15, 1985; November 29, 1985; October
29, 1986; June 23, 1992; December 8, 1992

WILSON, Michael. *Minister of finance*
June 13, 1990

The Patronage Machine

———

Secret Memos

DOCUMENT I
(Retyped for legibility from original copy)

PROGRESSIVE CONSERVATIVE PARTY OF CANADA
PARTI PROGRESSISTE-CONSERVATEUR DU CANADA

<u>FOR THE LEADER'S EYES ONLY</u>

May 25, 1984

MEMORANDUM TO: Hon. Brian Mulroney, P.C., M.P.
FROM: Hon. Erik Nielsen, P.C., M.P.

Unless otherwise directed by you, it is my intention to proceed immediately with the Appointments process as herein outlined.

Throughout, I am assuming certain priority objectives that you wish to achieve and be perceived as characterizing your administration in the first stage.

1. Economic management and Parliament accountability
2. Industrial revival—jobs
3. Trade expansion
4. Technological opportunities
5. The resurrection of cooperative federalism
6. External affairs

There would, of course, be subsequent objectives which you will wish to pursue which would be reflected by later changes.

APPOINTMENTS ADVISORY COMMITTEE

To plan the process for change I intend to implement with one or two minor exceptions, the "Nomination Model" presented to you for approval by Finlay MacDonald and Peter Harder. This includes the establishment of a small Appointments Advisory Committee composed of Finlay MacDonald, Guy Charbonneau and Janis Johnson. You would probably want to add Norm Atkins and perhaps others post election day.

SECRETARIAT TO ADVISORY COMMITTEE

This committee is to be assisted by a small secretariat of five persons. David Dyer will propose the names of these persons who would be drawn from existing Ottawa resources so that, when selected, they could carry on their work, in training, in addition to their regular jobs. The Secretariat would eventually be located in the P.M.O. to maintain liaison with the Chairmen of Provincial Advisory Committees. The five regional groupings in the Secretariat will be Atlantic, Quebec, Ontario, Prairies and British Columbia. Dyer will provide job description and suggested compensation prior to recommendation.

PROVINCIAL CHAIRMEN

I believe we should now, in the utmost confidence, identify the Provincial Chairmen so that they can be in place and prepared to function on day one. We would make them aware now of what is expected of them as to methodology and the qualifications and balance we expect from their provincial committee members. They would come to Ottawa immediately following the election for extensive briefings. They would bring with them their recommendations, for your approval, of those persons they would like to see serving on their respective provincial committees. Under no circumstances would they discuss the matter with anyone prior to your approval of their nominees. There should be a member from each provincial caucus on the provincial committee.

GOVERNOR IN-COUNCIL APPOINTMENTS

(a) Deputy Ministers
Changes or reassignments in certain key departments would follow immediately the swearing in of your Cabinet. I have in mind the following for first stage—others would follow:

(i)   Finance
(ii)   Treasury Board
(iii)   External Affairs (Under-Secretary)
(iv)   Energy
(v)   Revenue (Income Tax and Customs and Excise)
(vi)   DRIE (Industry and Commerce)
(vii)   Agriculture
(viii)   International Trade
(ix)   Science and Technology
(x)   Employment and Immigration
(xi)   Transport

The new Deputy Minister would come from the existing public service, or very highly recommended senior provincial bureaucrats and possibly the private sector. I believe that it is necessary to proceed as far as we possibly can now to identify these persons. In this regard, I have commenced a collation of the recommendations of our caucus critics. In addition, I propose to put in place a small committee of three professionals to commence this urgent work.

Included in this stage would be certain A.D.M.s [Assistant Deputy Ministers] in the foregoing key departments. These are as follows:

(i)   Finance—Associate Deputy Minister
(ii)   Treasury Board – Deputy Secretary Personnel and
                Collective Bargaining.
(iii) External Affairs – Deputy Minister (Marchand)
                – Ambassador to Washington
                – Ambassador to the United Nations
(iv)   DRIE – Associate Deputy Minister

I will be suggesting others after my review of critic reports has been completed.

In addition to the two HOP [Head of Post] changes suggested in External, which will signal the importance of changes in policy direction you will be making, I would also plan now for the replacement of Jamieson in London, Dupuy in Paris, Benson in Dublin, Béchard in New Orleans, Danson in Boston and Steers in Japan.

Unless you direct me otherwise, I will assume you approve and will proceed with planning for the identification of potential nominees.

(b) "Other" G.I.C. Appointments
Here the question arises as to what appointments should be planned to be made within the first sixty days with or without the benefit of input from the provincial committees. The assumption has been that it would take approximately 60 days for provincial committees to be in operation. I believe that by identifying the provincial chairmen now, this time lag can be substantially shortened.

I would suggest that no announcements of any changes be made in this category within the first week. Needless to say, if you announce the changes I have already suggested, it will take a week or two for the tremors to subside. There is one exception and that is C.D.I.C. [the Canada Deposit Insurance Corporation]. I propose an immediate replacement of [Joel] Bell and [Maurice] Strong. It goes without saying that [Senator Jack] Austin goes. The recruitment prior to the election, of proposed heads of the remainder of the crown corporations and agencies would, in my view, be dangerous. C.D.I.C. is the obvious exception.

One other area where change should be affected immediately is P.C.O. [Privy Council Office]. I propose that Osbaldeston remain. Both Deputy Secretaries (Operations and Planning) however, should be changed. I will proceed to identify proposed replacements, unless otherwise directed by you.

I have spoken with Bill Jarvis. He has agreed to assist. I propose, initially, to have him focus on Staffing and, once that is under control he will assume direction of the Appointments planning. In both cases, directly responsible to me. This should free me to concentrate on the vital work of machinery.

Erik

———

DOCUMENT 2

(Scanned from copy of the original)

Minutes from a meeting of the National Appointments Committee, November 30, 1984. Attendees were David Angus, Erik Nielsen, Bernard Roy, Peter White, Kay Stanley and Marjory LeBreton. Norman Atkins sent regrets.

NAC Meeting #3
Friday, November 30, 1984, 8 a.m.

MINUTES

Attendance: N. Atkins was unable to attend.
            L. O'Connor took minutes.

E.N. informs NAC that P.M. would like 50 appointments per week, until the backlog is eliminated.

Returning Officers
General agreement was to wait for a decision on redistribution of electoral boundaries before discussing the appointment of new returning officers. Discussion of returning officers put over to first meeting in 1985.

I.   PENDING BUSINESS

1)   Advisory Council on the Status of Women
     D.A. suggests Denise Angers. He will provide C.V.
     B.R. brought up the sensitive nature of this appointment, and suggests that NAC 'red flag' this appointment and wait on it.

2)   Standards Council of Canada
     Georges Archer appointed President (November 29, 1984).

3)   Tax Court of Canada
     Donald Christie (Chief Judge) wishes to become Associate Chief Judge. B.R. suggests that Jean-Claude Couture be appointed Chief Judge. Should the Minister reduce the powers of the Tax Court, B.R. indicates the possible necessity of finding something else for Couture. NAC acknowledges this as a potential problem, but suggests we go ahead on Couture nonetheless.

4)   Comptroller General
     Name of Lawrence Hanigan was raised. Jean Lanctôt suggested by the Québec PAC. E.N. suggests that the Canadian Organization of Management Consultants be approached for names. P.W. suggests Gordon Riehl, a senior C.A. who writes a column for The Globe and Mail. E.N. suggests Richard Geren, former president of IOC now living in Oromucto (P.M. thinks highly of his management ability). NAC suggests the desirability of a female. E.N. to send some information to P.W. regarding a French Businesswoman from Toronto; Lise Chartrand was also mentioned.

5)   Canadian Commercial Corporation
     B.R. mentions Guy D'Avignon, but P.M. may have something else in mind. D.A. to look into a few names, including Mr. Tooley. NAC discussed the difficulty of persuading successful business people to take this position. The name of Fred McCaffrey was also suggested.

6) **Canadian Security Intelligence Service**
D.A. suggests Cliff Kennedy, but he is not experienced in
security. E.N. suggests Bill Palk, a retired, fit, active
Winnipeg lawyer experienced in security. E.N. also
suggests Richard Rohmer. P.W. to check with Hon. Elmer
MacKay, and have him contact Mr. Barr regarding candidates
with a background in military intelligence. K.S. to check
High Flyer's list.

7) **Cape Breton Development Corporation**
Appointment of Dr. William Shaw has been put on hold
as the Chairmanship is not vacant.

8) **International Joint Commission**
NAC agrees to send the name of Hon. Davie Fulton as a
formal recommendation to P.M. Since the present vacancy
was held by a francophone, NAC agrees to propose a
francophone to replace Blair Seaborn in December, 1985.

9) **Public Archives**
P.W. to get suggestions from Quebec Archivists
Association.

10) **Petro Canada**
Recognize the need for high profile people to fill these
prestigious positions. NAC suggests soliciting firm
recommendations from PACs. P.W. will check the
possibility of reducing the number of Public Service
positions (Remove Tellier and Stewart, not Cohen). D.A.
and J.L. suggest Chester Johnson. Possibly add a Yukon
Director. E.N. suggests Art Collin.

11) **Supreme Court of Canada**
Registrar (B. Hofley-$63 to $75K) is sick, but is to
resume work in January, 1985. Note that Deputy Registrar
may become Registrar. NAC suggests a lawyer from the
Ottawa region, as salary is not too high (currently $58K).
B.R. and D.A. to check with Bar Association and report
back.

12) **War Veterans Allowance Board**
K.S. will check for possible women from High Flyers list.
Norma Walmsley was suggested.

13) **Canadian Livestock Feed Board**
Hon. John Wise to send names. B.R. suggests P.W. consult
Clement Vincent. J.C. Pelletier should contact U.P.A. and
Coop. Fed.

14) **Chief Pensions Advocate**
NAC agrees with name of André Lemieux suggested by Hon.
George Hees.

446

- 3 -

15) National Arts Centre Corporation
Pierre Boutin appointed as Chairman (November 29, 1984).

16) Canadian Livestock Feed Board Advisory Committee
P.W. to consult Hon. John Wise. Ask U.P.A. (Clement
Vincent).

17) Canadian Centre for Occupational Health and Safety
NAC suggests consultation with PACs. K.S. suggests Ann
Elizabeth (Betty) Smith (Toronto) and Karen Goldenberg.

18) Canada Ports Corporation
Hon. Ron Huntington appointed Chairman (November 29,
1984).

19) Economic Council of Canada
Name of Galynn Bennett (Toronto) was suggested. B.R. to
get P.M.'s views.

20) Restrictive Trade Practices Commission
Richard Holden appointed Vice-Chairman and member
(November 29, 1984). E.N. points out that it is bad for
morale in Ministry and in Caucus to be uninformed
regarding an appointment. PACs will still continue to
report directly to P.W., but PACs must inform their
caucus member of all recommendations.

21) Canada-United States Permanent Joint Board on Defence
Hon. Allan Lawrence appointed Canadian representative
(November 29, 1984).

22) Export Development Corporation
Put Over.

23) Canadian Security Intelligence Review Committee
Review Committee appointed (November 29, 1984).

24) National Capital Commission
Jean Pigott appointed member and Chairman (November 29,
1984).

25) World Bank
P.W. reported the Hon. Michael Wilson is prepared to:
a) ignore Search Committee that has been set up, b) move
Inter-American Bank individual to the World Bank vacancy
or, c) take NAC suggestions. P.W. will consult him
concerning Alain Gersten-Briand. E.N. suggests Pierre
Lassande, an engineer and economic consultant to Hon.
David Crombie.

- 4 -

II. NEW BUSINESS

26) Auditors
     Put over.

27) PACs Status Report
     L. O'Connor to provide accurate information.

28) Atomic Energy Control Board
     K.S. suggested Dr. Nancy Elgie from Ontario, where there
     will be a vacancy in February, 1985. For present Quebec
     vacancy, B.R. to report back.

29) C.B.C.
     K.S. suggested Nancy Kent (Prince Albert), Suzanne Olaski
     (Saskatoon), Margaret Strongitharm (B.C.). D.A. suggested
     Bruce Ledain (Montreal). P.W. to consult with ~~Gerard~~ Edward
     DesRosiers, M.P. Hochelaga, as well as P.M. and Hon.
     Marcel Masse. D.A. questioned Archambault. Names of
     Roger Régimbal and Georges Valade were also suggested.
     E.N. reported that the Responsible Minister is to inform
     Caucus Representative on PAC of every appointment.
     Regional Secretary is to inform PACs of selected vacancies
     being considered by NAC.

30) Immigration Appeal Board
     NAC agrees with John Weisdorf.

31) International Development Research Centre
     Check Wardlaw as possible Chairman. K.S. to recommend
     possible females. Chairman should be appointed first.

32) National Parole Board
     P.W. to report with additional vacancies sent to PACs.
     E.N. suggested Guy Marcoux (54); but may replace
     Simmons (will not know for 6 months) P.W. to ask P.M.
     D.A. suggested Judy Hendin (to get C.V.). J.L.
     suggested we consider unsuccessful candidates.

33) Teleglobe Canada
     Suggestion was made to send this to BC and NS PACs. P.W.
     to check with Hon. Sinclair Stevens and P.M. regarding
     need for Public Servants. Names of Bob Lloyd and Peter
     Pocklington were suggested.

34) National Farm Products Marketing Council
     P.W. to check with Hon. John Wise.

- 5 -

34) Tariff Board
Traditionally used to place a senior Public Servant. Put
over.

35) Tax Court of Canada
Marcel Lambert was suggested by E.N.

36) Federal Court of Canada
P.W. to check with Hon. John Crosbie and with James
Jerome.

37) Canada Labour Relations Board
Marie Marchand (Northern Ontario) was suggested by K.S.
P.W. to check with Hon. William McKnight.

DOCUMENT 3
(Retyped from original copy)

Patronage Tally
Aug. 29, 1985

From September 17, 1984 to Aug. 14, 1985, the government
made 1,337 Governor-In-Council appointments. Of this total
of 1,337 appointments, 326 (24 per cent) were routine or
administrative appointments. This category included judges
made acting administrators for lieutenant-governors; RCMP
promotions; regular consular postings for career diplomats
and commissioners empowered to take oaths.

The remaining 1,011 (76 per cent) appointments made by the
government were political.

- 550 appointments to various agencies, boards and
  commissions.
- Forty-one appointments of Parliamentary Secretaries,
  House of Commons Commissioners, and the Speaker of
  the Senate.
- Eighty Honourary Consuls abroad.
- Twelve staff members of the Prime Minister's residences.
- Twenty-six appointments of Queen's Counsel.
- Fifty-four Judicial appointments.
- Forty-five appointments of Senior Public Servants—DM
  [Deputy Minister] level.
- Forty appointments of Public Servants to directorships
  of Crown Corporations.
- Twelve appointments of auditors.
- Four appointments to Royal Commissions or
  Commissions of Inquiry.
- Two appointments of Lieutenant-Governors.
- 217 Reappointments of incumbents.

Using the 550 *very political discretionary appointments*
[emphasis added] as a base, the appointments break down
as follows:

Male:	73.7%	
Female:	25.4%	
Anglophone:	76.7%	
Francophone:	22.5%	
Ethnic:	10.2%	

	Percentage of Discretionary Appointments	Percentage of the Canadian Population
Yukon	.08	.08
NWT	.02	.02
B.C.	11.20	11.40
Alberta	5.70	9.30
Sask.	2.50	4.00
Manitoba	3.60	4.20
Ontario	36.60	35.50
Quebec	20.10	26.00
PEI	1.90	.40
N.B.	5.10	2.80
N.S.	6.10	3.40
Nfld.	6.10	2.30

Secret Strategy Memo

Gaining Control of the Senior Civil Service

Office of the
Prime Minister

Cabinet du
Premier ministre

1484

MEMORANDUM FOR THE PRIME MINISTER

DATE: December 11, 1985

FROM: Peter G. White

SUBJECT: The Senior Public Service

On September 4, 1984, 50% of the Canadian electorate voted for change. According to polling done at the time, one of their major concerns was process - the way the public service of Canada dealt with issues and with the public.

Over the past year it has become all too evident that you cannot change process and attitudes without changing personnel - especially at the top. It is not enough simply to shuffle some of the old faces around; they just take their old attitudes and biases with them to their new assignments, and the old networks and loyalties remain intact. What is needed, over time, is a massive infusion of new blood - and more importantly, new blood that is compatible with the new government.

Happily, our system is intended to provide for just such an infusion. Since well before Confederation, it has been clearly established that the Cabinet, and more particularly the Prime Minister, can appoint whomever they choose to the key senior positions in the public service. All deputy ministers and associate deputy ministers, and most heads of agencies, boards and commissions, serve at the pleasure of the government. This practice has stood the test of time because it is clearly essential for any government to have its own people in these key positions. If the ministers are the chief executive officers, clearly they must have compatible people as their chief operating officers - people who share the goals and convictions of the government.

.../2

Memorandum for the Prime Minister
Page 2
December 11, 1985

The Liberal Party, in office for 20 years out of 21 up to 1984,
built the public service that we have inherited. There are
very few public servants left who where brought into the
service during the Diefenbaker era. A number survive from the
Pearson years of 1963 to 1968, but most - and at senior levels,
nearly all - were recruited and promoted by Trudeau, or more
precisely by Pitfield. These appointments were made in a
conscious and perfectly proper effort to fashion a senior
public service that would be compatible with Trudeau's style
and approach - the very style and approach that Canadian voters
so emphatically rejected in September 1984. It is idle to
think that these men and women, who have spent most of their
public service careers designing and implementing the Trudeau/
Pitfield approach to government, could suddenly become strongly
committed to radically altering their own creation.

The "pink slips and running shoes" analysis was fundamentally
correct - that is why it was so popular. One of the main
reasons for our current difficulties is that we have not
followed through on its inescapable implications.

In my view there are three reasons why we have not done so:

(1) our initial failure to appreciate the fundamental
    importance of bringing in our own people at the top, which
    translated into insufficient political will to make the
    necessary changes;
(2) the jealously-guarded monopoly of advice to the Prime
    Minister on this issue from the Clerk of the Privy Council,
    speaking for "the system" and its preservation; and
(3) our own failure to establish an adequate structure and plan
    on the political side within the PMO to identify and
    recruit candidates for these key positions.

It is not too late to recover the lost ground, provided we act
quickly. The following steps are necessary:

(1) Give a clear mandate to the PMO to duplicate from the
    political perspective the work being done in the PCO (by
    the Senior Personnel Secretariat under George Post,
    reporting to the Clerk) and by COSO (the Committee of
    Senior Officials, an advisory commitee to the Clerk on
    personnel matters). This mandate should include:

.../2

Memorandum for the Prime Minister
Page 3
December 11, 1985

(a) Ongoing <u>assessments</u> of all senior officials, in
collaboration with the responsible ministers and their
staffs, based chiefly on the following test: does the
performance of this official contribute to or hinder
the government's achievement of its political goals?

(b) The <u>identification</u> of suitable candidates for all
senior positions (i.e. succession planning), from both
within and without the federal public service; and the
maintenance of an up-to-date <u>inventory</u> of the best
talent in Canada that would be compatible with the
government's political objectives.

(c) The <u>recommendation</u> of appropriate candidates to the
Prime Minister, and subsequently the <u>recruitment</u> of the
Prime Minister's choice. This can require up to six
months of advance planning, which is not now being done
anywhere in the government as nobody has been assigned
this specific mandate. This oversight has severely
limited our ability to recruit from outside the federal
public service. I have recently sent you a memorandum
concerning Peter Lougheed's offer to assist in this
area.

(d) The <u>integration</u> of new recruits into the system, so
that they are not prevented by the bureaucracy from
performing effectively; and the ongoing monitoring of
their progress.

(e) The <u>outplacement</u> of officials whose services are no
longer required. This should be done in close
cooperation with the Senior Personnel Secretariat.

(2) Determine whether the Prime Minister prefers to receive a
<u>single</u> stream of advice on personnel matters, melding both
the public service (PCO) and political (PMO) perspectives;
or a <u>dual</u> stream of advice, with possibly conflicting views
emanating from each source. In the former case, a
mechanism will have to be found for reconciling the two
perspectives before the resulting advice goes forward to
the Prime Minister. At the very least, this would involve
the appointment of a PMO representative on COSO. A better
solution would be to establish a new <u>Senior Personnel
Office</u> reporting directly to the Prime Minister, with equal
input from the bureaucracy and the political side.

.../4

(3) Whether the preference be for a single or a dual stream of personnel advice, a senior person in the PMO must be formally designated and authorized by the Prime Minister or the Principal Secretary to assume the responsibilities outlined above. This function would fall most naturally to the undersigned as Special Assistant for Governor-in-Council Appointments, since all the officials in question are in fact GIC appointments. As I have previously indicated to you, I would be delighted to assume these responsibilities if you wish. As you know, I have already done much of the preparatory work.

No single area of government is more important than the management or deployment of senior personnel. Since government is largely concerned with service to the public, it is at least as true of government as of business that "people are our most important product", and unquestionably more true that "people are our most important asset". As I have pointed out in several previous memoranda, the record of the federal bureaucracy in managing its senior personnel is a lamentable one: recruitment, training, career planning, evaluation, succession planning and outplacement planning are all shockingly inadequate. Unfortunately, we cannot yet claim to have improved matters much since the election. One result of our failure to act in this vital area is the apparent domination of more than half the Cabinet by bureaucrats inherited from the Trudeau years, and the consequent frustration of our caucus and our party as they see us succumbing to this domination. As for the Canadians who voted for change, many are beginning to wonder whether it will ever happen.

To reassure them, we must make an early start on gaining control of the bureaucracy by identifying and installing some of our own chief operating officers as outlined above. This should not be done with fanfare and only at long intervals, but routinely and continuously over the government's mandate. We must also bear in mind that a handful of positions, in the PCO, the PSC, the Treasury Board, DRIE, etc., are the key to effective control of the bureaucracy.

Please let me know your reaction to these suggestions.

Peter W.

Paying Their Own Way

———

EXCHANGES OF CORRESPONDENCE CONCERNING
RENOVATIONS AT MULRONEY'S OFFICIAL RESIDENCES
(Retyped from original copies for legibility)

<u>PC CANADA FUND</u>

February 18, 1987

<u>PERSONAL AND CONFIDENTIAL</u>

Rt. Hon. Brian Mulroney, P.C., M. P.
Prime Minister of Canada
24 Sussex Drive
Ottawa, Ontario
K1M 1M4

Dear Prime Minister:

I refer to your letter of March 5, 1984, a copy of which
is attached.

As requested, I attach an invoice addressed to you
personally representing the balance of advances made on
your behalf by the Party in respect to residences.

Please arrange to forward me a cheque in the sum of
$211,796.18 payable to PC Canada Fund (the Party's chief
registered agent) at your convenience.

With warm regards,

Yours sincerely,

W. David Angus, Q.C.

encl.

INVOICE to Rt. Hon. Brian Mulroney

 To reimburse the Progressive Conservative Party of
Canada for the balance of sums advanced in respect of
decoration and furnishing your residences at Stornoway,
24 Sussex Drive and Harrington Lake..........

$211,796.18

April 13, 1987

<u>BY COURIER</u>
<u>PERSONAL & CONFIDENTIAL</u>

Mr. W. David Angus, Q.C.
Stikeman Elliott
1155 Dorchester Blvd. West
Suite 3900
Montreal, Quebec
H3B 3V2

Dear David:

Find enclosed herewith a cheque of $211,796.18 payable to P.C. Canada Fund.

Brian had impressed upon me to issue this cheque as soon as possible after a meeting I had with him in Quebec in the latter part of February of this year. Unfortunately, I was unable to comply with this request earlier, due to extensive travelling at the time and an unfortunate ski accident that kept me in a Vancouver hospital for 12 days in March.

Nevertheless, the first thing I am doing now that I am back at the office, is forwarding to you this cheque.

I hope that this involuntary delay will not create any difficulty for you.

Best personal regards,

Alain Parais

Partner,
   Poissant Richard Thorne Ernst & Whinney
     Chartered Accountants
      2000, Ave. McGill College
       Bureau 1900
        Montreal, Quebec H3A 3H8

June 8, 1994

Dr. Jean-Pierre Wallot
National Archivist
395 Wellington St.
Ottawa, Ont. K1A 0N3

Dear Dr. Wallot:

After a great deal of work by my staff and your representatives, I note that the process of transferring archival material from my office to the Archives is well in train. Marilyn Burke informs me that everything is proceeding quite smoothly and her expectation is that, in an orderly and appropriate way, all of the documents from my time as Prime Minister of Canada will be transferred to the National Archives.

I would now, therefore, like to turn to another matter.

When we left office, the gifts and souvenirs that we had received over the years were transferred to a warehouse where we were able to review and categorize them. As you know, while they are not by and large of significant value, some may be of considerable historical interest. It is my intention to begin now the process of transferring much, if not all, of this material to the Archives, pursuant to the same criteria followed above. In some cases we shall choose to retain these items in our personal residence for sentimental reasons. These, however, will be sent along to you in future years and shall be transferred to you in their entirety upon the closing of our Montreal residence or, of course, my death.

I have conveyed this information to Marilyn Burke and have instructed her to begin this process at a time of your mutual convenience. Please feel free to call on me in this regard at any time.

Yours sincerely,

Brian Mulroney

August 16, 1994

Mr. Marcel Beaudry
Chairman and Chief Executive Officer
National Capital Commission
161 Laurier Ave. West
Ottawa K1P 6J6

Dear Mr. Beaudry:

In the twelve months since we left Ottawa, I have been
kept busy getting four children installed in schools, making
living arrangements in Montreal, while rebuilding my own
professional career. Only very recently have I had the
opportunity to consider how I should deal with some other
less urgent matters that arose because of our move from
Ottawa after a decade of living there.

In particular, I have decided to leave at 24 Sussex and
Harrington Lake those furnishings that belonged to me but
that I did not remove when my husband left office. For your
information and records, I enclose a list of these items that
have an appraised value in excess of $100,000. I shall not be
requesting a tax receipt for any of these items that I hope
future Prime Ministers and their families may enjoy.

Yours sincerely,

Mila Mulroney

Index